CARLA WAAL

HARRIET BOSSE

Strindberg's Muse and Interpreter

Southern Illinois University Press
Carbondale and Edwardsville

93   92   91   90   4   3   2   1

Library of Congress Cataloging-in-Publication Data

   Waal, Carla, 1933–
     Harriet Bosse: Strindberg's muse and interpreter / by Carla Waal.
       p. cm.
     Bibliography: p.
     Includes index.
     1. Bosse, Harriet, 1878–1961. 2. Strindberg, August, 1849–1912—
Biography—Marriage. 3. Strindberg, August, 1849–1912—Stage
history. 4. Actors—Sweden—Biography. 5. Dramatists,
Swedish—19th century—Biography. I. Title.
     PN2778.B65W33 1990
839.7'26—dc20
[B]
ISBN   0-8093-1548-3
                                    89-32971
                                         CIP

To Anne Marie Wyller Hagelin

CONTENTS

Preface   ix

Acknowledgments   xi

1. Debut of a Princess   1

2. Debut in Sweden   12

3. The Ingenue and the Playwright   25

4. Reaching Out   41

5. Stardom   54

6. Reign at the Royal Theatre   69

7. The Turning Point   126

8. Independence   146

9. Bitter Homecoming   171

10. After the Final Curtain   186

11. Inspiration and Interpreter   203

Appendix A: First Performances of Roles Played by
          Harriet Bosse   239

Appendix B: "Strindberg as I Knew Him" by Harriet Bosse   246

Abbreviations of the Names of Libraries, Archives,
  and Private Collections   247

Notes   248

Bibliography   277

Index   291

Plates appear on pages 85–125

PREFACE

A photograph of Harriet Bosse as Elektra first drew my attention to the charismatic actress. While doing research on the Norwegian actress Johanne Dybwad, I often encountered Bosse's name since they performed many of the same roles. Later, when asked to review the English translation of the Bosse-Strindberg correspondence and selections from his *Occult Diary*, I learned that much of what August Strindberg wrote after meeting her reflects his adoration of Bosse and his despair over the problems of their marriage. The haunting image of the beautiful Elektra merged with scenes from a complex relationship, and I wanted to know more about her achievements as an independent artist. I learned that Harriet Bosse's identity in the public view and in literary history is as the wife of a literary genius. She saw herself as both an independent professional and as guardian of the Strindberg legend.

Thanks to a grant funded by the Swedish Institute, in cooperation with the Society for the Advancement of Scandinavian Study, I visited Sweden in 1968 and began to familiarize myself with Strindberg bibliography. I also had the pleasure of meeting Torsten Eklund, who encouraged me in my hope to write a biography of Bosse. In 1981 and 1983 other grants from the Swedish Institute enabled me to return to Sweden for extended stays. Not only did they provide funding for research on Bosse, the Swedish Institute enabled me to meet Anne Marie Wyller Hagelin, Bosse and Strindberg's daughter. She has provided invaluable information and encouragement, as have other members of Bosse's family. The process of gathering material for this book has been an adventure, as I have met actors, critics, directors, scholars, and others who have shared their memories.

In addition to information obtained through interviews, this biography draws upon published and unpublished sources from libraries, archives, and private collections, primarily in Scandinavia. Most of the material was in Swedish or Norwegian. Unless otherwise noted, translations of quotations are my own.

When this study began, I wanted to separate Harriet Bosse from her romanticized image in the shadow of August Strindberg and to credit her with self-sufficiency and individuality. She was a fascinating person. As her daughter-in-law Randi Wingård has said, "Harriet was a great personality, and even if she was tiny, one could not help noticing her in any gathering.

She attracted everyone's attention" (Letter to author, 9 May 1987). While trying to do justice to her as an individual and as an artist, this book must emphasize her role as interpreter of Strindberg, the man and the playwright. Just as Bosse discovered, I found that their marriage and her relationship to his writing are an integral part of her story. Keeping the proper proportion so that the story will be presented in a new light has been my task. In presenting her life of hard work, of triumphs and disappointments, I also tell about a number of major developments in Swedish theatre and film during more than four decades.

ACKNOWLEDGMENTS

Research for this study has been financed in part by the Swedish Institute, the Swedish Foreign Ministry (in cooperation with the Society for the Advancement of Scandinavian Study), and the University of Missouri-Columbia Research Council.

I am grateful to the staffs of all the libraries and archives I have visited. In the United States these include the libraries of the University of Missouri-Columbia, the University of Minnesota, the University of Wisconsin-Madison, Indiana University, Harvard College, and the Lincoln Center Library of the Performing Arts (New York Public Library). In Sweden I have used material in the archives of the Royal Dramatic Theatre (Dramaten), the Drottningholm Theatre Museum, the Gothenburg Theatre Museum, and the libraries of the Universities of Uppsala, Lund, and Gothenburg. While in Stockholm I have also consulted books and documents at the Royal Library, the Swedish Film Institute, the Strindberg Museum, the Statistical Central Bureau, the Swedish Academy of Music, the Swedish Music Archive, the Archive for Sound and Images, and the Archive of the City of Stockholm. In Helsinki I used the collections of the Theatre Museum, the Swedish Theatre, and the university. In Turku I worked at the Sibelius Museum and the Åbo Academy. Research also led to the libraries of the Universities of Oslo, Bergen, and Copenhagen and to the Oslo Theatre Museum. I want to thank especially Margareta Brundin of the Royal Library in Stockholm, and the staffs of the Royal Dramatic Theatre Archive (Dr. Tom Olsson, Sten Rhodin, Nea Cleve, Margareta Rörby) and the University of Oslo Library (Øyvind Anker, Trine Næss, Jaga Kvadheim).

This study uses rare printed material and handwritten documents located in libraries and archives, private papers and photographs loaned or given to me, and information gathered in interviews. My heartfelt appreciation goes to the family of Harriet Bosse and above all to her daughter, Anne Marie Wyller Hagelin. In addition I thank other members of the family: Randi Wingård, Dagny Bull Heyerdahl, Jørgen and Wenche Wyller, Bo Wingård, and Kaare Backer. Information obtained from the family through letters and interviews is often interwoven with the narrative and not identified with separate footnotes. Other people who graciously granted interviews are listed in the bibliography.

It is impossible to mention everyone who has contributed to my research, but I wish to express my gratitude to: Stephen M. Archer, Liisa Byckling, Lena Daun, Marna Feldt, Bengt Forslund, Anne-Charlotte Harvey, Kerstin Gram Holmström, Helene Høverstad, Harry Järv, Anna-Lena Järvstrand, Inga Grabe Lewenhaupt, James Walter McFarlane, Marianne Norlin, Irmeli Niemi, Anita Persson, Tage Ringheim, Eva Stellby, Marianne Tiblin, the late Timo Tiusanen, Erkki Virkkunen, Inga Lill Westblom, Clas Zilliacus, and my mother Esther Christiansen Waal.

CHAPTER ONE

Debut of a Princess

"Once upon a time there was a princess in our land,"[1] wrote a Norwegian theatre critic, and that princess was the actress Harriet Bosse. Audiences first saw her as Shakespeare's Juliet and as the Princess in *Once Upon a Time — (Der var engang —)* by Holger Drachmann. With her delicate beauty and rich talent she might have become a leading actress at the National Theatre (Nationaltheatret) when it opened in 1899. There she would have competed with other contenders for the royal crown; instead she became for a decade the "queen" of Swedish theatre.

Fate led the young actress to Stockholm and into the life of the prominent and controversial playwright August Strindberg. She became his wife, his inspiration, and his interpreter. Much of what he wrote after meeting her reflects his adoration of Bosse and his despair over the problems of their relationship. The influence of their legendary courtship and marriage on each other's work is indisputable. When she no longer interpreted Strindberg's plays in the theatre, Harriet Bosse continued to interpret his life, realizing that it was inextricably interwoven with hers. She saw herself as a guardian of the Strindberg legend.

This is the story of an artist, her triumphs and disappointments, her life in and away from the theatre. Bosse's relationship to Strindberg permeates the story, but the story has other themes as well. Although marriage and motherhood made their demands, work dominated her life. Theatre historians are interested in the conditions that determined what choices she could make in accepting engagements. By noting the dozens of roles she played, we learn about trends in repertory at various theatres and about the power exercised by managers and directors. As we study the development of Bosse as an artist, we learn how she aimed for certain stylistic goals, building on spontaneous responses to material and developing a marked technique.

Although she appeared in plays by many authors, Harriet Bosse deserves

1

recognition for her Strindberg roles. Throughout the chronological narrative there are references to the playwright, but an extensive analysis of Harriet Bosse's interpretations of Strindberg on stage is presented in the concluding chapter. In that way, her importance as his muse and the continuity and significance of her work as Strindberg interpreter can be seen more clearly.

GROWING UP

Harriet Bosse was born at 15 Karl XII Street in Kristiania (now Oslo), Norway, on 19 February 1878.[2] The Bosse family had come to Norway from Denmark in 1867 because of her father's business as publisher and bookseller. Johann Heinrich Wilhelm Bosse was born in 1836 in the town of Celle, in Hanover, Germany.[3] He moved to Skanderborg near Aarhus, Denmark, and there he married Anne Marie Lehman (1836–93). They had fourteen children; only seven survived childhood. Harriet recalled her mother as "an unbelievably sweet, well-educated woman,"[4] who shared with the children her love of Danish literature.

Two of Harriet's older sisters were performers who helped to launch her on stage. The year Harriet was born, Alma (1863–1947) made her debut as an actress at the Christiania Theatre, the leading theatre in the capital. Alma eventually gave Harriet her first role and taught her the fundamentals of acting. Dagmar (1866–1954), another talented sister, was a concert and opera singer who offered Harriet artistic inspiration and guidance. Harriet and Dagmar bore a striking resemblance to each other. Dagmar was taller and had a more oval face, but both had dark eyes, pronounced curving eyebrows, and a beautiful profile. Seeing Alma as a successful comedienne and Dagmar as an acclaimed soprano, Harriet had role models who showed her what could be accomplished by a talented, disciplined young woman.

Little is known about the early years of Harriet's life other than simple anecdotes she told in her unpublished memoirs. Because of her father's work the family resided alternately in Norway and Sweden. Harriet attended two schools in Kristiania and two in Stockholm.[5] One of her earliest memories was of traveling alone on the train from Kristiania to Stockholm at the age of six. Throughout her life she made the trip between the two cities countless times. This led to some confusion of identity, for she had close emotional ties to Norway, yet she felt more Swedish than Norwegian.

Music was important to the Bosse family. The father sang with a choral society in Stockholm whose members included King Oscar II. Alma earned money as a piano teacher, and Dagmar studied and taught voice while still a teenager. Both Alma and Dagmar sang in operettas at the Christiania Theatre. Harriet and her brother Ewald (1880–1956) studied piano as children. For a while it seemed that music would be Harriet's lifework.

Harriet claimed that she was never stagestruck as a child, since she could not remember dressing up in costumes or putting on plays at home. With some coaxing and a twenty-five *øre* bribe from her mother, she might reluctantly recite a poem for company. Because of Alma's employment at the Christiania Theatre, Harriet probably saw a number of performances there when she was a child. Later she could recall only Henrik Ibsen's *Peer Gynt*, starring Bjørn Bjørnson and Johanne Dybwad. Eventually she and Dybwad were compared by the critics, for they played many of the same roles.[6]

At sixteen Harriet went to Stockholm to follow in Dagmar's footsteps. She studied at the conservatory, primarily to please her father, who wanted her to earn a certificate as a teacher. The Royal Conservatory of Music (Kongl. Musik-Konservatorium), where she enrolled in the fall of 1894, was administered by the Royal Musical Academy. The conservatory trained organists, church soloists, teachers for the public schools, and directors for military bands. Of the 164 students at the conservatory that year, 67 were women.[7] The only Norwegian in her class, Harriet was one of 31 students majoring in song. She studied voice with Ellen Bergman, who had been Dagmar's first teacher at the conservatory.[8] Bergman was praised as a singer for her "unusually distinct declamation and expressive, intelligent inter-pretation."[9] These characteristics were later typical of Harriet's acting.

The conservatory presented frequent student recitals, but Harriet was not considered ready to participate until 1896. That year she sang songs by French and Norwegian composers in three programs. She also performed declamation, which she was studying with Bertha Tammelin. In December Harriet presented a reading of Carl David af Wirsén's "Christmas Angel."[10] While Harriet was singing modest solos at student recitals, Dagmar was giving frequent concerts. After her debut at the Royal Opera in Stockholm in 1887, Dagmar had played such roles as Mignon and Cherubino. She appeared in concerts in Scandinavia, Germany, and France, and became well known for her interpretation of art songs. Edvard Grieg dedicated to Dagmar his "Haugtussa" song cycle. Critics wrote about Dagmar's singing in some of the same terms used later about Harriet's acting: her voice had "a silvery radiance," her diction was exemplary, and her interpretations were "fresh and unsentimental—so completely natural." Early in her career Harriet may have been coached by Dagmar, who began teaching voice, makeup, and scenic deportment at the Opera School and Conservatory in 1899.[11]

In the spring of 1897, after six semesters of study, Harriet passed her final examination and received a certificate in voice. Although she did not prepare for a certificate in piano, she was an excellent pianist. Music was an important part of her life. She occasionally sang in dramatic productions, but she much preferred instrumental music. Her favorite composers were Grieg, Beethoven, and Chopin. Among the pieces she played often were Grieg's Piano Sonata in E Minor, Norwegian composer Peder (Per) Carl Lasson's "Crescendo," and the *Appassionata* Sonata by Beethoven, which Strindberg liked to hear her play.[12] Her father's vision of Harriet as a teacher of music was never realized.

THE FAHLSTRØMS

While Harriet was still a schoolgirl, Strindberg had contact with some members of her family. He had been a customer at her father's bookshop on Mäster Samuelsgatan in Stockholm. In 1894 he met Alma and her husband Johan Fahlstrøm (1867–1938) in Paris. Many Scandinavian authors and artists visited Paris in the 1890s, encountering each other at restaurants and hotels. The Fahlstrøms stayed at the same place as Strindberg, the Hôtel des Américains in the Latin Quarter. Alma and Johan helped Strindberg send some of his paintings to Kristiania and received one of them, "Snow Storm at Sea," as a gift.[13]

The Fahlstrøms later became known for the fine quality of productions at their own theatres, but at the time they met Strindberg, they were both members of the Christiania Theatre ensemble. After being forced to resign in 1895, they sought out audiences by touring the provinces or working as guests for other managements. They also tried their first venture as independent producers. Without the enterprise of Alma and her husband, Harriet might never have made her stage debut. And without Alma's jealousy and temper, Harriet might never have left Norway.

THE FIRST DEBUT

For five evenings in mid-August 1896, the Fahlstrøms presented an abbreviated version of *Romeo and Juliet (Romeo og Julie)* at the old Tivoli Theatre in Kristiania. The tragedy was preceded by a curtain raiser—some evenings the fourth act of Ibsen's *Brand*, featuring Johan, and other evenings *Thunder*

Storm (Tordenveir) by Abraham Dreyfus, a tour de force for Alma as a jealous wife who talked nonstop. In *Romeo and Juliet* Alma did another comic role, the Nurse, and Johan played the young lover. His sister-in-law was invited to play Juliet.

Harriet Bosse was almost paralyzed by stage fright, but she reported to her sister in Stockholm, "You must believe it was a lovely evening, Inez!!!!!!"[14] The Fahlstrøms used a cutting of the Shakespeare play that included only five scenes, starting with the balcony scene. Scene 2 took place in Friar Lawrence's cell, scenes 3 and 4 in Juliet's chamber, and the last scene in the chapel. Harriet wrote to Inez: "I walked around there the whole time as if in a dream and wasn't aware enough to be really scared. After my big scene with the poison, I took 3 curtain calls but I still don't have any clear idea of how I got on and off, just a vague feeling that Alma pushed me . . . and that I stood bowing like a dunce." After signing herself "your radiantly happy sister Harriet," she added three postscripts: "People really stare at me on the street now. But it is just fun." She was embarrassed about her brother's publicity tactics: "That shameless Heinrich has put in the newspaper that I am seventeen"; she was really eighteen.[15] And finally, "Five curtain calls after the last act. Fourteen calls in all." Her sisters Inez and Dagmar shared the happiness, sending a telegram from Stockholm with the brief message "Hipp hurra!" Alma was proud of her protégée. The morning after the debut Alma awakened her: "Sit up, Harriet. Here are roses and gold for you!" Alma spread out the newspapers saying, "These are the roses, and here is the gold!" Then she showered onto the quilt ten shining crowns, Harriet's first salary.[16]

The thrill of opening night wore off during the weeks from 31 August to 7 October, when Harriet toured by boat and train to fourteen towns in Norway. First she had to notify the conservatory that she would arrive late for the fall term; then she set off with the Fahlstrøm troupe in a spirit of adventure, which is reflected in the tiny diary she kept.[17] Writing informally, with a disregard for punctuation, she filled the pages with impressions of the towns they visited, performing conditions, and her own progress as an actress. The diary also contains many practical details—attendance figures, ticket sales and expenses, her share of the receipts, and supplies she needed to take along such as "soap, curling iron, sponge, perfume."

At this time there was no union and no legal protection for actors. Harriet had an opportunity to see the Fahlstrøms' good managerial practices firsthand. To counteract the reputation that touring companies had for being unreliable, they paid their company's salaries in each town along the route. Long before it became a mandatory provision in contracts, they paid for everyone's travel, lodging, and meals. Harriet shared their concerns about box office income and public relations. She wrote in her diary upon arriving in Sandefjord: "Gives the impression of being a boring little town. Dirty and sad. Don't think we'll sell 4 tickets." Yet the next day she was happy to record, "Were in Sandefjord yesterday and despite all expectations a good house. Almost full."

The ensemble seemed to fill a cultural need in the provinces, and the Fahlstrøms had a loyal following. Audiences did not come just to see the handsome leading man; they also looked forward to seeing Alma in comic character roles. This was evident in Hamar where patrons were indignant because she did not appear. She had to stay home with her sick son, and there was a heated public protest.

Harriet was beginning to understand the dynamics of the performance environment and its effect on her work. She notes about an evening in Drammen: "I have never played so well there was nothing strange about that it was a proper and attractive theatre." Sometimes the group worked on tiny stages that allowed space to set up only two scenes of *Romeo and Juliet*. Harriet tells about the theatre in Sandefjord: "Played *terribly* but who can act in a theatre where one must put on makeup at a coffee table and fly across the passageway when we were supposed to go into the theatre. . . ." Conditions were even worse in Holmestrand: "The stage was made of small crates nailed together and we had to walk through closed doors when we wanted to get on stage because there were no such luxuries as entrances. And for the curtain a man had to stand off the stage and drag it up and down since it was so low he could reach up and pull it as he stood on his toes."

The Fahlstrøms persevered, presenting a varied program in each town. The scenes from *Romeo and Juliet* were advertised as being done "in costume" or with "new decorations and costumes." In addition the repertory contained declamation, comedy, music, and another serious play. Sometimes they competed with vaudevilles or a circus, but audiences came and Harriet noted in her diary the curtain calls, flowers, and shouts of "bravo!"

Although Harriet Bosse later claimed that she paid little attention to reviews during her forty-seven years in the theatre, this first season she made a scrapbook of critical notices. Johan and Harriet were commended for playing Shakespeare capably. Some reviews pointed out Harriet's lack of experience and control; others praised her talent and promise. While she may have seemed too frail and subdued to do justice to Juliet's passion,

Harriet was admired for her attractive appearance, clear voice, intelligence, and stage presence. A critic in Buskerud wrote: "She performed Juliet's big role with sensitivity, taste, and good understanding. Her performance of the scene where she is alone in her chamber and takes the sleeping potion was especially effective." Probably because she was Dagmar Bosse Möller's sister, Swedish newspapers noted her debut: "There was delicacy and grace in the image she presented, there was intelligence in the interpretation, and—for her age—a respectable ability to shape dialogue naturally and expressively. In addition Miss Bosse has a charming appearance, and there is much indication that she will have a beautiful future on the stage."[18]

Each day on the tour Harriet learned more about loyalty and hard work. Comments in her diary reveal that she was charmed by sentimentality and eager for exciting experiences. When sightseeing at the Nidaros Cathedral in Trondheim, the young girl climbed up the tower as far as she could go. She wrote in her diary: "The editor and I went higher than the others, and balanced on two beams that were laid across a deep abyss above the church. It was fun to stand there."

THE INGENUE

Johann Heinrich Bosse died on 5 November 1896. With the three thousand crowns she inherited, Alma decided to renovate the Alhambra Theatre. They would open with *Once Upon a Time—*. Johan would be perfect as the Prince and Alma as the comic servant. Who was to play the young Princess? A telegram was sent to Dagmar in Stockholm: "Ingenue needed. Send Harriet." Harriet rushed to Kristiania to rehearse for her first full-length play. Naming it the Central Theatre (Centralteatret), the Fahlstrøms opened their intimate and elegant theatre on 17 August 1897.[19]

For the grand opening the Fahlstrøms had hired an orchestra and ordered sets from Copenhagen. Alma, who later became an outstanding director, not only trained the motley cast and rehearsed her own major role, she attended to every detail. The morning of the premiere found her out in the house, pasting numbers from old calendars on the chairs. Opening night drew a large crowd. Despite the "tropical heat," there was a cordial mood and the audience stayed until the final curtain fell at 11:30 P.M.[20]

The action of *Once Upon a Time—* is reminiscent of *The Taming of the Shrew*; the princess is even called Kathrine. The play opens in a rococo palace in Illyria. The Princess is banished from court because of suspicious circumstances arranged by the prince. She must labor in a humble cottage in the woods and learn to love the disguised Prince while maturing as a woman. Johan Fahlstrøm dominated every scene and was acknowledged by the press to be a capable veteran of the stage. Harriet struggled with the demands of her role. In the first act she looked as dainty as a porcelain doll. It was difficult for the inexperienced actress to be convincing as both a capricious, pampered darling of the court and as a mistreated, hardworking peasant. Describing the evening years later, Sigurd Bødtker recalled the promising talent of the ingenue and her face "which—even with the soft features of a child—could express what a woman feels in her soul. . . ."[21]

Under her sister's demanding tutelage, Harriet learned the fundamentals of acting and clear diction. Olof Molander calls Alma Harriet Bosse's first and only teacher of acting.[22] Harriet said later: "I had great respect for Alma, who was 18 years older than I. Although she was always right when she commented on something, it wasn't easy . . . to hear her shouting at me during rehearsal from the orchestra . . . as I stood grieving, bent over my beloved Axel's grave in Adam Oehlenschläger's *Axel and Valborg [Axel og Valborg]*, 'Harriet, don't stand there looking like a boiled shrimp.'"[23]

One of Alma Fahlstrøm's greatest gifts was her ability to bring out the best in individual actors. She demanded more of her husband than anyone else, and with him she achieved her best results. When the Central Theatre opened in 1897, most of the company members had no previous profession-al acting experience. They included a dentist, a printer, an acrobat, and a music student—Harriet. Alma shaped them into a firmly controlled ensem-ble. She had a quick-witted, commanding personality and a fiery temper; often she would swear and shout when things went wrong.[24] A review in 1898 commented about her directing, "One notices at all points a strong guiding hand which must be characterized as a man's, even though it is a woman's."[25] Because Alma had been influenced by the new realism that Bjørn Bjørnson introduced at the Christiania Theatre, Harriet Bosse's early training stressed careful attention to details.

Harriet recalled her time at the Central Theatre: "I got all the leading roles—naturally with the help of my wise sister." Actually she did not get "all" the leads, but she had many opportunities to perform. During the season in Kristiania and on tour in May and June 1898, Harriet played approximately a dozen roles, including Thérèse in Strindberg's *Facing Death (Ved dødens port)*. Some roles she learned during this period remained in her repertory for years.

When Harriet appeared in Ludvig Holberg's *Pernille's Brief Time as a Lady (Pernilles korte fröykenstand)*, the audience could note both the family resemblance and the difference between the two sisters. Like Harriet, Alma was thought to look somewhat Japanese. She had a cute nose, pert face, and animated manner suited to comedy, while Harriet was "a dark, beautified version of her sister."[26] Leonore is usually a stereotyped and colorless young lover, but Harriet was so delicate and sincere that "Father Holberg's often rather dry words vibrated in her mouth like lovely, subdued music." When she and Alma as Pernille appeared together, their scene "was played so naturally and yet totally in the traditional style that the audience was completely carried away and began to applaud in the middle of the performance."[27]

Harriet Bosse had a unique ability to portray teenage girls convincingly. One of her first such characters, Lena in *The Christening Gift (Faddergaven)* by Peder Egge, foreshadowed her touching portrayal of Ibsen's Hedvig. Fernanda Nissen wrote: "Her face had the strangely old, worn-out expression which such an older daughter gets, when there is little food and many children in the house."[28]

One of Harriet's most demanding roles was Oehlenschläger's heroine Valborg, in the historical tragedy *Axel and Valborg* which takes place in Nidaros Cathedral in Trondheim in 1162. Valborg loves her kinsman Axel, but is betrothed to King Haakon. Amid villainy, pageantry, ritual, and warfare, she remains true to her love, but they both die — he in the service of the king, and she for love. Valborg says to Axel, "I am your Valkyrie." Harriet Bosse's interpretation was charming and conscientious, but an actress playing a Valkyrie needs a powerful personality and a commanding stage presence. Harriet was much better suited to the role of Skovstjernelil (Rautendelein), the sprightly elf in Gerhart Hauptmann's *The Sunken Bell (Klokken som sank)*. In this opening production of the 1898–99 season, Harriet was very good: "There was freshness, mischievousness, and passionate fervor in her playing."[29]

Since Alma's acting was limited to character roles, she frequently cast Harriet in romantic leads opposite Johan Fahlstrøm. Playing Romeo to her Juliet, the Prince to her Princess, and Axel to her Valborg, Johan served as an acting teacher by his example and gave Harriet her first experience of performing successfully opposite a partner. Throughout his career Fahlstrøm created a wide range of characterizations, including Osvald, Bluntschli, Luka, Shylock, and Falstaff. The public had first become aware of his remarkable talents when he played Krogstad in *A Doll House* in 1890. He developed a powerful voice, skill at speaking verse, and a forceful personality. In his best performances technique and emotion were kept in perfect balance. Johan Fahlstrøm always gave full credit to his wife for being the major influence on his acting.

On 19 February 1898, Alma hastily wrote a greeting in pencil on the letterhead of the Central Theatre for Harriet's twentieth birthday:

If I had time, I would write a poem to you in thanks for
all that is fine and beautiful that you have created in
your art — Take all our heartfelt wishes for sunshine and
flowers for your youth, my very dear little sister.

A thousand wishes for happiness
from
the three
of us.[30]

This harmonious relationship became strained in the months ahead, when Alma discovered that Johan was not only Harriet's leading man, but her passionate admirer offstage. The most vivid proof of his infatuation is the beautiful oil portrait he painted in 1897. Johan must have been proud of his work, for he sent the portrait to the Exposition Universelle in Paris in 1900. In the portrait Harriet is wearing a deep red dress trimmed with white lace. With soft, irregular curls falling on the forehead, her face and neck fill the canvas in a direct frontal view. Using bright tones of red and green, Johan captured the freshness and vitality of the young woman. Harriet learned to present herself to photographers in character, in sophisticated poses, usually in profile. In this little-known portrait, now stored at the Nordic Museum (Nordiska Museet) in Stockholm, she is looking straight ahead with a frank, open, and innocent gaze.[31] After the start of the fall season in 1898, Alma decided she did not want to see Harriet's face around the theatre. Displeased with Johan's infatuation, she told Harriet to leave. In November another young actress, Dina Nissen, made her debut at the Central Theatre, obviously replacing Harriet as the ingenue. In her memoirs Alma implies that Harriet was partly to blame for the ensemble's disbanding as the National Theatre neared completion. "Bjørn Bjørnson engaged for it [the National Theatre] almost all our leading talent — Harriet Bosse had already left for Paris. Thus our ensemble was broken up."[32] Harriet never saw the Fahlstrøms when she returned to Norway for visits.

Harriet could have taken refuge in Stockholm with her sister Dagmar and brother-in-law Calle (Carl) Möller, but she decided to travel and study. Her self-confidence and zest for adventure developed as she found herself facing the world alone. She also had moments of melancholy and doubt. On one page of her poetry album she entered a verse of her own composition:

Ingen far og ingen mor
Ingen på den hele jor
Har jeg, som mig ret kan läre
Livsens håb og lifsmod näre.[33]

No father and no mother
No one in all the world
Have I, who can teach me what is right
Or nourish hope and courage for life.

Harriet Bosse set out alone for Stockholm, Copenhagen, and Paris. It was a daring step, but perhaps not so surprising for someone who had ventured onto a lofty beam in the Nidaros Cathedral. There were admirers who were sorry to see her leave Kristiania. As critic Sigurd Bødtker wrote later,

— — —Once upon a time there was a princess in our land. She was a princess on the stage, and the art of acting expected great things from her. But it did not work out as it should have. No one bound the princess fast, and she went her way.

And now the princess is the queen in a foreign kingdom.[34]

CHAPTER TWO

Debut in Sweden

A modest inheritance from her father enabled Harriet Bosse to finance a stay in Paris. One evening in late November 1898 she arrived at the pension Moulinier at 6 rue de Mézières. She was greeted by the daughter, who invited her to join the family at a service in the nearby church of St. Sulpice. At bedtime Harriet recalled the excitement and apprehension of the train journey, glimpses of Paris from the taxi, and the sound of the organ and the fragrance of incense from her first visit to a Catholic church. As she stood on her balcony gazing at St. Sulpice bathed in moonlight, she was overjoyed to find herself in such an impressive city.[1]

Harriet soon felt at home. One of the lodgers was a massage therapist from Finland, Agda Söderman, who remained a friend for years. There were also two men from Germany, one of whom was studying art. On Christmas Eve the ladies from the pension attended midnight mass at St. Sulpice and returned to find that the men had set the stage for a party. There were glowing candles, a small Christmas tree, and an abundance of presents. The art student gave Harriet a sketch of herself as Skovstjernelil in *The Sunken Bell*, which he had created from her description. Away from the pension, Harriet became acquainted with Ida Molard, at whose salon artists and authors gathered.[2]

PREPARATION

From December 1898 through May 1899 Harriet had an opportunity to observe the contrast between traditional and innovative styles of production at Paris theatres and to study the craft of acting. She received permission to observe the classes of Maurice de Féraudy at the Conservatory of the Comédie-Française. Dominique–Marie–Maurice de Féraudy (1859–1932) had been acting at the Comédie-Française since 1880. From 1894 to 1905 he was a professor at the conservatory, where once he had been a student of the prominent actor Edmond Got. Féraudy was known as an elegant comedian and a versatile character actor, and above all as an interpreter of contemporary French bourgeois drama. His approach to acting was intellectual, marked by subtlety and restraint. Since her teacher was an active member of the ensemble, the Norwegian visitor undoubtedly saw him onstage in both the classical and modern repertory. Surely Bosse saw Féraudy in *Mercadet* by Honoré de Balzac, for on 30 January 1899, he took over the leading role formerly played by Got.[3]

Féraudy made an indelible impression on her, but when they were seated together at a banquet in Stockholm after World War I, he did not recall Harriet's having been in his classes. He had introduced her to the other students as "a little lady from the North Pole, who at home is always accompanied by a polar bear when she is out for a promenade."[4] Bosse credited Féraudy with teaching her how to play comedy. Especially as Marthe Bourdier in *The King (Kungen)* by G.A. de Caillavet and Robert de Flers and as Hélène de Trévillac in *The Adventure (Äfventyret)* by the same authors (with Étienne Rey), she recalled Féraudy's advice to put "both heart and elegance" into her delivery of lines.[5]

While in Paris Harriet Bosse went to the theatre frequently. An acquaintance arranged for her to receive free tickets from Aurélien Lugné-Poe and André Antoine.[6] At the Théâtre Antoine she had a box, which she shared with everyone from the pension. Later Bosse recalled that Antoine's productions were those she admired most in Paris, because his actors were the "most natural."[7] After her first visit, she wrote to assure Antoine that she admired his work and talent: "je me promet d'aller souvent étudier chez vous. j'aime votre art si speciel."[8] Bosse dreamed some day of playing Hedvig in *The Wild Duck* and Mélisande with Antoine's ensemble.[9]

Having founded his experimental Théâtre Libre in 1887, Antoine achieved artistic success while producing a great number of plays. At the Théâtre Antoine from 1897 until 1906, he provided vigorous leadership and stressed the importance of meticulous attention to detail.[10] That Bosse should prefer Antoine's naturalistic style explains in part the artistic goals she set for herself. During the early months of 1899 Harriet could have seen at the Théâtre Antoine *Mademoiselle Julie* by Strindberg, *La Parisienne* by Henri Becque, and the very successful *La Nouvelle Idole* by François de Curel.[11]

Lugné-Poe, manager of the Théâtre de l'Œuvre, did memorable productions in the 1890s of such Scandinavian plays as Ibsen's *Rosmersholm* and Bjørnstjerne Bjørnson's *Beyond Human Power*, although he is better known for innovative productions of Maurice Mæterlinck's *Pelléas and Mélisande* and Alfred Jarry's *Ubu Roi*. Harriet Bosse saw Lugné-Poe's outstanding ensemble not only during this stay in Paris, but on later visits and when his company came to Stockholm. During the early months of 1899 the Théâtre de l'Œuvre was playing Shakespeare's *Measure for Measure* at the Cirque d'Été and—on the stage of the Renaissance—a revival of Ibsen's *Enemy of the People*, whose popularity could be credited to its relevance to the Dreyfus affair.[12]

Bosse never considered Sarah Bernhardt an influence on her acting, although she had opportunities to see her in both Paris and Stockholm. She probably first saw the renowned star at her own theatre, which opened on 21 January 1899 in the former Théâtre des Nations. Bernhardt presented revivals of earlier successes, such as *La Tosca* by Victorien Sardou. Harriet may have taken advantage of Bernhardt's popular performances at 5:00 P.M. on Saturdays when the tickets cost only one franc.

The 1898–99 season in Paris offered a wealth of entertainment at thirty-eight different theatres, most of which presented several productions each week. Harriet may have seen the season's big hit at the Odéon, *La Reine Fiammette* by Catulle Mendès. At the Comédie-Française she could have seen classics such as Racine's *Phèdre* or contemporary plays like Brieux's *Le Berceau*.[13] Harriet must have seen Constant Coquelin as Cyrano during her stay in Paris, for that popular production had been running steadily at the Porte-Saint-Martin since its premiere in 1897. She could also have seen Coquelin as Napoleon in *Plus que reine* by Émile Bergerat, which opened on 4 April.

The months in Paris were joyful for Harriet. Crossing the Pont des Arts one sunny day, she felt inspired to write the following poem:

Har du kjent en deilig, svulmende fölelse
Vokse sig frem av din sjel,
Som om himmel og hav,
Som om höj og lav,
Som om allt der levet i verden var
Et eneste takk til Gud

Til Gud, der har givet oss alle den trang
Til at elske og glädes på jord,
Til at juble og le,
Til at frydes og se,
Til at synge det ud over bjerg og dal,
I en evig tonende sang.[14]

Have you known a lovely, swelling feeling
growing within your soul,
as if earth and sea,
as if high and low,
as if all that lived in the world were
but thanks to God.

To God, who has given us all the longing
to love and be happy on earth,
to rejoice and laugh,
to delight and see,
to sing it out over hill and vale,
in an everlasting resounding song.

When sending the poem to one of her sisters, Harriet hastened to reassure her that she had not become pious.

Harriet Bosse frequently returned to Paris in the years ahead. She became well acquainted with French production standards, acting style, and repertory. When a play she saw there had a good role for her, she suggested it to managers in Stockholm. In 1904 Harriet expressed admiration for Simone Le Bargy, the first really modern actress she had seen in France—without affectation and poses, coldness or formality. Madame Le Bargy came to life on stage like a real human being, Bosse said. Le Bargy was acclaimed as an interpreter of the plays of Henri Bernstein, for performances characterized by "her intelligence, her control, her nuanced and subtle diction." Although Bosse respected the excellent diction of French actors and the subtle good taste of certain productions, she always thought of her own temperament and acting style as Germanic.[15]

DEBUT IN STOCKHOLM

In the spring of 1899 Harriet Bosse faced a decision: Where should she continue her career? Should she return to Norway? Bjørn Bjørnson may have offered her a position at the new National Theatre.[16] She did receive a letter from a former colleague at the Central Theatre, trying to entice her back to Kristiania. Rudolf Rasmussen, who had played her father in *Once Upon a Time*—, sent a letter to Paris in March 1899:

Next season I am taking over the theatre on Akersgaden. I want to turn it into an elegant little theatre—completely artistic. As a director I have engaged the painter and author Otto Sinding, now a director at the Christiania Theatre. Mr Sinding has just enjoyed great success with *Romeo and Juliet*, a production which the newspapers say ranks with the most beautiful ever seen in this city. Backing my theatre venture are several of the richest men in town. But now, in short, dear young lady, will you return home and be the "Prima donna" at the theatre? You know I am kind and likeable, and you shall have a repertory which will bring you joy and pleasure. . . . Do come home again to the city which has missed you and your art for all too long. You will not regret it.[17]

Harriet declined Rasmussen's offer and returned to Stockholm in May. Dagmar persuaded her to try her luck as an actress in Stockholm, where there were more theatres than in Kristiania and where "things are on a larger scale." Admitting that Harriet spoke very poor Swedish, Dagmar was sure that she could learn the language with a good teacher. Nils Personne of Dramaten, the Royal Dramatic Theatre, granted an audition, at which Harriet read a fairy tale by Hans Christian Andersen. Personne told her she would be accepted into the company if she could "learn to talk like a human being." A few days later he offered her a one-year contract with a salary of eighteen hundred crowns.[18]

To clear away the confusion of Norwegian and Swedish, Harriet Bosse turned to her former declamation teacher, Bertha Tammelin. Once a successful actress, she was highly respected as a diction coach. At a summer cottage in the skerries, Tammelin, who was almost blind, worked for two months until the young woman's pronunciation was polished. She announced that Bosse was now ready to make her debut at Dramaten. On 22 August 1899, Bosse appeared with the prestigious ensemble as Loyse in the play *Gringoire* by Théodore Faullain de Banville.[19] Her work on the language continued, as she wrote an admirer that September. During the daytime she was still struggling with Swedish, "which I can't get into my head, as is only reasonable considering that previously I spoke the loveliest language in the world." Harriet expected to speak Swedish like a native one day, when her years in Kristiania were only a memory.[20] Eventually she used Swedish in private life, but for many years she spoke Norwegian at home with her sisters.[21]

Although Dramaten regularly staged new productions, they also kept in their repertory standard works like *Gringoire* that had been popular for years. This romantic historical play, first performed there in 1866, became an old standby that the management dusted off for one or two performances at intervals to please the public. Between its premiere and the winter of

1904, it was presented sixty-six times. Harriet had six predecessors as Loyse.[22] Of course she preferred being the first to create a role in a new production, but as a young member of the ensemble she was expected to accept any assignment. During the first season she played seven roles, winning most attention as Anna in *First Violin (Första fiolen)* by Gustav Wied and Jens Petersen and Puck in *A Midsummer Night's Dream (En midsommarnattsdröm)*.

DRAMATEN

The Royal Dramatic Theatre, usually referred to as Dramaten, traces its history to the era of Gustav III, an ardent patron of the performing arts in the late eighteenth century. In 1788 the king established a dramatic theatre intended primarily to present Swedish-language plays, but French theatre had a strong influence on its operation and repertory. The Royal Dramatic Theatre went through numerous changes during the next century—in financing, administration, location, and organization.

The first private theatre in Stockholm was founded in 1842, ending the monopoly and providing stimulating competition for the Royal Theatre. By the end of the century Stockholm had a number of private theatres, as well as variety houses offering light entertainment. Cancan dancers, tightrope walkers, fire-eaters, folk comedies, and other shows were calculated to win audiences with simple tastes. The supposedly low moral level of this entertainment caused consternation in religious circles, as did an occasional play at Dramaten that ran counter to bourgeois ideals of proper family life. Operettas by Offenbach did wonders for the box office but were considered unworthy of a national theatre and off-limits for any proper lady. Criticism also was directed against the practice of serving alcoholic beverages during intermissions.

The decades preceding Harriet Bosse's debut in Sweden saw heated public and parliamentary debates about theatre, tied to various social and political issues. There was the perennial controversy about whether theatre performs the useful social function of educating the public and setting a high standard of linguistic usage or whether it simply provides entertainment for the privileged few. Economic conditions reached a crisis during these years, leading to a large immigration to the United States. Farmers and urban laborers were often in direct need, and some argued that it was unfair for tax money received from the entire population to be used in part to subsidize a leisure pastime of the elite.

Whether Dramaten was truly a national theatre was frequently debated. In the neighboring countries of Norway and Finland the champions of a national theatre were fighting for the use of native-born actors, the predominant spoken language, and production of native drama. In Sweden the debate usually focused on administration and economics. Dramaten was expected to be the nation's outstanding theatre, maintaining high artistic standards. Some critics found that it fell far short of being national in the sense of a folk theatre, for Dramaten did not serve a broad cross section of the population, except perhaps with Christmas productions.

The typical patrons of the Royal Dramatic Theatre and the Opera were upper class for most of the nineteenth century, and many considered the royal theatres to be extensions of the social life at court. However, there was some diversity in the audience, which tended to be grouped by social class according to seat location. By the time Bosse joined the company in 1899, the audience was changing, as seen in the list of season ticket holders. Whereas earlier the list had been dominated by court officials, by 1900 merchants and members of the business community were in the majority. Changes in the composition of the audience reflected developments in society as a whole.

King Oscar II, who reigned from 1872 to 1907, was avidly interested in theatre. Some critics thought he appointed managers who had noble rank or previous service in the military or at court, but who knew little about the art of theatre. The king preferred French comedies, which were performed with excellent ensemble playing and polished delivery of dialogue when Dramaten was under the direction of Gustaf Fredrikson from 1888 to 1898. The theatre produced some works of Ibsen, including *The Vikings at Helgeland, Lady Inger of Østraat, A Doll House*, and *The Wild Duck*. Dramaten usually avoided anything that might prove offensive, especially by unknown or controversial playwrights like August Strindberg. The king sometimes intervened if he considered a production radical. The theatre had a literary advisor or censor, who judged whether scripts were acceptable morally and aesthetically. During Bosse's first engagement, Carl Carlsson Bonde held the position and vetoed any plays that did not suit his conservative standards. Eric Wennerholm has described the climate at Dramaten in the late nineteenth century as "conventional and rigid." Lucrative farces and insignificant French and German drawing room comedies outweighed great drama in the repertory, he wrote, while tiresome and constrained mannerisms were all that remained of the traditional French acting style.[23]

Edvard Stjernström opened an excellent private theatre in 1875, the New

Theatre (Nya Teatern). Under Ludvig Josephson, who managed the theatre effectively from 1879 to 1887,[24] the New Theatre produced Swedish classics and new plays, and on the whole had a repertory of more substance and merit than Dramaten's. The New Theatre, later known as the Swedish Theatre (Svenska Teatern), dominated the theatre scene in Stockholm in the 1880s, presenting serious classical drama, including Goethe's *Faust*, and contemporary plays of ideas, such as those by Bjørnson.

The building where Bosse made her debut was located at Kungsträd-gården. Constructed in 1842, it had been known as both the New Theatre and the Smaller Theatre (Mindre Teatern). The building was sold to the government by Edvard Stjernström in 1863 to serve as the Royal Dramatic Theatre for the next forty-five years. In 1898 the building underwent urgently needed repairs and electric lighting was installed, but the theatre was constantly threatened with closure because of its dilapidated condition.

Political arguments, financial problems, and moral issues all played a role when the Parliament (Riksdag) voted in 1888 to withdraw financial support from the Royal Dramatic Theatre. The king appointed Gustaf Fredrikson to lead what is known as the first association. In effect the theatre continued to be partially subsidized since it was charged very low rent for the building. A new association was established in 1898 led by Nils Personne with all members of the company sharing financial responsibility. Dramaten was totally divorced from its former status as a royal or court theatre.

Harriet Bosse found herself contending with a powerful administrative structure controlled, not surprisingly, by men. The highest-ranking administrator (*inspektör*) was the censor, Bonde. Next in rank were the managers Nils Personne and Gustaf Fredrikson. Under their administration many favorite productions were revived and occasional new plays introduced. Full-length works alternated with programs of two or three short plays. While both men were noted for presenting French, German, and Scandinavian comedies, Personne also produced a few contemporary Swedish plays and plays of literary value, especially by Shakespeare. The Ibsen works he scheduled sometimes featured visiting artists, including Johanne Dybwad from Norway and Betty Hennings from Denmark.

Nils Personne began his career in 1876 and worked with industry and intelligence to develop a polished technique and a specialization of playing fools and buffoons. He was an able translator, theatre historian, director, teacher, and administrator. After serving as head of Dramaten's training school for actors from 1890–98, he managed the theatre until the second actors' association was disbanded in 1904. By the time Harriet Bosse auditioned, Personne had played a variety of character parts, such as Malvolio in *Twelfth Night*. One of his greatest successes was the lead in *Cyrano de Bergerac*, a production that illustrates the tendency of major theatres in Stockholm to compete by producing plays that had been successful in Paris or Berlin. Bosse attended Personne's lectures on theatre history and was influenced by his meticulous coaching in proper period mannerisms. As a director he stressed pacing and cut scripts to quicken the tempo. His productions have been credited with "consistency and integration" of action.[25]

Gustaf Fredrikson's acting career began in 1862 and spanned more than fifty years. Having studied in Paris, Vienna, and Berlin, he brought to the Swedish stage a modern realistic style, elegant manner, and conversational delivery. Henrik Ibsen asked that he play Helmer in the first Swedish production of *A Doll House*. Evert Sprinchorn comments that "Fredrikson was to the Stockholm stage of the 1870s what Cary Grant was to the Hollywood film of the 1930s and the 1940s . . . a matinee idol before there was such a thing, the popular star of drawing-room comedy and light melodrama, admired for his elegance and charm. . . ." In his memoirs Fredrikson looked back fondly on his administrative work at Dramaten (1888–98 and 1904–7). He thought of the turn of the century as a happy period for the ensemble, who felt there was something special about playing at "Gamla Dramaten"—the old building—in its final years. Perhaps because the theatre's days were numbered, "interest on both sides of the footlights was so strong and vital." Fredrikson's acting was marked by elegance and vigor, even when he represented the last glimmer of the golden age of French comedy. When Fredrikson resumed his position as head of Dramaten in 1904, the association was disbanded and the theatre was without royal sponsorship.[26]

By the end of the nineteenth century the trend in Scandinavia was toward a more modern approach to directing. Directors using newer methods included Bjørn Bjørnson and Gunnar Heiberg in Norway, William Bloch and Herman Bang in Denmark and Ludvig Josephson, August Lindberg, and Harald Molander in Sweden.[27] Not all directors, however, were innovative and effective. One of their most perceptive critics was the playwright Tor Hedberg, who became a director and head of Dramaten in 1910. Hedberg maintained that there was an urgent need for improved planning and consistent quality in the choice of repertory and preparation of productions. It seemed to him that theatres left everything to chance and that buying a ticket to any theatre in Stockholm was as much a gamble as buying a lottery ticket.[28] Some Dramaten directors began to use a new approach in

the early years of the twentieth century, working with psychological relationships and individual roles. This approach proved compatible with
Harriet Bosse's preferred method of working.

Bosse started her Swedish stage career at a time when critics were
demanding reform. It was traditional for an adoring public to come to see
their favorite singers and actors, regardless of the literary merit of a
production. The public's attraction to stars and virtuoso acting was inten-
sified after they saw impressive guest performers such as Sarah Bernhardt,
Eleonora Duse, Constant Coquelin, and the company of the Duke of Saxe-
Meiningen. Stockholm critics realized that many Swedish actors lacked the
skill to speak verse in classical plays, while others needed to learn a new
performance style for innovative contemporary drama. The critics demanded less focus on stars and elegant costuming, and more on characterization and other values in the scripts.

The most notable actresses who had preceded Harriet Bosse at Dramaten
were Elise Hwasser, Lina Sandell, and Ellen Hartman. Hwasser, who
retired in 1888, played a number of leading Ibsen roles, including Nora,
Mrs. Alving, Hjørdis, and Lady Inger of Østraat. One of her most acclaimed
characterizations was Queen Anne in Eugene Scribe's *Glass of Water*. Harriet
would not be expected to do all the same roles, for Elise Hwasser was
majestic and monumental. She played strong, independent women—Jane
Eyre, Lona Hessel, and Bjørnson's Maria Stuart. Like Bosse in her later
years, Hwasser experienced the bitterness of being pushed aside in favor of
younger talent, when she could still have played with vigor and outstanding
technique.[29]

Lina Sandell, who was petite and energetic, played a wide range of roles,
in which she was interesting, sensitive, natural, and, above all, intelligent.
After her debut in 1884, she played numerous ingenues, including Ophelia,
Hedvig in *The Wild Duck,* and Svanhild in *Love's Comedy* by Ibsen, but she
demonstrated versatility in a variety of other roles. Later she specialized in
older characters, notably Queen Christina in the play *A Phantom (En
skugga)* by Knut Michaelson.[30]

The public loved Ellen Hartman, who made her debut in 1877. She had
round cheeks, big childlike eyes, and a charming, bright personality suited
to modern comedy and to the role of Puck in *A Midsummer Night's Dream.*
For a while Hartman studied acting in Paris and performed in the French
language. Returning to Stockholm in 1894, she was a box office draw for
Dramaten until her retirement in 1898 and was especially popular in
Victorien Sardou's *Madame Sans-Gêne*.[31]

Sandell had not played ingenues for years. Hartman's acting featured technique, personality, and superficial effects, quite different from Bosse's simple, natural style. Nevertheless Harriet Bosse resembled those actresses in her dainty appearance and charm, and was considered their successor.

TALENT AND DETERMINATION

Arriving at Dramaten with some stage experience, training given her by Alma Fahlstrøm, and ideas acquired in Paris, Harriet Bosse also brought natural potential that was recognized immediately by some critics. About five feet tall, she had a well-proportioned, rounded figure, which showed off elaborate costumes to fine effect and looked charming in fantasy and children's costumes. Because she was petite and delicate, Harriet was often cast as a young girl or fairy-tale figure.

An olive complexion, dark hair, roundish face, straight nose, almond-shaped eyes, and arching eyebrows set Harriet Bosse apart from other Scandinavian actresses. When a journalist told her she looked French, she replied that people usually said she looked Japanese.[32] Her exotic beauty — suggesting an Oriental or Middle Eastern origin — suited her for the roles of Sakuntala and Chitra in Indian plays, Biskra in Strindberg's *Simoon (Samum)*, Salome in Sudermann's *Johannes*, and Gulnare in Oehlenschläger's *Aladdin*. The distinctive dark beauty also was appropriate for Spanish, Italian, and French characters. Although her exotic looks were an advantage, they excluded her from certain roles. With the aid of wigs, however, her appearance could be remarkably transformed — even to Nordic beauty.

August Strindberg often mentioned Bosse's tiny hands. Actually they were broad and strong, probably because of many hours spent playing the piano. She used her hands beautifully. They were never still but moved gracefully or were held in poses that revealed the French and Italian training in vogue at the turn of the century.[33]

Bosse had an exquisite and silvery voice. The images of silver and crystal used to describe Sarah Bernhardt's voice were evoked constantly by critics describing Bosse. When young, she spoke in a light, high-pitched voice. As the voice matured, it maintained the quality of a beautiful musical instrument. She developed remarkable vocal control and precision of articulation that were commended throughout her career. Those who remember her say that no one speaks that clearly any more. Her voice was resonant and easily heard throughout the theatre. Partly as her individual manner of bringing out the lyrical quality of dialogue and partly because of a love for music,

Bosse spoke almost musically, another point of comparison between her vocal technique and that of Bernhardt. Bosse would cling to certain words for emphasis; some say that she "sang" on the vowels. However, this unique feature of her acting seemed stylized or artificial to some critics.[34]

The most decisive attribute Harriet Bosse brought to Dramaten was strength of personality. She was determined to succeed, not by imitating established actresses but by developing a new style—quiet, natural, and subtle. She considered the predominant broad style to be "artificial, declamatory, and false," and she disliked the popular repertory of French drawing-room comedies and sentimental German plays. There were so many approaches to acting at Dramaten that productions seldom achieved unity of style. Each performer worked individually, ignoring the director and fellow actors. One could see the grand bravura style of older stars, the sophisticated salon mannerisms of Gustaf Fredrikson, the neoclassical precise and polished performances of Nils Personne, and the intense, almost undisciplined power of Anders de Wahl. Harriet also encountered a spirit of competition. Herbert Grevenius has described the company's attitude toward ensemble acting: "If you don't get in my way, I won't get in yours."[35]

Critics expected actors to exercise good judgment and taste in developing their talents. There was no formal instruction for young members of the company; they learned by observing more experienced performers and by working under various directors.[36] Years later Harriet Bosse recalled being impressed by the genius and power of Strindberg's *Crimes and Crimes (Brott och brott)*, which opened on 26 February 1900, starring Augusta Lindberg as Henriette. Bosse sat in the auditorium at rehearsals, trembling with admiration and excitement.[37] The production was significant because it established Strindberg as a major playwright whose works deserved inclusion in Dramaten's repertory. That thirty-one performances were given is evidence the public shared Harriet's enthusiasm about *Crimes and Crimes*.[38] With the courage of her convictions and this production as inspiration, Harriet felt justified in continuing toward her goal—to play with intimate and subdued realism.

Harriet Bosse's debut coincided with a year of achievement and good will for Dramaten. Nineteen productions were presented in 1899–1900, with leading roles played mostly by older members of the company. Harriet had several young rivals. One was Valborg Holmlund, later known as Valborg Hansson, who was lovely that year as Karin Månsdotter in a play by Adolf Paul.[39] The casting of young actresses was probably often affected by offstage relationships with authors, critics, managers, directors, and other company members. Memoirs and newspaper reviews are subjective and incomplete, since they do not divulge backstage gossip or the personal prejudice of the writers. Intrigues and power struggles at the theatre were discussed and sometimes decided in the city's cafés, yet they are not recorded. It is impossible to trace definitively the effect of flirtations, jealousies, and favoritism. For example, Amanda Janson was presumed to enjoy special advantages because of her relationship with Nils Personne, whom she married in 1905.[40] Harriet also gained a favored position because of her relationship with a man. We may only speculate about what she would have achieved without an identity as the third wife of August Strindberg.

CHAPTER THREE

The Ingenue and the Playwright

Before he met Harriet Bosse, August Strindberg had lived through more than fifty years of intellectual growth, artistic achievement, and private anguish. Born on 22 January 1849, he grew up in a household in which his mother's illness, his father's remarriage to the housekeeper, and unjust discipline became his most vivid memories of childhood. Strindberg was ambitious, but it took years of effort as a teacher, actor, journalist, and librarian before he found success in the field of literature. The novel *The Red Room (Röda rummet)*, published in 1879, brought him recognition and marked an important milestone in the history of modern Swedish literature.

Strindberg was unbelievably prolific. Although he is best known in English-speaking countries for his drama, he also wrote fiction, poetry, and essays.[1] In the 1880s most of the novels he wrote used autobiographical material and reflected his ambition to be part of the naturalistic movement. The same may be said of major plays such as *The Father (Fadren)* and *Miss Julie (Fröken Julie)*. In the 1890s Strindberg continued experimenting with dramatic form, but he was also obsessed with scientific experiments. Illness, an interest in the occult, and other stressful experiences caused a period of crisis referred to as the Inferno. As he recovered his mental balance, Strindberg's zest for writing returned, and he began a productive decade of writing more novels, innovative plays, and reflective essays. After he met Harriet Bosse, he wrote many works with thoughts of her foremost in his mind.

The marriage to Bosse was Strindberg's third. His first marriage in 1877 to the beautiful Siri von Essen was made possible when she divorced her husband, Carl Gustav Wrangel. She and Strindberg intended to have a modern marriage, maintaining their independence, each busy with a successful career. To protect their reputations, they gave away the child born shortly after the wedding, and within two days the premature infant was dead. There were happy interludes when Strindberg supported Siri's acting career and enjoyed family life with their three children. There were also years of exile, suspicion, and disillusionment. Siri declared, "I am not born to be a *woman* — God intended me to be an artist. . . ."[2] For Siri, who considered herself a bad wife, mother, and homemaker, it was frustrating to lose her beauty and health. After their divorce in 1891, Siri received custody of the children.[3] She returned to her native Finland to cope with family responsibilities and economic hardship. Most people, including Harriet Bosse, believed that Siri was the one of Strindberg's wives whom he loved the most. He was deeply moved at news of Siri's death twenty-three days before his own.

Frida Uhl was Strindberg's second wife. His reaction to their marriage is fictionalized in the play *To Damascus (Till Damaskus)* and in the novel *The Cloister (Klostret)*. Frida's story of the marriage was published in 1933–34 as *Strindberg and His Second Wife (Strindberg och hans andra hustru)*.[4] Her account is sentimental and unreliable, but contains "sudden flashes of insight. Frida definitely was the most intelligent of Strindberg's wives," according to Olof Lagercrantz, who describes her as "emancipated, ambitious and independent" — a combination of "all the traits Strindberg condemned in women."[5] The author was forty-four and Frida twenty-one when they married in May 1893. They lived together briefly, spending part of their marriage in London and part in Austria, where their daughter Kerstin was born in May 1894. There were some happy weeks that spring and summer, but after separation and an unsuccessful reconciliation in Paris, Frida filed for divorce. The failure of the intense relationship can be explained by repercussions from Strindberg's first marrriage, his apprehension about Frida's ambitions for a career in journalism, their inability to agree on a life-style, anxiety about finances, and his craving for success as a scientist and an artist. Ironically, Frida Uhl's literary image as The Lady in *To Damascus I* became the vehicle by which Harriet Bosse entered the imagination and affections of the playwright.

COURTSHIP

In early January 1900 Harriet Bosse was studying a role that would change her life: Puck in *A Midsummer Night's Dream*. She was eager to try her conception of the character as a will-o'-the-wisp, "dressed," as she put it,

in something gray, colorless, with an electric lamp on my forehead, so that when I flew over the dim forest scene, only the light would show. But they refused at the Opera's costume shop. "Miss Bosse is just a beginner, so you have nothing to say about it. You will be dressed like your predecessors in the role, that is, like a girl in a tulle dress." I was unhappy, but kind Emil Grandinson the director helped me so that I didn't have to wear tulle, but the costume they put on me became feminine anyway. In my opinion Puck should be a rascal, with lots of mad pranks . . . like Barrie's Peter Pan.[6]

The costume was a modest sailor dress with a pert elf's cap. Bosse's eyebrows were drawn with an amusing slant extending upward. A production photo of the court setting shows a large, columned construction on two levels against a painted backdrop. Since the other women in the cast wore formal, draped Greek costumes, Bosse was strikingly different. The eye is drawn to Bosse's tiny figure, posed gracefully in the downstage area, with her left foot turned out and pointed.[7]

The opening night audience on 6 February was charmed by her dainty, impish Puck. In this three-act adaptation by F. A. Dahlgren,[8] Puck first appeared at the start of act 2, seated on a flower. Harriet invented the pantomime of capturing and releasing a fly, then following its flight with her eyes as Mendelssohn's music filled the theatre. Music was heard throughout the production, often accompanying Puck's gestures, entrances, and exits. In many of her scenes the prompt script is labeled "melodram," meaning that music is played under the dialogue. The scenery changed frequently, sometimes by simple means, as when Puck cast the spell, waved her hands, and bushes were pushed in to hide the sleeping lovers.[9]

August Palme, who played Lysander, thought that several of the young actresses in the cast might be suited for the lead in August Strindberg's new play, *To Damascus I*. Palme, a handsome, pleasant actor admired for his speaking of lyrical dialogue, had played Gringoire when Harriet made her debut at Dramaten and was her leading man in several major productions during the next few years. She later expressed appreciation of "his distinctive acting style, which evinced goodness and warmth."[10] Now the actor played a role in her private life, for he visited Strindberg and urged him to see the Shakespearean comedy.

Strindberg went to *A Midsummer Night's Dream* with his sister Anna von Philp and her family. Usually he did not remain in a theatre throughout a performance, for the many eyes turned his way made him feel uncomfortable, but that evening he was spellbound and stayed until Puck brought the dream to its close and bid a bright farewell to the audience.[11]

The next day Strindberg asked his sister to get him a photograph of "Puck." Later he teased Bosse by saying that her shapely legs had impressed him; she would have preferred to capture his attention with her talent.[12]

Others appreciated that talent, saying, when *A Midsummer Night's Dream* was revived in 1903, that Bosse stood out as the bright spot in the production. She was the only cast member responsive to Mendelssohn's music and the only one deserving applause, wrote a critic. "Her imaginative movement as the wonderful dream figure characterized, in a charming way, life in the forest on a midsummer night."[13] Strindberg always remembered Harriet's Puck as playful and good-natured—"wanting to play the *troll* and be wicked, but not able to."[14]

Although Strindberg knew little about Harriet Bosse before she delighted him as Puck, she was already fascinated by his life and works. She knew the Fahlstrøms had met him in Paris. Now in Stockholm she heard a great deal about the famous author and attended the successful premiere of his *Gustav Vasa* at the Swedish Theatre in 1899. Bosse recalled later that she read as much as she could by Strindberg, becoming fascinated with his work and feeling sympathy for the unhappiness he had suffered. On New Year's Eve, 1899, as she and her brother Ewald were returning from a celebration at Skansen, Harriet impulsively suggested they go to the building on Banérgatan where Strindberg lived on the ground floor. The apartment was dark and quiet. The two young people pressed their noses against the windowpane, and Harriet whispered, "Happy New Year."[15]

In April Bosse was successful in a much larger role, Anna in the Danish play *First Violin*. She had the fun of appearing disguised as a young man applying for a place in a string quartet. Later Anna was revealed to be a vivacious and irresistible girl, plotting to win not only the first chair, but also permission to marry the pharmacist son of one of the musicians. This was the first role for which Bosse received extensive commentary from the Stockholm critics.

Meanwhile Strindberg had not forgotten her as Puck. Using Palme as intermediary, he invited her to visit at his apartment on 31 May. Since she could not call on the author in her dowdy gray walking suit, Dagmar came to the rescue, lending her a black dress that made Harriet feel slender and sophisticated. With the jacket buttoned, no one would guess that the dress was held together by pins. Although she had hesitated before ringing the bell, Harriet was soon charmed by Strindberg's smile and fascinating talk. The table was set with wine, flowers, and fruit. Conversation covered "everything between heaven and earth," including his experiments with alchemy. She agreed that the sample he showed her must be gold, although she commented later that if he had shown her a dog and said it was a cat, she would have agreed. The visit has become part of the Strindberg legend.

According to Bosse, the playwright asked for the feather from her hat to make a pen with which to write his plays.[16]

Strindberg wanted Harriet to play The Lady in *To Damascus*. She visited him on 5 July and agreed to accept the honor, then sent a brief note to Nils Personne on 18 July: "After having read through the role of The Lady in 'To Damascus,' I just want to notify you, that I have decided to try to do it as well as I can."[17]

Details of the progress of their courtship are found in Strindberg's diary and correspondence and have been frequently reported by biographers.[18] One of the most intriguing incidents occurred on 15 November 1900 when Strindberg was observing a dress rehearsal of *To Damascus*. He came on stage to talk to Bosse, and as he stood facing her, he felt mesmerized by her eyes, spellbound as though she had actually kissed him. We know from his diary that he fantasized that he had become her husband long before their wedding night.

The premiere of *To Damascus* was 19 November 1900, a significant date in the history of Swedish theatre.[19] As usual the playwright did not come to the theatre on opening night, but he sent Harriet red roses and a letter thanking her for the beautiful things he had seen at dress rehearsal. He wished her luck on her journey "among thorns and stones," offering the flowers to place on her path.[20]

Being singled out to play the lead in *To Damascus* did not immediately elevate Harriet Bosse to a privileged position. She still had to accept any assignment, including such bit parts as a page in *Cyrano de Bergerac*, which opened a remarkably successful run on 9 March 1901. In *Cyrano* another young actress, Valborg Hansson, stood center stage with Nils Personne. Bosse remarked more than fifty years later, "Her Roxane still lives in . . . memory."[21] We may judge the size of roles by the number of pages (or "sides") a performer received, as noted in the theatre's "Role Book." As Marie-Louise in *Mammon*, for example, Harriet's role was only two and one-eighth pages long.[22]

While Harriet continued to appear in roles selected by the management, Strindberg was determined to have her as Eleonora, the delicate young girl in his new play *Easter (Påsk)*. Two days after the opening of *To Damascus* Strindberg proposed to Personne that Bosse play Eleonora. It is customary to say that the role was written for her, but the model for the character was Strindberg's sister Elisabeth. Like Eleonora, she was confined to a mental hospital. Despite doubts that she was ready to play the role, Bosse accepted. The premiere took place at a matinee on Maundy Thursday, 4 April 1901.

By then the twenty-three-year-old actress and the fifty-two-year-old playwright were engaged. Their relationship developed as they shared thoughts on literature and theatre. The playwright revealed his need for someone to brighten his life and restore his faith in humanity. Using images from *To Damascus*, Strindberg offered Bosse the opportunity to encourage him to face life hand in hand with her, rather than letting him turn his back on the world to enter a monastery. According to tradition, often confirmed by Bosse, Strindberg proposed on 5 March 1901, by asking, "Will you have a little child with me, Miss Bosse?" She curtsied and answered, "Yes, thank you." On 6 March they bought rings for each other, and the next day their engagement announcement appeared in the newspaper with the notice that they would not be paying or receiving calls.

Harriet was busy at the theatre in April, although she was replaced in the cast of *Cyrano*. Because of a question about the legality of Strindberg's divorce from Frida Uhl, it appeared for a while that a new marriage might not be sanctioned. Strindberg dreamed of going with Harriet to a church one evening after vespers and kneeling at the altar to promise fidelity and exchange rings, praying God to bless their union. He visualized opening the windows of their home the next morning to sunshine and mild breezes—a sign from a "smiling" God. On 6 May Bosse and Strindberg were married, with his brother Axel and her brother-in-law Carl Möller as witnesses. Now she could never escape the public eye. "To be August Strindberg's wife is a high position in society; it is as good as a queen's crown," wrote Anna Branting.[23] The couple began living together at Karlavägen 40 in a five-room apartment furnished elaborately by Strindberg, according to his taste. The cover of the May issue of the periodical *Teatern* featured the bride as Puck. This image would be enshrined on Strindberg's wall, in life size, when the marriage ended and he was once again alone.

THE MARRIAGE

Perhaps it was inevitable that the marriage would not last. The great age difference, Strindberg's previous marital discord, and Bosse's career ambitions foreshadowed the unhappy ending of what in the spring of 1901 was a beautiful romance. Harriet Bosse came to her marriage, at Strindberg's request, bringing none of her own furnishings. He would create the setting in which to nurture and dominate her. At his insistence she was to study languages and literature, learn to sculpt, and do whatever else would preserve her image as the pure and exquisite creature he idolized. (Biographers and psychiatrists have narrated and analyzed the episodes of the marriage at great length.[24] Further comments on the marriage's significance for Strindberg's work and Bosse's career are found in chapter II.)

Harriet grew depressed in the dark apartment, in which she felt like a caged bird. At least the summer would allow her to spread her wings, she thought. Plans were to travel to the Continent, but on the morning they were to depart, Strindberg announced that "the Powers" had conveyed a psychic message to cancel the trip. Harriet was to content herself with viewing people at a distance from the window of their apartment and traveling vicariously through pictures and descriptions in a Baedeker guidebook. Instead, on 26 June she left alone for her "honeymoon" at the beach resort of Hornbæk in Denmark. Strindberg arrived in July. He grimly endured socializing with other vacationers and drove away a photographer who intruded on their privacy at the beach. This was a happy interlude, of which one souvenir is a tiny drawing by Harriet: a heart with Strindberg's face in its center.[25] Later, writing on 4 September, Strindberg described this tranquil time in a letter to his unborn child:

And your lovely Mother cradled you upon the blue waters that sweep three kingdoms . . . and in the evenings, when the sun was about to set, then—then she sat in the garden, looking the sun in the face, that you might be given the sun to drink of.

Child of the sea and the sun, you slept your first slumber in a little red cottage of ivy, in a white room, where words of hate were not even whispered and where nothing impure was even thought.[26]

At the beginning of August the couple traveled to Berlin—and began to quarrel. Harriet wanted to visit a nightspot; Strindberg was shocked at her willingness to appear in a place he considered beneath her. While still in Germany, she felt ill. Her husband guessed the cause, and on 9 August a doctor confirmed that she was pregnant. Harriet began the new season at Dramaten by playing Eleonora several times. On 23 August the performance of *Easter* was cancelled. She had left Karlavägen the day before, no longer able to tolerate her husband's jealousy and unreasonable moods. Harriet's closeness to her sisters annoyed Strindberg, but she needed their emotional support. Determined to start an independent life, she even threatened to use Bosse as her child's last name.

Harriet stayed away for more than six weeks, during which Strindberg was tormented by vacillating moods. He called on her at Dagmar's home, and she visited him at their apartment. It was a time of great longing and emotional stress for them both. Strindberg suggested they spend the winter in Switzerland or take a trip to Paris, but she would not leave her work. Harriet feared that her youthful exuberance and Strindberg's complexity and sensitivity would never harmonize, yet she admired and sympathized with him. He persuaded her to return to Karlavägen in early October, and they enjoyed a tranquil time as Harriet continued to perform until late in her pregnancy. While she sculpted and read, Strindberg painted and wrote, and cheered her with promises of wonderful roles in his new plays. He enjoyed hearing her play the piano and occasionally played himself.

During the fall of 1901 Harriet appeared in four productions. Her schedule was busy, sometimes including matinee and evening performances in two different productions on the same day. She was intended to play Emerentia Polhem in Strindberg's *Charles XII (Karl XII)*, but the premiere was delayed so long that she had to request sick leave as of 3:00 P.M. 3 February. On 25 March 1902, Harriet gave birth to a daughter, named Anne Marie in honor of her maternal grandmother. According to family tradition, Harriet's sister Inez was allowed to choose the name. If the child had been a boy, the parents were planning to name him Örn (Eagle). The birth was agonizing and one of Harriet's sisters made sure that Strindberg heard every cry of pain. Anne Marie was cherished by both her parents. Strindberg was very fond of his youngest daughter, as he was of all his children. Harriet was an affectionate mother, even though she often had to be away because of an engagement.

During their marriage Strindberg rarely went to the theatre with Harriet. They did see Wilhelm Meyer-Foerster's *Old Heidelberg (Gamla Heidelberg)*, starring Anders de Wahl and Astri Torsell, and Strindberg's *Lucky Per's Journey (Lycko-Pers resa)*, with his daughter Greta as Lisa. When Harriet was in a play or when one of his own works had a premiere, Strindberg stayed home, pacing back and forth and receiving a report by telephone during each intermission.

The couple tried to establish a social life with a circle of friends, including artists and actors, but Strindberg wanted a much more private and quiet existence than did his young wife. Once he even turned away a visitor, the women's advocate Ellen Key. From a humble post in the corner, Harriet observed the pleasant mood of her husband's Beethoven evenings with friends and his brother Axel, who came for chamber music and supper. While she tried to share his interest in psychic phenomena, Harriet's thoughts were concentrated on the theatre. She was ambitious and assertive, fighting for the opportunity to play challenging roles. Strindberg worried about his wife's socializing with colleagues from Dramaten. He would usually retire before she arrived home in the evening. Although he bought her soft slippers to put on at the door, he was often awakened by the sound of clacking footsteps. That source of friction is typical of the lack of harmony and companionship in the marriage.

Both partners were determined to maintain their sense of individuality, and for Harriet this meant pursuing her career rather than settling into domesticity. A series of separations began in the summer of 1902, when Harriet took the baby to the skerries for fresh air and sunshine. The family enjoyed some happy days of summer vacation together at Furusund in 1903, but Harriet and Anne Marie spent much of that year in a furnished apartment. The strain of living apart and constantly disagreeing caused Harriet to suffer a nervous breakdown in 1904. After three weeks in bed that spring, she knew that a divorce was essential for her peace of mind. To overcome her depression she visited Paris, leaving Anne Marie in Strindberg's care. They stayed for a time in a cottage at Furusund, where his sister Anna and family also spent the summer. Harriet visited there for a few weeks after returning from Paris. It was the most peaceful interlude of their marriage. In the fall of 1904 she went to Helsinki for her first engagement as a guest star. On 6 September she wrote to her husband and offered to give up her career for the sake of reconciliation, but Strindberg had already begun divorce proceedings and would not change his course. The divorce was granted on 22 November.

Strindberg felt hurt and lonely. Harriet felt lonely at times too, but she regained her peace of mind and ability to concentrate on her work. Their lives were still interwoven, for Harriet brought Anne Marie on Sunday visits, and they conferred on plans for productions of his plays. The visits also were a time for physical intimacy. When Harriet was traveling, Strindberg assumed responsibility for the little girl, and later he was generous with her financial support. He tried to work out his feelings of loneliness and resentment through his writing, and eventually he found consolation in the productions of the Intimate Theatre and in the companionship of others. Bosse became more successful and popular and eventually she remarried, but she always remained associated in the public's mind with her illustrious first husband.

GROWING AMBITION

When Strindberg biographers write about the period from the spring of

1901 to the fall of 1904, they emphasize his literary output and the domestic tensions of his marriage. However, for Bosse these were years of maturing artistically and developing a strong sense of individuality. She did not dwell on marital problems: "One important role after another took up my time, and I had literally none to spare for pondering my misfortune."[27]

From her debut at Dramaten in 1899 until she went to Helsinki five years later, Bosse played twenty-nine roles. Some were modest supporting parts, others were leads. Even featured roles did not please her if they were stereotyped ingenues in scripts without literary merit. Playing Jolanta was an opportunity many actresses would have envied, for the role of the blind princess allowed her to sing and to touch hearts with her pathos and innocence. Yet, Harriet wrote to Strindberg, "I am . . . completely without feeling for *King René's Daughter [Kung Renés dotter* by Henrik Hertz]. Possibly this is because I cannot endure its old-fashioned, stilted language. It makes me feel clumsy and unnatural. I am probably being very ungrateful, for everybody says that the role is 'so sweet.'"[28] She also felt "ungrateful" for all her assignments in French and German comedies, commenting that it might be fun to see others in those plays, but she loathed doing them herself.[29]

Later she glossed over her discontentment: "I was happy at the Royal Theatre. The roles alloted to me were to my liking, and I had no reason whatever to complain."[30] In actuality she complained forcefully. One of her most eloquent pleas was written to Carl Carlsson Bonde in November 1902. That season she had appeared in a reprise of *King René's Daughter*, and had played Emerentia Polhem in *Charles XII*, Biskra in Strindberg's *Simoon*, Hero in *Much Ado About Nothing*, and Bessy in *Miss Hobbs* by Jerome K. Jerome, a total of thirty-eight performances. Nevertheless, she asked Bonde to release her from a two-year contract after one year so that she could "gain" a year:

I say *gained*, for I am only losing time at the theatre where I never have any major work that interests me; all I get are small things which any young student could do just as well.

When I entered into contract with Director Personne, he gave me a *verbal* agreement in which he promised that my talent would be allowed to develop during the year through good and suitable assignments.

Not *one* of the roles he suggested has been given to me; on the contrary, there does not seem to be any prospect for improvement. This spring it will be two years since I have had a good assignment, Eleonora in *Easter*, and interest dies completely if there are to be such endless intervals between roles. . . .

It is clear that the Dramatic Theatre does not need me; otherwise it would presumably make use of my assistance to a greater degree.

With conditions as they are now, there are so many others who could fill my place just as well, but I neither can nor will endure it. I have such an unbelievably strong desire to work, so much yet undone, and year after year is passing while I am forced to remain inactive.[31]

Bosse was not the only actress who felt unappreciated. Valborg Hansson and Augusta Lindberg voiced their grievances too. All three thought that Amanda Janson was favored, even though critics often commented on her acting only in terms of her radiant appearance and gorgeous costumes. The actresses and management aired their views to the press. Everyone learned that Bosse, Lindberg, and Hansson had requested release from their contracts. Nils Personne summoned them to a hearing where he tried to prove with statistics that they had been treated just as well as Janson. Lindberg resigned, but Bosse and Hansson were more conciliatory. Although Bonde negotiated an amicable resolution, the public and the company were now aware of widespread discontent behind the scenes.[32]

In addition to improving morale, how could Dramaten improve the quality of its work and become a worthy national theatre? One answer would be to end the association and appoint a strong artistic director. The need for a new manager was presented in a petition to Bonde dated 14 January 1904, signed by twenty-seven members of the ensemble including Harriet Bosse. They were alarmed about the threat of financial collapse, blamed on mismanagement by Nils Personne. After negotiations, meetings, and the king's intervention, immediate monetary problems were solved, the association dissolved, and Gustaf Fredrikson appointed to head the theatre. Starting in the fall of 1904, he managed Dramaten as a private theatre for three years, an interlude of relative calm and popularity with anticipation of a fresh start in a new building.[33]

Bosse was not shy about requesting favorable salaries, as well as better roles. On 31 March 1902, Personne wrote: "Fru Bosse has demanded a raise of 2,000 crowns. I have offered her 1,000. It would be a great loss for us if she went to the Swedish Theatre."[34] In a gesture of good will the management gave her six roles for the remainder of the 1902–3 season, including Hedvig in *The Wild Duck (Vildanden)* and Juliet. Bosse continued to threaten to leave unless she was granted more challenging assignments. In September 1903 Personne wrote to Bonde:

I therefore set forth a proposal that she should sign a contract for 1904–1905 "on the basis of important repertory conditions." She vacillated and made a fuss. I was unyielding. Today I at last received her conditions: (1) 6,000 crowns guaranteed— 1,000 crowns for costumes (2) a month's leave of absence (3) three roles: "Méli- sande" by Mæterlinck; "The Crown Bride" by Strindberg; "Maria Stuart" (!!) by Bjørnson. She wants an answer soon, "since she has received offers of engagements and is anxious to get the matter settled."

What to say? She is not shy. I think, however, that there is reason to meet her halfway despite her exaggerated demands, but at least try to get her to forget about "Maria Stuart" and perhaps substitute something newer for "Mélisande."[35]

All three roles were denied her, casting a shadow over the success she enjoyed in other roles. Her frustration surfaced periodically as long as she remained at Dramaten. Now that assertive behavior by women is seen in a more positive light, Harriet Bosse deserves credit for trying to obtain artisti- cally worthy roles and to negotiate with management for fair treatment.

While her self-confidence grew during the first five seasons at Dramaten, Harriet Bosse sensed that she had not reached her artistic potential. She became a celebrity whose photograph appeared often in theatrical maga- zines. The change in her status is reflected in the records of the costume department. When playing modest ingenue roles she dressed simply, some- times in recycled costumes from other shows. After she was cast in the leads of major productions, she wore frequent changes in costumes of costly fabrics. But these outward signs of success did not mean as much to Bosse as the progress she was making toward her goal of naturalness on stage.

Strindberg challenged Bosse to be "the actress of the new century." He encouraged her to bring something new to theatre: "You seem to be born with all the fresh ideas of the new century."[36] Responsibility for development rested with the actress herself. Tor Hedberg wrote in 1900 that he hoped she had "enough self-criticism" to correct certain habits and not misuse her talent.[37] The naturalness she set as her ideal was used as a measure of success by some critics. Of her performance as Bessy in *Miss Hobbs*, one wrote: "Fru Bosse's delivery of speeches is a model of calm control and appears truly natural, to the fullest extent. That is the finest one can desire of an artist."[38]

Bosse continued developing an ability to create the illusion of naturalness, described in a review of Giuseppe Giacosa's *As Leaves before the Storm (Som blad för stormen)* in 1903:

In order not to repeat what can always indisputably be said of Fru Bosse's perfor- mances: attractive appearance, excellent diction, artistic temperament, etc., the reviewer this time will add something which to him is even more significant—a role played with real emotion. Or in any case: a presentation of emotion creating such an illusion that it cannot be distinguished from the real thing.[39]

To achieve a natural effect Harriet Bosse played in a manner some considered monotonous and stylized, while others praised the simplicity and restraint.

Many roles in Bosse's first five years at Dramaten featured her delicate beauty and natural charm. One of the most successful was Isotta in *A Venetian Comedy (En veneziansk komedi)*, which opened on 1 March 1904. The playwright Per Hallström suggested Bosse for the lead, "if she thinks she could be interested in the role."[40] She was. Later Bosse called Isotta her favorite role that season because of its great artistic distinction, a contrast to many roles she played only to please the management.[41]

In a season of precarious finances, *A Venetian Comedy*, with almost fifty performances, was Dramaten's only success.[42] Hallström based his script on a short novel by Matteo Bandello, published in 1554 and entitled "Two Gentlemen of Venice Are Honourably Cozened by Their Wives."[43] One critic wrote that it was a long time since there had been such a sunny mood on both sides of the footlights.[44] Isotta is colorful and aggressive, dominating each scene with her merry disposition. After episodes of flirtation, intrigue, deception, and despair, she appears at a trial in the final scene and discourses with remarkable poise on women and their reputations. She tells the Doge's court about the well-intentioned trick she played on her husband and a neighbor, pronounces a moral lesson, and urges all present to enjoy the happiness and beauty of life.

The production was a beautiful spectacle, with three large Renaissance settings and elaborate costumes. Bosse found a portrait by Domenico Ghirlandajo at the National Museum from which she copied an amusing coiffure with her hair frizzed out to the side.[45] One of her costumes was covered with appliqued butterflies, especially appropriate considering her closing speech: "This is a world where we should do our best, and enjoy our youth and watch butterflies soar through the air. . . ."

The bright and lively character of Isotta so captivated audiences and critics that other cast members received little attention. August Palme, playing her husband, was lauded for his delivery of lyrical passages and for accepting with good cheer the lesson taught him by his delightful wife.[46] Bosse was perfect in that role—charming, delicate, intelligent, effervescent. "She sparkled—her eyes, her teeth, but above all the words sparkled."

Unfortunately, however, the long run took its toll on her health. On 25 April a doctor was summoned in the middle of the performance when Bosse became convinced that her jaw was locked and that she could not speak.[47]

Because of the lyricism and wit of the script and Harriet Bosse's vivacious presence, *A Venetian Comedy* was memorable. Theatre historian Agne Beijer suggests that the reason for its phenomenal success was the blending of neoromanticism and realism—and Bosse's ability to maintain a paradoxical balance between the artificial and the real. People loved period costumes because they suggested a masquerade and playful emotions. "The historical costume not only provided brilliance and festivity, it allowed one to capture something that had vanished." Hallström had combined the traditions of the costume play and verse drama with characters expressing the spirit of the 1890s. *A Venetian Comedy* represented the cult of beauty of that decade, combining sensualism with escape from reality. Harriet Bosse was the ideal interpreter of that spirit.[48]

CRITICISM AND SELF-CRITICISM

In the first five seasons at Dramaten, Harriet Bosse established her talent and charisma, but she did not convince the management or critics that she was a mature artist. Because of the large, elaborate settings and general illumination, she appears on photographs as a tiny and modest figure in the overall stage picture. She commanded attention through energetic movement and clarity of speech, yet she did not have the strength and authority that the Stockholm public saw in Johanne Dybwad or Eleonora Duse. Being singled out by August Strindberg gave Bosse social prominence and the opportunity to star in his plays. Without him she would probably still have enjoyed a long, pleasant career in Swedish theatre, but it is impossible to determine if she would have earned the same prestige. An analysis of critical responses indicates that her achievements were appreciated on their own merits, just as her shortcomings were criticized without deference to her celebrity status.

Anna Branting, writing in 1904, acknowledged that Bosse was "still so young. She is experimenting and seeking, perhaps not convinced of the precision of her work." Still, Branting concluded, her performances always deserved respect, and she had plenty of time to reach her peak. Anna Branting had met Harriet when she was a sixteen-year-old music student; ten years later she still looked like a delicate child. Branting described her vivid impressions of Bosse's ingenue roles: "She was something completely new, which we had never beheld. She awakened the feeling of feminine tenderness, she brought tears to our eyes, with just the sound of her voice." Paying the kind of compliment the actress most appreciated, Branting praised the realism of her characterizations: she presented human beings on stage—"never puppets or automatons."[49]

In September 1904 Victor Sjöberg also praised the realism of her work:

The secret of Harriet Bosse's art seems to me to lie in its being . . . free from all affectation and artificiality, in its being fresh, clear and natural as water . . . on a beautiful day in spring, when the lark warbles in the sparkling sunshine. She can, when needed, reveal her deepest intimate emotion, but she is never sentimental.[50]

After Bosse's performance as Juliet in 1903, Tor Hedberg wrote a negative but sympathetic review. He praised the potential of her voice, the fascinating expressiveness of her face, her intelligence, and the wide range of her talent, but he found fault with some restrained and stiff movements, an occasional "frozen" facial expression, lack of technique, and overacting. Hedberg realized that Bosse had received little guidance; responsibility for developing technique and for making wise decisions was her own.

It is probable that not very many rehearsals were granted to the actress. One hopes that the theatre will keep the play in its repertory and let fru Bosse completely work out the characterization for which she is so beautifully suited. It can be of major significance for her development, and is a consideration the theatre should show to the greatest dramatic talent it now has.[51]

A week later Hedberg saw *Romeo and Juliet* again and praised Bosse in glowing terms in a new review, which encouraged her and pleased Strindberg.

Harriet Bosse realized she needed more time to develop. She played instinctively and spontaneously, drawing upon the resources of her charm and personality, working on roles until she discovered what felt right. Much later she said that in the early years she had acted "on sheer nerves, straining and dangerously near a breakdown," in doubt that she had enough strength for demanding roles.[52]

In 1901 a reporter had asked whether she knew as soon as she read a role how she would do it. The actress answered: "Oh, no, I might immediately feel that I grasp the proper mood in the role. But the concept I get later on. What is most fun is working out the role. You seem to grow through the part."[53] In 1904 she was ready to venture out as a guest prima donna, yet Bosse confessed: "Despite everything I don't really have self-confidence. I know when I do something, that I cannot interpret it any other way. But I am still not sure of myself."[54]

CHAPTER FOUR

Reaching Out

FIRST GUEST APPEARANCE

"I have never been on tour before," Harriet Bosse told a journalist in August 1904. Obviously she considered her travels with the Fahlstrøm troupe unworthy of mention. Featuring her visit to Finland, the periodical *Teatern* carried an article and twelve photos of Bosse in September. Describing her as "an unusually versatile and deep, delicate and poetic actress,"[1] a journalist reported that she felt unsure of herself. This would have surprised Conny (Konni) Wetzer, head of the Swedish Theatre. Their correspondence reveals Bosse's strong opinions about salary, repertory, and the sequence in which her vehicles should be scheduled. In coming to Helsinki, Bosse was not a pioneer, for many Swedish performers, directors, and managers made brief visits or stayed for long engagements. She was compared to both Scandinavian prima donnas and Continental guest stars.

Wetzer took over leadership of the theatre shortly before Bosse's arrival. A native of Finland, in contrast to previous managers from Sweden, Wetzer made his debut as an actor in 1892. He studied with Harald Molander, whose example inspired him to go into directing. Although sometimes arrogant and cutting, Wetzer managed the theatre with efficiency and fairness until 1916. A noteworthy feature of his tenure was the presentation of works composed and conducted by Jean Sibelius.[2] Morale was good, for Wetzer kept the ensemble working so hard that there was no time for backstage intrigues.[3] However, there was controversy over the appropriate language for the stage. Some patrons wanted to hear Finno-Swedish, but the theatre manager and a majority of the board of directors preferred the language as it was spoken in Sweden.

Bosse's appearance had an ironic personal dimension, since Helsinki was the home of Strindberg's first wife, Siri von Essen, and their children. After a debut on 22 November 1900, Greta, a daughter from that marriage, was engaged at the Swedish Theatre. She was a charming ingenue, a favorite with the public. Unpretentious and attractive, Greta Strindberg played with warmth and sweetness; there seemed to be "sunshine surrounding her on stage."[4] During Bosse's 1904 engagement, Greta appeared with her in two supporting roles.

Besides working with an ensemble that was fond of Greta Strindberg, Bosse encountered people sympathetic to Siri von Essen. Since 1893 Siri had lived in Finland, supporting her family with various jobs, including that of prompter. After working briefly at a theatre school in the 1890s, Siri continued teaching movement and diction at home, as well as directing a Catholic church choir, translating, and offering classes in dance. While married to Strindberg, Siri had enjoyed some success as an actress, but she never had the outstanding career for which she longed. Early in her career she appeared at the Swedish Theatre in Helsinki in *Jane Eyre* and in François-Joachim-Edouard Coppée's *Pater Noster*. Now she only occasionally performed in public, giving readings of poetry to musical accompaniment.[5] For Bosse to arrive as an honored guest at the Swedish Theatre, where Siri von Essen held the humble position of prompter, must have created tension for them both.

Bosse received a cordial welcome at the newly painted theatre on Teateresplanaden. She found a lifelong friend in Ida Brander, who played the Nurse to Bosse's Juliet and Gina to her Hedvig. Brander had been trained in Stockholm and had begun acting at Dramaten under Gustaf Fredrikson. During her career she played close to five hundred roles, of which the most successful were strong, dignified women, like Ibsen's Mrs. Alving and Gunhild Borkman.[6]

Bosse reluctantly submitted to Wetzer's wishes about the repertory. She had hoped to play Puck, but the play had recently been done elsewhere in Helsinki in Finnish, and the Swedish Theatre did not have an orchestra available to play the Mendelssohn music. Expecting Mélisande to be one of her six roles, Bosse asked Wetzer to send the translation since she urgently needed to study the script during the summer.

I am very excited about the music, especially since Sibelius is doing it. I love music as dearly as my own art, and think the ideal is a combination of the two.

In anticipation of and grateful for an answer to all these questions, I first want to remind you that *you are not allowed to cut A Venetian Comedy* from the repertory.

She presented persuasive arguments: first, that she was doing other roles only to please Wetzer, second, "as Isotta I have had my most recent and greatest triumph, third, the play is cheerful, which is needed since most of the plays are quite gloomy. And then—a Swedish original."[7] Wetzer let her play Isotta, but not Mélisande.

A guest appearance by Harriet Bosse was guaranteed to launch the fall season successfully. The theatre could thank her for healthy income at the box office from her thirty-five performances.[8] Word of her sensitive acting style had preceded her. She opened on 1 September as Ilka in *War in Peace*, Gustav von Moser and Franz von Schönthan's popular comedy, which she had done in Stockholm in 1903. Now she charmed the Helsinki audience with her grace, childish näiveté, and spontaneity. Knowing that more serious and demanding works were to follow, they applauded this opening piece wholeheartedly. The occasion was a victory for both Bosse and Wetzer.

As Hedvig in *The Wild Duck* Bosse was praised for her "large, wise, expressive eyes" and for keeping the characterization honest and natural. "Her interpretation is clear and intelligent, the performance logical and carefully worked out to the smallest detail." Julius Hirn, critic for the *Helsingfors-Posten*, recommended seeing Bosse several times as Hedvig, "in order to grasp all the finely observed details in this simple and striking performance."[9]

Per Hallström was known in Finland for his fiction. Now Bosse had the honor of introducing him as a dramatist. Although *A Venetian Comedy* was too "literary" to have broad appeal, its witty dialogue, comical situations, and carefree mood worked well at the Swedish Theatre's first new production of the season, opening 16 September. In her Dramaten costumes, Bosse was just as beautiful, merry, and gracious an Isotta as she had been in Stockholm.[10]

After Hallström's bright and robust play, audiences had difficulty adjusting to the abstract quality of *To Damasus I*. Critics had to defend the merits of the script. The intense mood and Bosse's simple "stylized" manner as The Lady struck some viewers as monotonous and tiresome,[11] but others called the performance inspired and warm. The beautiful music of her voice was singled out, as was her appearance—"a vision, elevated and mild as the holy *Madonna*."[12] Konrad Tallroth, who had done Hjalmar Ekdal in *The Wild Duck*, was effective here as The Stranger. A capable actor, more popular in the provinces than in the capital, Tallroth later became noted for playing major Strindberg roles.[13]

Bosse wrote an affectionate letter to Anne Marie ["Lillan"] about *To*

Damascus: "Mother has acted in your Papa's play, which has been done awfully many times, and the theatre has been full of people who have been there every evening. . . . Everyone here is so kind and sweet to Lillan's mother. . . ."[14] Harriet wrote to her daughter often and told her about the gifts she would bring back from Finland—a doll in national costume, a necklace with blue stones, and a toy piano.

After a contrast of style in the domestic drama *The Mannequin (Sky-ltdockan)* by François de Curel, the engagement ended with *Romeo and Juliet*. The production received more than the usual care in preparation, and the authentic decor, careful staging, and effective duel scenes won critical praise.[15] The audience listened reverently, almost mesmerized as Harriet Bosse spoke her lines from Dramaten's Hagberg translation, while the rest of the cast used a different version. Bosse considered this a justifiable privilege: "*I* did it because a *guest* has the right to keep his or her own language, as well as the interpretation with which the role was originally done. Since if a guest were to visit several cities . . . and all had different translations, it would be a Herculean task to re-do the role for each place." To maintain the rhythm of Hagberg's translation and to achieve an Italian sound, she pronounced the name Romeo with stress on the second syllable, the customary pronunciation at Dramaten.[16]

Julius Hirn considered Bosse's Juliet a triumph. While she looked like a young girl, she revealed depth and realism in her portrayal. "How simply and movingly she made the difficult transition from the emotions of a young, infatuated girl to the tragic greatness which surrounds the figure in the drama's later acts. The scenes with her parents, the nurse, the rejected suitor, the confessor along with the final death scene with her lover were genuine pearls of effective art."[17] Hjalmar Lenning wrote in *Hufvudstad-bladet* that she had "saved the best [role] till last." He found Bosse convincing first as a naive and eager girl, and later as a "strong, energetic, fully developed woman." Above all he praised the beautiful tone quality and diction that enhanced the lyricism of the love scenes. Bosse extended her stay, and extra performances of *Romeo and Juliet* were scheduled. The evening of her benefit, there was warm applause on her first entrance as Juliet and throughout the performance.[18]

The visit to Helsinki was significant professionally, for it demonstrated to Bosse that she could win acclaim away from home. It also coincided with the end of her marriage to Strindberg and introduced her to Gunnar Wingård, who later became her second husband.

A NEW FRIENDSHIP

While Strindberg was legally ending their marriage, Bosse was establishing herself as a star and as an independent professional. New acquaintances in Helsinki treated her graciously. While actor Gunnar Wingård eventually became her husband, another admirer became an attentive friend. He was Gunnar Castrén (1878–1959), an aristocratic-looking intellectual.

Son of a newspaper editor, Castrén earned a Doctor of Philosophy degree in 1902. He was working as a librarian in 1904, but was also a critic, literary scholar, and leading contributor to the journal *Euterpe*. Castrén began teaching aesthetics and modern literature in 1907 and enjoyed a long career as a university professor and literary historian. He became an outstanding cultural figure, known for his devotion to tolerance and democracy.[19]

Extant letters from Bosse to Castrén are evidence that their friendship, which caused Strindberg pangs of jealousy,[20] continued until she decided to marry someone else. The scholar called on Bosse when he was studying literary history in Uppsala in 1905 and later when he had occasion to be in Stockholm. In her letters we encounter a woman who is capricious at times; serious and responsible when discussing her daughter, career decisions, and literature; and always appreciative of his thoughtfulness.[21]

Castrén's reviews of Bosse's performances in Helsinki are sensitive and perceptive. Describing her as The Lady in *To Damascus,* he credits her with establishing the style of the play, true to the author's intentions, and bringing the entire performance into a harmonious whole through the exquisite simplicity of her stylized manner. He describes Bosse sitting quite still, "but against this background of immobility even the slightest expression is effective: a movement of the hand, a turn of the head. The same with her voice." Castrén praises the control of every detail, as Bosse created a role portrait with clarity, beauty, and quiet rhythm. Her most prominent trait, he wrote, was intelligence.[22] We may imagine the actress and scholar discussing the nuances of her interpretation as their acquaintance began. As the friendship developed, she expressed her longing to work with a repertory of quality and voiced appreciation for his support: "It pleased me *enormously* amidst so much lack of understanding to hear a voice express in regard to art and literature what I myself have wanted to scream into every ear!! *Thanks*!!"[23]

LEAVING DRAMATEN

Before going to Finland, Harriet Bosse had rehearsed day and night for Dramaten's revivals of *War in Peace, A Venetian Comedy,* and *The Mannequin,* but she was "full of energy and desire to work despite her fatigue."[24] Returning to Stockholm and a new status as the former wife of Strindberg, she repeated two popular roles and created three new ones that season. The most unusual was the title role in the Hindu drama *Sakuntala* by Vasantasena, adapted by Max Müller. Unfortunately the production was not a success, but the role foreshadowed one of her most famous characters — Indra's Daughter in *A Dream Play*.[25]

By the time Dramaten closed for the summer of 1905, Harriet Bosse had decided to leave. A specific complaint was the theatre's failure to produce *Pelléas and Mélisande*. She was not counting on a vague verbal commitment. Her contract for 1904–5 specifies: "Mrs. Bosse-Strindberg is granted the right to play Mélisande's role in *Pelléas and Mélisande* by Mæterlinck."[26] Bosse had campaigned ardently to do a play by Mæterlinck, whom she called "the greatest contemporary author." The theatre had obtained performance rights for the play in October 1903, and in March 1905 they even bought scene designs from Germany, but the production never reached opening night, a bitter disappointment for Bosse.[27] Her discontent went deeper, as she told Castrén:

If one wants to introduce modern authors at the Dramatic Theatre, the theatre's traditions forbid any extravagances in that direction.

Traditions — *traditions* — I abhor the word with all my soul. Is there anything more limiting for theatrical art — yes, art in general!

All *contemporary* art, that which seeks to appear in *a new form*, even if the action is drawn from the time of Moses, *shall* thus be forced into narrow boundaries which our forefathers considered appropriate.

Such art decays and becomes unwholesome, like stagnant water.[28]

Bosse and Castrén shared an interest in the German actress Gertrude Eysoldt. Bosse called her "the only female artist I really admire" — even though she had not seen Eysoldt perform.

But from everything I have heard about her, read about her, by studying the program she loves to appear in, along with her art of transforming her appearance — the imagination she develops — all this suffices to tell what a great artist she is; and that is — and has *always* been my dream — to introduce just that sort of art here in Sweden.

But unfortunately—people *don't want* theatre here to be anything more than high-class variety [entertainment].

Therefore it is terribly discouraging to want [to create] *art* and remain completely powerless.[29]

Bosse chose to set out on her own, seeking opportunities to play the type of roles she preferred. Although she would one day return to the Dramaten company, she would never again play on the old stage where her Swedish career began. Dramaten lost Harriet Bosse at a time when she was acknowledged as a major artist. An encyclopedia entry in 1905 stated that she had been a foremost performer at the theatre since shortly after her debut. Eleven of her "more significant" roles were named, including Puck, Juliet, Hedvig, and The Lady in *To Damascus*. The clear diction and beautiful voice were praised, and her acting described as "fresh, natural, pleasant and intelligent."[30] Bosse felt no regrets: "Thank Heaven I have now bid farewell to Dramaten until it pleases them to change their repertory in favor of more artistic and literary plays."[31]

SEARCH FOR OPPORTUNITIES

Memories of her honeymoon must have been vivid when Harriet took Anne Marie to Hornbæk for the summer of 1905. She thought Hornbæk had everything—"sky, sea, woods, the most wonderful sunsets."[32] After the vacation she began free-lancing in Gothenburg, Sweden, at the Large Theatre (Stora Teatern).

When Conny Wetzer became head of the Swedish Theatre in Helsinki in 1904, he succeeded Victor Castegren, who had held the position since 1899.[33] Castegren went to Gothenburg to head the Large Theatre. His tenure (1904–6) is considered "one of the great epochs in the theatre's history, because of the many new productions and his ability to gather around him an excellent ensemble."[34]

Rather than expecting the company to stand back submissively while the visiting star dominated center stage, as many international prima donnas did, Harriet Bosse came for the first rehearsals in September. A journalist reported: "She does not think it is completely fair to the public that one of the performers, through the blocking, shall be effective at the expense of the others. No, a good ensemble is foremost." She expressed confidence in Castegren as a director, praising his assurance and energy.[35]

Bosse recreated some established roles, and she discovered that the

Gothenburg audience did not necessarily like performances that had been well received in Stockholm. Beginning 20 September, she did Anna in *First Violin,* Juliet, Ilka in *War in Peace,* and Eleonora. On 24 October she played Mélisande, in a new production with the music of Jean Sibelius. This was the first performance of *Pelléas and Mélisande* in Sweden. Bosse fulfilled a dream and proved she was perfect for the leading role. Her appearance, voice, and ethereal quality brought the naive and loving heroine to life in a deeply touching way. The male leads were Ivar Kåge and Ivan Hedqvist, with whom she performed at other theatres in the years ahead. Critics had reservations about the production, but the company played with dedication and vitality. Bosse was "so successful in dragging the cast members with her, that the overall impression was completely overwhelming." This production was more "realistic" than Lugné-Poe's at the Théâtre de l'Œuvre, yet its mystical overtones and delicate mood were so effective that the audience sat in "devout silence" after the final curtain.[36] Of all productions during this guest engagement *Pelléas and Mélisande* was the most popular. Bosse often returned to Gothenburg, where she always felt welcome and appreciated.

Harriet kept in touch with Strindberg, who was caring for Anne Marie. He offered advice about her career, told about the five-act monodrama he was writing for her, and expressed concern about the royalties he was to receive from Castegren. Harriet sent affectionate messages to Anne Marie, and on 15 September wrote in a brief note to Strindberg: "Gusten, I am so fond of you. Good Night, Harriet."[37]

Bosse traveled to Germany in late November to "study" theatre but primarily to look for plays with roles she might like. Later she claimed to have seen forty productions, mostly of plays by established German playwrights such as Goethe, von Kleist, and Hebbel.[38] She sent Anne Marie a postcard showing the little girls at Isadora Duncan's dancing school and corresponded with Strindberg, who urged her to improve her fluency in German and explore the possibility of making a debut on the German stage. In 1904 she had been asked to play Eleonora at the Lessing Theatre in Berlin but did not have time to learn the role in German.[39] Strindberg asked his conscientious translator Emil Schering to introduce Bosse to prominent theatre people. Visiting the Scherings allowed Harriet an opportunity to see their daughter, born in 1904 and named Harriet in her honor.[40]

The director Richard Vallentin became rather interested in Bosse when she met him in Vienna. Although he was noncommital about her audition as Biskra in *Simoon,* in 1906 Vallentin offered her a five-year engagement at the

Hebbel Theatre in Berlin, starting with a salary of fifteen thousand marks, increasing to twenty-two thousand by the fifth year. She was invited to live with the Vallentins during the summer of 1907, in order to practice German stage diction. She would begin by playing Mariamne in Friedrich Hebbel's *Herodes und Mariamne*. By then, however, she had promised to join Albert Ranft's ensemble at the Swedish Theatre in Stockholm. Although tempted to move to Berlin, Bosse felt she would be happier in Sweden. Later she was philosophical about the course of events, for it would have been difficult to master the German language, and it happened that Vallentin died within less than a year.[41]

RETURN TO FINLAND

In March 1906 Harriet Bosse played Mélisande again but not under ideal conditions. After ten days of rehearsal she opened her guest engagement at the Swedish Theatre in Helsinki. Conny Wetzer had contacted Bosse a year earlier, offering a full year's contract. Weighing several options, she chose instead to appear for six weeks.[42] Bosse set her own conditions regarding salary, percentage of the house, repertory, and translations. She proposed several serious or classical roles, including Elektra in either Sophocles' or von Hofmannsthal's version of the story, Salome in *Johannes* by Hermann Sudermann or Oscar Wilde's *Salome*, Puck, the title role in *Elga* by Gerhart Hauptmann, and in Strindberg's plays, The Lady in *To Damascus III*, Biskra, Queen Christina, and Swan White.[43] The list is proof that she preferred challenging and significant work. It was years before she persuaded a manager to produce certain of these plays; in Helsinki only Mélisande remained of her original suggestions. Although she was ambitious, Bosse knew her limitations. She turned down Wetzer's proposal to play Ellida in Ibsen's *Lady from the Sea*, commenting that it would be twenty years before she was mature enough. Instead she offered to play Hilda in *The Master Builder* or her old role of Valborg. Bosse argued persuasively for plays that could be done with one simple setting and that had not been performed often in Helsinki. About one role she was adamant—she would not play Anna in *First Violin*.[44] But Wetzer insisted, and *First Violin* followed *Pelléas and Mélisande* during her engagement. Differences of opinion continued and led to such a clash at rehearsal on 9 March that Bosse threatened to leave. Wetzer had accused her of putting "theatrical effects" above regard for Mæterlinck's script. She felt she deserved respect for the interpretation she had already developed and insisted on being treated with courtesy.[45] Obviously Wetzer made amends, for she did not break her contract, but she felt that the theatre had "turned its back" on her. It also distressed her that there were many competing artistic events in the city. Only the kindness of friends made her visit pleasant.[46]

Pelléas and Mélisande, with Sibelius' score, had been successfully produced at the theatre a year earlier. Bosse stepped into a production directed by Wetzer and into a role shaped by Gabrielle Tavaststjerna and proved that Mélisande was a perfect role for her beauty and acting style. "Her tiny girlish figure, the individual timbre of her voice and the childlike inflections, the graceful and nimble walk" created a perfect image. She also brought a "shimmer of poetry and mysticism" to the role. The distinctive qualities of Harriet Bosse's style were appreciated during this visit to Helsinki. As Hjalmar Lenning wrote, "The artist's way of acting with stylized, economical gestures and monochromatic diction was naturally now, if ever, completely appropriate and . . . effective."[47]

Wetzer knew what the fans wanted, for *First Violin* proved to be the most popular of Bosse's six shows. The audience laughed heartily at the comedy and enjoyed the energy and lively pace of the production. Bosse was the midpoint of the action—graceful, coquettish, high-spirited. Because they had played many of the same roles, she and the Norwegian actress Johanne Dybwad were compared by critics.[48] Georg Henrik Theslöf wrote, "Fru Bosse's performance deserves in all ways to be ranked with fru Dybwad's famous interpretation of the same role."[49]

Familiar with Dybwad's success at Dramaten as Sara in *Merry Wives (Glada fruar* or *Lystige koner)* by Norwegian author Jonas Lie, Bosse obtained the script from Gustaf Fredrikson.[50] The performance in Helsinki displayed her command of technique in the service of realism. With small but effective means, the way jealousy began to cast its shadow over Sara's life was conveyed, and the sobs when her husband confessed were not just executed with virtuosity but also gave the effect of expressing thoroughly genuine emotion.[51] Bosse also appeared in *Romeo and Juliet* and in two Strindberg plays—*Easter* and *The Crown Bride*. Her first appearance as Kersti, the Crown Bride, was on 24 April. The production was a great triumph for its star, who used the play for her farewell performance. With quite a change of mood and style, the stage the next evening was set for the farce *Charley's Aunt (Charleys tant)* by Brandon Thomas, starring Gunnar Wingård.[52]

GUNNAR WINGÅRD

During her first engagement in Helsinki, Bosse played opposite the charming Gunnar Wingård. Hjalmar Lenning in a review of *Romeo and Juliet* wrote: "In Mr. Wingård as Romeo Mrs. Bosse had found a partner who with his youthful appearance, vigorous, elegant bearing, and flowing, well-nuanced diction offered many important qualities for the role."[53] Julius Hirn, however, found Wingård to be more a melancholy Hamlet than a convincing, romantic Romeo. The actor also played Anselmo, her husband in *A Venetian Comedy,* and some minor roles in her other plays. When she returned in 1906, they costarred in *The Crown Bride, Merry Wives, Pelléas and Mélisande,* and once again in *Romeo and Juliet.* Rumors of a romance circulated backstage. Some thought they played love scenes with an involvement and intensity that suggested more than acting.[54]

Anders Gunnar Wingård, oldest of three children, was born 30 September 1878, in a house on Nybrogatan in Stockholm.[55] His father, Johan Alfred Wingård, was a pharmacist, and his brother Nils Åke chose to become a pharmacist as well.[56] The actor Nils Arehn, a close friend, said that Gunnar began acting as a schoolboy in Sundsvall. Classmates enjoyed his excellent portrayals of old men.[57]

After passing the *student* examination, Wingård worked with the railroad for two years. He and Arehn took acting lessons from Charlotte Winterhjelm (1838–1907). Born and trained in Stockholm, Winterhjelm spent the decisive years of her career in Helsinki. From 1867 to 1872, with her first husband Frithiof Raa she helped to develop the Swedish Theatre (Arkadiateatern) to a high standard. Outstanding in tragedies and serious modern plays, she was excellent as Schiller's Joan of Arc and Queen Elizabeth, and as Lady Macbeth and Desdemona. Although otherwise she spoke Swedish on stage, Winterhjelm triumphed when she played the title role in Alexander Kivi's *Lea* in Finnish. Another triumph was as Mrs. Alving in August Lindberg's production of *Ghosts* in 1883. Despite her petite size she commanded attention through carefully planned gestures and hard-won vocal technique. When teaching acting, she shared her idealism and sensitivity to poetry as well as her method of developing characterizations with an aura of fate.[58] Wingård was influenced by Winterhjelm's instruction and example and by other actors with whom he worked.

Following the death of his mother, Gunnar Wingård became a professional actor. At twenty-one he made his debut in Nyköping with the Selander touring company, playing the old servant Daniel in *Life in the Country (Lifvet på landet)*. After three years of touring he joined the Swedish Theatre in Helsinki.[59] Wingård was not immediately successful. One critic commented that in Ernst Didring's *Midnight Sun (Midnattssol)* he seemed "to be more at home in Lapland than in the salons of Faubourg Saint Germain."[60] From 1902 to 1906, he polished his craft and won the hearts of the Swedish-Finnish theatre-goers. The young actor was hired by Victor Castegren, but his success came under the management of Conny Wetzer. Because of Wingård's attractive appearance and charming personality, Wetzer found him well suited to play young lovers. As though by magic, he became a star when he did the prince, Karl-Henrik, in *Old Heidelberg*. Wingård was a favorite with the ladies. In fact, he was so popular socially that his performances might have suffered, but he never allowed a party or rendezvous to interfere with his work. He was a conscientious, modest, and courteous member of the company.[61]

The repertory of the Swedish Theatre included farces and traditional audience favorites imported from France, England, and Germany, as well as Scandinavian realistic social plays, light entertainment, and dramas based on historical material. Gunnar Wingård developed versatility in this repertory, in roles ranging from Percinet in *Les romanesques (Romantik)* by Edmond Rostand, to Falk in *Love's Comedy (Kärlekens komedi)* by Ibsen, to Boberley in *Charley's Aunt*.[62]

In 1906 Wingård accepted an offer from Albert Ranft to join the Vasa Theatre in Stockholm. On 15 May the Swedish Theatre granted him a benefit in *Old Heidelberg*, and on 1 June 1906, he gave a farewell performance as Hugo Bendler in a three-act farce, *Misstep (Snedsprång)* by Gustav Kadelburg. Wingård left a void in the hearts of the public and the ensemble that was difficult to fill. One of his most brilliant characterizations had been as Hlestakoff [Khlestakov] in Gogol's *Inspector (Revisorn)*. When Hugo Sandell played the role in 1910–11, he could not compare with everyone's memory of Gunnar Wingård.[63]

Albert Ranft persuaded Gunnar Wingård to leave Helsinki and Harriet Bosse to give up free-lancing. He would bring them together again after Wingård had played a year at the Vasa Theatre.

A NEED FOR PRIVACY

In the summer of 1906 Harriet could feel a sense of accomplishment. She had proved that she was in demand beyond the confines of Dramaten. She had learned to negotiate for excellent salaries and the right to play roles of her choice. She came to Stockholm's Swedish Theatre self-confident and eager to work hard, but first she needed "sun, sea and woods" to restore her peace of mind: "Yes, now summer is here, and one is freed from going to the theatre, putting on makeup, and sharing oneself with an audience which may be more or less understanding, freed from selling one's soul, one's thoughts, one's being. . . ."[64]

To preserve emotional balance, Harriet Bosse always maintained some distance from the audience. She was aware that critics used the term "stylization" to describe the uniqueness of her acting. "I have held onto my individuality so strongly," she wrote, "that at times on stage I have had a sense—when I shared my innermost feelings—of spiritually prostituting myself. Anyone could sit there and buy what is deep within me for a coin." At such times she realized that she "closed up like a clam. . . . Then the critics said I was stylizing—they didn't understand. And how could they?"[65]

CHAPTER FIVE

Stardom

The achievements of women in Scandinavian theatre deserve study as part of women's history. At the turn of the century, an acting career was one of the best ways for women to achieve recognition and financial independence. For several decades before Harriet Bosse began her engagement at the Swedish Theatre, women had been asserting their rights individually and through organizations. Although she was not a crusader for women's rights or an outspoken feminist, Bosse believed it was important for women to be independent and self-supporting.[1]

CELEBRITY AND PROFESSIONAL

A book on Swedish career women published in 1914 lists a variety of professions, including sculpture, medicine, building inspection, fabric design, and university teaching. Two Bosse sisters, Dagmar and Harriet, are included, along with at least eight other actresses.[2] They were in a privileged position compared to the many women doing manual labor and housework. When Bosse was hired by Albert Ranft in 1907, the average annual salary for an unmarried woman in Sweden was 330 crowns.[3] Among the lowest paid workers were maids and cooks, whose wages ranged from 10 to 30 crowns per month. The average annual income of a seamstress was 936 crowns, while a woman working in a textile factory might earn 800.[4]

Ranft, who paid well compared to other theatre managers, started inexperienced actors at salaries close to industry wages. Lars Hanson, who became one of Sweden's most distinguished actors, began working for Ranft at 1,200 crowns per year. The average well-established actor in the first decade of the twentieth century could earn at least three times as much as a factory worker. Harriet Bosse's salary with Ranft was 10,000 crowns per year. This may be compared to 5,000 crowns paid to Charles Magnusson when he became head of a Swedish film company during that same period, and to Strindberg's income, which is said to have fluctuated between 4,000 crowns in 1906 and 32,000 in 1907.[5]

Standard contracts specified that a company member must agree to accept all types of roles and provide his own costumes. Undoubtedly Ranft excused Bosse from having to accept nonspeaking roles. In 1910 an actress might spend 1,000 to 1,500 crowns per year on costumes. At the Swedish Theatre Bosse wore elegant costumes, for which she sometimes paid 3,000 crowns per year. A contract ran for eight or nine months, beginning 1 September, with two weeks of rehearsal in August without pay. As at Dramaten, Harriet Bosse found at the Swedish Theatre a system of fines for such offenses as being late for an entrance or performing when intoxicated.[6] Though conscientious and hardworking, Bosse enjoyed a privileged position in the company. Others remained standing in the actors' foyer ("green room") until she took a seat and stepped aside to let her go first through the stage door.[7]

Michael Hays speculates that leading actors at the turn of the century were models for the middle-class ideal of the "successful competitor, the free individual who acquires that which he desires."[8] Harriet Bosse was such a model, enjoying celebrity status. However, throughout European theatre during that era, Hays maintains, the creative process allowed actors only the "illusion of freedom." As the position of the director became stronger, "creativity and freedom for the actor existed only within the context of the director's organization of the working space." The division of labor gave an actor the illusion of freedom, "but only within the context established by the invisible but omnipresent decision-maker at the top of the hierarchy in each productive unit."[9] For women the lack of freedom in an acting career was even greater than for men. Unlike her sister Alma Fahlstrøm, who was a strong-willed manager-director, as well as an actress, Bosse worked within hierarchies dominated by men and was not truly "free."

According to many reports, Harriet Bosse was strong-willed and opinionated. It was often uncomfortable for her to accept the power of managers and directors. Because she did not want to become a manager or a director herself, she asserted her rights by proposing roles to play and by developing characterizations independently. When repertory did not measure up to her standards, she moved to another company or resumed free-lance negotiations.

ALBERT RANFT

Stockholm offered a rich diversity of theatrical entertainment in the first decade of the twentieth century. People could see folk comedies, realistic drama, or conventional sophisticated salon plays. During this era of social debate and struggles in labor and politics, controversial current issues were not reflected much in literature or the arts. Still influenced by the optimism of the 1880s and the aestheticism of the 1890s, Swedish theatre concentrated on commercial success, artistic standards, and individual talent.[10]

Since the reign of Gustav III, no one individual had exercised so much influence over Swedish theatre as the entrepreneur Albert Ranft. Starting as an actor with provincial touring companies in 1875, he established himself as a manager in the 1880s. By the 1890s "the theatre king" expanded his activities, buying theatres and managing companies in Stockholm, Gothenburg, and the provinces. When Harriet Bosse was in his employ, Ranft ran seven theatres in Stockholm, the Large Theatre in Gothenburg, and several touring companies.[11]

A dictator with a pleasant disposition, Ranft was a clever business executive, diversifying the repertory at his theatres so that the popular, lucrative ventures could support more exclusive, artistic productions. Ranft let his taste and an intuitive understanding of the middle-class audience be his guides. Although sometimes scorned for his choice of plays, accused of promoting immorality, and criticized for treating employees unfairly, he had the warm support of a broad cross section of the public. Ranft's career flourished during a period of prosperity when people could afford to spend money on entertainment. When times changed during and after World War I, his success began to fade. After the Swedish Theatre burned in 1925, Ranft never recovered, and by 1931 his theatrical empire was just a memory.[12]

THE SWEDISH THEATRE IN STOCKHOLM

The Swedish Theatre, formerly called the New Theatre, changed hands several times before Albert Ranft purchased the building in 1898. It had been the site of an important production of *Hedda Gabler* and an appearance by the Duke of Saxe-Meiningen's troupe. Ranft redecorated the theatre beautifully and dedicated it to drama of quality and significance. There were, for instance, successful productions in 1899 of Gerhart Hauptmann's *Weavers (Vävarna)* and Strindberg's *Gustav Vasa*.[13] Until about 1910 the level of repertory was generally superior to Dramaten's, and the work of the Swedish Theatre's directors, actors, and scene designers was excellent. Scandinavian playwrights Ibsen, Bjørnson, Strindberg, and Tor Hedberg were quite well represented, while foreign dramatists included Shakespeare, Shaw, and Gorky. The Parisian comedy team of Caillavet and Flers was introduced in 1908 with *Woman's Weapon (Kvinnans vapen)*, followed the next year by *The King,* both starring Bosse. Other French boulevard drama was done, as well as the sentimental favorite *Old Heidelberg*, starring Anders de Wahl as the prince.[14] Ranft's policy was to present plays on a rotating schedule. Rather than offering the same program every evening, he opened a new production as quickly as possible.[15]

Bosse worked with several directors at the Swedish Theatre. One of the most important was Gunnar Klintberg, whose work was "marked by a painstaking and decorous conservatism."[16] The director Bosse preferred was Victor Castegren. They made theatre history with the world premiere of Strindberg's *A Dream Play* in 1907.

DEBUT AT THE SWEDISH THEATRE

Harriet Bosse joined her new colleagues in August 1906. At first it was difficult to submit to the discipline of rehearsals: "Åreskutan's mountains, woods, lakes, meadows, sky are still so much a part of me, that I can't in an instant throw myself into the dust, grease paint, filth, unnaturalness, wretchedness of Theatre."[17] And Bosse did not find much comradeship in the company. Rather than socializing, she wrote to Gunnar Castrén, "my orgies are limited to bacchanals alone with Anne Marie." She worked hard, with a performance almost every evening for months. The program satisfied her longing for a good repertory, and at first she did not miss Dramaten.[18]

Bosse's inauspicious debut at the Swedish Theatre was as Tove, opposite Anders de Wahl, in Holger Drachmann's verse drama *Gurre*. The action, based on a popular romantic saga, takes place in the fourteenth century at the castle Gurre. Sven Söderman praised Bosse's beauty and innocence, especially in the scene when she realized the queen had condemned her to be scalded in the sauna: "Then her fragile little being was filled with great courage, making the character significant."[19] The most memorable moments occurred in the wings, when she used a technique similar to one taught by Constantin Stanislavsky:

I was supposed to scream offstage, but how should I do it? I didn't want to stand among a lot of people backstage at such a moment, so they built me a little booth where I sat alone and screamed. Of course I didn't know how it feels to be boiled in oil [sic], but all I needed to do was think of how it felt to give birth to my daughter. . . . They have said that people fainted in the auditorium, so my screams must have been effective.[20]

Most critics felt the bone-chilling screams exceeded the limits of art. Bosse also received negative reviews for speaking in an artificial, musical pitch pattern, but spectators were captivated by her delicate and ethereal qualities.[21]

The premiere was a gala event with the author in attendance. Bosse confided to Castrén that she was unimpressed by the extravagant and gallant poet, considering it a dubious pleasure to perform in his worst play, "where the interest—at least for me—focused on the boiling point in the 3rd act, where I, after justifiable hysteria, got to disappear."[22] Some praised Bosse in the last act, where Tove appears in a vision to the aged, dying king. *Gurre,* which Bosse called *"mischmaasch,"* drew audiences for twenty-five performances, after which she did a small role in a play by Maxim Gorky. Then she had the pleasure of showing Stockholm why she should have been allowed to play Mélisande years before.

Pelléas and Mélisande opened on 29 November 1906. Once again Bosse worked with Castegren, who had directed her in Gothenburg. Some theatregoers remembered Lugné-Poe's highly stylized version of the play in 1894. Expectations were not completely realized because of the length of the script and some inadequacies in the lighting and scenery. On the whole this was considered a fine production, with Bosse an almost ideal Mélisande. Tor Hedberg described the submissive, fragile qualities of the character, reminiscent of a "frightened bird and fragrant flower," and thought that Bosse's "sensitive and pure" performance, especially in her gestures and movement, was "a genuinely artistic creation."[23]

Nonnaturalistic pitch patterns were acceptable for this role. Carl Laurin wrote, "Some of fru Bosse's inflections, full of dreams and foreboding, raised us for a few moments above the world of reality."[24] Bosse has commented, "What was said with the speeches was not the most important thing—the air around them trembled and spoke. It was probably after this role that the critics and the public said I stylized. I was not to blame; it was the most sensitive role—I did not dare touch it with careless hands—then I would have torn to pieces the veil of mysticism which Mæterlinck had woven with a masterhand."[25] Gustaf Collijn focused on Mélisande's speech,

"Jag är inte lycklig" ("I am not happy"): "No Duse would be capable of pouring more unfathomable mysticism, more life and modulation into those words than fru Bosse did, and never has she herself interpreted a speech with more wonderful inflection. It became a melody, one . . . which cannot be written down, but which perhaps exists that much more intensely, Bosse-Mélisande's: I am — not — — happy."[26]

Bosse vividly recalled her enchantment with the Sibelius score: "As I lay on my death bed in the last act, and the orchestra played 'Mélisande's Death,' I was so affected by the mood that I cried—every evening." In retrospective articles on Bosse's career, Mélisande was always praised as one of her most admirable achievements. She called it "one of my dearest roles."[27]

GUNNAR WINGÅRD AS COSTAR

After one season at Ranft's Vasa Theatre, Gunnar Wingård joined the company at the Swedish Theatre and found himself on stage again with Harriet Bosse. Although he was engaged to replace Anders de Wahl, Wingård did not receive the red carpet treatment accorded to Bosse. She was the one who inherited de Wahl's large, pleasant dressing room. Because of his handsome appearance, expressive face and eyes, rich voice, and refined manner, Wingård was expected to step into the line of roles classified as "first lover." His sharp powers of observation and tendency toward satire suggested that he was even better suited for character parts. In that field critics praised his outstanding Doktor Jura in Hermann Bahr's *Concert (Konserten)*, a talkative, philosophical, charming figure.[28]

Gunnar Wingård was assumed not to be popular. In 1910 a columnist for *Dagens Nyheter* theorized that popularity required establishing a personality that won the public's sympathy, then modifying details from role to role. Wingård developed a wider range through hard work and won respect and admiration rather than superficial popularity.[29] Working with a distinctive broad Nordic face and large eyes, he could vary his looks remarkably with facial hair, makeup, and wigs. His aristocratic Gustav III, intense John the Baptist, saintly Rogers in Charles Rann Kennedy's *Servant in the House (Tjänaren i huset)*, and youthful peasant Matts in Strindberg's *Crown Bride* were among the intriguing images in his role gallery.

Bosse and Wingård were an attractive team. They traveled with the Swedish Theatre troupe to Finland in 1909[30] and pleased audiences who had first seen them there as costars. Wingård admired Bosse's poise and capacity for hard work and praised her confidence and powers of concentration. He also worked hard, studying all his roles diligently. A review of *The Thief (Tjufven)* by Henri Bernstein describes the team: "Herr Wingård was natural, controlled, and—in the big scenes—strong and masculine; fru Bosse was tender, yielding, passionately and recklessly in love. . . . The demanding second act had a powerful effect because of their acting."[31] Bosse was not always paired with Wingård. She played with other actors whom she encountered on various stages later in her career, including Tore Svennberg, Ivar Kåge, Nils Arehn, and Ivan Hedqvist, but there would never be a partnership with the charisma and popular appeal that she and Gunnar Wingård shared.

GUNNAR WINGÅRD AS HUSBAND

Harriet Bosse's life followed a pattern of hard work during the theatre season and refreshing vacations during the summer. At the beach she loved the salt breeze off the water; in the mountains she loved the invigorating air she thought beneficial to her throat. She went for long hikes, pausing to dip her feet in icy mountain lakes.[32] Anne Marie spent her vacations with Aunt Inez, who was a devoted "summer mama."

Although Harriet often felt lonely, her life in Stockholm was pleasant. She confided to Gunnar Castrén:

Last night, New Year's Eve 1906–1907, I sat totally alone, meditating over the past year's sunshine and shadow. . . . Nothing particular had happened, nothing occurred which deeply affected my destiny and left its mark—in a word, I was very glad that 1906 was finished and that 1907 was at the door. . . . And this morning I went to the Djurgård Park. You *cannot* believe how beautiful it was. The most dazzling winter weather, with a fiery red . . . sun which colored everything—people, bushes, snow, water.[33]

Bosse began to dream of living near the Djurgård Park. That dream was later fulfilled when she shared an apartment with her second husband, Gunnar Wingård.

Harriet was still involved with Strindberg, visiting him and corresponding when they were separated. In June 1907 she shared with him her ennui and melancholy: "You think I am having fun out among people. *Having fun.* —No, it is to have something to do, to numb myself, since, like you, I long so much to leave all this, that if I did not have our child to keep me, I would long ago have freed myself." Harriet assured Strindberg that she would never forget him, even if she married someone else: "I hold you dear, perhaps because you—through a deep sorrow—have given meaning to my life."[34]

In fact, before her marriage to Wingård, Bosse found it easier to end the friendship with Gunnar Castrén than to sever ties with Strindberg. Writing to Castrén in March 1908 Harriet suggested paying him a surprise visit that summer: "No, I shall surely find something else instead, travel to Italy (you *mustn't* laugh!) or to Paris—or perhaps sail directly into the safe harbor of marriage—hm! Who knows — — We are all a *little* mad!"[35] Signing off with the phrase "Live well," she proceeded with plans for a future with Wingård.

Harriet was determined to begin this marriage with optimism and peace of mind. When she visited Strindberg in April to tell about her plans, he was too overcome by emotion to wish her well. Within a few days he wrote to thank her for those happy spring months "when after 20 years of misery, I got to see a little of life's radiance."[36] He fantasized that they might remarry, that once again she would say, "Yes, thank you," if he proposed that they have a child. Exhilarated by unrealistic hopes, Strindberg tormented her with pleas and accusations. On 4 May she wrote that all contact between them must cease: "I belong to another man—shall marry him in June. Put yourself in his place—how you would suffer—."[37] This letter is with Strindberg's papers at the Royal Library in Stockholm; in the envelope is a photograph of the newlyweds at Hornbæk in July 1901 with her head cut off. On 13 May Harriet again reminded Strindberg that he must not write. She ended, "Wish me all happiness—I believe—in happiness—."[38]

At a performance of *Two Kings (Två konungar)* on 4 April 1908, Gunnar Wingård for the first time wore the gold ring that marked his engagement and that became his wedding band. Colleagues were not surprised by the engagement, which was announced the next day. The bans were published at Hedvig Eleonora Church on 2 May, and the wedding ceremony was performed there on 24 May. Harriet and Gunnar went to England for their honeymoon.[39]

A kind and generous father, Strindberg feared that Anne Marie would transfer her affections to her stepfather. She recalls receiving a beautiful red leather letter case from Strindberg: "When I came home with it, Wingård took me aside and said that he had bought something similar for me and 'if you give me yours, you can have this one from me instead.' But nothing came of it, no matter how he tried to persuade me—I have always been very stubborn, so of course I kept the one from my father."[40]

Anne Marie welcomed a brother, Bo Gunnarsson Wingård, born 9

January 1909. That year the family moved to an apartment in a large red brick building at Strandvägen 57.[41] The apartment was attractive: "The milieu was superb: the large, bright, elegant salon—comfortable and artistically arranged. . . ." One snowy day a journalist stood inside with Bosse, looking at Anne Marie playing beneath the window and beyond her at the entrance to the Djurgård Park.[42] Until the Wingårds moved in 1910 to Valhallavägen 107, Strindberg avoided Strandvägen and the bridge leading into the park.

THE DEMANDS OF STARDOM

Of the thirty roles Harriet Bosse played at the Swedish Theatre, many emphasized her attractive appearance in glamorous costumes more than her acting ability. In Paris the height of elegant fashions could be seen in productions at major theatres, and actresses like Cécile Sorel were acclaimed for being well dressed and setting fashion trends. In Stockholm actresses emulated French fashions on a modest scale, sometimes ordering an exact copy of a dress worn on the Paris stage. Good taste in fashion did not necessarily correspond to talent, but actresses knew they would be judged by the costumes they ordered from their dressmakers. An article on fashion in 1908 praised Harriet Bosse for having worn many excellent toilettes in recent seasons. "It doesn't interest me terribly much . . . , but I have that type of role, and since Jahnke sews for me, the costumes turn out so well that I think it's really fun," she remarked. Photographs showing her in exquisitely detailed dresses and hats for the role of Giselle Vaudreuil in *Woman's Weapon* accompanied the article, with commentary on the décolletage, linen and chiffon fabrics, and gores in the skirt.[43] The dominance of costuming is evident in a portrait of Bosse in *The King*, where her gaze is fixed on the elaborate train of her ball gown.

Bosse accepted many assignments that did not measure up to her artistic standards, but she also tried to negotiate for roles she wanted to play. A letter to Norwegian author Johan Bojer exemplifies the effort she probably often made. She had persuaded Ranft to ask for rights to Bojer's *Eyes of Love* (*Kjærlighedens Øjne*), in which she would play Ovidia, but the script was already sold to another producer.[44] It is likely that Bosse exerted an influence on the choice of repertory. She probably persuaded Ranft to produce, among other works, *The Crown Bride, Elga,* and *Johannes,* in which she was featured as Salome.

Opening 26 November 1907, the production of *Johannes* was weak, especially the crowd scenes. Photos show Bosse with a brazen tilt of the chin, frizzy hair, a filmy veil over her shoulders, and breasts decorated with beading and a metallic star pattern. The daring costume revealed Bosse's graceful body and the final act focused on her talent as a dancer, which would be crucial to her success as Elektra.

According to her daughter, Bosse was coached for Salome's dance by the outstanding teacher Signe Hebbe (1837–1925). There is no evidence that Bosse studied with her otherwise, but the expressive movement Hebbe taught established standards that Bosse observed in the deportment of her colleagues. Hebbe's numerous students included Gerda Lundequist, Manda Björling, Hilda Borgström, and Anders de Wahl. To harmonize with the style of fellow players and appear graceful in the eyes of the public, Bosse must have conformed to the principles of Hebbe's method.

Signe Hebbe was a talented individual—"diva, fury, and angel in one person."[45] Although her voice was small, she gave memorable performances on the concert and opera stage, being especially acclaimed as Marguerite in *Faust*. Hebbe taught an approach to declamation and acting derived from the traditional Italian system, based on her study with Adelaide Ristori, Ernesto Rossi, and teachers at the Paris Conservatory. She emphasized thought, the body being the "servant" of intelligence and will. According to Olga Raphael:

The basic idea was that the thought should be born first and shown in the gaze, and then in the total attitude of the body and spontaneous gesture of the hands, followed by speech and steps. Posture rested on invisible support through the body's midline, which should be touched by each movement of the hand, and a step should never be taken before the weight of the body had been moved so far forward that the step *had to* be taken for the sake of balance.[46]

Hebbe also taught students to walk in certain rhythms, to sit properly, and to acknowledge applause, always stressing intensive practice to gain control of the body.[47]

Salome's dance is performed in the final act of *Johannes*. Unfortunately the setting had distracting, stylistically incorrect details, and the lighting was poor. If "used correctly," wrote Carl Laurin, the lighting "could have helped to reinforce the impression of beauty and concentrate the gaze on Salome."[48] Still Bosse's dance was praised for its beauty and emotional effect, as she performed with grace and self-hypnotic abandon. The playwright describes the scene: "Her dance becomes wilder and more abandoned; she gradually loosens her veil, then covers herself with it again in voluptuous playfulness, till at last, quite unveiled, she stands with the upper part of her body apparently unclothed. She sinks on her knees half exhausted, half in homage, before Herod. . . . All break into ecstasies of applause."[49] Herod is obligated to offer what she demands, and of course that is the head of John the Baptist. The Stockholm audience did not respond with "ecstasies of applause." Bosse's work was acknowledged to have fine moments, but Gunnar Wingård received more critical praise in the role of John. Bosse complained: "Too much Bible history and too little a work of art, I believe was the general opinion. Too bad it was not Wilde's *Salome* instead."[50]

In terms of significance and artistic merit, Bosse's major roles at the Swedish Theatre were Mélisande, Indra's Daughter, and Kersti. Her versatility and skill were also revealed in a number of English comedies, which she approached as studiously as any serious play. One of the public's favorites was George Bernard Shaw's *Man and Superman (Mannen och hans öfverman)*, opening 27 September 1907, with Tore Svennberg as Jack Tanner. In a letter written in July, she complained that she did not understand the play or the character of Ann Whitfield, "but I hope it will become clearer for me toward autumn. The woman is so immensely contrived. He has patched together everything bad about our sex, and on this hodgepodge set a halo." She thought Shaw's treatment of Ann showed poor taste, but she admitted the script was very witty in places.[51] Critics compared Bosse's Ann to a kitten or "a young tigress," combining "coolness and egoism," obstinacy and smugness. Sven Söderman called the portrayal "an adorable presentation of a woman as a boa constrictor."[52] Bosse could report to Castrén that 3 December would be the forty-second performance: "It has been a raging success, and I suppose we shall live on it all season."[53] Obviously Ranft was willing to bend his policy against long runs when he had a box office smash. Bosse followed her success with starring roles in other English comedies, like Somerset Maugham's *Mrs. Dot*, which was produced in February 1909. Its similarity to *Man and Superman* was obvious, as Svenberg did "a lightly caricatured edition" of Jack Tanner and Bosse did "a fresh and playful variation" of Ann.[54]

While Bosse held center stage at the Swedish Theatre, her former colleagues were preparing for the opening of a magnificent building designed by Frederik Lilljekvist. The first performance at the new Dramaten on 18 February 1908 was the verse version of Strindberg's *Master Olof*.[55] Ranft renovated the Swedish Theatre in 1909, making the vestibule spacious and the auditorium splendid with a decor of red, white, and gold.[56] Bosse continued to play variations on popular roles and to dazzle the public with fashionable costumes, but this could not satisfy her for long.

COMPETITION

While Dramaten and the Swedish Theatre were the major legitimate houses, there was other entertainment competing for audiences in Stockholm. Folk comedies, operettas, and variety shows attracted crowds. No other endeavor during these years was as significant as the Intimate Theatre, founded by Strindberg and the young actor August Falck.

In December 1907 Harriet Bosse confided to Castrén: "The Intimate Theatre—was a fiasco, as you perhaps read. I have not been there yet, but have been told that the whole thing is something dreadful. The locale, on the other hand, I have seen, and it was very lovely."[57] She was accustomed to massive, cluttered stage settings and the social rituals of a major commercial theatre. Years later she mused: "I wonder if a great author—Shakespeare, Ibsen, Strindberg—could be played well without decorations—just in drapes."[58] Actually that was the approach used by Strindberg and Falck for their production of *Queen Christina*. Strindberg's advice to the company and his theories of production are published in *Open Letters to the Intimate Theatre*.[59] The artistic achievements and financial struggles of the theatre until it closed in 1910 make an important chapter in Swedish theatre history. Audiences could see old and new Strindberg plays and feel the psychological power of the form he called the chamber play. Capable actresses won acclaim in roles originally intended for Bosse: Anna Flygare as Eleonora, Manda Björling as Queen Christina and The Lady, Fanny Falkner and Anna Flygare as Swan White.

The Intimate Theatre stimulated Strindberg's creativity at a time when he needed to overcome his longing for Harriet Bosse. He often spoke with Falck of his third wife and asked for any gossip about her circulating among the theatre crowd. Falck has left a description of Strindberg excusing himself and going into another room to gaze at the portrait of Bosse as Puck. The sound of brass rings as Strindberg pushed aside the drape, his reappearance with right hand pressed against his eyes, and his habitual anxious ritual of washing his hands in ice water persuaded Falck that Strindberg was still distressed about having lost Harriet.[60] He tried to forget her by taking a sweet young girl under his wing, encouraging her to become an actress. Having first seen Fanny Falkner as an infant, Strindberg met her again at the Intimate Theatre. Her father became Strindberg's landlord at Drottninggatan 85, where he moved to get away from memories of Harriet associated with the apartment on Karlavägen. The only memento he brought with him was a death mask of Beethoven. Fanny was shy—more talented as a painter than as an actress. Her natural qualities inspired Strindberg to visualize her as Eleonora, but she lacked the poise and vocal technique for the role. Fanny was quite charming when she played Swan White. Although they were engaged briefly, Strindberg was primarily her mentor and benefactor. Encouraging her to find friends and become independent, he showed Fanny the greatest consideration, even while suffering through his final illness.[61]

DEPARTURE

The Wingårds stayed busy learning new roles. In November 1910, they opened in *The Concert*, which spotlighted Gunnar's talents as a character actor. While that production ran for forty-eight performances, they moved to Riddargatan 55. Two weeks later they appeared in the opening of *My Niece (Min niece)* by Gustaf von Horn. Harriet worked in two more new productions during the spring of 1911, as well as in a revival of *Gurre*. Life was about to change, for she had decided to return to Dramaten and to end her marriage.

The cause of the divorce is rumored to have been Wingård's infidelity. Strindberg heard another rumor—that Wingård had run up large debts, which threatened to ruin Harriet financially.[62] Using one of the few available legal avenues to divorce, Harriet went to Denmark, and Gunnar claimed she had deserted him "out of malice and antipathy," intending never to live with him again. He was granted a divorce on 16 January 1912. Harriet proposed to care for and educate Bo; Gunnar did not contest custody.[63] Harriet would not permit visits to her home, so little Bo, in the company of a nursemaid, would meet his father elsewhere. Later Bo recalled that his father gave him exciting presents, including a toy fire engine that sprayed real water.[64]

After the new building opened on 18 February 1908, Dramaten's repertory began to improve. The theatre presented major Scandinavian works, such as Ibsen's *Ghosts* and *John Gabriel Borkman*, and classics by Shakespeare and Schiller. Bosse may have envied some actresses their major roles: Gerda Lundequist's Lady Macbeth and Maria Stuart, Augusta Lindberg's Queen

Elizabeth and Ella Rentheim, Lina Sandell's Anna Pedersdotter, Julia Håkansson's Helene Alving, Hilda Borgström's Candida.[65] Many talented performers left the employ of Albert Ranft to join Dramaten when the new building opened. The responsibility of drawing patrons to the box office of the Swedish Theatre rested primarily on Harriet Bosse's shoulders. People had assumed that she was not versatile: "She cannot support the repertory by herself, they objected. She has her very limited specialization. She can't play everything. — [But] fru Bosse has shown that she can. . . . She has developed into an artist who is second to none as regards intelligence and flexibility, and to few as regards imagination and charm."[66]

Being a public figure, wearing elegant costumes, and sparkling as the star of a series of comedies was not satisfying, for she no longer found the repertory artistically challenging. Her position was analyzed by Helge Wahlgren: "It seems that the Swedish Theatre is leaning more and more every year toward international comedies and folk plays; certainly even in such plays fru Bosse, with her distinctive spirituality and brilliant virtuosity, has often made the worthless worthwhile, but from a general theatrical perspective it must seem an unforgivable waste, and from a personal perspective an outrage, . . . to exploit a genius." Another journalist, writing about Bosse's resignation, asserted that Ranft was expert at "exploiting an artist who he knows is highly regarded by the public."[67]

In 1907 Bosse had enjoyed a triumph as Agda Gauvin in Tor Hedberg's *Johan Ulfstjerna*. In 1910 Hedberg succeeded Knut Michaelson as head of Dramaten, and Bosse gladly accepted his invitation to rejoin the company. She looked forward to working with the versatile playwright, who was a competent manager with an appreciation for dramatic literature of quality. She made the change in order to work with what she called "the great repertory" and not for financial advantage.[68]

After Bosse's departure, Pauline Brunius took her place as prima donna at the Swedish Theatre, and Tora Teje began to develop the skill and individuality that would bring her to the top of the profession. Although the theatre still had artistic ambitions, its repertory after 1910 tended toward light comedies, classics, and spectacles, such as *Quo Vadis?*, with which Klintberg tried to emulate Max Reinhardt.[69] Gunnar Wingård was featured in many leading roles, and the public anticipated that he would enjoy a long and successful career.

She had appeared on stage hundreds of times, but Harriet Bosse still suffered from anxiety attacks on opening nights: "I always felt as though I were crossing Niagara on a tightrope."[70] Nevertheless she arrived at

Dramaten's grand new building with more self-assurance and technical virtuosity than when she left the company in 1905. Unfortunately the divorce cast a shadow over her personal life, and she found herself enduring a year of illness, deaths, and scandal.

CHAPTER SIX

Reign at the Royal Theatre

RETURN TO DRAMATEN

Harriet Bosse's return to Dramaten coincided with a period of prosperity and artistic vitality for Swedish theatre. In 1910 there were ten permanent theatres in Stockholm, presenting four thousand performances of 250 productions.[1] The new Dramaten was built in Östermalm at the outskirts of the city. Within a few years, like most other legitimate theatres, it was considered to be centrally located. By 1911 there were about five thousand seats in Stockholm movie houses, usually constructed in local neighborhoods. Drama competed with film, cabaret, and organized sports, along with traditional operas, operettas, revues, and folk comedies. Competition affected Dramaten's repertory, which could not be entirely serious or "literary." World War I whetted the public's appetite for light entertainment, and the labor movement supported the concept of *folkteater*, theatre for the people. The *folkteater* movement and fresh artistic impulses for directors and designers came from France, Germany, and Russia. Visits by choreographer Michel Fokine and director Max Reinhardt inspired Swedish theatre artists to reinterpret classics and the plays of Strindberg. New ideas from abroad and vital Swedish issues were debated in theatre journals, where some of the best articles were by Gustaf Collijn and Olof Molander, who played important roles in Bosse's career.[2]

Despite its traditional—and undemocratic—auditorium with boxes, tiers, and limited seating on the main floor, the old Dramaten had been a popular theatre. The new structure was so formal and imposing that Bernard Shaw mistook it for a bank when he visited Stockholm in 1909.[3] Bosse, with her petite stature and silvery voice, was more in her element in an intimate theatre, and that is what she preferred. However, Tor Hedberg's promise that she would play significant roles in plays of literary quality had lured Bosse back to Dramaten. The size of the ensemble varied, but in 1914, a typical year, there were thirteen women and eighteen men.[4]

Tor Hedberg was a sophisticated, intellectual critic and author. Having written about the need for reform and modern directing methods, Hedberg got to try out his ideas when he was artistic director of Dramaten from 1910 to 1921. As an administrator he was rather despotic, cool, and conservative; as a director he excelled at working with actors on role analysis and characterization. "He was a fine and cultivated director with the imagination of a poet and the sensitivity of a theatre artist regarding psychological values and relationships."[5] Bosse described Hedberg as "the most honorable, most honest general manager" she ever had at Dramaten.[6] He gave Bosse star status, but she was not always pleased with her roles. When she left the Swedish Theatre, Bosse commented that she did not like to tie herself down with a long-term contract: "At least I feel: one should get out and move now and then. I am not made to get stuck anywhere."[7] She stayed at Dramaten for seven seasons.

A YEAR OF CRISIS

Strindberg was fatally ill. Anne Marie visited him whenever his health permitted. She stood with her father on the balcony of the "Blue Tower" when a crowd of about ten thousand laborers carrying torches paid homage to the author on his sixty-third birthday. Strindberg had suffered the agony of separation from the children of his first marriage. Now he was reconciled with them and sent funds to their mother. He could afford to be generous. To Harriet he gave money for a grand piano. She sometimes had to curb his generosity, begging him not to give Anne Marie new bedroom furniture or too much spending money.[8] Bosse accepted with gratitude Strindberg's efforts to assure the girl's future financial security: "Since I have assumed all the expenses for little Bo, perhaps in time it would have been difficult for me to maintain Anne Marie in the position she deserves."[9]

The Bosse and Strindberg families suffered five bereavements in 1912. First Arne Fahlstrøm went down with the Titanic on 15 April. Later that month Siri von Essen died in Helsinki. On 14 May Strindberg succumbed to cancer. He was spared the grief of the death of his daughter Greta, who was crushed in a train wreck on 16 June. The fifth death was Gunnar Wingård's.

Fortunately, Bo was too young to understand why he would never see his father again. Anne Marie did understand that her father was seriously ill and that he did not want visits after a certain point but preferred her to remember him as he had been. During the final months of his illness, Harriet sent a flower each day—anonymously.[10] The day of Strindberg's funeral, which was a national event rather than the modest occasion he had requested, Harriet escorted her daughter to Drottninggatan 85. While Anne Marie walked in the procession to the Norra kyrkogård cemetery with other family members, Harriet sat alone in the Djurgård Park, looking at the water and meditating. She stayed away from the theatre for a few days but otherwise had a busy month appearing in three productions.

Many times during his life Strindberg had felt unappreciated. He had to contend with the rejection of his plays by theatres and the rejection of his books by publishers, but his genius and originality were finally appreciated. Although Strindberg had a gift for alienating individuals and groups, he also won the admiration and support of many. This was evident at his funeral, when government officials, Social Democratic politicians, labor organizations, theatre artists, and students were among the large number of mourners paying their respects. In the years since his death Strindberg's works have been analyzed, interpreted, and performed throughout the world. No one would deny his influence on twentieth-century drama or his fascination as a personality.

While Harriet Bosse was concentrating on her career and her children, Gunnar Wingård was becoming increasingly tense and dissatisfied with his work. Although he enjoyed a vacation in an island setting that summer, Wingård's friends noticed his bitterness and pessimism.[11] After leaving the home he had shared briefly with Harriet at Riddargatan 55, he moved three times, finally settling into an apartment on Grefmagnigatan in October. Three days later he killed himself.

Wingård seemed to be in a good mood the last few days of his life. After a busy Sunday doing a matinee of *Monna Vanna* by Mæterlinck, dinner at the Strand Hotel with Valborg Hansson, and an evening performance of another play, he returned home around II:00 P.M. After the housekeeper retired, Wingård remained in his study, working on a new role. He then wrote a note, saying that "the captain of the ship" could not go on: "My life is of benefit to no one; at least someone will benefit from my death." He made a phone call, believed to have been to Harriet Bosse. Without returning the phone to the receiver, he bared his chest and fired a single shot to the heart, then fell to the floor and died.[12]

That morning, 7 October, the company at the Swedish Theatre became alarmed when Wingård did not report for a rehearsal of *Anna Karenina*. The housekeeper, noticing his bed had not been slept in, discovered the body and summoned help. Nils Arehn and Gunnar Klintberg, Wingård's close friends, went to the apartment, which was swarming with police, a doctor, and reporters. Harriet wanted to rush there too, but friends restrained her. Anne Marie, called home from school, found her mother in bed, distraught and grief-stricken.[13]

There was an outpouring of grief from colleagues, friends, and the public. Pauline Brunius recalled later, "He was such an amiable and honorable friend—we were so fond of him and grieved for him deeply for a long time."[14] Wingård had been cast too often as the protagonist when character roles were probably more appropriate, since his powers of observation and gift for satire were outstanding. Among the roles singled out for praise after his death were the lead in Shaw's *Devil's Disciple (Djäfvulens lärjunge)* and Frank in *Mrs. Warren's Profession (Mrs. Warrens yrke)*, Gustav III in *Two Kings* by Ernst Didring and Oginski in *Elga*.[15] Rudolf Björkman's tribute is representative: "His personality was rich, his manner refined and pleasant, and in happy moments humor played upon his lips and in his smile. His notable appearance on stage, the honesty which characterized his artistic work, won him not just the applause of the moment but also warm sympathy and many silent admirers."[16]

On Thursday, 10 October, extra streetcars were scheduled and "all the automobiles in the city" drove to the Norra kyrkogård as an enormous crowd—mostly women—found their way to Gunnar Wingård's funeral. Many members of the companies at the Vasa and Swedish Theatres were in attendance, listening to tributes and to pleas for tolerance of the "desperate act" that ended his life. Later in the afternoon, when the crowd had left, Harriet Bosse visited the cemetery and laid two pink dahlias on the grave.[17]

After missing several performances following Wingård's death, Bosse returned to work on 11 October, rehearsing Elektra, one of the most remarkable roles of her career and performing alternately in *Johan Ulfstjerna* and *Trial by Fire (Eldprofvet)* by Henry Kistemaeker. The tension she had felt all year was increased by gossip that blamed her for Wingård's suicide. She received anonymous letters daily, as well as threatening phone calls. On 7 November her attorney issued a press release asking for information as to the identity of the persons conducting the campaign of rumors and persecution.[18] Bosse was on the verge of a nervous breakdown. In the spring it helped her to take a leave of absence and travel with Dagmar and Carl Möller to Spain, where she could come to terms with the memories of her two husbands.

ACHIEVEMENTS

When she returned to Dramaten in 1911, Harriet Bosse was a single mother responsible for the welfare of two children, a professional determined to assert her individuality, and an actress with polished technique. She competed with excellent actresses such as Signe Kolthoff and Maria Schildknecht and guest star Astri Torsell. Some promising younger actresses took over Bosse's roles when she was ill, away on leave, or busy with other performances. They included Olga Raphael, Anna (Nickan) Lindskog, Stina Hedberg, Jessie Wessel, and Tora Teje. The latter became more and more competent and popular, and eventually she inherited Bosse's diadem as the leading lady of Dramaten.

Although in her thirties, Bosse usually played younger characters—even adolescent girls twenty years younger than her actual age, like Erika Larsson in Frans Hedberg's *Hothouse Flowers (Blommor i drifbänk)*. Critics became divided: some praised her youthful appearance, while others dared to write that she was too old for certain roles. Although Bosse still admired naturalness, technique sometimes dominated her performances. Critical reaction focused on whether she created a convincing illusion or whether her technique was distracting. On her portrayal of Maria Stuart in the play by Bjørnstjerne Bjørnson, a critic wrote, "The tragic despair in the last act offered the technique of suffering more than its reality."[19] Technique was her defense against revealing private emotions. When she confided to Anders de Wahl that acting sometimes made her feel exposed and cheapened, he urged her: "Instead, imagine that you have a sack full of gold coins, and you take fistfuls of them and throw them out to the hungry audience."[20] After *First Violin* was revived briefly in May 1912, a critic called Bosse's performance "a display of theatrical bravura, which certainly is closely tied to external effects, but is irresistible in its piquancy and refined expressiveness. . . ."[21] Some of Bosse's vehicles were shallow or melodramatic, and it was to her credit that she overcame the material to achieve a realistic effect. Of *Trial by Fire,* a critic wrote, "What one especially enjoyed was her way of delivering the long, trailing and rattling speeches, which must be said with great art in order not to . . . sound completely unnatural."[22] Her performance in *The Wedding March (Bröllopsmarschen)* by Henri Bataille evoked praise: "Bosse is a master of the art of making the uninteresting interesting, the unnatural natural."[23]

The role of Elektra is one of Bosse's most significant, even though she played it relatively few times,[24] for it displayed emotional dynamics she usually kept strictly under control. Harriet Bosse had been interested in Elektra for seven years, yet she felt apprehensive when Hedberg offered her the role. She recalled in her memoirs:

I hesitated, for I had never previously done anything so tempestuously dramatic; I didn't believe I could carry such a powerful role. But Hedberg asked me—he thought that now I had done so many comic roles to court the public, I should show that I also could manage this great tragic role. And I succeeded. The audience was never more spontaneous, more enthusiastic. But it was only Tor Hedberg's persistence—and friendliness—which compelled me to give the best I had to offer as an artist in the role.[25]

Thanks to reviews and a thorough description by Olof Molander, it is possible to present a composite picture of Bosse in Hugo von Hofmannsthal's *Elektra,* which she first played on 19 November 1912. The actress emerged with faltering steps from the dark hall of the royal palace. A brownish gray gown hung in rags over her tiny body. Dirty, matted hair fell in wisps over her forehead. Her eyes—sunk into dark sockets—glanced restlessly around. Her face glowed pale gray in the moonlight, and her hands trembled with hate and vengefulness. Her bearing was noble, despite the degradation of her condition. Clinging to the massive wall, she crept down the stairs on bare feet, like a wounded wild animal or a spirit from the underworld. A shriek of pain burst from her throat, carried away as by the wind, dying to a whimper when she lamented:

Alone, as always. Alas. My father gone,
cast forever into the dark chasm.[26]

This was no splendid Greek heroine, but a human being scorned and disowned, for whom "hate had become the melody of her life."[27] Hate had made her hideous, yet there was "passionate loftiness" in the determination to avenge her father's death.[28] Elektra listened to her mother Clytemnestra's tormented confession with the "rigidity of a sleepwalker." With her sister Chrysotomis she was ingratiating and threatening; with her brother Orestes she shared tenderness and triumph.[29]

The role was a test of strength, for Bosse was on stage almost two hours, executing long harangues with "dizzying speed," playing with "terrifying intensity" that kept the audience in breathless suspense. With "furious energy" and a "wealth of delicate . . . details," Bosse showed a creative imagination as inexhaustible as Elektra's passion for revenge.[30] Bosse recalled that she played the role in a "state of delirium from the first to the last speech. Since I had laid the foundation for the role during rehearsals, I played with complete abandon and trusted to nerves—and inspiration."[31]

The expressive voice and body were at her command. As she poured forth her grief, the voice had a darker tone than usual. She would whisper to Orestes of the joy she once felt over her youthful body and dreams of love. The voice would rise and fall, harden and scream, yet it never broke.[32] Einar Skavlan compared the voice to flames: "Now playing the fiery-red and sulfur-yellow tones of hate, then ash-gray with sorrow, then charred black by powerless despair."

Early in the play Bosse's Elektra performed a strange ritual at her father's burial mound, an exotic and violent dance with knees lifted high. That step was expanded in the final scene as she rose on wobbling legs, clinging to the walls for support. Lifting a torch from its sconce, she staggered down the stairs to provocative music by flutes and cymbals. Head flung back like an intoxicated maenad, she raised her knees, stretched the torch high, and danced in ghastly, wild leaps. People streamed through the palace doors, then backed away from the frightening dance. Her sister called anxiously and Elektra stopped, every sinew of her emaciated body taut, every nerve quivering with elation. Her eyes were glazed, her voice distant as she challenged the others to join her. Again she lifted her knee, swung the torch overhead, and launched a victory dance in wide circles around the grave. Suddenly, as the wild rhythm pounded, devoured by the passion of jubilation, Elektra fell to the ground, collapsing without a sound like the ash from a huge bonfire.[33]

When she played Elektra for Hofmannsthal, he praised her "as one of the best interpreters of the role he had seen."[34] Norwegian critic Fernanda Nissen wrote that only after the curtain went down was there any thought of Bosse's technical proficiency: "As long as one was watching her, one was simply enthralled by Elektra." Created in a year of private tension and grief, the brilliant performance combined intense personal involvement with perfection of form.[35]

Bosse rehearsed *Pygmalion* during a busy month when she was playing Gulnare in *Aladdin*. She worked with a favorite partner, Ivan Hedqvist, as Professor Higgins. Bosse thought Hedqvist "was wonderful to play opposite. If you were nervous on opening night, you just needed to look into his calm, grayish-blue eyes, and you regained your equilibrium."[36] She also worked with a favorite director, Gustaf (Muck) Linden, who introduced

George Bernard Shaw to the Swedish public. His career is significant because he had studied with Max Reinhardt and brought to Dramaten some of the skill and vision of his teacher, as was evident in his production of *Everyman*. The opening of *Pygmalion*, translated by Hugo Vallentin, took place in Stockholm on 7 April 1914, five days before the London premiere. The show was a popular success, running almost continuously in April and May.[37] Audiences especially enjoyed the rainstorm and the appearance of an automobile in the first act, where the decor was based on photographs sent by Shaw.[38]

Bosse pushed the outer limits of her range in this role, for she was probably too delicate and refined to do the unpolished Liza. August Brunius told that it took several minutes before the audience recognized her in the first scene. He praised her comic talent and bold energy. Her climactic outburst of anger in act 4 was the high point of the performance, "prepared through lively pantomime."[39] Daniel Fallström, who enjoyed the contrast of vigor and refinement, declared he had seldom seen Bosse "more piquant and radiant."[40] Sven Söderman found her so convincing at first that it seemed impossible she could ever be civilized. He especially liked the scene "when the well-instructed doll suddenly forgets her role" and reverts to her former jargon. As she became a lady, she also learned "to feel and think in a new way. Here was sincerity and seriousness, instinctive womanly cunning, and a naively touching need for tenderness."[41] Liza joined the gallery of Harriet Bosse's outstanding roles.

DIVIDED LOYALTIES

While it was pleasant to have a secure position and occasional artistic challenge at Dramaten, Harriet Bosse could imagine a career with some of the glamour and variety enjoyed by international stars. She had become acquainted with Max Reinhardt and Alexander Moissi when they were in Stockholm in 1911 to present *Oedipus* at the Djurgård Circus; both visitors found her captivating. The Stockholm public enjoyed performances by Sarah Bernhardt, Eleonora Duse, Suzanne Després, Constant Coquelin, and other stars from the Continent. Bosse may not have dreamed of their flamboyant life-style and extensive touring, but she could picture herself on a Scandinavian circuit, with a stature comparable to Johanne Dybwad, Ida Aalberg from Finland, and Danish actresses Betty Hennings and Betty Nansen. Organizing a tour and negotiating for engagements was not easy, however, for an actress who functioned as her own manager.

Bosse established a compatible relationship with "the theatre king of the provinces," Allan Ryding. She supplemented her income handsomely and expanded her repertory by touring Sweden under his management. After studying acting at Dramaten and privately with Signe Hebbe and Hedvig Charlotte Winterhjelm, Ryding began his career, as had Gunnar Wingård, by touring with the Selander company. He then became manager of his own provincial tours, an enterprise which flourished for several decades. Under his management from 1909 to 1937, his wife Margot played many leading roles, as did some of the elite among theatre artists, in productions of high quality.[42]

Ryding booked his companies on a rigorous schedule in theatres throughout Sweden. Bosse went wherever Ryding sent her, never gaining any mastery of geography. Some evenings she was unsure as to what town she found herself in. "Just so I had a stage on which to stand and fairly pleasant scenery, I always did my best wherever I was, and was so caught up in my role that it didn't matter to me where I was acting."[43] Bosse called Ryding "Caesar," for he made an imposing sight as he marched ahead of his "troops," wearing a broad-brimmed hat and gesturing grandiosely. She appreciated his kindness and sense of humor, which helped to lighten the mood during long hours of travel. Actually Bosse did not find touring overly strenuous in southern and central Sweden. Only in the northern region did the distances necessitate rising at 3:00 or 4:00 A.M. to travel to the next town to play that evening.[44] Although Bosse received red carpet treatment, she often felt exhausted and bored when touring. Once in Skåne she met one of the earliest Swedish pilots and begged him for a ride in a tiny open plane. Ryding was horrified to think his star might be in no condition to perform for a sold-out house. Before the plane took off from Höganäs, he wrapped all the scarves and shawls he could find around her head, then greeted her with relief when the plane landed at Ljungbyhed.

Ryding was a clever businessman who chose stars and their vehicles with an eye to commercial success. Bosse was paid handsomely for working with him, but she had to appear in some plays Ryding produced for box office appeal rather than for artistic merit. Always considerate and cheerful, he made Bosse's engagements as pleasant as possible. In the fall of 1914 she repeated two successful roles from her Dramaten repertory, Monique in *Trial by Fire* and Liza Doolittle.[45] The next fall she played Hélène de Trévillac in *The Adventure,* which she had done that February at Dramaten, and a new role, Jacqueline Gautier in *One Wife Too Many (En hustru för mycket)* by Francis de Croisset. On and off Bosse would tour with Ryding, sometimes in roles such as Marguerite Gautier, which she never had an opportunity to play in Stockholm. Provincial audiences considered it an honor to see a star of her calibre.

Bosse always felt welcome in Gothenburg. She appeared there regularly on Ryding tours and went with the Dramaten company in May 1914 to present *Pygmalion*. In the fall of 1917 she was warmly received at the Lorensberg Theatre as Erika Larsson in *Hothouse Flowers* and Kersti in *The Crown Bride,* directed by Gustaf Linden. Bosse called him "irrefutably the most outstanding in his field in Sweden." She half promised a reporter to consider moving to Gothenburg.

"Things have been quite tedious for me in Stockholm the last few years. And I have wondered about it a little . . . But I do have my little ones in Stockholm, and they go to school there, and . . ."

"There are schools in Gothenburg too. Excellent ones . . ."

"Well, one never knows what might happen."[46]

Bosse never moved to Gothenburg, but she enjoyed other successful visits at the Lorensberg Theatre on a free-lance basis.

In December 1914 Bosse performed in Denmark for the first time at the Dagmar Theatre. The manager, Holger Hofman, who had seen her play Liza Doolittle in Gothenburg, extended the invitation. Although he helped her substitute Copenhagen slang for some phrases, she spoke Swedish. It was ironic that her first appearance before a Danish audience was in a play where the humor depended on understanding nuances and inflections of speech. Although subtleties may have been lost, she was understood sufficiently to support her belief in "Scandinavianism" in art. Referring to her Danish mother and to her childhood in Norway, she remarked, "I am a kind of Scandinavian: but I consider myself Swedish, because the Swedes have been so good to me." Since she had labored to learn pure Swedish, she understood Liza: "I haven't sold flowers on the street—and my diction errors were different; but I have experienced the same work with language that she did." For three performances Bosse stepped into an established production where she found the cast presenting "the most human *Pygmalion*" she had seen.[47]

The consensus was that Liza was the wrong role for Bosse to play in Copenhagen, despite her "strong temperament, brilliant technique, and great skill." Critics called the performance disappointing, and the audience gave a lukewarm response. There was much confusion over her Stockholm dialect, which forced the Danish actors to answer occasionally in Swedish. Since to Danish ears "all Swedish sounds like music," only Bosse's tone of voice hinted at lack of refinement in the early scenes. Overreliance on technique was also a problem: "First she scratched her head, then she fingered a little toothpick after an exaggerated enjoyment of chocolates." The business was clever and technically brilliant, "but the flower girl's basic nature disappeared beneath all the fireworks." After Liza became an aristocrat, Bosse could show "how much tenderness and refinement she commands, behind a slightly artificial or stylized charm, which is characteristic of Swedish actresses."[48]

THE "PRINCESS" RETURNS

Harriet Bosse enjoyed a much warmer reception when she returned to her birthplace. From 22 May to 9 June 1916, the Swedish Royal Dramatic Theatre and the Norwegian National Theatre exchanged stages. The public could compare the artistic calibre of the companies and the brilliance of their stars, Johanne Dybwad and Harriet Bosse. Playwright Gunnar Heiberg, comparing their ensembles, praised the naturalness of the Swedish style of acting. Heiberg saw greater "depth of characterization" among Norwegian actors but more color and intensity in the Swedes. Johanne Dybwad was sometimes bigger than life and tended to push a performance beyond naturalness. Heiberg found that Dramaten achieved consistent realism not through the "talent and will power" of individual performers, but thanks to the "guiding hand" of the directors.[49]

It must have meant a great deal to Bosse to return as a celebrity to the city where she first appeared on stage. She was featured in three revivals: *Johan Ulfstjerna*, *Twelfth Night (Trettondagsafton)*, and *Elektra*. She also played a new role, Henriette in Strindberg's *Crimes and Crimes*. Dybwad had recently played Henriette and Rosalind in *As You Like It (Som Ni behagar)*, a role comparable to Viola. Bosse found the Kristiania public receptive and enthusiastic. Unfortunately she became ill and had to cancel the second performance of *Elektra*, but she never forgot the thunderous applause after her appearance in that play on 31 May.[50]

Critics wrote thoughtful reviews that impressed Bosse, for they based their comments on repeated viewings of the Swedish productions. One of the most glowing tributes of her career was written by Sigurd Bødtker, who recalled her debut almost twenty years earlier. Now the talented "princess" had become the "queen" of Swedish theatre. Bødtker described her achievement in widely different roles—Agda in *Johan Ulfstjerna,* inspired by love and patriotism; Henriette, recklessly daring fate; Viola, playing with love; Elektra, burning with passion. Compared to Dybwad, Bødtker found Bosse more feminine and delicate in her Shakespeare role, more believably Parisian, trusting, and submissive as Henriette. Bosse had demonstrated the wide range of her art, which spanned comedy and tragedy, the classics and contemporary literature.[51]

Harriet Bosse returned to her birthplace as a representative of the Swedish nation. King Gustav V sent along two gold medals—*Pro Litteris et Artibus* (For Service to Literature and Art)—which Tor Hedberg presented on 6 June to Bosse and Ivan Hedqvist. She suggested that the glaring blue ribbon might be replaced by a color that would look better with her violet taffeta dress, but Hedberg hastened to convince her that the blue color was the most beautiful feature of the decoration.[52]

One of the highlights of the visit was a banquet at the Grand Hotel. Gunnar Heiberg and Tor Hedberg gave speeches highlighting the artistic and political significance of the occasion. The two nations were at the brink of war a decade earlier; now they were separated politically but bound together through literature and theatre.[53] Bosse's table partner was the Arctic explorer Fridtjof Nansen.[54] While on her first tour in 1896, Bosse had joined the crowds welcoming Nansen home after his successful expedition with the "Fram." Then she was a face in the crowd; now she too was a celebrity enjoying a triumphant homecoming.

CONTROVERSY

The life of a leading lady was strenuous. Harriet Bosse worked very hard during the nine or ten months of the theatre season, giving as many as twenty-six performances per month. She seldom missed a performance because of illness. In January 1916 while doing a lively dance in *Hothouse Flowers,* she tore a muscle in her leg, but a doctor bound it tightly at intermission, and the audience never realized the seriousness of her injury.[55] She had no choice but to cancel a performance of *Elektra* in December that year; the next day she underwent an appendectomy.[56] On the whole Bosse was energetic and healthy, thanks in part to refreshing summer vacations at favorite resorts such as Marstrand. Writing to Tor Hedberg in July 1916, she explained she was canceling plans to go on tour that September because she was still exhausted from the engagement in Kristiania: "It is painful, you understand, to have to give up so much money, especially when one has two children to work for, but that is wiser than getting sick and not being able to work."[57]

Tor Hedberg was usually gracious about granting Bosse leaves of absence to go on tour. She later recalled the seasons from 1911 to 1918 as her happiest at Dramaten.[58] Gradually, however, she became displeased with her roles and felt her salary did not keep pace with expenses.[59] This discontent could not be kept confidential. In October 1916 the press learned that Bosse had written to Hedberg asking to be released from her contract:

I cannot figure out why I have been so pushed aside, especially the last few years. The public is fond of me, and I am sure that I have not done any work so bad that the theatre would consider it necessary to keep me out of the repertory. That this inactivity—or obligation to carry out uninteresting assignments—finally generated ill feeling is not surprising. What is even worse is that I risk a decline in the execution of my work through this lack of training.

She assured Hedberg that she did not expect to have all the big roles, but at least a few—if only he would relax his policy of not choosing a play to feature a specific performer. Bosse was prepared to sign a contract with another theatre. According to rumor, she was negotiating with the National Theatre in Norway, a possibility viewed with optimism by Kristiania theatregoers. If Dramaten considered her a "good artist worth keeping," she wanted to negotiate for challenging roles, such as Shakespeare's Portia or Cleopatra. "My existence as an artist is at stake—and I do not have the right to jeopardize it."[60]

Soon her complaints were a topic of public controversy. Hedberg released his reply to the press, which also quoted Bosse's letter. The manager let her know that the board would not grant her release from her contract, nor would he allow her to set conditions for repertory unless they were compatible with the interests of the theatre. *Dagens Nyheter* described unhappy working conditions and wondered whether other artists might join Bosse in resigning. *Social-Demokraten* defended her motivation, asserting that she was an artist of stature, not a prima donna making unfair demands. Any serious artist would find it depressing to be inactive. Bosse deserved understanding from the theatre's administration, not discipline and bureaucratic pressure.[61]

Expressing no sympathy, *Stockholms Dagblad* found that Bosse had played many good roles in eleven seasons at Dramaten. The paper reported the rumor that Tor Hedberg had reluctantly gone along with Bosse's idea of alternating with Signe Kolthoff as Hebbel's Judith. After participating in several rehearsals, Bosse announced she did not want to continue. She did not want to be in a secondary position to Kolthoff, who created the role and played it on opening night.[62] The paper pointed out the theatre's generosity in complying with her demands. She had requested a leave of several months for the fall of 1916. When she felt too exhausted to tour, she asked to be put back on Dramaten's payroll with time off because of ill health. The theatre agreed but could not on short notice feature her in a major new production. In recent seasons a number of Bosse's roles had been old or inconsequential. Tro in *Everyman (Det gamla spelet om Envar)* and Erna in *The Far Country (Det vida landet)* by Arthur Schnitzler, did not "count," she said, nor did any repetition of an earlier role. Later that season she would probably appear only in one act of Schnitzler's *Anatol*. The Princess in *Once Upon a Time — (Det var en gång)*, which would not be a major new role, had been promised for three years without materializing. Enumerating many roles they considered "major," *Stockholms Dagblad* concluded that Bosse "was one of those most favored with roles — if not the most favored — at the Dramatic Theatre."[63]

The crisis in Bosse's career was symptomatic of a general crisis in Stockholm theatre life caused by questionable repertory policies.[64] Georg Nordensvan wrote that there was no truly "national" theatre other than the Opera. Critics wanted more original Swedish plays and a rotating repertory schedule. Audiences still came to theatres like Dramaten because they enjoyed the talented performers and the luxury on stage and in the auditorium. Instead of the sense of comradeship and painstaking work once found at Dramaten, individual performers seemed to be isolated. Bosse's actions were typical of a trend for actors to avoid a binding contract in order to be free for tours or guest engagements.[65] For a time she and Hedberg tried to cooperate. *Once Upon a Time —* was produced splendidly for her in the spring of 1917, but after an engagement at the Lorensberg Theatre that fall, she finally left Dramaten in the summer of 1918. Since returning in 1911, she had revived four roles from her earlier repertory and created twenty-two new characters. Those mentioned most often in retrospect are Bjørnson's Maria Stuart, Liza Doolittle, Kersti in *The Crown Bride,* and Elektra.

Grace de Plessans in *The Wedding March* was Harriet Bosse's last major role before leaving Dramaten. It demanded a virtuoso performance, both musical and dramatic, for Grace is the focal point of the play. The unhappy young woman plays the Mendelssohn wedding march as a piano duet with her lover when they are defiantly in love, suffers the attentions of a seducer, and sings as she makes her final desperate exit before committing suicide.[66] Carl Laurin commented on the appropriateness of Bosse's farewell role. "She, who excels in humility—on stage," could flavor the performance with touches of "justifiable pride": "Divas love to appear as scapegoats. It would be incorrect and unkind to call fru Bosse a diva. She is not yet 'sufficient unto herself,' whereby one loses one's most valuable identity as an actress. . . . But the departure of this beautiful, intelligent and talented artist brings with it some worry that she will now become a diva. . . ."[67]

START OF A FREE-LANCE CAREER

Since leaving the Swedish Theatre, Harriet Bosse had played such a variety of roles and achieved such stature that it was difficult to summarize her achievements. An encyclopedia article in 1915 described her as "fresh, natural, charming and intelligent; she has an unusually well-developed artistic sense and can infuse the strength of her temperament into both impish and . . . touching characterizations. Her diction is especially clear and her voice beautiful."[68] In a summary of her work from 1911 to 1918, Stig Torsslow wrote that Bosse "maintained a leading position; with the deepened artistic maturity she achieved, in the judgment of many she appeared to be at the height of her career and was widely considered our foremost actress. Her most brilliant characterization during this time might be considered Hofmannsthal's 'Elektra,' in which she combined perfect form with harrowing emotional intensity."[69]

There had been few roles besides Elektra that offered Bosse the opportunity to be so innovative and physically expressive. She had reached the critical age for an actress who feels too young to play middle-aged character roles. On her fortieth birthday in February 1918 an article began, "Is she so old. . . . Is she so young. . . . One question seems just as appropriate as the other." The public admired Bosse's image of beauty and elegance, both on stage and in society. Her olive complexion was augmented by the lingering hue of a summer suntan. Countless photographs show the classic profile, almost always with a serious expression. Weight was sometimes a problem, but generally she was proud of her youthful figure. Despite her Norwegian origins, the birthday tribute claimed she was truly a "Swedish actress," for about one third of her roles had been in Swedish plays. Praising Bosse as "our most versatile actress," the writer suggested the time had come for her to consider acting in films.[70] Victor Sjöström, an actor with whom she had appeared on a Ryding tour, now offered her a movie debut. Film might have turned her career in a new direction, but it instead provided an isolated artistic achievement. Harriet Bosse chose to concentrate on the stage, where there were brilliant episodes. Offstage her life was filled with discontinuity and stress as she struggled to manage the career of a free-lance artist.

Harriet Bosse (*left*) and her sister Dagmar. (Courtesy Anne Marie Wyller Hagelin.)

Alma Fahlstrøm—sketch by her husband, 1914

Johan Fahlstrøm

Alma and Johan Fahlstrøm and their son Arne

Gunnar Wingård. (Courtesy Randi Wingård.)

Anne Marie Strindberg and Bo Wingård. (Courtesy Randi Wingård.)

Edvin Adolphson. (Photograph by Benkow.)

August Strindberg—sketch by Anders Zorn. (Courtesy Dramaten.)

Strindberg in his study. (Courtesy Dramaten.)

Strindberg. (Courtesy Dramaten.)

Puck in *A Midsummer Night's Dream*, 1900.
(Photograph by Herm. Hamnqvist.)

The Lady in *To Damascus I*, 1900

Eleonora in *Easter*, 1901

Biskra in *Simoon*, 1902. (Photograph by Florman.)

Hedvig in *The Wild Duck*, 1903. (Photograph by Herm. Hamnqvist, courtesy Randi Wingård.)

Isotta in *A Venetian Comedy*, 1904. (Photograph by
Herm. Hamnqvist.)

Title role in *Sakuntala*, 1905. (Photograph by Herm. Hamnqvist.)

Mélisande in *Pelléas and Mélisande,* 1906. (Photograph by A. Jonason, courtesy Anne Marie Wyller Hagelin.)

Indra's Daughter in *A Dream Play,* 1907. (Courtesy Dramaten.)

Ann Whitfield in *Man and Superman*, 1907. (Photograph by
Atelier Jaeger.)

Marthe Bourdier in *The King*, 1909. (Photograph by Atelier Jaeger.)

Title role in *Elektra*, photographed in 1917. (Photograph by
Ferd. Flodin.)

Steinunn in *The Wish*, 1917. (Photograph by Ferd. Flodin, courtesy Dramaten.)

Kersti in *The Crown Bride*, 1918. (Photograph by Herm. Hamnqvist.)

Bosse and Victor Sjöström in *The Ingmarssons,* 1918. (Courtesy Swedish Film Institute.)

Title role in *Queen Christina*, 1926. (Courtesy Dramaten.)

Gerda in *Storm Weather,* 1933

Bosse as Franskan with Bertil Ehrenmark (*left*) and John Ekman in *Bombi Bitt and I*, 1936. (Courtesy Randi Wingård.)

Bosse as Henriette with Uno Henning in *Crimes and Crimes*, 1936. (Photograph by Almberg & Preinitz, courtesy Dramaten.)

Madame Thiers in *The Defeat,* 1939. (Photograph by Almberg & Preinitz, courtesy Dramaten.)

Caricature of Bosse by Gösta Säfbom. (Courtesy Dramaten.)

Portrait of Bosse as Indra's Daughter by Greta Gerell. (Courtesy Dramaten.)

Dramaten—the Royal Dramatic Theatre, Stockholm. (Photograph by Arne Enander, courtesy Dramaten.)

The Red House—apartment building at Karlavägen 40. (Courtesy Dramaten.)

Central Teatret

Chef: Johan Fahlström.   Instruktør: Alma Fahlström.
Kapelmester: Gaston Borch.

Tirsdag den 17de August Kl. 7½

„Der var engang —"

Eventyrkomedie i 5 Akter — 8 Billeder — af Holger Drachmann.
Musiken af P. E. Lange-Müller, med tilhørende Dans, komponeret af Augusta Johannesen.

Personerne:

I Kongeriget Illyrien:

[cast list largely illegible]

I Danmark:

[cast list largely illegible]

Soledansen i 4de Akt danses af Frk. Augusta Johannesen.

Dekorationerne af Carl Lund.   Dragterne efter Tegning af Andreas Bloch.

Mellemaktsmusik;

NB. Det længste Ophold er mellem 3tou Akta tree og 2det Billeds skeen ikke og ejes Akt.

Central Teatets Belysning besørget af 1ste Svenstaen Udstyrsmagazin. Det elektriske Lysanlæg fra Bahne & Comp.
NB. Publikum anmodes velvilligst om at hænge Yderiøtoi af.

Billetpriserne er:

1ste Parket A 2.50, 1ste Parket B 2.00, 2det Parket 1.50, Staaende Parket 1.50, Sniploger 2.50
Logerækken 2.00, Logerækken 2 Side-Bænk 1.25, Balcon, Front, 1ste Bænk 1.25, Balcon, Front,
2den Bænk 1.00, Balcon, Sidepladse 0.75, Galleriet (staaende) 0.50.

Billetter faaes i Teatrets Billetkontor Mandag 12—3 til en Overpris à 50 Øre for Parket og Loge-
række, 25 Øre for de øvrige Pladse Forestillingsdagen til ordinære Priser fra Kl. 9—10, 12—3
samt fra Kl. 5.

Playbill—*Once Upon a Time*—, 1897

Playbill—Bosse's benefit performance, *A Dream Play,* 1907.
(Courtesy Dramaten.)

Bosse's letter accepting role in *To Damascus I*. (Courtesy Swedish
Royal Library.)

SLUTSCENEN I "FÖRSTA FIOLEN"

Rydin fo

G. Bergström   O. Bæckström   A. G. Adamsen   O. Hamrin   H. Bosse
J. Hagman   N. Personne   A. Hansson

Final scene in *First Violin*, 1900. (Photograph by Rydin.)

Bosse and August Palme in *To Damascus I*, 1900. (Courtesy Dramaten.)

Carl Grabow scene design for *A Dream Play,* 1907. (Courtesy Dramaten.)

To Damascus III, designed by Jon-And, 1926

The Turning Point

Once again Harriet Bosse had turned her back on Dramaten, choosing freedom and self-reliance rather than stability and institutional discipline. She trusted her own artistic judgment and business instincts. With a mentor to advise her about choosing roles, negotiating contracts, and renewing her acting style, she might have accomplished more. Only rarely did she encounter a stimulating new playwright like Pär Lagerkvist, an innovative director like Per Lindberg, or an idealistic theatre manager like Gustaf Collijn. At her best Bosse deserved the welcome audiences gave her, and the tribute paid by Olof Molander in his book about her. Bosse's delicate beauty, enchanting voice, intelligence, and versatility usually overcame the doubts of critics. In her first film she found a director and a costar who could match her in creativity and dynamics and challenge her to develop a technique suited to the new medium.

FILM DEBUT

In 1919 newspapers carried ads for fifty-four movie houses, which vied with palatial banks as landmarks in Stockholm. Early films attracted mostly lower-class audiences because of reasonable ticket prices. Eventually elegant cinemas were constructed in an effort to attract an affluent audience. The Red Mill (Röda Kvarn) on Biblioteksgatan, with 860 seats, was the largest movie theatre in Sweden. Built in 1915, it was obviously intended to compete with Dramaten.[1] Carl David Marcus wrote a protest for *Scenen* in 1919:

One could close all the theatres [in Stockholm] tomorrow and—with a few exceptions—none of the public would even notice. At this moment there is no European capital with cultural traditions which has been caught in the grip of film like Stockholm. The city reminds you of an American gold-mining town, where the war speculators — miners, I mean — after finishing their work in the evening want to have fun in the most pleasant way. Film — not theatre, not books — is the Stockholmer's cultural ideal.[2]

August Strindberg praised films for their artistic innovation and the democracy of the social setting in which they were viewed, but most cultural leaders debated whether film was an art form worthy of the efforts of theatre artists. Tor Hedberg added a paragraph to Dramaten contracts in 1914 forbidding actors to make films during their summer vacations.[3] Those from the theatre world who "capitulated" and went into movies were assumed to be eager to earn high salaries. Harriet Bosse adamantly maintained that she agreed to make a film because of the youthful vitality of the new art form, not for money. That she would even consider making a film enhanced the prestige of the industry.

The premiere of *The Ingmarssons (Ingmarssönerna)*, Bosse's film debut, took place at the Red Mill on New Year's Day, 1919.[4] This was a major event in the history of Swedish film. One critic found it refreshing, after being exposed "ad nauseam" to publicity for American films, "to encounter a work of art, a film masterpiece, where one can justifiably say, 'This is Swedish.'"[5] Critics have praised Sjöström's use of symbolic images and his bold imagination in scenes of fantasy, such as the ascent to a heavenly farmhouse. The authentic settings, respectful rendering of Selma Lagerlöf's book, and natural acting won high praise for director-actor Victor Sjöström. Sjöström as Lill Ingmar, the shy and awkward farmer, and Bosse as Brita, his fiancée, made such a perfect team one would have thought "they had never done anything else but act in films together."[6] Years later Ingmar Bergman called *The Ingmarssons* a "magnificent, remarkable film. He [Sjöström] works there with Harriet Bosse, and one sees that they . . . found each other artistically. It is not a bit condescending; there is no sentimentality."[7]

Bosse was fortunate to work with Sjöström, an excellent actor and a pioneer director who understood the potential of film.[8] His career spanned six decades, from apprenticeship in a company touring Finland before the turn of the century to his portrayal of Professor Isak Borg in *Wild Strawberries,* directed by Ingmar Bergman in 1957. Bergman acknowledges that Sjöström's example, collaboration, and advice were an important influence on his development. In the 1920s Sjöström directed some important films in Hollywood, including *He Who Gets Slapped* and *The Scarlet Letter,* but his achievements in acting and directing occurred primarily in Sweden.[9]

The film script was adapted from the novel *Jerusalem* by Lagerlöf, the first Swedish author to receive the Nobel Prize. In 1918 Sjöström directed films based on parts 1 and 2 of the novel; Bosse appears in part 1, drawn from the brief narrative showing farm life and folk beliefs in the province of Dalarna. The dialogue, inserted as printed titles, consists of direct quotations from the book. The novel begins with Lill Ingmar at his plow, imagining a visit to heaven to confer with a council of his forefathers. He seeks advice about whether he has any obligation to share his life with Brita. She has been sentenced to three years in prison for murdering their newborn child. Brita's father exonerates Ingmar from any responsibility and arranges to send his daughter to America when she is released. The day her term ends, Ingmar is waiting for Brita, but each hesitates to make a claim on the other's affection. Stopping at church, they realize she is a social outcast. They also receive a cold reception from Ingmar's mother, who refuses to have the "sinner" under her roof. Ingmar learns that Brita has come to love him, a confession she makes in a letter he was to receive after she sailed. Stopping in the forest, the young people are drawn to each other. A local gossip brings word that they must rush home, for the pastor has come to praise Ingmar for bringing Brita to church. Now his mother is ready to welcome her, and Ingmar will enjoy a position of respect in the community.

The script builds faithfully on the naive and moving story, adding episodes of rural social life, the routine of farm work, and the unhappiness of the reluctant fiancée. One might expect Harriet Bosse to look too exotic for a simple country girl, but the color of her hair fits the author's description: "She had dark hair and bright eyes and rosy cheeks." The novel describes facial expressions ("He looked up into her face, upon which suffering had wrought a new kind of beauty") and haunting eyes ("like the eyes of a poor, hunted fawn").[10] Bosse could do justice to Lagerlöf's intentions and to the demands of a new medium.

In the spring of 1918 Sjöström traveled through Dalarna to study the way of life and search for locations for *The Ingmarssons*. He was determined to film Bosse against a splendid background of hills, woods, and lakes. Photographer Julius Jaenzon, for the first time in any Swedish film, used a moving camera. All wooden furniture and utensils were handmade, and the costumes were homespun.[11] Eight leading actors were making their film debut. One of the most remarkable was Hildur Carlberg, aged eighty-four, who played Ingmar's mother.[12]

The company spent approximately six weeks on location, working under conditions that could be rigorous. They had to be there in the summer for the extended daylight and wildflowers. Sometimes the company would lumber up a hillside in wagons and on bicycles—in costumes and makeup—only to wait in vain until twilight for the rain to stop. While drying her woolen stockings by an open fire, Bosse told a journalist that the local citizenry, who were extras in a scene depicting the wedding of Lill Ingmar's daydreams, dressed in finery brought out of old trunks. Some thought the couple was really getting married. The actress said, "They came up to me as we sat in the wagon and shook hands and offered congratulations, and one wished me many children."[13]

Bosse commented later that she would rather prepare for ten theatre premieres than work on one film: "It is a psychic and physical strain you cannot imagine if you haven't tried it. You must constantly exert your strength to the utmost, and you do not always do that on stage."[14] Bosse found it difficult to shoot scenes out of chronological sequence and to plunge from one emotion to another, knowing she would not have a chance to do the scene better the next day. "Therefore the stage undeniably offers more joy while the work is taking place—in film the joy comes afterward."[15]

Although Bosse's acting in *The Ingmarssons* was superb, she would have been more suitably cast in a sophisticated role. She was even criticized for not holding the needles correctly as she knit a stocking.[16] The natural exterior light and closeup shots made her age more obvious than it was on stage, yet reviewers found no fault with her appearance. They praised Bosse for understanding that film required a new approach to acting: "Her hair lay dark and smooth around the tiny round face—no painted lips, no drawn eyes, nothing reminiscent of theatre. But what a wonderfully changing face."[17] Another wrote: "No matter how many times one has seen this actress' stage portrayals, it will nevertheless be a new experience for the Swedish public, undisturbed by distance and disadvantageous lighting, to be able to enjoy this exceptionally soulful face. She has a capacity to make her face radiant without smiling—it seems to be illuminated from within—to become ethereal, transfigured." Another review called her performance "a picture from real life."[18]

When filming began, Bosse used the method she had polished for years in the theatre. She was appalled to see herself in screen tests. With Sjöström's instruction and reassurance, Bosse set to work to develop a new technique. Later she explained how she had learned to use her eyes for what she would express with words and gestures on stage: "Every glance one uses on stage is enlarged on film. I am accustomed to walking freely on stage; here it becomes impossible and grotesque. . . . To act for film is an art in itself . . . it is distinct from the art of the stage, just as painting and sculpture are two separate branches of art." She longed for reassurance that the new technique had worked:

If with my eyes and facial expressions I have been able to reveal all that Brita feels when she leaves the prison—wondering whether Lill Ingmar is kind to her out of pity or whether the little bouquet on the carriage might mean something. If in the scene at court I could show with my face how all the troubled thoughts are lifted from Brita as though by a miracle when Lill Ingmar says: "I consider her so innocent that I want to marry her when she has had her punishment." Do you think I succeeded? Oh, how happy I am.[19]

Bosse expressed heartfelt appreciation of Sjöström: "I cannot say how happy I am that I had my first film experience with him." After seeing *The Ingmarssons,* Bosse said, "At least it was not a disappointment." She was not enthusiastic about the first half, where she was crying and desperate and "hard as flint," but she liked the second half very much—especially the letter scene in prison.[20] A critic describes her sensitive facial expressions "when with her eyes she follows the movement of a ray of sunshine—how it slowly creeps down the wall and stops over the paper—the letter she is writing to Ingmar. The tiny sunbeam becomes for her the symbol of the new life which may begin after she is set free. The dawning of happiness shines in her eyes—and one sees it, feels it with her. It is well done . . . and above all, it is art."[21]

It was my privilege to view part 1 of *The Ingmarssons* at the Swedish Film Institute. Victor Sjöström deserves praise for his acting and for his ambitious, imaginative directing. He brings out the human qualities of the characters and gives the film exciting dimensions through flashbacks, visions representing characters' thoughts, and vignettes.[22] His Lill Ingmar is an indecisive, stolid peasant, whose integrity is threatened by social pressure. Bosse's Brita is a melancholy and anxious young girl, at the mercy of her parents' matchmaking and her fiancé's advances. Her expression of emotion is somewhat quaint and slightly melodramatic, but there is clarity and variety in her performance. Emotional moments are intense and touching and not at all ludicrous. Sjöström obviously wanted to depict authentically the confining, drab milieu that the young fiancée enters. When Lill Ingmar drives into his farmyard, his mother comes to greet Brita, who must jump down from the wagon unassisted. She and the mother stand knitting busily, not smiling; they pause only momentarily to shake hands.

Bosse shows Brita's realization of her pregnancy in a scene when she becomes dizzy while stacking linens. Her eyes roll up, and she falls on the floor, then is helped to bed, where she overhears with alarm that Ingmar might postpone their wedding another year. Bosse uses her hands expressively. She reveals nervousness by clasping the edge of a table, squeezing and twisting a pillow, or grasping her skirt and wrinkling it. Sometimes she raises a hand to her hair and brings it down along her cheek. Often she sits calmly with hands clasped in her lap. When her brow furrows or her bosom heaves, it is convincing that she is agitated. Bosse succeeds in showing how touched and appreciative Brita is at Lill Ingmar's statement on her behalf in the courtroom. She looks calm and peaceful, as though transformed by a mystical experience.

In the prison Bosse uses her eyes effectively while considering whether or not to write the letter telling Ingmar she has come to love him. She moves her head slowly and watches the beam of sunlight seeming to signal that she should take up the quill pen and write. As she leaves prison, Ingmar fantasizes about the wedding they might have had. Bosse smiles broadly in that imaginary scene for the only time in the film. Their meeting, the tentative clasping of hands as they walk down the cobblestone street, the feeling of shame and ostracism at church, the painful rejection by Ingmar's mother, all prepare for the most touching scene. In the woods, where somehow the letter carrier finds them, Ingmar reads Brita's letter, despite her protestations. Her shoulders sag and energy seems to leave her body, but she comes to life when she realizes that Ingmar is angry about her trying to leave for America without confessing her love. Bosse almost laughs as she hops down from the wagon and approaches Sjöström, who is stretched out on the forest floor, sobbing. She takes off his hat and gently strokes his forehead. Gradually he shows that Ingmar is prepared to defy society for her sake. In their last scene he sweetly caresses her hand, she leans her forehead against his head, and they laugh when they notice a dozen cows watching them. Bosse and Sjöström create an affirmation of the transforming power of love.

Everyone wondered if this was only the first of many films in which Bosse would appear. She expressed some interest in continuing if she could work with material that met her artistic standards:

One thing is totally clear: how extremely important it is to have a really good script—absorbing action, a true depiction of people—only when the director has this to build upon can he accomplish anything of artistic value. Film is not just "light reading," although all the American action films and those from other countries have established that impression with the general public. Film has artistic possibilities just as much as theatre—if only artists take charge. I think our best Swedish film production has proved that fully.[23]

It was seventeen years before Harriet Bosse made another film in Sweden. In her memoirs she wrote: "I don't know how it happened, but it [*The Ingmarssons*] was the only worthwhile Swedish film I was involved in. Possibly it was because I was possessive about my summers, when I wanted to travel, and not make movies."[24]

THE INTIMATE THEATRE

Although Bosse did not capitalize on her film debut, she was a prominent figure in the public eye. In the 1920s she, Naima Wifstrand, Tora Teje, and Anders de Wahl were the most often photographed theatre artists.[25] Except for a film made in Germany in 1919, her livelihood depended on tours and guest engagements. Her most important work was done at a theatre with the name used by Strindberg and Falck—The Intimate Theatre. Gustaf Collijn, the artistic manager, was talented and intellectual, and well acquainted with new developments in European theatre. In 1910 he founded the first significant Swedish theatre journal, *Thalia*.

Beginning in September 1911, Collijn and Knut Michaelson, Tor Hedberg's predecessor at Dramaten, managed the second Intimate Theatre. From 1914 to 1921 Collijn was sole administrator of the theatre on Birger Jarlsgatan near the Royal Library. He presented a repertory of high quality, regardless of financial risk, and tried to create an ensemble style comparable to that of the Moscow Art Theatre. Established stars and young talent were featured. Outstanding performers who appeared at the Intimate Theatre were Victor Sjöström, Edith Erastoff, Karin Molander, Doris Nelson, and—above all—Lars Hanson. An acting style patterned after French models still dominated the Swedish stage, especially because Dramaten students were taught those principles. People were growing aware that the times demanded a new approach, which they had glimpsed in the work of certain actors. The Intimate Theatre replaced the technique of polished diction and graceful gestures with a "psychological" style of acting—careful character analysis, individualized details, and internal truthfulness. The word *intimate* in the name of the theatre expressed the artistic concept on which its work was based.[26]

Although most of the repertory was modern, there were also Swedish classics and plays by Holberg, Molière, and Sheridan. The directors were Michaelson, Einar Fröberg, Emil Grandinson, and Rune Carlsten. "A kind of 'group staging' developed at the New Intimate Theatre. During many long nights of conversation and rehearsal, productions were worked out by the ensemble and director together. . . . In contemporary theatre debate the New Intimate Theatre's ensemble was held out as a model."[27] Because of limited space and technical resources, productions were of necessity "intimate." Bosse told a reporter before her engagement: "The stage is small— but, my Lord, I am not so terribly large myself. And the Intimate Theatre is, in my opinion, a little pearl. Striving forward in every way and with an excellent repertory."[28] After her first performance a critic commented that she had never managed her voice so effectively: "The excellent acoustics of the theatre must explain the remarkable result Bosse achieved."[29] The Intimate Theatre provided stimulating competition for Dramaten and for Ranft's Swedish Theatre.[30] A loyal audience seriously interested in art came to performances, and during intermissions there was a kind of "literary salon," as the audience discussed the plays. "It was intimate even beyond the stage."[31]

Harriet Bosse conferred frequently with Gustaf Collijn, proposing roles she would like to play. Her first appearance at the theatre was in two Norwegian plays with which she had become familiar in Kristiania in the 1890s: *The Master Builder (Byggmästare Solness)* by Ibsen and *The Balcony* by Gunnar Heiberg. Bosse prepared to play Hilda [Hilde] Wangel appropriately, while sledding and skiing in Norway during the Christmas holidays, but she was worried that Hilda would not interest the public as much as the character deserved.[32] Audiences saw Bosse in a curly blond wig and a striped sailor blouse, and the cap and knapsack she used herself when hiking in the Norwegian mountains. The play was considered puzzling because of its symbolic and mystical dimensions, and its revival now provoked Pär Lagerkvist to attack Ibsen as passé and the play as improbable and artificial. Nevertheless, Lagerkvist said of Bosse that "a better Hilda Wangel could hardly be imagined, at least none so charming."[33] Lars Hanson played a Solness who was clearly neurotic, but with convincing traces of genius. Hilda was a role in which Johanne Dybwad had been triumphant when a guest at Dramaten in 1900. Daniel Fallström wrote: "Harriet Bosse's Hilda was both fresh and captivating. Her first act had the same effect as Johanne Dybwad's—mountain breeze."[34] Although some critics objected that Bosse tried to appear too young, naive, and delicate, others called this one of the best performances she had ever given. Since Bosse had been seen so little in Stockholm in recent years, Hilda's speech had a double meaning: "I almost think you don't recognize me." Now the public welcomed her back warmly, filling the house for more than sixty performances of *The Master Builder*.[35]

The Balcony was considered scandalous when it appeared in 1894, for the leading female character is reckless and egotistical, following primitive passionate impulses regardless of who gets hurt. As a literary work, the play won many admirers for its pathos and poetic mysticism. Opening on 1 April 1919, the Intimate Theatre production was directed by Rune Carlsten, who also played the husband effectively. Lars Hanson as the lover completed the triangle, but Bosse as Julia was the focus of attention. Julia is an Eve figure, reminiscent of Wedekind's Lulu, symbolizing sensual charm and obsession with love. With mature femininity, seductiveness, and a brilliant range of emotional color, Bosse brought out nuances that would have been lost in a larger theatre. Once again she used a touch of the stylization for which she was noted.[36] Opinion was divided about the production and even about Bosse's interpretation, which some found too soft, charming, and refined. Sven Söderman wrote, "The final impression was that fru Bosse presented a masterful characterization, but that Heiberg's play should be read and not seen."[37] Bosse did not report that comment when she sent the playwright a photograph of herself as Julia and told him that the play received a great deal of attention during its run of eighteen sold-out performances.[38]

Harriet's second season at the Intimate Theatre was jeopardized when she broke her leg skiing in Norway on Christmas Eve, 1919. Although newspapers reported her in great pain, Harriet assured Collijn that she would be ready to work on 6 January, although she might have to sit through rehearsals until the break healed.[39] This season Harriet appeared in two rather shallow but entertaining plays: *The Plume (Aigretten)* by Dario Niccodemi and *Home and Beauty (Änkleken)* by W. Somerset Maugham. The productions were popular, running for twenty-eight and fifty-two performances respectively. Bosse's interpretation of the role of Suzanne Leblanc, originally written for Réjane, was psychologically clear and emotionally intense. The play by Maugham gave Bosse her first chance at this theatre to display her skill as a comedienne. The plot revolves around the complications when a husband who was believed killed in World War I returns to find his wife married to someone else. Bosse played with humor and a touch of satire the pampered social butterfly who solves her dilemma by choosing a third man.[40]

Despite illness during the spring of 1920, Bosse was busy making plans for the next season. Disappointed that Collijn would not produce *Lysistrata*, she hoped to do the play elsewhere, but that production never materialized.[41] In the winter of 1921 Bosse appeared in six productions, including Strindberg's *Easter*.

In *Nju* by Russian author Ossip Dymov, Bosse used a style reminiscent of *Pelléas and Mélisande*. This was the first time she worked with her future husband, Edvin Adolphson, who had joined the company in 1920.[42] He was dazzled and frightened to learn that he was to appear opposite the illustrious fru Bosse, but he gave in to her persuasion to rehearse the role for at least one week. While Adolphson found rehearsals inspiring, he felt ill at ease about a scene in which he was to pull Bosse out of bed and throw her on the floor. She complained that he was obviously holding back and letting her control the fall. On 18 January 1921, the public saw Bosse and Adolphson together for the first time; they probably never again saw them in such a violent scene. Adolphson lost control and threw Bosse so far that she flew across the floor and stopped only when she hit the wall. The audience sat gaping, almost too stunned to applaud.[43] Söderman commented on the "sensual charm" of her "youthful body," and Inga Tidblad, who was one of the leading actresses of the next generation, has written that she would never forget how beautiful Harriet Bosse looked in *Nju* in a white costume, reading a book aloud "with silver bells in her voice."[44]

Members of the ensemble were responsible for their own modern costumes. Bosse had her clothes made by the best seamstresses in Stockholm, but for those with modest salaries it was a financial burden to provide clothes, shoes, wigs, and makeup. Adolphson thought it was catastrophic to appear in a premiere two months in a row, for he often used half his salary for clothes. The public was unaware that some members of the Intimate Theatre company were poor, because they always looked elegant.[45]

Bosse and Adolphson made an attractive and intriguing couple in the episodic, romantic one-act play *Chitra* by Indian author Rabindranath Tagore. The role belongs to the series of Bosse's exotic Oriental characters. The setting and the presence of the gods Madana and Vasanta must have reminded spectators of Bosse's association with *A Dream Play*. Chitra appears in two guises—the hunter, who is dressed as a man, and the seductive and mysterious mistress, who is granted perfect beauty by the gods for one year. Arjuna, the warrior prince played by Adolphson, is smitten by Chitra's illusory beauty but also fascinated by the legend of the proud and strong hunter. At the end the young woman appears as her true self, offering to work side by side with Arjuna and bear his son.[46] Adolphson and Bosse had to be convincing as passionate lovers, she tormented by deceitfulness, he adoring and accepting of her in both identities. Bosse commented that no one would dream how much work she did to draw out the nuances of the character and convey the delicate poetic quality of the script. "There is a floral fragrance, a charming lyricism about the little play which enchanted me."[47] The beautiful production, unusual because it was a double bill of very different works, drew a full house.

During intermission Bosse transformed herself from a legendary Indian Amazon to a mad young girl with flowing hair, barefoot, wearing a shawl and a simple dress. This was the world premiere of *The Secret of Heaven (Himlens hemlighet)* by Pär Lagerkvist. The mood on stage changed from the dreamlike enchantment of *Chitra's* fairy tale to the bleakness and despair of a grotesque nightmare. The audience was unable to adjust; they found Lagerkvist's play puzzling and offensive. Conservatives hissed vigorously, while the Lagerkvist faction applauded just as vigorously. The production, directed by Einar Fröberg, used excellent new music composed by Ture Rangström. The music established a mystical atmosphere and seemed to allow some penetration of the "secret" of the script. Yngve Berg, making his debut as a scene designer that evening, was responsible for the simple setting—an isolated platform suggesting a sphere floating in a void.[48]

Although critics considered *Chitra* more significant, Harriet Bosse was captivated by *The Secret of Heaven,* with "all that is new" and "all its supernatural, powerful symbolism."[49] She played one of the individuals encountered by a young man newly arrived in a macabre heaven. She is searching for a golden string for her guitar; if she could find it, trees would blossom, birds would sing, and the whole world would become beautiful. Bosse recalled later: "The stage was built up like a globe, and we wandered on it with rubber soles to keep our footing. Some in the audience left demonstratively, others did not understand a thing but stayed in their seats, wondering what the play meant." Critics described her characterization as "a figure of wild, moving tragedy," "touching and frightening in her helplessness." The most haunting detail of her performance was a heartrending laugh. Bosse was brilliant during momentary wild outbursts, but she was criticized because the scene with the young man was reminiscent of the way she played a similar scene in *Easter*.[50]

Harriet Bosse's marathon engagement closed at the end of April with a benefit performance of the Tagore-Lagerkvist bill for an audience that showered her with applause and bouquets. This was the last production under Collijn's management, which ended in May 1921. Bosse reflected later: "Gustaf succeeded in a great achievement at the Intimate Theatre, and I consider that, unfortunately, no one has taken his place." Working with Collijn, she said, gave her the opportunity to fulfill her "artistic desires":

There I got to develop what is for me an especially suitable form of theatre. Drama which I loved, a form of intimate art which has meant the most to me — where heart speaks to heart, and that which lies above and behind the dialogue is brought out. This is, in my opinion, what is most important in all acting. To boom out a speech, and later find nothing remains — that is sterile.

The little Intimate Theatre was a jewel box whose contents were most often sublime spirit — the innermost essence of theatre. Without spirit — no art.[51]

A survey of Bosse's career appeared in March 1919, praising the success of her performances as Hilda at the Intimate Theatre and Brita on film. "But in the long run Swedish theatre naturally cannot do without this intellectual and imaginative talent, and the occasional reappearances as a guest are a meagre substitute for what the actress offered during the recent golden age of the Swedish stage."[52]

Occasional guest appearances were the pattern of Bosse's professional life in the 1920s. A "golden age" of Swedish theatre had passed. Bosse was alarmed to see competition and commercialism, artistic and financial crises. A younger generation of directors and actors created a new "golden age" in the 1930s, but by then she was relegated to the sidelines and her work at the Intimate Theatre was a fond and happy memory.

AWAY FROM STOCKHOLM

In 1921, when the Intimate Theatre was forced to close, theatre in Stockholm was experiencing "a classical financial crisis."[53] There was a sense of solidarity among actors, who formed Skådespelarföreningen, their own section within the association called Svenska Teaterförbundet. The group worked for actors' rights and standard terms in contracts, for example, uniform fees for matinees and extra performances. When in Stockholm, members of the theatre community saw each other's dress rehearsals and met at morning lectures, such as those given by Max Reinhardt.[54] Harriet Bosse had many acquaintances in Stockholm theatre circles, but she was quite independent. Not limiting her engagements to Stockholm, she sought opportunities away from the capital.

In the years between 1901 and 1915, the touring circuit was expanded, as at least sixteen fine provincial theatres were constructed. There was also a summer circuit of parks called Folkets Parker, but it was out of the question for a star of Bosse's stature to appear at these parks.[55] Scheduling troupes for both parks and formal theatres, Allan Ryding remained a successful entrepreneur, with whom Bosse continued to accept engagements.[56] Tours could be exhausting, as she confided to Gustaf Collijn: "It is very hard work to travel on tour and have 3 new roles to learn. I am very tired, but as I was, unfortunately, born with a duty-motor that can't be switched off, there's nothing to do but keep working."[57] She earned well and usually enjoyed the attention accorded her:

The public was most often wonderfully kind and interested. Except for one time in a city in the North, when I did "The Lady of the Camellias," a role I did not want to do but was forced to because of my contract with Ryding. In the last act, when The Lady of the Camellias lies dying and reads, from memory, her beloved Armand's letter, I happend to cast my tear-drenched gaze at the first row of the orchestra—there sat a man reading the newspaper *Aftonbladet*. I was probably not especially good as The Lady of the Camellias.[58]

Bosse played a variety of roles with Ryding. Sometimes she revived successes, such as Jolanta in *King René's Daughter* and Grace in *The Wedding March*. She was identified with Strindberg in the mind of the public, who always welcomed a chance to see her as Eleonora. After she had played that role in the fall of 1920, Ryding stated, "During four years as theatre manager in the Swedish provinces, I have never before had such a brilliant artistic as well as financial success as Harriet Bosse's latest guest appearance, and I want to hereby publicly express my most sincere thanks to the theatre managers in the capital, who have until now not discovered and stolen from the provinces our country's most outstanding scenic artist."[59] For Ryding she also played a new Strindberg role, Judith in part 2 of *The Dance of Death (Dödsdansen)*. Like Sarah Bernhardt, who found it easier to please audiences on tour than those in Paris, Harriet Bosse enjoyed the warm reception she received away from Stockholm.

Having received a cordial welcome when she appeared at the National Theatre in Kristiania in 1916, Bosse returned to play with their ensemble in 1923, her first time to appear with a Norwegian company since 1898. She played Elektra once again and demonstrated the other extreme of her range as Victoria in Maugham's comedy *Home and Beauty,* which in Kristiania was called *Victoria's Men (Victorias mæand)*. Bosse enjoyed playing in Norway: "They were all so nice — both the public and colleagues. I became more and more fond of the latter. I would have nothing against returning there soon. I have really always loved the country."[60]

The idea of establishing herself as an international star attracted Harriet Bosse, but she was never lucky enough to find a manager to promote her successfully. In 1924 it appeared that she might be able to follow in the footsteps of European prima donnas who had toured the United States. She arrived in New York aboard the Swedish-American liner *Drottningholm* in early May. The *New York Times* heralded her as "one of Sweden's foremost actresses" and announced that she would give "a series of recitals" during a three-month visit.[61] In her memoirs Bosse does not name the managers who invited her to appear on a variety bill. She says they managed musical comedies, but vaudeville is probably the correct term. Having prepared a monologue by Johan Ludvig Heiberg, Bosse went to audition. One of the managers sat down at the piano and improvised a jazz accompaniment that he proposed to liven up the performance. While trying to decide whether to accept the engagement, Bosse went to see one of the firm's programs:

The performances began at noon, and continued uninterrupted all day. People were packed into the theatre. They were obviously prepared for a long program, for they had brought their lunch with them. . . . First a cyclist came in and swept across the stage like a tempest. He called out as he pedaled. "Mary, where are you?" The answer from the wings: "Here I am." There followed a demonstration of the wildest swoops with the bikes. Next came a man on roller skates . . . and all this was accompanied by jazz. My mood and my expectations sank considerably. But my decision was settled with the third number — a seal entered and played with a ball, which he balanced on his nose. No, I did not fit into that milieu.[62]

After turning down the "fantastically high salary," Bosse learned that Sarah Bernhardt and Eleonora Duse had performed small numbers from their repertory in that very milieu, and she wondered if she had been foolish not to do the same. Fortunately her acquaintance with American theatre was not limited to vaudeville. She saw good productions while in New York, such as *All God's Chillun Got Wings, Hedda Gabler,* and *Rain,* and left with a vivid impression of Manhattan's excitement and the "excellent organization of these millions of people."[63]

As soon as she returned from the States, Bosse was deeply involved in arrangements to manage her own tour: plays by Ibsen and Strindberg and an itinerary in Sweden and Norway. This was her way to strike a blow in the battle for serious drama of merit.

PERSONAL LIFE

Harriet Bosse often returned to Norway for vacations to see family and friends and to hike in the mountains. She was never invited to visit Alma and Johan Fahlstrøm, but her brother Ewald frequently offered her the hospitality of his home. After studying and teaching at the University of Kiel, Ewald returned to Norway in 1924 and became noted for his research in labor relations. Harriet and her children frequently visited him and his wife Margit at their beautiful estate at Voksenkollen, on a mountainside overlooking Oslo.[64] Anne Marie was confirmed in Norway. She recalls her mother coming for the occasion and helping with a last-minute review of the catechism. After Anne Marie spent the school year of 1919–20 in Oxford, her mother met her and they visited London and Paris for sightseeing, shopping, and theatregoing. Traveling regularly to England and the Continent was part of Bosse's life-style.[65]

In June 1922 Anne Marie persuaded her mother to buy a vacation place with a house and two cottages in the Stockholm archipelago at Gällnö near Vaxholm. The summer home was christened "Ning-e-Nang." This phrase had evolved from Bo's crooning as a baby when he cuddled with a favorite blanket, and it became the family's term for anything cozy and pleasant. Bosse threw herself energetically into redecorating, sewing curtains, and planting flowers. The island retreat always meant more to Anne Marie than to her mother, who alternated quiet vacations there with travels to Norway, Italy, and other favorite destinations.[66]

Bo Wingård attended an exclusive boarding school starting at the age of ten. Because he was away and his mother was busy working during the theatre season, summer offered the best opportunity for them to be together. In 1923 she invited a tutor to join the family on the island, since Bo had been having difficulty with his schoolwork. She declined an invitation to visit Norway that year, explaining that she needed to spend time with her son.[67]

In the city Anne Marie always had the responsibility of helping her mother memorize lines and keeping the house quiet so that Bosse could rest when she came home from rehearsals. Bo sometimes met his mother after performances to walk her home. He later recalled her constant hard work, rather than what some would have assumed was the glamorous social life of an actress. Harriet socialized mostly with musicians and theatre artists. Her closest friends were the actress Tyra Zanderholm and Ellen Appelberg-Collijn, a former actress married to the librarian Isak Collijn. To them she could confide private concerns and professional frustrations and hopes. In 1923 she wrote to Ellen about plans to appear at an interesting private theatre managed by Ernst Eklund. The play was *East of Suez (Öster om Suez)* by W. Somerset Maugham. "The role is so enormous that I need a lot of time. . . . I have promised to rehearse 8 days without pay, but it is impossible to get it ready in such a short time, so I shall probably offer 8 more days."[68]

Eklund began his theatrical career with the traveling company of Hjalmar Selander. By the early 1920s he was an actor-manager-director, leading the Blanche Theatre (Blancheteatern) in Stockholm, where he presented some outstanding foreign artists, including Alexander Moissi in *Ghosts*. In 1923 he took over Collijn's Intimate Theatre and renamed it the Comedy Theatre (Komediteatern). The repertory at both Eklund's theatres included popular foreign comedies, an occasional serious drama, and new Swedish works. One interesting production was Brecht's *Three Penny Opera (Tolvskillings-operan)* in 1929, in which he played Mack the Knife and his wife, Alice, appeared as Polly. His company included Carl-Gunnar Wingård, a cousin of Gunnar Wingård. With Ernst Eklund playing opposite her, Bosse's appearance as Daisy in *East of Suez* in August and September 1923 was not as noteworthy as her later work with Eklund when he presented some ambitious productions at Stockholm's new concert hall.[69]

A GUEST AT DRAMATEN

After leaving Dramaten in 1918, Harriet Bosse first returned as a guest star after an absence of almost four years.[70] She was invited to play three roles, of which Rosalind in *As You Like It,* directed by Olof Molander, was most significant. The successful production opened on 21 April 1922 and was revived in the fall, as was *The Adventure,* which she had first done in 1915. Continuing to appear as Hélène in *The Adventure* at Dramaten in the winter of 1923, she also created two new roles: Varvara Aleksejevna in the serious drama *The Labyrinth (Labyrinten)* by S. L. Poljakov and Phaethusa in the comedy *Aiolos the Shoemaker (Skomaker Aiolos)* by Arnold Kübler. After her engagement at the Comedy Theatre in 1923, Bosse returned to Dramaten to play Kate Hardcastle in *She Stoops to Conquer (Värdshuset Råbocken)* by Oliver Goldsmith. In March 1924 she appeared as the intense, exotic Acacia in *Mother's Rival (Mors rival* or *La Malquerida)* by Jacinto Benavente.

Dramaten acquired a new artistic director in 1922, when Tore Svennberg took the position. He seemed to favor a younger generation of actresses, giving leading roles to Märta Ekström, Jessie Wessel, and above all, Tora Teje. Bosse worked with some outstanding mature actresses, such as Thekla Åhlander, Signe Kolthoff, Hilda Borgström, and Julia Håkansson, and she was sometimes reunited with old acquaintances, including Lars Hanson, Ivan Hedqvist, and Anders de Wahl. Harriet Bosse did not feel that Svennberg offered her attractive roles, and as long as he was head of the theatre, she was unlikely to appear there very often.[71]

Whenever Bosse appeared at Dramaten, critics and audience members gladly welcomed her back. Opinion was still divided as to the degree of naturalness with which she played. Her subtle and discreet technique might be praised, or she might be said not to be acting but to be living a role. When she did the young aristocratic Elsa in *Pension Bellevue* by Ernst Didring, Bo Bergman wrote: "It has been a long time since I saw the actress so completely free from the artificial, so thoroughly true and genuine. Her voice has always been an unusually well-managed instrument; now this instrument also gives tones from deep within."[72] She continued to show her emotional range, as in *The Labyrinth,* with its contrast between the sunny joy of the first act and the tragic pain of the later acts.[73] An occasional objection was raised about Bosse's having been miscast. Clarissa in Alfred Sutro's *Choice (Valet)*, for example, could have been done by any young girl, and it was hoped that Bosse would "soon appear in a more significant role."[74] There was a tendency to keep her in ingenue roles but whether in blond wig, lace, and straw hat as Kate Hardcastle, velvet doublet and hose as Rosalind, or peasant blouse and shawl as Acacia, she looked amazingly young. When she returned to Dramaten in 1922, a poem in *Svenska Dagbladet* welcomed her back from her long "exile" and proclaimed that she still looked as though she were in her twenties. Such return engagements at Dramaten put her in direct competition with "a whole army of very beautiful young actresses."[75]

The importance of Harriet Bosse's career and the unique qualities of her acting were the subject of a book published in 1920 by Olof Molander, who was then her ardent admirer. A translation appeared in Germany in 1922. Molander had begun his training at Dramaten in 1912, studying diction, pauses, and tempo with Thekla Åhlander, facial expressions, gestures, and deportment with Nils Personne.[76] He began his directing career with *The Merchant of Venice* in 1919 and became known for radically simplifying the decor, using new lighting effects, and reinterpreting the major works of

Shakespeare and Strindberg.[77] As an experienced actor and promising director, Molander was qualified to describe Bosse's achievements and understand her artistic independence and individuality. She allowed him to quote from a scrapbook of the early days in Norway and from Strindberg's letters. The resulting slim volume presented a chronological overview of her career, some glimpses of her personal life, and a tribute to her artistry. Molander defended and praised Bosse in an almost poetic style, as illustrated by his comments on her voice, after referring to her speech as Mélisande, "I am — — not — — happy":

Like a rare bird's resonant song, her voice rang with the musical nuances which are her own, and which sometimes are so criticized.

Justifiably and—unjustifiably. It is true that there is something unnatural, I am tempted to say beyond natural in these nuances, which does not always permit us to understand the meaning, since many are unfamiliar with the style. But is that our fault or hers? Nothing is more relative than the concept of "nature" in regard to theatre. Harriet Bosse's voice reaches our ear in a soundwave with musical nuances, which raises her characterizations above the ordinary to a plane where only our purest intuition and most active fantasy might perceive it.[78]

Molander describes the sense of isolation and mystery that Bosse often conveyed in performance, through not only her voice but through shifting facial expressions and harmonious movements. She had a charisma or magical power that made her the darling of the public.

"THALIA IS DYING"

It was pleasant to know that she was popular, but Harriet Bosse had other concerns that mirrored the achievements and struggles of Swedish theatre. A primary concern was the tension between commercialism and art, certainly not limited to Swedish theatre nor to the era in which Bosse lived, but especially relevant during the 1920s. In the struggle to survive financially, she tried to balance the need for income against good taste and a preference for drama of literary quality. It was not always possible to appear in significant works or to create new roles, yet she tried to resist the trend toward light entertainment and the misuse of talent. Sources vary as to what worried her. It may have been the overwhelming popularity of American films or her consternation at Gösta Ekman's appearance in light comedies such as André Picard's *Gentleman in Tails (En herre i frack)*.[79] Bosse's reaction to alarming trends inspired the following statement, which appeared in the theatre magazine *Scenen* on 15 October 1923:

THALIA IS DYING—
  We, her children, stand by helplessly and can do nothing.
  Thalia is dying—of grief—since she feels that her time has passed.
  Everyone is forgetting her—no one inquires about her—she has been driven off the pedestal which was hers, where she sat safely in the awareness that the holiness she represented—art, culture, beauty—could never die.
  She did not think that these three fragile things could be easily swept away by a football, a boxing glove. She cannot bear to do battle with her humble weapons—those of the spirit—in this age of physical strength and disrespect. She realizes that one cannot fight a cannon with a foil.

*

  We say: let us try to help her—perhaps people are not yet so unreceptive toward beauty in our art. Perhaps amidst all the rush and superficiality of our day one may find time to awaken and find within oneself the spark of the divine which is granted to all human beings and which expresses itself in a need for art—in whatever genre it may appear.
  It is not art people want—the kind of theatre in demand now is degrading—thoughts *cannot* take flight—the beauty of the spirit *cannot* be seen.
  The managers must have people [audiences]—the public's taste is brought down to one level—and the repertory corresponds to it.

*

  But do not let Thalia die. I, one of her children, pray for her so earnestly. I beg the public, the critics to support her—help her.
  Let us regain the great joy of going to our work with the firm belief that the masterpieces of dramatic art we so much want to have the honor of presenting, must not be crushed against a wall of cynicism, disrespect—and ignorance.[80]

Bosse's meditation on the decline of theatre did not meet with universal sympathy. A perceptive critic named Sven Stål dared to respond with a harsh essay, published in 1925, analyzing what he considered to be a mid-life crisis. If Bosse looked at herself honestly, she would discover that she was still using the same old techniques: "While her fellow actors speak, she rests until, on signal, she breaks into the conversation, changes the tone, and does solo pirouettes." Stål admired Bosse in his youth, but he had found nothing creative in her work in the previous ten years. He blamed her for distancing herself from theatre and mourning its decline like a Greek chorus, criticizing not just her performance style but the shape of her career. There were countless roles, such as Swan White, which might have been worth her effort, but she had yielded to public taste: "Fru Bosse has not just betrayed her craft, she has betrayed dramatic art, her own development, and she has won nothing from her choice." Having spent some time in the United States, Stål named Maud Adams as an admirable actress whom Bosse might emulate. The critic urged her to exercise strict self-discipline so that her individual performance would be subordinate to the work of the ensemble and the author's words. He challenged her: "Try to create a work of art. Forget about whether the wrinkles show and the years make their claim. . . . For once, be natural."[81]

Whose judgment could she trust? Ultimately Harriet Bosse had to be self-reliant, negotiating contracts and seeking challenging roles for two more decades. She began to see herself as a figure in the history of Swedish theatre and in the legend of August Strindberg.

CHAPTER EIGHT

Independence

During the years from 1924 to 1933 Harriet Bosse courageously tried new ventures—managing her own tour, appearing on a large concert stage, marrying a younger man, preparing for a London debut, living on a farm, editing a book, planning an experimental theatre. She felt ambitious, energetic, and youthful, but economic hardship and professional disappointments gradually narrowed her options.

LIFE OFFSTAGE

In the 1920s Harriet Bosse's children established lives of their own. Neither had an artistic temperament, nor considered a career in theatre. That was just as well, for Bosse would have adamantly opposed their following in her footsteps.

Anne Marie was a gentle young woman who was happy spending her summers at the home on Gällnö. She had always enjoyed spending the day alone fishing, ever since Aunt Inez let her go off alone in a boat at the age of ten. On a visit to Norway in 1925, she attended a university student dance where she met Anders Wyller, a scholar of language and literature. Three days later she wrote to her mother that they were engaged. Anne Marie and Anders married on Gällnö in June 1926. The ceremony took place outdoors among the roses, and an archway of wildflowers adorned the door to the cottage. It amused Bosse to realize that she and her daughter had traded countries. Born in Norway, she needed a Swedish passport to travel there; Anne Marie, born in Sweden, needed a Norwegian passport to travel home to Stockholm. After Wyller took part in the Scandinavian student movement, he and Anne Marie moved to Paris, where their two sons, Arne and Jørgen, were born. Wyller wrote a dissertation on Paul Claudel and taught Norwegian literature and language at the Sorbonne from 1933 to 1936. Since Anne Marie and her family could not conveniently spend summers in

Sweden, Harriet sold the property on Gällnö. While in Paris, Anders Wyller kept in touch with cultural and political developments at home. Inspired by a humanistic philosophy, he returned to Norway and in 1938, with his friend Kristian Schjelderup, founded the Nansen School in Lillehammer.

In the mid-1920s, the family recalls, Harriet Bosse was courted by a wealthy American. Anne Marie and Bo had visions of moving to America, but their mother was not in love. Instead she became interested in Edvin Adolphson, with whom she had been costarring. He had found her striking from the first: "Harriet Bosse was at an age when a woman is most tempting to a man—a 40-year-old, beautiful, shapely woman, who seemed at least ten years younger." There was no doubt that he admired her versatility and achievement as an actress, but a personal relationship evolved slowly: "Her experiences in life probably contributed to her seeming a little aloof and reserved toward people she did not know."[1] According to Adolphson, the romance began when they met by chance in London at a performance of a play by Shaw.

Gustav Edvin Adolphson was born in Furingstad, Sweden, in 1893, the oldest of seven children. While working in a shipyard, he made his debut at the Norrköping Workers' Theatre at the age of nineteen. From 1916 to 1925 he was married to the actress Margot de Chergé, with whom he had a daughter and two sons. After engagements with several provincial ensembles, he was hired by Skådebanan's People's Theatre (Folkets Teater) in Stockholm in 1918. Following his appearances with Bosse at the Intimate Theatre, Adolphson stayed in Stockholm to play at the Mosebacke revue theatre and at Ranft's Vasa Theatre. In the 1926–27 season he was at the Lorensberg Theatre in Gothenburg, where he won the hearts of their patrons. Adolphson was happy there, appearing in almost every production while looking forward to the arrival of his fiancée. The engagement was secret; people knew only that Harriet Bosse was coming to play Cleopatra in Shaw's *Caesar and Cleopatra,* opening 21 February. Adolphson hoped to play Antony, but had to be content to do Apollodorus, the Sicilian who smuggles Cleopatra on board Caesar's ship rolled up in a rug.[2]

When they married on 11 January 1927[3] Harriet Bosse was a glamorous artist fifteen years his senior, while Adolphson's success as a matinee idol and his recognition as a character actor lay in the future. He later commented: "When, in the breathless excitement of youth, I read the plays which the great master [Strindberg] had written expressly for his very young wife Harriet Bosse, I could not have dreamed that nineteen years later she would be mine." Bosse's youthfulness and Adolphson's good looks made them an attractive couple. Unfortunately her career was rather at a standstill, while Adolphson was busy with pioneering work in films. He philosophized later about the friction that occurs when both a husband and wife have an acting career, if one of them succeeds while the other becomes depressed and temperamental.[4] All was harmonious as long as Harriet had good roles. He moved from a modest bachelor apartment to Harriet's large, attractive apartment on Östermalmsgatan in an exclusive area called Lärkstaden—and Bo moved out. The apartment was on the top story of a red brick Tudor building in the shadow of the Engelbrekt Church, whose bells reverberated dolefully when funerals were scheduled. From their balcony the couple looked out on an idyllic view of flowers, greenery, gently curving streets, and residences reflecting the influence of national romanticism.[5]

Traveling in an imposing black Dodge, Bosse took her handsome husband to Norway to visit relatives and see the mountains. He also vacationed on Gällnö and tried fishing and boating. Much of the time they were separated, and Harriet felt her husband was too busy to miss her. Their personalities and careers were not compatible. Bosse considered stage work more dignified than film, yet it was difficult for her to obtain roles. Filming still had to be done during the summer when sunlight and theatre personnel were available. She preferred to vacation in Norway and Sweden rather than to join Adolphson on location in England or France. He felt that his wife did not take any interest or pleasure in his success with films, while she felt that he was unwilling to accept the help she offered. Harriet confided to her sister Dagmar, "I *never* get to help him," yet he felt that he could help her. "Eyvind [Edvin] wants the best for me—but he uses the wrong approach. I will not improve through his pointing out weaknesses which I know so well myself that I have."[6]

Adolphson made film history by directing the first Scandinavian sound film, *Say It With Music (Säg det med toner)*, which had its premiere on 2 January 1929. This was a technically complicated project, since the sound, music, and images were not recorded simultaneously but had to be put together in the editing process. With sound films in their infancy, Adolphson predicted that silent films would become laughable. He directed the cast for the first film with spoken Swedish dialogue, *When the Roses Bloom (När rosorna slå ut)*, produced by Paramount in a studio near Paris. Sensing the potential for an international market, Adolphson anticipated importing foreign actors to make sound tracks so that Swedish films could be sold in other countries. Film was still not considered an art form, but he believed it was becoming acceptable and attracting a better audience.[7] Bosse to some extent shared his belief in the potential of film. She told a journalist in 1929 that there were more good movies than good stage plays and that she was optimistic about the future of sound films.[8]

Adolphson also added to his stature in the theatre. His triumphant breakthrough as a serious dramatic actor came with his playing the role of Claude Vallée in *The Play of Life and Death (Spelet om kärleken och döden)* by Romain Rolland at the Oscar Theatre (Oscarsteatern) late in 1927. Adolphson worked there for five seasons, proving himself a worthy colleague and a friendly rival to Gösta Ekman. His leading ladies were most often Pauline Brunius and Inga Tidblad. Adolphson believed that his wife was depressed about not being invited to join the company.[9]

The marriage ended officially on 9 June 1932, although Harriet and Edvin had been legally separated since 28 April 1931.[10] There were no legal or financial complications, since they had made a premarital agreement keeping their property separate. It is ironic that Harriet Bosse, like Strindberg, had three marriages. Adolphson was married four times. Bosse maintained a discreet silence about their marriage, but for Adolphson it became the subject of anecdotes with which he entertained listeners, probably stretching the truth. He would say that Bosse was totally impractical in domestic matters, accustomed to playing the piano while a maid did the cooking, but almost thirty years after the divorce, Adolphson encountered Bo Wingård and spoke cordially about the years with Harriet.[11]

After the divorce Adolphson continued his busy career in films, on stage, and finally on television. With his wholesome and sometimes unpolished approach, he was the essence of masculinity: a combination of "apache, gangster and gigolo."[12] On the screen he was the most popular leading man and a sex symbol during the 1930s and 1940s, with an appearance reminiscent of that of Ronald Colman. Although Hollywood producers were interested in Swedish actresses like Greta Garbo, Ingrid Bergman, and Viveca Lindfors, they did not open their doors to Adolphson.[13] Nevertheless he had an outstanding career in Sweden where his performances were noted for their versatility and naturalness. "The strength, assurance, and ease of his acting lend themselves just as well to dramatic tasks as to comedy."[14] He was a member of the Dramaten ensemble for three seasons, starting in 1932, and later appeared as a guest star there and at many other theatres, playing such roles as Adam in *Green Pastures (Guds gröna ängar)*, Adam Brant in *Mourning Becomes Electra (Klaga månde Elektra)*, Jason in *Medea*, Petruchio in *The Taming of the Shrew (Så tuktas en argbigga)*, and Cyrano de Bergerac.[15]

Bo Wingård was at loose ends when his mother married for the third time. She arranged for him to work his way to Colombia on a ship, thinking it might be a beneficial experience.[16] Unfortunately he suffered a back injury while working on deck. After arriving in Colombia in 1928, Bo refused surgery but recovered after painful months in a hospital bed. His mother worried about Bo's tolerance of the tropical heat but was pleased to receive his cheerful letters.[17] Bo went to Canada, where he worked for about three years. Then he went to Oslo and lived with his Uncle Ewald, who encouraged him to study agronomy. At the agriculture school he met Randi Iversen, a student of home economics. They married in 1936 and had three children. Wingård used his knowledge of agriculture on his uncle's farms for a while; then he worked for the government. Producing documentary films on agriculture led to his lifework as a film archivist. In April 1951 he established a library, Statens Filmbibliotek, and in 1956 he became chief administrator of the new Norsk Filminstitutt. Bo Wingård died in 1976.

No matter what her marital or financial worries, Harriet could turn to close friends for understanding. Her sister Dagmar was a loyal confidante. When they were apart, Harriet said Dagmar's letters were "like sunshine."[18] It also helped to confide in Ellen Collijn about the disappointments of her career. When her courage waned, Bosse told Ellen that she would try to "be patient and wait" for things to "become brighter again — and then perhaps I can progress a step further."[19]

There were clouds on the horizon in Sweden in the 1930s. The optimism and "psychological, sexual and artistic experiments" of the 1920s belonged to a decade of economic prosperity followed by the threat of unemployment and Nazism. The public still saw Harriet Bosse as a glamorous celebrity, but she faced limited financial circumstances. She enjoyed a pleasant social life, primarily with friends in the arts, such as Olga Raphael and Gustaf Linden. Her favorite host was Anders de Wahl, who planned many festive occasions. Olof Lagercrantz met and danced with Bosse at the home of his cousin, the author Agnes von Krusenstjerna. He recalls how young, beautiful, and graceful the actress was, although she was approaching the age of sixty.[20]

TOURING

Whenever her prospects in Stockholm looked bleak, Harriet Bosse could count on a cordial reception and a steady income on tour. Many ensembles touring the Swedish provinces presented light entertainment — French farces or witty comedies. Although experienced managers could have warned her that she was taking a financial risk, Bosse presented two substantial plays, *A Doll House* and *Easter,* under her own management.[21] Gustaf Linden directed both plays. The tour was to begin 6 September 1924 in Norrköping and to continue throughout Sweden for two months and Norway for one month. For Norwegian audiences Bosse provided program notes written by Martin Lamm. She discovered that the role of managing director was not one of her favorites. "It is a confounded nuisance to have one's own tour," she remarked privately. "One has to think of everything between heaven and earth—not to talk of one's own role."[22]

The leading man of the troupe was Edvin Adolphson, who played Torvald and Elis. Bosse wished her friend Ellen Collijn had been free to play Mrs. Linde and Kristina, but instead she placed an ad in the paper and chose an applicant named Magda Englund. At a rehearsal of *Easter* Adolphson put his arms around her and started to kiss her. Bosse protested. "Never mind that, Mr. Adolphson, it isn't at all necessary." When Adolphson replied that he thought it was natural for Elis to kiss his fiancée, Bosse maintained that Strindberg had never said anything about it. The episode ended angrily, and Englund had to be content with some kisses in the wings.[23] Fifty-four years later Englund wrote an article recalling the tour. Bosse traveled first class and sent the other five company members by third class. After performances she usually ordered a simple supper in her hotel room; however, in some places she joined the company for festive champagne suppers. Wearing a black velvet dress, pearls, and a ring Strindberg had given her, she would enter the restaurant on Adolphson's arm.

Bosse smiled, and a murmur filled the room. One heard the ladies whisper: "Oh, how exquisite she looks—like a young girl."

And during the supper, gentlemen and officers came over to our table and asked to toast the prima donna. With a delighted smile she responded to their toasts. They thanked her for a wonderful evening. And she got many compliments which made her extremely happy.

One day when the prima donna and Englund were walking in the woods, Bosse reminisced about her marriages. She never visited the cemetery where her husbands were buried, for it made her ill to do so. Although, Englund said, some members of the audience in Karlstad laughed at the most tragic scenes, the tour throughout Sweden was generally successful. In town after town the public applauded Bosse warmly and inundated her with flowers.[24] Bosse had to cope with the unexpected when on the road. Once during a performance of *A Doll House* in Karlshamn, a maid was asked to empty a chamber pot from the women's dressing room.

The old woman, who both saw and heard poorly, had not noticed that the curtain had gone up for the second act—where Nora is pacing anxiously back and forth in the dark. The old woman takes the shortcut straight across the stage to reach the sink, but when she reaches the prompter's box, she notices that the curtain is up. She stands paralyzed—holding the pot with outstretched arms. Time stands still a moment! Then Bosse's pulse returns and she hisses:
"Out! Out!!"
But the old woman is rooted to the spot.

In order to break the spell, the leading lady had to take her by the arm and push her offstage.[25]
Bosse arranged another Swedish tour in the fall of 1925. Hugo Bolander, who also appeared in minor roles, was listed on the program as tour leader. Bosse was credited with directing *Friend Lorel (Vännen Lorel)* by Vély and Géradet. Edvin Adolphson played the title role in the French comedy. He also played Elis and Antonio in the other two plays on the bill, *Easter* and *The Balcony*. Otherwise Bosse toured under Ryding's management, repeating the perennial favorite *Easter,* and adding two other Strindberg roles to her touring repertory, Queen Christina and the title role in *Sir Bengt's Wife (Herr Bengts hustru)*.

THE LORENSBERG THEATRE

On 20 September 1954, a Museum of Theatre History opened on Berzelii-gaten in Gothenburg, its exhibits displayed in the dressing rooms and on the stage of the old Lorensberg Theatre. It had been abandoned in 1934 when the City Theatre (Stadsteatern) opened a large complex nearby. The Lorensberg Theatre was founded in 1916, and its managers, in succession, were Mauritz Stiller, Gustaf Linden, Per Lindberg, Knut Ström, and Torsten Hammarén. The theatre's most noteworthy period occurred with Lindberg at the helm, from 1919 to 1923. A leading personality in Swedish theatre during the 1920s and 1930s, Lindberg (1890–1944) was the son of actor-director August Lindberg and actress Augusta Lindberg. In one sense he revived the concept of a people's theatre debated in Sweden in the 1800s, yet he was also a man of the twentieth century. Some of his ideas were derived from Max Reinhardt, whose work he studied in Berlin in 1918–19. Lindberg was quite a scholar and theorist, who plunged into debates with members of the theatre establishment, particularly Albert Ranft. Lindberg dreamed of a theatre with reasonable ticket prices, modern staging techniques, and an excellent repertory.[26]

The Lorensberg Theatre was well equipped technically, with a cyclorama, revolving stage, and advanced lighting equipment. In terms of technical resources and its ambitious choice of repertory, it was often far ahead of theatres in Stockholm, especially in producing the classics. Lindberg invited Knut Ström, who had been a director and designer in Düsseldorf, to join the staff as scene designer. Influenced primarily by German theatre and to some extent Russian theatre, they mounted productions that were outstanding visually, with three-dimensional scenery, a sense of unlimited space, and the actors sculpted by skillfully differentiated light. With Lindberg leading the way, the Lorensberg Theatre was a laboratory for experiments that influenced theatre artists throughout Sweden.[27] Lindberg presented not only visually exciting productions, but also intimate plays with excellent acting influenced by his observation of Reinhardt's work with individual actors. Unfortunately the enthusiasm, tremendous workload, and ambitious repertory of Lindberg's first few seasons could not be sustained when the theatre's ledgers went into the red.[28]

Public receptivity to theatrical experiments and the generally liberal cultural milieu made Gothenburg an exciting city for artists. Harriet Bosse had appeared at the Lorensberg Theatre earlier, both as a guest and on tour. She was invited to return in 1926 to play Shaw's Saint Joan and Strindberg's Queen Christina, and in 1927, Shaw's young Cleopatra.

The premiere of *Saint Joan (Sankta Johanna)* on 9 February 1926 was a triumphant occasion for the director, Knut Ström, and the theatre, which needed to prove that it could still do outstanding work. Harriet Bosse was thought to be too feminine and mature and her voice too light to fit the preconceived image of the vigorous and heroic saint, but she more than compensated for the miscasting through her intelligent interpretation, masterful technique, and sincerity. Having failed to persuade Gustaf Linden and Tore Svennberg to produce *Saint Joan* for her in Stockholm, she welcomed this chance to prove herself. After her retirement she recalled Joan as the only role she ever played in which she felt completely calm on opening night.[29]

Bosse made her Joan a bourgeois, sympathetic character, in contrast to Tora Teje's portrayal of her the previous November in Stockholm as a robust peasant.[30] She may not have looked like a teenager, but Bosse was "fresh and natural and eager, forgetful of herself and irresistible in her naive assurance."[31] The critic for *Ny Tid* comments that in the first scene the actress was "without a doubt exactly Shaw's Joan, the wholesome farm girl capable of strong willpower and action, completely in the grip of her zeal to set in motion the task 'the voices' gave her, without a thought of any difficulties. . . . In this scene fru Bosse fully presented all the characteristics of the Maiden."[32] The *Göteborgs-Posten* describes her as "natural and visionary at the same time; she was so filled with her mission but still so simple, so unaffected, so beautiful. . . . One felt just as willing and confident as her comrades about following her to the ends of the earth." As the evening went on, Bosse's characterization was not totally convincing, except when she spoke to the judges in a resonant and flexible voice, making clear the doubt and sense of isolation that counterbalanced her zeal, regaining the courage and strength that was both "superhuman and yet deeply human." The epilogue was well done, as Bosse spoke the famous final speech: "How long, Oh Lord, how long?" Critics complained about the length of the performances and touches of sentimentality in Bosse's voice, but the theatre and Bosse received credit for an excellent achievement.[33] She wished Ellen Collijn could have shared the excitement of opening night: "I had no one to hold my hand."[34]

People in Gothenburg were cordial to Bosse, but playing Joan was strenuous and she was learning Christina, so she declined social invitations.[35] Christina was one of the major roles of Bosse's career as an interpreter of Strindberg. *Queen Christina* opened on 26 March 1926 under the direction of Rudolf Wendbladh. Strindberg had a dominant position in Gothenburg repertory in the 1920s. Bosse believed that he was more appreciated there than in Stockholm.

The Lorensberg Theatre had experienced some weak productions and poor attendance before Bosse arrived to play the lead in *Caesar and Cleopatra*, directed by Knut Ström in the winter of 1927. She was aware of the objections to bringing in a guest star instead of choosing a play more suited to the talents of the resident company:

It's a little unpleasant for me, especially since I did not ask to come here but simply accepted an invitation. . . . Naturally the concept of guest appearances can damage an ensemble if it is pushed toward a cult for stars, but on the other hand I find it completely natural if there is an occasional guest engagement at a theatre which does not have sufficient financial resources to engage as large and specialized a personnel as one needs to present the repertory expected at a theatre with public subsidy.[36]

The Shaw production was luxuriant visually, and Bosse's fourteen performances as Cleopatra were the high point of the season. Bosse found the discipline of the company a sharp contrast with that of the previous year. With nothing ready for dress rehearsal and some of the cast stumbling over their lines, Bosse felt she had never worked in such a hectic atmosphere.[37] Having just done Shakespeare's mature Cleopatra five months earlier, Bosse demonstrated once again her uncanny ability to play a lively teenager who moves with catlike grace. Under the tutelage of the aging emperor, the naive child became the proud and cruel ruler. Outacting Olof Sandborg as Caesar, Bosse dominated the performance.[38] Erik Brogren praised her crystal clear diction and singled out her playfulness and fear at the foot of the Sphinx, the pantomime when she realized Caesar's identity, and her emotional outburst at the murder of Pothinus as unforgettable moments. "Perhaps the historical Cleopatra later in life was more impressive, but as a young girl she could well have been exactly as fru Bosse created her."[39]

THE CONCERT HOUSE THEATRE

A few years after his notable achievements at the Lorensberg Theatre, Per Lindberg conceived of using the two-thousand-seat auditorium of the new Concert House (Konserthus) in Stockholm as the arena for his experiments. This venture had the financial and moral support of producer-manager Ernst Eklund. Although the large hall, opened 7 April 1926, was intended for musical programs, Lindberg staged several dramatic productions on the concert platform, which had no proscenium arch and no curtain. He thought it would be stimulating to work in an architectural space reminiscent of pre-Baroque theatre and free from reliance on the illusion conveyed by painted scenery. Even in that large hall he believed intimacy could be achieved, with the aid of sculptural lighting that would appear to bring the actors closer to the audience. The Concert House was the best space available in Stockholm to demonstrate the artistic and theatrical superiority of a "formal stage." Lindberg's enthusiasm was boundless, but his plans for reform and innovation were met with conservative reservations and some animosity.[40]

Despite her status and reputation, Harriet Bosse did not wait to be asked to take part in Lindberg's idealistic experiment. She wrote from Gothenburg on 13 February 1926: "Desire terribly much to work with you next season. Your theatre will surely be what we have long been waiting and yearning for in Stockholm."[41] Assuming that she simply needed an engagement, Lindberg suggested she contact Ernst Eklund. Bosse replied that she was on good terms with Eklund, but a year earlier he had turned down her proposal to play Queen Christina, and she doubted he would hire her now. Instead, she reassured Lindberg that she had written impulsively because she wanted to be involved when the person who would "renew" theatre appeared in Stockholm.[42] Convinced of her zeal, Lindberg cast Bosse in starring roles in Shakespeare's *Antony and Cleopatra (Antonius och Kleopatra)* and Strindberg's *To Damascus III*.

Whether Lindberg was a good director is debatable. In his work at the Lorensberg Theatre he had maintained strict control over every speech and gesture, and yet created a stimulating and festive atmosphere for the company. He could elicit from a "young actress an expressiveness and brilliant intensity" that suddenly raised the artistic level of her work.[43] He was scholarly, demanding, and inventive. Although Lindberg considered himself in conflict with the "older generation" of actors because he insisted on a unified concept and style of production, actors who were receptive found it inspiring to work with him.[44] Designers were also inspired by his innovative ideas, appreciation of color, and rejection of "barren naturalism and sterile illusionism."[45]

The Shakespeare tragedy, translated by Per Hallström, was an ambitious choice for the first Concert House production, which had to compete for rehearsal time and space with musicians preparing concerts. The unique physical characteristics of the hall required a new technique that Lindberg did not fully develop.[46] Using three levels, he kept the action flowing, letting costumed extras move the set pieces. He conceived of composition and movement on a grand scale and sometimes made nearly inhuman demands on the performers who had to pose and climb on the stairs. The large cast included more than sixty university students working without pay. At one rehearsal of *Antony and Cleopatra,* Lindberg defied gravity by demonstrating a spectacular run up a staircase on a row of shields, only to fall with a crash in a jumble of shields, swords, and bit players.[47] Lindberg had visualized Bosse entering on those shields. She wrote later: "The men knelt. My friends said: 'Don't do it. You'll kill yourself.' But I went, and one shield slipped. Since I am rather agile, I quickly got on my feet again. But Lindberg's sensible wife, who realized it was dangerous, whispered to him: 'I don't think it looks good.' And so I entered through a door, instead of on the perilous shields." Bosse was good-natured: "It was so crowded backstage that one felt flat as a flounder, pressed against the wall waiting for an entrance—but what did that matter, when it all was so successful. There wasn't room or time to place on stage a chair for me, so one of the extras formed a stool—hands and knees on the floor—I sat on her back. We sometimes rehearsed until 3:00 or 4:00 in the morning, but we didn't feel tired."[48]

Isaac Grünewald, then working in Paris, was engaged as costume designer. When his sketches arrived, the actresses turned pale as they saw they were to wear small metal bras and scanty skirts draped around their hips. Harriet Bosse declared that she would not appear on stage "half-naked." After their costumes arrived, Bosse along with Doris Nelson and Mimi Pollak, playing her handmaidens, discovered that they were not to appear with naked midriffs and bare legs, for there were flesh-colored tricot undergarments and tights sewed to the costumes. Then Bosse declared she would not appear on stage in sagging tricot, and she snipped off the flesh-colored fabric with a scissors. When the costume designer came to the dress rehearsal, he was delighted with the effect of all the colorful costumes— purple for the Oriental scenes, steel blue for the Roman ones—but indignant to see that his tricot had been cut away. To show so much bare flesh on stage was quite daring in that era, but Grünewald finally told the actresses they looked wonderful.[49] The daring beaded dress probably brought back memories to Bosse of other exotic Oriental costumes, such as Salome's, nineteen years earlier.

With her short stature and silvery voice, Harriet Bosse was nearly lost amid the massive pillars and platforms. Critics were divided as to whether her emotional intensity and resonant voice were sufficient to convey the pride and passion of the legendary queen. Sven Stål was totally displeased, acknowledging that Bosse was best in the death scene, but even then, he wrote, she elicited no interest or sympathy. Sigfrid Siwertz described her Cleopatra as "a coquette, sensual, soft as a cat, sometimes touching," but he found no sense of "fate and power." Since, according to Erik Wettergren, "just barely two of the participants knew their craft," he did not linger on Bosse's inadequacies but praised the freshness and precise details of her presentation.[50]

During his only season at the Concert House Lindberg produced five other plays. Harriet Bosse stepped into the autobiographical episodes of the third part of *To Damascus*. The season also included *Hamlet* and *Oedipus,* but *Antony and Cleopatra* was considered to be Lindberg's greatest success. In March 1928 Bosse returned to the Concert House stage in another Strindberg play, *Queen Christina,* under the management of Ernst Eklund. She and Lindberg considered working together again several times, but their ideas were never realized. In 1928, for example, he considered starting a theatre at which she would play Bjørnson's Maria Stuart. Bosse weighed the possibility seriously. She admired Lindberg's "unbelievable imagination" as a director and felt she could have done the role much better than she had in 1911.[51]

Harriet Bosse summarized her experience at the Concert House positively. She was pleased with the acoustics, thought she established good contact with audiences despite the large dimensions of the hall, and was glad she did not panic when maneuvering on the stairs and platforms.[52] The Concert House venture was a significant part of Swedish theatre history. The public was quite interested in the productions but thought of them as isolated experiments and not theatre in the usual sense. Instead there seemed to be more interest in the Oscar Theatre established at the same time by John and Pauline Brunius and Gösta Ekman; it attracted the type of audience that had previously attended the Swedish Theatre. Lindberg's Concert House productions were conceived idealistically, but the press did not support his vision and casts could not adapt to the space and new style of directing. Nevertheless Lindberg and Eklund had at least laid a foundation for future developments in the folk theatre movement and the "New Stagecraft."[53]

At both the Lorensberg and Concert House theatres, Harriet Bosse had appeared in extravagant productions, dressed in splendid costumes and surrounded by monumental scenery. She felt, however, that the essence of a theatrical performance was the spiritual dimension provided by the actor: "Everyone has his own Thalia—mine has been a search for something that lay behind the dialogue, above and beyond the words, independent of time, costumes, and scenery. As far as I am concerned, one can perform theatre in any impersonal milieu. . . ."[54]

GUEST ARTIST

The Concert House and the Lorensberg Theatre were the scenes of her most significant achievements during the late 1920s and early 1930s, but Harriet Bosse sought and accepted a variety of other engagements. She remarked, "I must find something, because I—who have always had so much to do— can't survive being idle."[55] No matter what she believed about the primacy of the actor, Bosse needed to work within a structure of theatres that would open their doors to her. She was skeptical about trends: "Nowadays to have any effect one has to somehow come up with something really novel, and as long as this works one is noticed, only to be forgotten just as quickly for someone new, who has found an even more ingenious approach for his novelties." She considered this an indication of the hectic mood of the age: "People want change, and they so easily forget old ideals while searching for fleeting innovations." Bosse felt that people too easily forgot "those who have made real contributions on the thorn-covered path called acting."[56] There was no doubt she included herself among those whose contributions had been forgotten.

On her fiftieth birthday, in January 1928, an article in *Göteborgs-Posten* presented a laudatory survey of her career and reflected that "she is still needed for many years even if she finally must give up ingenue roles as she passes the half-century mark." The writer pointed out the injustice of Bosse's position: "She is still youthful and eager to work, and it is almost with astonishment one hears that no Swedish stage, after the closing of the Concert House Theatre, considers that it needs her. Because she still has much to give. It does not speak well for the organization of our Swedish theatre system that both Gerda Lundequist and Harriet Bosse are kept away from practical work."[57]

There were only a few occasions when Bosse walked through the stage door of Dramaten. She played Nora for a few evenings, starting 10 January 1925. Although the play was daring when it appeared more than forty years earlier, by now its indebtedness to the French well-made play tradition was obvious, and some thought it quaint and dated. With Gustaf Linden as director and a strong supporting cast, the production built on Scandinavian tradition. Strangely enough, Bosse wore short dresses while the rest of the cast were in correct period costumes. Their characterizations also had the flavor of a bygone era. Critics were divided as to whether Bosse succeeded in making credible both Nora's early childlike dreams and her final cold realism.[58] There was also disagreement about the terms of her contract. Bosse had proposed playing Shaw's Saint Joan. When that was rejected, she thought an understanding was reached that she would play Strindberg's Christina and the daughter in Pirandello's *Six Characters in Search of an Author (Sex roller utan författare)*. While she was on her fall tour, *Queen Christina* was being prepared by Gustaf Linden for an observance of the playwright's birthday in January, but Tore Svennberg did not honor the commitment. *A Doll House* was substituted hastily with insufficient rehearsal. She called the situation "a total inferno," and requested immediate release from her three-month contract at the end of January.[59]

Bosse confided to Ellen Collijn that a sense of honor had driven her away from Dramaten. "I could not work amidst lies and intrigue." Even before the *Doll House* episode she had told Ellen that if only she had money, she wouldn't "give a damn about any theatre here in this country. It is all just intrigue." It was painful to be excluded from Stockholm's major stage, and she turned for a while to Christian Science for comfort: "sometimes I feel so discouraged—give up and have no faith. I know that such relapses must occur now and then. . . ."[60] Bosse asked Crown Prince Gustav Adolf early in 1928 whether he could help to get her readmitted to the Dramaten ensemble—not as long as Svennberg was head of the theatre, but when he stepped down from the position. She also considered writing to Ingolf Schanche about the possibility of working for him in Oslo at the New Theatre (Oslo Nye Teater), which was to open in 1929.[61]

In 1925 Bosse appeared twice in Copenhagen. That April she brought the company that had won praise on its fall tour of Sweden and Norway to the Betty Nansen Theatre for two performances of *Easter*. Once again the matter of language intrigued the Danes, who were impressed by her excellent Norwegian in private conversation. She assured them she would never try to learn Danish, even though that had been her mother's native tongue. One journalist called her language "neither Swedish, Norwegian or Danish, but a mixture—Scandinavian." He claimed that her voice was so much better than those of most Danish actresses that Bosse's pure and beautiful tone quality was reason enough to go to the theatre.[62] Away from Sweden, Bosse seemed to be more marketable in Strindberg roles. She expressed a wish to return to Copenhagen to play Swan White and Henriette. *Swan White* was Strindberg's "wedding present to me," she explained, but "I have never been allowed to play in it."[63]

Henriette she did play in Copenhagen in November that year. *Crimes and Crimes* was called *Intoxication (Rus)* in the translation by Sven Lange used at the Dagmar Theatre (Dagmartheatret). The director and manager of the theatre, Holger Hofman, commented that Bosse helped him and the Danish cast to realize they had been taking Strindberg too seriously: "One can also find the smile in Strindberg's writing."[64] Bosse remarked that she considered this play more optimistic than most of what Strindberg wrote. She had felt some apprehension about fitting in with a Danish cast, but her fellow actors were so helpful that she was comfortable and delighted with the experience. To her friend Ellen Collijn she wrote, "Thank goodness, I have had a great success—it was not too soon after all my troubles in Stockholm."[65] Although she was pleased about her appearances in Copenhagen,

Bosse never enjoyed the honor of an invitation to play at the Royal Theatre (Det kongelige Teater).

In Stockholm it was painful for Harriet Bosse to see Tora Teje playing roles she felt she could do better. In *Love (Älska)* by Paul Géraldy, Teje played opposite Anders de Wahl. Critics called the performance a triumph for Teje—impressive in her spontaneity and ability to convey the subtext.[66] Bosse commented privately that she could not understand why Teje was not "exposed as the worst and most artificial actress in Sweden!" She felt de Wahl was "the only one . . . who was natural."[67] Bosse always thought that Teje's playing was artificial and unimaginative and that she forced her voice into a low register.[68] Having begun her career at the Swedish Theatre in 1913, Teje had her first major success as Wilde's Salome in 1915. After coming to Dramaten in 1923, she was given many substantial leading roles, such as Rebekka West in *Rosmersholm,* Nina Leeds in *Strange Interlude (Sällsamt mellanspel)*, and Phèdre. She also played a number of Strindberg roles, including Alice in *The Dance of Death* and Indra's Daughter. There was something new and modern about Teje's acting style. She seemed to combine the grandeur and expansiveness of classical acting with the unrestrained psychological depth appropriate to contemporary plays. This unique combination worked effectively when she played Christine Mannon in *Mourning Becomes Electra* and Queen Elizabeth in Schiller's *Maria Stuart*. With her wide range, Teje enjoyed success not only in tragedy but in romantic melodramas, satiric comedies, and realistic dramas.[69]

At the end of the 1927–28 season Tore Svennberg turned over the leadership of Dramaten to Erik Wettergren, who began planning a repertory in which the featured actresses would be Tora Teje, Signe Kolthoff, Hilda Borgström, Stina Hedberg, and Märta Ekström. His directing staff consisted of Per Lindberg, Olof Molander, and Gustaf Linden. Productions in the first season included *King Lear, Peer Gynt,* Pär Lagerkvist's *He Who Lives His Life Over Again (Han som fick leva om sitt liv)*, and several French plays. At her husband Edvin's insistence, Bosse phoned Wettergren in April 1928 to ask about rejoining the company, but she was told he had already drawn up the contracts for the next year. Wettergren offered her a minor role in a comedy as a limited engagement, but she was not interested. If she had been a permanent member of the ensemble, she might have considered the part, but it was not at all appropriate for a guest appearance. People assumed that Bosse was willing to play only young women, that she would not acknowledge the time had come to play older characters. She maintained she would never play "kaffetanter" (old ladies sipping coffee) but insisted it was totally wrong to say that she wanted to play ingenues. "What I long for is to do *character roles*, to be what I am—a mature woman." She could visualize herself in "transitional roles," such as Hedda Gabler, Medea, and Lady Macbeth.[70] Within a few years Tora Teje played both Medea and Lady Macbeth.

In 1929 Bosse returned to Dramaten to do Germaine de la Cognac, the only female role in *What Price Glory? (Ärans fält)* by Laurence Stallings and Maxwell Anderson. She looked forward to appearing before the Dramaten audience again, but not necessarily because the auditorium had better dimensions than the Concert House:

I do not think one can say, "That theatre always has good contact between stage and auditorium" or "In that play the actors could always be sure to draw their audience to them." Contact does not depend on just the actors, play, and locale. It depends at least as much on the audience itself. One evening you can despair—you feel separated from the audience, not just by a ramp but by a space of incomprehension. You stand there trying to get them interested in the human fate you are presenting—but from the auditorium you hear only coughing and the rustle of programs and candy bags, a hushed whispering, a scraping of feet. But the next evening it is the opposite—absolute silence, intense interest. Such a mood in the auditorium gives the actor very valuable help, it nourishes and supports.[71]

What Price Glory? gave her an opportunity to work again with Per Lindberg. Before rehearsals started she traveled to Berlin to see a production of the play. It had been four years since she appeared at the national theatre, "a dangerously long time for a theatre artist to be separated from her public, but in this case the impression of the actress' rich and intelligent art of characterization is probably strong enough to span . . . such an interval."[72] Most reviewers treated her kindly, but this was a rather stereotyped female role that featured her exotic appearance and "astonishingly authentic" French dialect, rather than any depth of characterization. One reviewer, describing Germaine's innocence and sensuality, wrote, "All this was shown to full advantage in Harriet Bosse's interpretation, where what was lacking in youthfulness was made up for by catlike grace."[73]

As Suzy Courtois, Bosse was reunited with Anders de Wahl in January 1930 for Dramaten's production of *Topaze* by Marcel Pagnol, directed by Gustaf Linden. Once again Bosse was typecast as a French femme fatale. The role, which she played with coldness and cynicism, was considered "too insignificant for an actress of her stature."[74]

Although it was for only one evening, Bosse finally appeared on stage in Berlin in November 1930. Rather than speaking German, which she had studied seriously with Strindberg's encouragement, she played Eleonora in Swedish for a performance of *Easter* presented by the Skandinavisches Theater at a large rented theatre. She brought along a Swedish cast that included Maria Schildknecht and Hugo Bolander. This was a new venture organized by Gösta Richter and two partners. They considered Bosse a pioneer whose example should encourage other Scandinavian artists to appear there. The audience for the sold-out performance included members of the Berlin diplomatic corps and her son-in-law, who came from Paris for the occasion. The evening was a splendid success for Bosse personally, but the Skandinavisches Theater did not become established.[75]

In 1933 talented and charming Gösta Ekman was manager and star at the Vasa Theatre. Harriet Bosse appeared there in March as Grusinskaja in the dramatization of Vicki Baum's novel *Grand Hotel,* directed by Gunnar Klintberg. Ekman was touching as the naive, dying Kringelein. Speaking with a Russian accent, Bosse was assured and intense, but the script was disappointing and the role did not seem worthy of her.[76] Playing a stereotyped aging ballerina, she was featured as a fashion plate in the program, which gave detailed comments on her elegant tailored costumes and none on the drama. One reviewer wondered what kind of "god always and everywhere grants protection to the mediocre and oppresses the talented? In recent years have we had so many real artists that there was absolutely no work for Bosse?"[77]

BOSSE'S ROLE AS A STRINDBERG AUTHORITY

While Harriet Bosse worked constantly to achieve something worthwhile as an independent artist, her identity as one of Strindberg's wives continued to fascinate the public. Reporters asked her about Strindberg and the theatre, and she tried to give thoughtful and interesting replies. To a Danish reporter's question as to whether Strindberg's plays were performed much in Sweden she replied: "No, I can't say that. And it is a shame—for he loved to have theatres present his plays. Often when small provincial troupes came and wanted to give one of his plays but could not afford to pay for it, he said, 'Take it. Just perform—it doesn't cost anything. But play it well.'"[78] To another Danish journalist she offered a comparison between Strindberg and Ibsen, who "strikes me as a mathematician," while Strindberg created characters who were more human, "for better or worse."[79] People frequently asked about their courtship and marriage, and she realized that the letters she had received from Strindberg would be of great general interest and would illuminate his personality from a new angle.

Whether Harriet should guard the confidentiality of her Strindberg letters provoked an incident that may have brought her third marriage to an end. Edvin Adolphson in his autobiography says that Harriet spoke with respect and warmth about Strindberg and mentioned the wonderful letters he had sent her. One day Adolphson noticed the letters lying in the safe deposit box he and Harriet shared at the bank. He asked if she would consider publishing them, but Harriet replied that this would not happen until after her death.

Because the playwright sounded quite different in Harriet's description from the familiar public image, Adolphson's curiosity grew about what the letters might reveal. The subject of the correspondence came up one day when the literary scholar Martin Lamm joined them for dinner. Lamm was eager to see the letters, according to Adolphson, but Bosse could not be persuaded. Later Adolphson says that he took two of the letters out of the safe deposit box and showed them to Lamm, making him promise not to tell anyone. Lamm thought the letters were wonderful because they revealed new aspects of Strindberg's personality. According to Adolphson, Lamm urged him to persuade Bosse to make the letters public.

Adolphson did something that proved disastrous. He brought up the sensitive subject of Harriet's relationship to Dramaten, trying to persuade her to ask for an engagement. He had talked to someone there on her behalf without her permission and had been told that the theatre would welcome her back, provided she made the first overture. When Adolphson confessed what he had done, Harriet was struck speechless:

And for the rest of the dinner all that was heard was the scraping of knives and forks on our plates. Before I left the table, I considered it my duty to speak openly. "You are just as stubborn in this regard as you are with the letters. It is dishonorable toward Strindberg to withhold them."

Harriet's brown eyes turned even darker when, with emphasis on each syllable, she asked, "How do you know?"

I rose from the table to avoid answering, but was overcome by a desperate honesty: "I have read some of them and I have also shown the same letters to a Strindberg expert who says that you are doing a confounded injustice to keep them lying in a bank vault."

Adolphson went to his room to ponder the day's events. Those who knew Bosse are divided as to whether the incident could have ended as he describes. According to Adolphson, his wife rushed in, took a beautiful mirror off the wall and smashed it down on his head. He writes, "I have never felt so stupid as when I sat there with the frame of the mirror around my neck, picking splinters of glass off my knees and shoulders." However Harriet actually expressed her indignation that evening, the marriage was finished.[80]

Although Adolphson's anecdote is entertaining, its accuracy is open to challenge. The actor did not give Martin Lamm his first opportunity to see the Bosse-Strindberg correspondence. In the winter of 1921–22 Lamm was preparing for Stockholms Högskola (now the University of Stockholm) a series of lectures that became the foundation for two volumes of Strindberg's drama, published in the mid-1920s.[81] Lamm obtained special permission to consult the collection of Strindberg papers at the Nordic Museum.[82] A letter dated 30 May 1922 is evidence that he also obtained access to Harriet Bosse's papers. She wrote after he had made excerpts from the collection:

From them I understand you have perhaps thought of directly *quoting* the letters in future lectures — which I beg you not to do. It would be detrimental to the collection in its entirety when it is eventually published. Neither do I want the copies to be shared with others for reading/printing or quoting. But there is so much material in these letters to support research on Strindberg's literary production during this period — and if I have helped you to shed light upon Strindberg during this period of his authorship, no one can be happier than
Your Harriet Bosse
I have taken the liberty of removing a certain amount which seems to me too personal to lecture on.[83]

As early as 1927, Bosse started work on an annotated edition of her letters from Strindberg. She told her sister Dagmar in January 1928 that she had shown a draft to the attorney Erik Lidforss, who had discussed the possibility that Bonniers might establish a pension of four thousand crowns per year with the understanding that the firm would publish the book after her death;[84] however, no such agreement was ever reached. Partly on the advice of Strindberg scholars and partly because of economic necessity, Harriet Bosse decided not to postpone publication of the correspondence.

In 1931 and 1932 she lived near Rena in Østerdal, Norway, at Øglegård, a small farm owned by her brother Ewald. The primitive living conditions were difficult for Bosse, especially during the winter. Her son Bo was working there, and part of the time Anne Marie, Anders Wyller, and their two sons were with her. One day a letter arrived from a friend, Jenny Bergqvist-Hansson, who was married to the publisher Johan Hansson of Natur och kultur. Mrs. Hansson wondered whether Bosse could come to the defense of Strindberg's reputation. When she learned that there were many beautiful letters, Mrs. Hansson asked to read them, and plans were soon underway for publication. Working at Øgle, Harriet prepared commentary and transitions for the volume published by Natur och kultur in 1932, entitled *Strindbergs brev till Harriet Bosse.*

Bosse was modest about the literary value of the hundreds of letters she wrote to Strindberg. Even though he had praised them for their purity and beauty,[85] she kept most of her own letters and eventually burned them.[86] She also destroyed three letters written by Strindberg: one about her sister, one that was unflattering toward Gunnar Wingård, and one that treated Frida Uhl negatively.[87] For the rest of her life Harriet Bosse tried to maintain control over the correspondence. She refused to read the letters on the radio and would not permit others to do so. Because of their intimacy, she preferred "that one be alone in a room with these letters, not that they be shouted on the radio. . . ."[88] She would be appalled to know that since her death the letters have been widely quoted on the radio and used as the material for stage and television scripts.

Through her book and public statements, Harriet Bosse painted a portrait of Strindberg as a good human being, as someone who was "often unhappy, almost always misunderstood, tender-hearted, self-sacrificing." She cast aside her doubts about publishing the letters because she thought they contained a valuable lesson: "Oh, how I hope that my Strindberg book can teach people to be less egotistical—as Strindberg showed he could be toward me—to be as compassionate as he, great in love as he. His letters have a great deal to say to many people in these times." Strindberg even provided insight to her own suffering and bitterness about being excluded from the mainstream of theatre in Sweden. "The older I become," Bosse said, "the better I understand Strindberg. Surely he has been—if not exactly like me—in a similar situation. If Strindberg had been given more love, encouragement and understanding by a number of his countrymen, his work would certainly have been in a brighter mood. But people did not try to understand, much less to help him." Bosse tried to have faith that the future would be better, both for herself and society. "I believe, therefore, that the Strindberg book has a mission to fulfill; I hope it will help to make people aware of what is most essential in life—to be true to yourself."[89]

In her foreword Bosse made it clear that she did not intend to write a detailed account of their marriage or to present a psychological analysis of Strindberg. "I have only wanted to contribute to a clearer understanding of this remarkable man, and I am glad to present some of the brightest and best of Strindberg—his letters to me." Although she might have preferred that attention be directed only to Strindberg's works, she realized that others analyzed and judged him as a private individual. Bosse considered it her obligation, as someone who had been close to "a great man," to contribute what she could so that the general understanding of his personality could be as correct as possible. She acknowledged that Strindberg had many facets. "This book tells how I perceived him, and how he appeared to me. Others might have experienced him quite differently."[90]

Bosse awaited anxiously the critical reception of her book. On 10 April 1932, she sent a letter to Martin Lamm, whom she had quoted in her introduction, requesting that he write a review or give a lecture on the book to help publicize it. When he replied that he could not because of ill health, she invited him to visit the farm in Norway to enjoy the peace, fresh air, and natural setting: "For me, who have rested for years, life here is too quiet, and especially now since the work on my book is finished. Now once again I am unemployed. I am in great suspense wondering how it will be received. I hope the critics do not take too formally my simple artless comments. They are meant only as a very slight accompaniment."[91]

The volume published in 1932 was significant for the insight it offered into Strindberg's personality and creative process. Harriet Bosse was established without any doubt as his muse, the inspiration for major plays and poems, and the model for characters in several of his plays. Whereas Strindberg's public image was that of a neurotic misogynist, this book revealed that he could be warm, tender, and generous. Bosse maintained that an evil spirit seemed to come over Strindberg when he wrote, while away from his desk he could enjoy friends and family and the disciplined routine of his workday. Although her testimony had no scientific credibility, Bosse's assertion that she had seen no signs of mental illness convinced some readers that the playwright "had strong reserves of psychic health."[92] Strindberg's dualistic personality, his naive happiness during their courtship, tension during the marriage, devotion to his youngest daughter, resignation in loneliness, dreams of reconciliation—all are revealed with comments by Bosse that critics found to be informative, appropriate, and discreet. Publication of the letters was an event of such popular appeal that the book was even mentioned by the cabaret singer Karl-Gerhard in one of his songs that season.[93] The letters have continued to be appreciated. In 1956 Bosse was pleased that they were praised on a Danish radio broadcast, but felt embarrassed by the assertion that her image would be immortalized like that of Dante's Beatrice: "I don't have any such pretensions—it is Strindberg who should receive credit for having seen me as so beautiful."[94]

FRUSTRATED HOPES

Whether Harriet Bosse could ever reach a wider audience by playing in German or English was a question that recurred periodically. Noting that she was able to appreciate great actors speaking Russian, she wished she could play in her own language in other countries. It had not been difficult to learn German and English fairly well, but she could not "feel and think" in those languages, as she would want to on stage.[95] Although she had given up hope of performing in the United States, Bosse considered appearing on the London stage in the 1930–31 season. Rumors had circulated a few years earlier that she was planning a guest appearance there but that she had decided against it because she felt insecure with the language. When it seemed that she might have a chance to play a major Strindberg role, however, she set to work in earnest.

Strindberg had a champion in London in the actor-director Robert Loraine (1876–1935), who produced *The Father* in August 1927 and revived it in August 1929.[96] Loraine, who had made his stage debut in 1889, had played countless roles in both period and modern plays. Among his successes were John Tanner in *Man and Superman,* Bluntschli in *Arms and the Man,* and Cyrano de Bergerac. One review of *The Father* described Loraine's "tormented study of Adolph, full of imagination and the fires of despair." Another praised the performance as "one of the strongest, most vivid, most terrifying feats of acting the contemporary stage can show." Yet another called this performance "the greatest of this generation," and said that anyone who loved acting "MUST see Loraine's performance. Not *should,* MUST."[97] Some Swedes who saw it were offended by liberties Loraine had taken with the script out of consideration for the English audience, but Bosse was tolerant of the changes.

Loraine ventured another Strindberg production—*The Dance of Death*—which had its premiere at the Apollo Theatre on 16 January 1928. The play was thought to be loosely structured and contradictory but admirable for its "beauty and dignity and power." Edgar in Loraine's interpretation, described as "evil" by several critics, was seen as "a fiend who seems to have visited the earth from another world."[98]

Working in Stockholm with Sallie Herrström as diction coach, Bosse learned the roles of Eleonora and Indra's Daughter in English.[99] She would have preferred to do *Easter,* but Loraine was more interested in *A Dream Play.*[100] During a visit to London in April 1930, Bosse joined him and his wife at lunch and read Indra's Daughter, with Loraine doing all other roles. It was settled that she would come to London the following season to star in *A Dream Play.* Unfortunately, Robert Loraine had to cancel his plans and travel to the United States. Someone else offered Bosse the opportunity to play Indra's Daughter at the Arts Theatre in London, but as she explained, "I realized that the stage was much too small, and I should get only a couple of rehearsals of this difficult play—that would kill both the play and myself, so I said, 'No, thank you.'"[101]

For a while there was hope that Bosse would star at a theatre in Stockholm embodying Per Lindberg's vision of a people's theatre, reaching all levels of society. Inspired by the Theatre Guild in New York, fifteen individuals, including Bosse, met in August 1932 to begin planning a new enterprise that would sell 70 percent of its tickets to organizations and 30 percent to the general public. The publisher Johan Hansson was a member of the group, which hoped to attract ten thousand subscribers for the project, referred to as both the Free Theatre (Den fria teatern) and the Theatre Guild (Teatergillet). Its organizers were concerned about the financial crisis facing subsidized and commercial theatres, and they envisioned the Theatre Guild as a way of restructuring theatre throughout the country while maintaining headquarters in Stockholm. The repertory would consist mostly of new plays on contemporary issues. *Mourning Becomes Electra* by Eugene O'Neill was purchased as a vehicle for Harriet Bosse.[102] She became involved in the group's financing by lending the Free Theatre a pearl necklace to use as collateral. The necklace was returned to her,[103] and the theatre never came into existence because of a change in government policy, initiated by Arthur Engberg. In March 1933 Tora Teje played the lead in *Mourning Becomes Electra* at Dramaten, in June Lindberg began producing plays for the People's Theatre (Folkets Teater),[104] and in August Harriet Bosse returned to Dramaten for the final phase of her career.

RETURN TO DRAMATEN

Before the meeting to plan the Free Theatre ever took place, Harriet Bosse had pleaded with the Royal Dramatic Theatre to take her back. She wrote from Öglegård to Erik Wettergren and the board of directors on 11 May 1932, reminding them that she had requested a permanent engagement at Dramaten each season for a number of years. Now she appealed to their sense of gratitude: "I permit myself to point out that I have belonged to the Swedish theatre for 30 years, and in this time have belonged to the Dramatic Theatre for 20. I have had the great honor and pleasure during these 20 years to take part in the theatre's best repertory and its many successes, and I believe that I can still give the theatre valuable support through my contribution." Bosse acknowledged that these were difficult times economically, and therefore she would not expect a high salary. "I have no pension to draw on, own no property, and am economically dependent on my work." She closed with an appeal to the chivalry of the board to consider that she was one of the leading figures in Swedish art and with another reminder that she had been part of Dramaten for many years.[105]

A year later Bosse signed a contract to return to Dramaten as a regular member of the company. She took part in a month of rehearsals starting on 14 May 1933, in anticipation of the fall season. After returning from a visit to Norway, she prepared to open in Strindberg's *Storm Weather (Oväder)* on 30 August. For the first time in fifteen years she was a member of a repertory company on an annual contract, but her position was humble. She was granted few major or challenging roles; instead, she watched from the sidelines Tora Teje's dominance of the stage and the developing careers of Märta Ekström and Inga Tidblad. Harriet Bosse had won reentry to her theatrical home because of skillful persuasion and the significance of her past achievements, but she would seldom stand at center stage in the remaining decade of her career.

CHAPTER NINE

Bitter Homecoming

Sweden felt the impact of the Depression as the 1930s witnessed the end of an epoch of industrial expansion and prosperity. An important era began in 1932 when the Social Democratic government came to power and established new domestic policies and programs. Political issues, concern for the working class, and conflict between conservative and progressive factions determined some major developments in the arts. A stylistic change took place in theatre, where the bold expressionism of the 1920s left a legacy of imaginative visual images in scenery and lighting. There was a revival of interest in realism. Directors allowed their interpretations to evolve organically from the scripts, and emphasis on decor was kept in better balance with focus on the actors.

Although not a central figure, Harriet Bosse was involved briefly with many notable theatrical trends and events of the prewar decade. One important event was the establishment in 1933 of the National Theatre (Riksteatern), a government program that sent productions on tour throughout the country. At first the organization, led by Gösta M. Bergman, sent out ensembles from established theatres; eventually the National Theatre would mount its own productions. Per Lindberg continued to be a dominating figure in Swedish theatre, experimenting artistically and working to bring theatre to a wider spectrum of the public. From 1929 to 1931 he was the first head of broadcasts for the Radio Theatre. He then served as artistic director and staged productions for several theatres managed by the brilliant actor Gösta Ekman. Among Lindberg's most interesting productions were John Masefield's *Japanese Tragedy (En japansk tragedi)*, *Hamlet*, and *The Hangman (Bödeln)* by Pär Lagerkvist. In 1937 Lindberg began directing for the National Theatre, where his most significant work was with Lagerkvist's plays.

DRAMATEN AGAIN

When Harriet Bosse returned to the Royal Dramatic Theatre to finish out her working life, she was reunited with people with whom she had appeared there and on other stages. Heading the theatre from 1934 to 1938 was Olof Molander, who played Mats to her Kersti in 1918 and wrote the beautiful book of tribute in 1920. Molander was doing important creative work as a director, emphasizing psychological analysis, discipline, and respect for the written text. Although he followed Stanislavsky's example in demanding truthful and believable acting, he also worked with the entire production team to achieve a harmonious, artistic whole of sound, color, and light. No longer Bosse's ardent admirer, he was in a position to control repertory and casting and to keep her waiting in the wings for good roles. In 1949 she wrote: "I have been dead a long time now—almost 20 years. It was Olof Molander who killed me. I hope he does not forget to tell his confessor about this—and beg for forgiveness."[1] She never gave up without a fight, but confrontations in Molander's office usually ended in her defeat. He was so strong-willed that some actors feared and hated him, especially when he found fault with any unmotivated gesture or inflection. He worked most successfully with younger performers, who trusted him to develop their talent. Tora Teje was already experienced and successful when she began working with Molander, but he guided her development into a unique modern tragedienne, in such roles as Marguerite Gautier, Phèdre, and Christine Mannon. Bosse was excluded from Molander's innovative and masterful Strindberg productions, which were among the most important theatrical achievements of the 1930s. It was especially difficult when Molander chose Teje as Indra's Daughter in 1935. Bosse asked to alternate in the role, which she considered "ageless," but the request was denied.[2]

A colleague from an even earlier period succeeded Molander in 1938. Pauline Brunius and Bosse had been together in the ensembles of Dramaten and the Swedish Theatre in the first decade of the century. Georg Rydeberg noted that one day Rune Carlsten interrupted a rehearsal and asked the cast to guess who had just been named the new head of Dramaten. When Carlsten said that Arthur Engberg had appointed Pauline Brunius, Bosse is supposed to have turned pale and sat down, saying, "This can't be true. It's not possible."[3] Rydeberg assumed she was shocked because she remembered competing with Brunius for leading roles many years before. After Bosse left the Swedish Theatre, Brunius was its undisputed leading lady for fourteen years. She also enjoyed a successful period as manager-star at the

Oscar Theatre from 1926 to 1932. On stage Brunius had a stately presence when playing noble heroines like Schiller's Joan of Arc and Bjørnson's Tora Parsberg. She demonstrated "bright and clear intelligence" and impressive technique in contemporary and period British comedies, such as *The School for Scandal (Skandalskolan)*.[4] Described by Viveca Lindfors as "a strong, active, attractive woman," Brunius had the commitment, "grace and conviction" for administrative work.[5] Under her management, marked by femininity and humor, Dramaten was popular with the public.[6] While Molander emphasized classics and serious drama, Brunius presented more comedies. Bosse actually welcomed Brunius to Dramaten. Their long-standing acquaintance, and perhaps the fact that both were women, enabled them to maintain a cordial relationship. Sending a birthday greeting in 1941, Bosse wrote to "Paula": "That I wish you everything good for the future, you know. Also that I admire your courage, your wisdom and perseverance. What I especially want to thank you for is the kindness you always showed when we had one thing or another to talk about." At the time of her retirement Bosse thanked Brunius again for always being "understanding and friendly."[7]

In addition to Molander, Alf Sjöberg and Rune Carlsten were major directors at Dramaten during Bosse's final years there. Sjöberg was more intellectual and innovative, but Carlsten was competent and able to work harmoniously with Bosse.[8] Perhaps it was because of his ties to older traditions that he and she were compatible. Public taste had changed, partly because of the prevalence of film and partly because of the influence of Stanislavsky; Lars Hanson replaced Anders de Wahl as the model of a great actor. Bosse rejoined Dramaten as the theatre observed its twenty-fifth anniversary in the new building. In an overview of the years since 1908, several productions in which she had appeared were mentioned as noteworthy, but Harriet Bosse was referred to by name only in connection with *Berg-Eyvind and His Wife (Berg-Eyvind och hans hustru)* by Johann Sigurjonsson from 1913 and *Pygmalion* from 1914.[9] Bosse was known for careful preparation, meticulous polishing of details, and her own conception of "realism." Like Gerda Lundequist, she represented the older generation. Nils Beyer has written that no matter how admirably they delivered lines, those two actresses "could not avoid appearing old-fashioned to a contemporary audience, which was accustomed to the inflections of everyday speech." According to Beyer, Hilda Borgström was the older actress who adapted best to the new era: "She [also] was a master of dialogue but at the same time possessing humor and modesty which enabled her to blend into a modern ensemble."[10] As Harriet Bosse and others of her generation neared retirement, Dramaten introduced attractive and talented new actresses, among them Karin Kavli, Hjördis Petterson, Birgitta Valberg, Signe Hasso, and Gunn Wållgren.

THE FINAL DRAMATEN YEARS

During her last ten seasons at Dramaten, Harriet Bosse had few opportunities to demonstrate creativity. Being cast in minor roles and kept inactive for months at a time wore on her nerves, and she simply tried to endure the bitterness of the situation. From the fall of 1933 to the spring of 1943, Bosse played fifteen roles. Two were repeated from her earlier repertory: Henriette in *Crimes and Crimes* and Tro in *Everyman*. Where once she had played the young heroine, Bosse now appeared as an older character in *Romeo and Juliet*, *The Master Builder*, *Gösta Berling's Saga* by Selma Lagerlöf, and *The Adventure*. Rarely the focal point of a production, she played supporting roles in comedies, such as *Claudia* by Rose Franken, *The Women (Kvinnorna)* by Clare Booth Luce, and *Dear Octopus (Guldbröllop)* by Dodie Smith, or she was one of many in such large spectacles as *The Defeat (Nederlaget)* by Nordahl Grieg and *Everyman*. Occasionally Bosse would request an extension of a leave when visiting Norway, and it would be granted, implying that she could easily be replaced in most of her roles.

Because she played minor parts, Bosse usually received little or no critical comment. Playing opposite Lars Hanson in *The Defeat*, which takes place in Paris in 1870, Bosse appeared as the President's wife, a cold, hateful, and derisive woman. Obviously accustomed to a privileged status and elegant clothing, Bosse's Madame Thiers "made a strong impression despite the smallness of the role."[11] Her excellent acting occasionally caused a critic to wonder aloud in a review why Bosse should be limited to minor roles. Carl Laurin expressed in his review of *Everyman* the hope that Bosse would be seen and heard more often.

Although she seemed weak in the early scenes, Bosse was praised by some for her performance in 1937 of Aline Solness in *The Master Builder*, which starred and was directed by her old friend Anders de Wahl. Signe Hasso was not as forceful a Hilda as Bosse had once been, but she was charming, and especially effective as she listened to Aline's story about the burning of the family home. That was also Bosse's strongest scene. As she told about losing her dolls, it became understandable why she had appeared to be a ghost or sleepwalker earlier in the performance. Obsessed by melancholy and a sense of duty, this Aline was clearly Solness' sickly conscience. Reviews were mixed, for some dared to write that Bosse's portrayal of Aline was too theatrical and extreme. While acknowledging her "almost unlimited" technical mastery, Agne Beijer asserted that Bosse had always used herself as the basis for her characters. Now that she had made the transition into character acting, it was "very tempting for her to push the performance too far."[12] Signe Hasso, one of Bosse's heirs in the role of Eleonora as well as Hilda, recalls little about *The Master Builder* other than Bosse's believability and de Wahl's upstaging, ad-libbing, and domineering personality. She remembers Bosse's offstage gentleness, lovely appearance, and sense of humor. Like other young performers in the 1930s, Hasso describes the strict discipline at Dramaten and the separation of generations. A student in the acting school had to sit in the hallway among coats and boots, waiting to play a role and earn the privilege of entering the green room. One day Hasso dared to ask if Strindberg really had asked, "Will you have a little child with me?," and Bosse assured her that was true.[13]

In 1915 Bosse played Hélène in the Swedish premiere of *The Adventure;* twenty-five years later Gunn Wållgren played Hélène, and Bosse appeared as her grandmother. Although it was rather inappropriate, Bosse requested that her costume be an elegant version of a peasant dress; the effect was delightful.[14] Her face was still unwrinkled, but she suggested age with a gray wig. More than forty years later, Wållgren recalled Bosse as "very modern" in her acting, much more like Hilda Borgström than Tora Teje in style. Carlo Keil-Möller, who directed *The Adventure,* did not offer Bosse any instruction but simply allowed her to do as she wished. Everyone in the cast respected Bosse and hesitated to approach her. According to Wållgren, one did not really play "with" Bosse. She had a commanding presence and charisma onstage, but there, as well as in the backstage social structure, Bosse was isolated. The older actress and Wållgren established rapport and mutual respect. Twenty years later, Bosse wrote to a friend that Gunn Wållgren had "soul and technique" and was "the truly great talent they have now in Stockholm."[15]

STRINDBERG'S WIDOW

After the death of Professor Vilhelm Carlheim-Gyllensköld in 1934, his family found and returned to the Royal Library a group of letters from Strindberg to Bosse. Carlheim-Gyllensköld, a physicist, had been a devoted friend of Strindberg, included in the Beethoven sonata evenings at the playwright's apartment. Strindberg's heirs had commissioned him to go through the author's belongings, partly to catalog papers but mainly to look for unpublished manuscripts that might be issued as a book.[16] While checking the manuscripts and assorted notes, he found an envelope labeled by Strindberg "Inferno II Aug.–Sept. 1901." It contained almost forty letters by Strindberg and nine by Bosse. Carlheim-Gyllensköld copied Bosse's letters by hand and at some time returned the originals to her. Although the professor did not receive a key to the atelier at the Blue Tower until November, he dated the copies of Bosse's letters 8 September 1912.

The large collection of papers went to the Nordic Museum (Nordiska Museet) in 1915 and was placed in a cold, damp room on ground level. To expedite his preparation of the edition of previously unpublished manuscripts in a more healthful environment, Carlheim-Gyllensköld took material home.[17] Intending also to publish a comprehensive collection of Strindberg's correspondence, he had a typist copy the "Inferno II" letters from Strindberg. Obviously he forgot to return them to the museum or give them to the Royal Library, which took over the collection in 1922. The letters lay in a wardrobe for years, wrapped in a handkerchief.[18] On 11 March 1935, Oscar Wieselgren, head of the manuscript collection at the library, found the "Inferno II" letters while sorting through the Strindbergiana from the Carlheim-Gyllensköld estate and made them available to Harriet Bosse.[19]

The majority of the rediscovered letters were from the end of August and all of September 1901, when Bosse was living at a boarding house and considering divorce. She had not told about this separation and crisis in the early months of her pregnancy in her book published in 1932. When Bosse checked her own letters from 1901, she could confirm that the newly discovered letters were Strindberg's answers to hers. He had insisted that she keep their letters collected and organized. It is likely that he marked the dates on these particular letters in pencil and tied them together, choosing not to return them to Bosse after the divorce, perhaps because he planned to write a book entitled *Inferno II*.

Harriet Bosse granted an interview to Märta Lindquist of *Svenska Dagbladet* in April 1935 and allowed her to quote a few of the letters and publish a photograph of two of the pages. Lindquist described her impressions: "It is the Strindberg of the Inferno who wrote some of them, but it is also Strindberg the great lover, and the enormous tension between the forces in his nature, the tug of war between good and evil, light and dark, is mirrored at times with overwhelming intensity in these deeply personal confessions—

one senses the Titan's flaming breath, although his hand never trembled for a moment. . . ."[20] Lindquist reported that Bosse did not intend to publish these letters separately but preferred to wait and add them to the second edition of her original Strindberg book. A second edition never appeared.

For safekeeping Harriet Bosse often kept her Strindberg papers on deposit at the Royal Library. In February 1925 she deposited a package of Strindbergiana accessible only to herself. After removing it in August 1928, she probably placed it in the safe deposit box shared with Edvin Adolphson.[21] It is not known when this package was returned to the library since there is no notation that the "Inferno II" items were redeposited after she borrowed them in 1937. Bosse later claimed they were accepted by a library employee; if so, they were not replaced in their proper location.[22]

Her Strindberg letters published in 1932, the unpublished "rediscovered letters," miscellaneous small manuscripts, and the manuscripts for *Swan White* and *The Crown Bride* were valuable acquisitions for the permanent collection of the Royal Library. Bosse's attorney, Harald Dahlin, advised her to approach the Wenner-Gren Foundation, asking them to pay her twenty-five thousand crowns for the collection and afterward donate it to the library. Isak Collijn, the head of the library, along with Oscar Wieselgren and Martin Lamm, wrote letters to accompany Bosse's appeal, which was rejected in October 1938.[23] She expressed her disappointment and financial worries in a letter to Torsten Nothin, governor of the city of Stockholm:

People perhaps wonder why I have not myself donated the collection under discussion to the Royal Library—I would of course have done so since the best place for this unique collection is undeniably the Royal Library—but my economy does not permit it. I have been part of Swedish theatre for forty years—[I] have since 1933 received a minimal salary at the Royal Theatre, and my pension does not become available for two years—after a lifetime of work [I shall receive] a second-class pension of 2,400 crowns. I have no private fortune, so this sum is what I have to live on. Would it not be possible to reach an agreement so that the government would arrange a pension for me based on the understanding that I would leave my Strindberg collection to the Royal Library?[24]

This appeal was turned down as well, and sale of the collection was delayed for another decade.

During the years of martyrdom when Harriet Bosse felt unappreciated as a theatre artist, she recognized that she was more celebrated as the widow of Strindberg. In 1937 the entertainer Karl-Gerhard invited her to contribute to a journal on acting, a project that seems not to have materialized. She offered him an unpublished letter from Strindberg to enhance any brief statement she might make. Limited to the periphery of what was happening in theatre, she asked:

What shall I write about? About my life? That would be too long and too complex, and many would surely not understand why I did *this* instead of *that*.

About my life as an artist? That I struggled, never thought I achieved what I wanted to, and when I now look back on the whole thing, I ask myself, what in the name of mercy I was doing there. That the happiest time of my life should be when I was freed from the love of my youth—the theatre. But it is often finances which hold a relationship together, and therefore the marriage continues.[25]

Rather than her half-century of marriage to the theatre, it was the brief marriage to Strindberg that fascinated the public. In addition to building the legend of their courtship and marriage, Bosse occasionally answered factual questions from scholars doing research. When her theatrical career came to a close, Bosse's thoughts often turned to the years with Strindberg.

OTHER ENGAGEMENTS

After an absence of seventeen years, Harriet Bosse returned to the screen in 1936. She played Franskan (the French woman) in *Bombi Bitt and I (Bombi Bitt och jag)*, which was called by one critic Sweden's first "Wild West film."[26] The film, produced by Triangelfilm and directed by Gösta Rodin, is lively and entertaining. Based on the debut novel of popular author Fritiof Nilsson Piraten, the movie shows the friendship of two young boys, played by actors in their twenties. "I" (Frank Sundström) is a decent young man from a conservative household; Bombi Bitt (Sture Lagerwall) is an impish, ragged urchin reminiscent of Huck Finn. Although the director tried to make a "family film," children were not allowed to see it.[27]

Bosse took part in location shooting in Simrishamn during the summer of 1936. Her salary was five hundred crowns per day, with a guaranteed minimum of twenty-five hundred crowns plus travel money and per diem expenses.[28] A reporter from the Kristianstad newspaper described Bosse as "tiny, dark and with a distinguished profile. She was dressed in a bright red blouse, which looked excellent next to her coffee-colored skin."[29] Bosse accepted working conditions patiently—waiting for the proper light and repeating scenes many times. Her presence was required only a few days, but she contributed to the quality of a film that many enjoyed because it captured the happy mood of summer in Sweden. Others were disappointed that it failed to convey the vitality and charm of the novel.

Bombi Bitt, released in November 1936, was Bosse's first talking film. Although her role was small, she created a "keen and pungent character study."[30] Franskan, Bombi Bitt's foster mother, gives him sleeping space in the attic and meager food. He lives with her in a cottage that is perhaps too idyllic in the film, but it clearly is a humble dwelling isolated from proper society and is a gathering place for rogues. Franskan and her cohorts plan to steal candlesticks and other silver from the local church, not realizing that their scheme has been overheard by the boys, who place hams in the chest in place of the silver. Because of a falling out among the thieves, Franskan is knifed to death.

Seeing the film now, one can appreciate Harriet Bosse's technique and discipline and total commitment to the character. She is dressed roughly, her figure is matronly, there are age lines on her face, her voice is strong and mature. The characteristic stance is with hands on hips, by which she conveys Franskan's roughness and tension. She uses simple gestures and masterful facial expressions. Her most emotional scenes occur after the theft, one when Franskan demands her share and becomes very agitated until she is given three hundred crowns, and the other when she is awakened the next day and denies knowing what has happened to the silver. The murder is not shown directly but is suggested by a shot of a cat being startled and a candle going out.[31] Bosse's excellent work prompted a critic to ask, "Why does one so seldom see fru Bosse on film?"[32]

Where she had once been the feted prima donna of the private commercial touring circuit, Bosse also experienced the new approach to touring under government auspices that developed during the 1930s. Bosse's first Dramaten show after her return, *Storm Weather,* went on tour for more than a month in September and October 1933. In an attempt to reach new and larger audiences, *Gösta Berling's Saga* was done out of town and in the Auditorium at Norra Bantorget in Stockholm in 1936. Immediately after her appearances as Märta Dohna, Bosse left with *Crimes and Crimes.* The premiere took place in Gävle 19 November at the start of visits to fourteen cities. The production, directed by Alf Sjöberg, was then presented for two performances at Dramaten, on 4 and 5 December.[33] In 1938 Rune Carlsten directed *The Play of Life and Death* by Romain Rolland, which takes place in Paris in 1794, for a National Theatre tour. In Stockholm the show was presented for two "school performances" at Dramaten. Bosse found herself reunited with an old acquaintance, Carl Ström, and working with one of the promising younger actors, Georg Rydeberg, as Claude Vallée, the role that had brought Edvin Adolphson his first critical acclaim. As Sophie, Harriet Bosse was also acclaimed for her diction, charisma, spontaneity, and youthful appearance.

Rydeberg has left an account of the formality and courtesy with which Bosse was treated during rehearsals and of her dignity and aloofness when they traveled by train. She never joined the cast after a performance, not even after the premiere in Sundsvall. One evening, however, she accepted his invitation for supper after a performance in Jönköping, and Rydeberg found her charming. On stage he thought she was "fantastic." Despite the difference in their ages, he could justify Vallée's infatuation: "And truly her acting was such that one found it natural that this man dashed over the seven seas to reach his most beloved woman. Fru Bosse offered warm-blooded, sensually intensive acting, which is why I look back with deep admiration and respect on the time when I had the honor of playing opposite one of the greatest actresses of this century."[34]

As the only other woman on the tour, Lisskulla Jobs-Berglund heard Bosse reminisce about Strindberg and the "ups and downs" of life. Bosse declared that she still felt youthful and that her life was not over, even though she was disappointed at not getting good roles. She gave the younger actress two pieces of advice: never read a review until after a production closes, and since you can't do anything about your age, always exaggerate. Bosse said she would tell people she was born in 1632.[35]

Years earlier it would have been unthinkable for Harriet Bosse to perform in a folk park. Finally she did so in 1939. Summer entertainment in "folk parks" had been an important part of Swedish life since the early twentieth century. Bosse traveled the park circuit as Valentine Bourjon in *The Lord's Vineyards (Herrens vingård)* by Robert de Flers and Francis de Croisset. The tour, managed by Nils Ekstam, included forty performances for a total of 44,301 spectators.[36] Bosse became fond of Inga Tidblad, who was excellent as her daughter in the production. Most reviewers found that the stars outshone the inconsequential play. They praised Bosse's vitality, "genuine French esprit," intelligence, and—as always—beautiful diction.[37]

Radio was a perfect medium for Bosse's diction and silvery voice. Her first broadcast may have been on 2 July 1933, when she read from the works of Strindberg on NRK, the Norwegian Broadcasting System. After that program she sent an urgent letter to Per Lindberg, asking him to suggest "newer Swedish literature" for another broadcast. It was probably because of his advice that she presented a Pär Lagerkvist program on 12 August.[38] The Swedish broadcasting company also provided an occasional outlet for Bosse's talents and a welcome supplement to her income, permitted by the terms of her contract with Dramaten. She sometimes read poetry by Swedish, Finnish,or Norwegian writers on programs featuring the work of one poet or a theme, such as "Swedish Summer in Music and Poetry." The author whose works she read most often was Strindberg. Some of his fairy tales, "The Big Gravel Screen" ("Stora grusharpan") for example, became standards she frequently read on the air. She also did Strindberg's satirical essays from *The New Kingdom (Det nya riket)*, "How One Becomes a Famous Author" and "How One Becomes an Important Singer."[39]

Recordings of Bosse's broadcasts are valuable historical artifacts, illustrating her technique and individuality. She took part in three dramatic productions directed by Olof Molander. In 1935 she recorded her role of Cleopatra in the Shakespearean drama, opposite Anders de Wahl as Mark Antony and Lars Hanson as Caesar. Bosse also played the minor role of Time, the Chorus, in *A Winter's Tale (En vintersaga)* early in 1938. In 1942, with Anders de Wahl as Maurice, Bosse recreated the role of Henriette in a Radio Theatre production of *Crimes and Crimes.* A critic praised her reading: "The microphone transmits exactly the degree of cold acerbity and intensive monomania which the role demands."[40] When performing on the air, Bosse refused to rub elbows with the other performers. She would stand apart, protecting her psychological space.[41] Radio permitted Bosse and the audience to forget for a while the tension of theatre politics and the appearance of aging and to concentrate on the music she created with her distinctive vocal instrument.

FAREWELL

Sometimes the drama of nations clashing upstaged what was happening inside Dramaten, as when *Dear Octopus* opened on 1 September 1939. During intermission the audience rushed out to buy extra editions for news of Hitler's invasion of Poland. The company would cluster around a radio backstage during performances to hear the latest war bulletins. While Sweden remained neutral during World War II, Harriet Bosse was intensely aware of the impact of the Nazi occupation in Norway and concerned about the welfare of family and friends there. She may have said later that she did not consider herself Norwegian, but during the war she identified with Norway and showed her concern by reading works of Norwegian poets such as Nordahl Grieg and Nils Collett Vogt on the radio. Among the artists from the National Theatre in Oslo who escaped to Sweden in 1943 were the actor-directors Gerda Ring and Halfdan Christiansen, whom Bosse invited to dinner in her apartment at Kammakaregatan 66.[42]

The war had a deep effect on Bosse's immediate family. When the Nazis invaded Norway on 9 April 1940, her son-in-law Anders Wyller was among those who escaped by ship to England with King Haakon, while his wife and sons joined Bosse in Stockholm. Shortly after arriving in London, Wyller was diagnosed as having cancer. He was flown to Sweden so that Anne Marie could be with him during the final critical weeks. His sister Ingrid, a nurse, managed to come from Norway to help with his care. It was a strain for Bosse to rehearse and perform *The Adventure* during Wyller's illness, yet she did not discuss the situation with the cast. Following his death on 2 October, Anne Marie went back to Norway for her husband's funeral, and Harriet found herself in the role of full-time grandmother. She attended a school play in which Jørgen played Olav Trygvesson, but her reluctance to see any younger members of the family choose a theatre career was probably the main reason she refused to give him permission to go on tour with the play. After living with her mother for a while, Anne Marie took the boys to Uppsala in 1941 to enroll them in a Norwegian school.[43] Wyller's articles and speeches on humanism were published in 1947.[44] Harriet Bosse paid him tribute in a letter: "Anders Wyller should have been exactly the right person — after the war — to help with rebuilding. We here in Scandinavia so desperately need his culture, his fine personality. They will never forget in Norway what he has already been able to accomplish for his country. What he sowed will grow among all Norwegians."[45]

Although the Board of Dramaten observed some courtesies, like sending her flowers for opening night of *Storm Weather* and greetings on her sixtieth birthday, Bosse felt unappreciated during the final decade. Once in her dressing room she was heard to say, "I am only a cleaning lady here."[46] She commented later that while still in her fifties she was forced to play "gumroller," old women's roles.[47] It was believed that Bosse refused to play characters appropriate to her age, but she denied this misconception: "I never demanded to play young roles (people say that) but I insisted on getting to play *worthy* roles, for example Maria Stuart (the last years of her life), but that was given to a student."[48] Among the roles Bosse refused to play was Julia in *Swedenhielms* by Hjalmar Bergman, because, according to her friend Olga Raphael, "she would not do a caricature of an actress."[49]

An indication of the lack of status was her salary. She no longer had her brother-in-law's advice when negotiating with the theatre, for Carl Möller died and was buried in Rome in 1933. Having enjoyed one of the highest salaries in the nation, Bosse accepted what she called student wages of 2,400 crowns when she returned to Dramaten, and 5,000 crowns for each of the next nine seasons. This may be compared to Tora Teje's salary of 28,000 crowns in 1931–32 and 22,800 in 1933–34. When rehearsing in the production that would be Bosse's farewell to the stage, Teje was paid 2,800 crowns per month. Bosse's pension was calculated on the basis of service from July 1911 through June 1918 and from July 1933 through June 1943. Having to accept a minimal salary to qualify for a pension was humiliating. What caused her more anguish was being overlooked: "Everything I had done as an artist, the level of roles which I deserved, in other words my position as a major force at the theatre, was taken from me. I was trampled down. . . ."[50] Bosse was made to feel Dramaten did not need her, that she was standing in the way of younger talent and being kept on simply as a kindness. A committee appointed by the king would have liked her to retire in 1938 when she turned sixty. When it appeared in 1940 that her salary would be cut almost in half, Bosse begged for consideration—and for the opportunity to do some decent roles. Dramaten replied that Bosse would receive a payment from the pension fund and the remainder as salary to keep the total at 5,000 crowns a year until 1943. Although practical economic problems were given as the excuse, she was told bluntly, "But then you must also agree to play the roles you are offered."[51]

It would have been possible to supplement her salary and influence the younger generation by teaching, but that never appealed to Bosse. She said, "I have never taken a student, just because I did not want to force my interpretation on another artist." Rather than accepting a teacher's ideas, she thought each artist should work independently.[52] This confirms the impression that Bosse expected to have autonomy when developing a characterization.

Harriet Bosse's career ended with the season of 1942–43, which included two Strindberg productions, *Swan White* and *The Ghost Sonata (Spöksonaten)*, as well as a significant play by Vilhelm Moberg, *Ride This Night! (Rid i natt!)*. *The Big Shadow (Den stora skuggan)* by Carlo Keil-Möller was the play, and Elsa Båge the role, chosen to bring Bosse's career to a beautiful and fitting close. This is a comedy about an aristocratic poet, Harald Båge; everyone realized the model was Verner von Heidenstam. The poet is a "shadow" or spirit who does not appear, but his impact on the lives of others dominates the action. Plans are being made to turn his home over to a foundation and to publish a national edition of his poetry. Keil-Möller, the play's author and director, created a rather contrived script and a lifeless production. The stage directions describe Elsa, the poet's sister-in-law, as around fifty-five years old, attractive and aristocratic. Bosse's best scene was a confrontation with Tora Teje as Helena Gardone, the woman Båge loved in the last years of his life. Bosse's last speech on the Dramaten stage was: "Now that's enough, Sven! You don't know what you are talking about! That is your only excuse!"[53] The production began rehearsing on 10 March and opened 9 April.

After performances almost constantly through 28 April, the evening of 3 May 1943, was planned as Harriet Bosse's farewell to the stage, but she was cheated of the occasion that is traditionally a highlight in the life of a Scandinavian actor. The farewell should be a gala occasion when family, friends, and fans have an opportunity to pay tribute. An official of the theatre makes a beautiful speech and leads the audience in a cheer, and many bouquets and wreaths are presented with good wishes. Friends had sent flowers in honor of the occasion, and Bosse had permitted herself to feel sentimental. In makeup and costume she was waiting in her dressing room when word came that Olof Bergström, who played Sven, had not arrived. According to Bergström, he had forgotten about the performance and gone to a movie. At 8:15 P.M. Pauline Brunius announced to the audience that the performance was cancelled. Harriet Bosse never went through the ritual of a "final" exit at the theatre where she made her first entrance forty-four years earlier, nor did she appear for curtain calls, surrounded by flowers, to receive applause and thank her admirers. Swallowing the disappointment, Bosse comforted herself with the thought that at least she had earned her pension. Two days later she wrote to thank Mrs. Brunius and the Board of Directors for the roses they sent: "It is gracious of you to tell me I am welcome to return, but I am firmly determined never again to act in a theatre." She wrote in her memoirs: "It was with a sigh of relief that I left my dearly beloved theatre, and although people later begged me to perform, I have never again wanted to set foot on a stage."[54]

Herbert Grevenius wrote that it was "grotesque" to talk about a pension for Bosse, for she seemed ageless. He recalled her cool, precise, controlled speeches in the scene with Teje as one of the best memories of the season.[55] In another tribute Harriet Bosse was praised for her achievements:

Stockholmers of a mature generation do not forget the brilliant star from the first quarter of this century, when she shone with intensity, intelligence, and the charm of her artistic personality in a whole series of major roles in both the dramatic repertory and comedy. Many are disappointed that she has had few opportunities in recent years to provide the evidence of her mature and cultivated artistry, but when it has happened, she has convinced us that the spark has never been extinguished.[56]

The following spring Bosse underwent major surgery. While recovering at the resort of Saltsjöbaden, she received an honor which softened to some extent the bitterness of the denouement of her stage career. The city of Stockholm presented her the Saint Erik's medal in gold on the Norwegian national holiday, 17 May. A speech by the Mayor, Carl Albert Anderson, summarized her achievements, praising her ability to express intensity, passion, lyricism, and playfulness, and her commitment to presenting contemporary problems in the theatre.[57] Bosse appreciated the honor, commenting shortly afterward: "The recognition came like a healing bandage on a wound after two operations, and also after my painful wandering through Golgotha these last ten years at Dramaten."[58]

CHAPTER TEN

After the Final Curtain

Retiring from Dramaten freed Harriet Bosse from a humble position and bitter disappointment. She had lost her sense of identity as a leading lady but not the conviction that her earlier achievements had earned her a prominent place in the history of Swedish theatre. A few performances in films and on radio drew upon her polished skills, but most of her attention centered on a quiet private life. She enjoyed traveling and her family, but the problems of aging and illness often depressed her. Recalling her life with Strindberg and sharing her recollections with the public took on great importance.

TAPERING OFF

During World War II Sweden's film industry produced a large number of movies, zealously checked by censors for controversial propaganda. There were films with serious themes related to politics and business, as well as light entertainment and romantic melodrama.[1] Harriet Bosse played small roles in two movies immediately after her retirement.[2] Viveca Lindfors, who starred in both films, recalls her as a charming person—delicate and beautiful—and a great actress. Like others who worked with her, Lindfors remembers Bosse being aloof and protective of her privacy when on the set.[3]

The first film, made in the late spring of 1943, was *Anna Lans,* the story of a troubled country girl who converts to the Salvation Army. The program described it as "the story of one woman and of thousands of women." Under the direction of Rune Carlsten, Bosse appeared as a baroness, Friherrinnan Löwenfeldt, who hires Anna as a maid shortly after her arrival in Stockholm. Bosse establishes a gracious, refined, generous, and rather frivolous character. She is first seen lounging in a long robe with flowing sleeves, eating chocolates as Anna helps her pack. While the baroness is out of town, her charming playboy son has an affair with Anna, who expects to marry him. Upon her return Bosse, dressed in an elegant black suit with furs, summons Lindfors as Anna to discuss the affair. Playing with restraint and compassion, Bosse makes clear the inappropriateness of the situation. She uses the light tone quality, musical inflections, and smooth phrasing for which she was famous. The gentle persuasion of the baroness and the son's failure to defend her cause Anna to leave the household in despair. There is nothing theatrical or dated in the size or style of Bosse's performance. Obviously she had mastered the subtlety and naturalness necessary for this medium.[4] After the premiere on 20 August 1943, critics found fault with the stereotyped characters and mediocre plot, but *Anna Lans* had commercial appeal and became the prototype for a genre popular in the 1940s. When the film was shown again on Swedish television in 1982, a new public could see Bosse's fading, delicate beauty and polished professionalism.

Bosse also had a minor role in the film *Appassionata,* the story of a temperamental and jealous concert pianist played by Georg Rydeberg. Lindfors was the pianist's wife and Bosse her aunt, fru Lenander. The film, directed with artistry by Olof Molander, had its premiere 2 February 1944. It was reviewed by music critics, who praised the piano playing, and by film critics, who commented on the beautiful photography and good, though melodramatic acting. Bosse appeared so briefly that she received little mention. Her cameo role was enjoyed in 1983 when the film was shown on television. For Viveca Lindfors *Appassionata* was a stepping stone to Hollywood; for Bosse it was the last time an audience would see her act.

RETIREMENT

Although her fans wished she would continue to act, Harriet Bosse felt relieved at being free of responsibility, backstage politics, and the anxiety of stage fright. When Georg Funkquist phoned to offer her a role in an English play at the Avenue Theatre (Alléteatern) in about 1951, she declined, saying she was "so tired of theatre that I feel tired all the way to the roots of my hair."[5] For her the joy of creativity had been the rehearsal process, as she searched for the underlying meaning of dialogue. Writing from Tyresö on 8 July 1943, Bosse reminisced about her career, sharing thoughts in a charming and humorous "vacation letter" to *Svenska Dagbladet.* She never had her heart set on being an actress but felt she could have fulfilled her purpose in life as a teacher of cooking (although she admitted that her only culinary skill was boiling potatoes). Immense ambition, capacity for work, and a need for privacy were the essential elements of her self-image. "For me life does not consist just of acting—I have countless other interests. . . . Living is an art in itself, if one views it with artistic and not materialistic eyes." Bosse reassured readers that she would find plenty to do in retirement. As a start "I'll clean out my dresser drawers!"

Harriet Bosse was still a celebrity. Journalists asked for comments on various events, but she was discreet and guarded her privacy. While reporters hoped for a sensational interview about her life with Strindberg, Bosse adamantly refused such requests. On the one-hundredth anniversary of Strindberg's birth in January 1949, she declined to be interviewed for a series of articles by Margit Siwert on "Strindberg and Actresses," which appeared in *Svenska Dagbladet,* nor would she participate in public festivities at Dramaten and the City Hall. While Strindberg's daughter Karin Smirnoff and twenty-three other relatives were in the spotlight, Harriet and Anne Marie observed the day at home. The actress contributed to the occasion by reading the prologue to *A Dream Play* on the radio.

The artist Greta Gerell was a friend of Harriet Bosse during the later years in Stockholm. She painted three role portraits: Eleonora, Indra's Daughter, and Kersti. Gerell could remember Bosse in *A Dream Play,* especially her facial expression as she descended from the cloud "like an exotic bird." Capturing the ethereal quality with "ordinary earthly colors" was frustrating. The artist labored for five months and did ten oil paintings, which she destroyed. As she posed tirelessly, Bosse read the entire role many times and offered abundant criticism of the portraits. Gerell used a delicate and simple technique that captured the radiance of the character. When thanking Bosse for giving the portrait to the theatre, Dramaten called it a reminder of her deep and moving art, which would show her always as "the interpreter of August Strindberg's thoughts."[6] This portrait, with the colors unfortunately dimmed, may be seen in a stairwell of the lobby.

Bosse and Gerell brought the portrait of Kersti to the City Theatre of Gothenburg in December 1950, before embarking on a voyage to the Canary Islands. The actress was shown in a simple dark habit with white headpiece and bib, hands at her waist, head tilted defiantly. Standing in front of a bust of Strindberg, Bosse presented the portrait with thanks for the kindness of theatre patrons and for "beautiful memories" of Gothenburg. She assumed it would remain on view as a reminder of her many performances there, especially in Gustaf Linden's production of *The Crown Bride*. The portrait has disappeared.[7]

RETURN TO NORWAY

When the war ended in 1945, Harriet Bosse began to consider moving to Norway to be near her children and grandchildren. Finances were limited, but she hoped to buy a small place to live and to use her pension for monthly expenses.[8] The move was delayed for ten years, during which she traveled whenever possible. Her favorite vacation was a three-month cruise to South America. When Arne and Jørgen Wyller were studying at the University of Oslo, their mother lived with Bosse for a while in a tiny efficiency apartment without a kitchen. Anne Marie slept on a sofa in the living room and during the day went to the Nordic Museum, where she painstakingly cataloged more than six thousand books in her father's library.[9] After major surgery in 1954 Bosse felt ill and lonely. Anne Marie came from Norway for her mother, took her by train to Oslo, and established her at the Smestad Hotel early in 1955. This was thought of as a temporary arrangement during convalescence, but then Bosse decided to settle in Norway. Her return was heralded by a long article in *Aftenposten* with the headline "Harriet Bosse back to Oslo for good" and a quote in bold type: "I think it is WONDER-FUL to be free of everything to do with theatre, says the queen of Swedish acting."[10]

Moving back to Norway proved a mistake, for Bosse never felt happy there. Dagmar Möller died in 1954, and Ewald Bosse, in 1956. Harriet was the only one left of the fourteen children born to Anne Marie and Johann Heinrich Bosse.[11] She wrote to a friend in 1958: "How I long desperately for Stockholm—my whole life is there. I *cannot* learn to be content here—the Norwegian temperament is completely different. And then they want to turn me into a *native* Norwegian—a mistake: my mother was Danish, my father was German, I was actually born in Oslo, but I could just as well have been born on the Atlantic—don't have a drop of Norwegian blood." Although she spoke Norwegian with her daughter-in-law, most of the time she continued speaking Swedish. She was tempted to move back to Stockholm and reside in a nice boarding house, but she felt she would not live much longer.[12] It was not unusual for her to say, "I won't live until summer" or "I may not live until fall."

Bosse managed on her "people's pension" from the Swedish government and the one she had earned at Dramaten. Failing health, bitter memories of her treatment at the theatre, and the fact that most people in Norway were unaware she had been a prominent celebrity all contributed to her chronic melancholy. It was as though she never accepted her fate. Ewald would tease her that happiness was always some place other than where Harriet was. She preferred a quiet, reclusive life; in fact, she was distressed when an Oslo newspaper published an article in observance of the sixtieth anniversary of her debut.

Mentz Schulerud of the Norwegian Broadcasting System proposed producing a radio program featuring Bosse, but she refused to be interviewed about her life or her interpretation of roles. She also refused to read scenes from Strindberg's plays, agreeing to use on the air nothing but selections from the fairy tales he wrote for Anne Marie in 1903. Obviously she wanted to present to the world only a bright and positive impression of Strindberg. Bosse's last public performance was twenty-three minutes and ten seconds of the fairy tales recorded on 17 April 1958 for broadcast on 21 April. Grandson Bo Wingård remembers her rehearsing for the broadcast in front of a mirror, a technique she probably had used when learning roles for the stage. Comparing the last recording with one she made in Oslo in 1952, it is obvious that she had more energy, a faster basic tempo, and more lilt to the pitch patterns in 1952. For both recordings she used her renowned precise diction, the technique of "singing" on long vowels, and perfect control of phrasing.[13]

Despite the housing shortage and red tape, Bosse found a roomy apartment on Kopperudvejen with the help of Randi Wingård. Her homes had always been decorated attractively. Once again the Dalarna grandfather clock, a chandelier from the Trondheim Cathedral, a large Watteau reproduction, a portrait by Greta Gerell, and other beautiful items created a pleasant effect. Still she was easily depressed. Bosse could surprise the family with a burst of energy, as when she agreed to travel to Stavanger for her granddaughter Janecke Wyller's christening. Members of the family, who called her by the nickname Snings, were attentive and helpful during medical emergencies or anxiety attacks. When feeling ill or upset, she would sometimes stay in the home of her son Bo or grandson Jørgen Wyller. When well enough to travel, she would vacation where she could enjoy the sun, preferring resorts on the Mediterranean, at Lugano in Switzerland, and at Marstrand in Sweden.

Harriet Bosse found it difficult to accept growing old, although she looked younger than her age. Her hair remained dark until the last years of her life. She appeared petite, partly because she wore flat shoes in private life and was careful about her diet. Bosse dressed stylishly in vivid colors and used brightly colored lipstick and nail polish. There was no doubt that her self-image was still that of a leading actress and alluring coquette.

Bosse usually did not attend the theatre or socialize with theatre person-alities. On a rare occasion in 1958, she decided to see a production of *Easter* directed by Olof Molander. Requesting three complimentary tickets from the Oslo New Theatre, she invited Jørgen Wyller and his wife Wenche to accompany her. An awkward scene was averted when a photographer approached during intermission. Not wanting to be photographed or interviewed, Bosse hid her face. The man tactfully went past and took a picture of the illustrious Norwegian actress Agnes Mowinckel, who was seated in the same row.[14]

The cast was probably unaware that the performance was being seen by the actress who had created the role of Eleonora. Bosse kept up a running commentary—mostly negative. Patrons seated nearby tried to hush her, but Bosse could not keep from exclaiming, "Oh, no!" at various moments. Her dismay may have been justified. Olof Molander, who had never directed *Easter* before, probably wanted to add it to the long list of Strindberg plays for which he had received acclaim. According to critic Paul Gjesdahl, this production did not establish the traditional peaceful mood; instead there was tension, neuroticism, and disharmony among the family members. While others praised Henny Moan for the sensitivity, spontaneity, and purity of her Eleonora, Gjesdahl found fault with her latent hysteria and "strangely constrained" manner of speaking, especially in scenes with Benjamin, where Molander's strong hand was too evident. The director's artistic judgment could also be questioned in his substitution of thin piano music for Haydn's "Seven Last Words of Christ."[15]

Although she must have enjoyed some of the triumphs of her career, Harriet Bosse did not encourage anyone in the family to follow in her footsteps. Janecke, one of her favorite grandchildren, came to visit at the age of four. With persuasion and the lure of a sweet drink, Harriet Bosse got the shy little girl onto her lap. She then said solemnly, "Janecke, one thing you must promise me: that you will never be an actress!" Theatre has turned out to be Janecke's consuming interest, but she is using her talent as a drama teacher.[16]

MEMOIRS

These were years for reminiscing. Although she told the *Aftenposten* report-er in 1955 that she would not write memoirs, the family encouraged her to record her recollections. For exact dates of certain productions Bosse requested information from Sweden, but mostly she relied on her memory.

The result was "Both—and: Some Sketches" ("Både—och: Några skisser"), a brief account of highlights of her life. The manuscript contains reflections on her career, favorite roles, and fellow theatre artists as well as glimpses of the friendships and adventures that brightened her private life. Strindberg is the only husband she mentions; nothing new or significant about their relationship is disclosed. Just as guarded as during interviews, Bosse chose not to reveal her feelings about bereavements, personality conflicts, or periods of despair and loneliness. The friend to whom she sent a copy of the manuscript did not see any potential for publication. Jenny Bergqvist-Hansson, who had been instrumental in getting the Strindberg letters published in 1932, expressed the opinion that the public would be interested only in an autobiography that told the intimate story of the three marriages. The rough draft was therefore set aside in Bosse's desk.

The memoirs are the musings of an artist who felt sentimental as she looked back on the great performers of an epoch that had faded away. She began by quoting from act 3 of Goethe's *Egmont* the words sung by Klärchen, a character she had portrayed in 1903:

In most cases one could set
as a motto for an artist's temperament:
"Himmelhoch jauchzend—zum Tode betrübt."
Thus it was for me.

Like Klärchen, whose love for Egmont brought her both glorious joy and grievous sorrow, Bosse reminisced about the happiness and suffering of her life in the theatre.

Those actors she recalled fondly were Anders de Wahl, Ivan Hedqvist, Emil Hillberg, Nils Personne, August Palme, and Oscar Bäckström. The actresses she singled out were Hilda Borgström, Tyra Dörum, Valborg Hansson, and Thekla Åhlander. Bosse recalled her colleagues with respect for their talents and distinctive personalities. Some memories were of temperamental performers who had behaved unreasonably, such as a costar who would lift her up during the curtain call and drop her like a sack of potatoes as soon as they reached the wings. She enjoyed describing moments when a cast could barely keep from bursting into laughter, like the evening they noticed that Augusta Lindberg had forgotten her slippers for a serious scene in *Trial by Fire* and was walking around in white cotton stockings with a rose embroidered on each big toe.

Harriet Bosse's brief autobiography includes informal theorizing about acting as an art, which she considered essentially to be beyond explanation. The great artist has God-given talent, she contended, "but one must nurture the gift—through work." Bosse thought that the proper balance of emotion and intelligence, inspiration and control, about which many have theorized, cannot be rationally explained. She observed: "The artist is an instrument— who plays on the instrument is a mystery. Of course there must be *control*, parallel with the role, but only in the subconscious." She agreed with a statement by Ludmilla Pitöeff: "Our art is a mystery which is just as inexplicable as life itself."[17]

STRINDBERG LETTERS

After the failure of negotiations to sell her Strindberg papers in 1938, Harriet Bosse continued to keep them on deposit at the Royal Library. In 1943 she tried to sell the collection in such a way that it would be donated to the library while she would receive funds to supplement her pension. Negotiations undertaken on her behalf by Fredrik Ström, a journalist and politician, were not successful.[18] In May 1945 Bosse contacted Ström again, with the suggestion that the Strindberg Society might be the appropriate custodian of her letters and manuscripts. Since she was in poor health and unable to earn money by working, Bosse hoped that sale of her papers might finance the purchase of a home in Norway.[19]

In addition to manuscripts of the letters published in 1932, Bosse offered for sale "The Dutchman in Front of the Window," selected passages of Mæterlinck's "Le Trésor des humbles" translated by Strindberg and dedi-cated to her, the poem Strindberg wrote to her with the eagle feather pen in April 1901, plus a couple of small items. Zeth Höglund, Commissioner of Finance for Stockholm, proposed that the city purchase Bosse's Strindberg letters and manuscripts for donation to the Royal Library.[20] On 5 Decem-ber 1949, twenty thousand crowns were made available to the Strindberg Society, which served as intermediary between the city and Harriet Bosse. City officials were favorably disposed, since in 1946 they had started subsidizing publication by the Society of Strindberg's correspondence, edited by Torsten Eklund.[21]

In 1952 Bosse checked out of the Royal Library her manuscripts of *Swan White* and *The Crown Bride*. She considered selling the latter to someone in America.[22] With her physician, Dr. Telemak Fredbärj, serving as intermediary, she sold it instead to a Swedish collector. Her manuscript of *Swan White* traveled to England and Norway before returning to the Royal Library, which purchased it in 1980 from Damm's, a bookstore in Oslo.[23]

There was a great deal of confusion about the "rediscovered letters," which Oscar Wieselgren listed in an inventory sent to Bosse in 1943.[24] Although she acknowledged receiving the list, she did not notice or remember that the letters had been "rediscovered" again sometime after being misplaced in 1938. Therefore, on a visit to the manuscript collection in February 1950, Bosse was surprised to find the letters that Professor Carlheim-Gyllensköld had kept at his house.[25] Bosse considered them her property, while the Royal Library claimed they were part of the collection for which she had received twenty thousand crowns. It required a meeting of several city officials and three representatives of the Strindberg Society in November 1952 for Bosse to assert her ownership rights, which continued to be disputed by the library.[26] After making a microfilm copy, the library allowed her to have the originals on 3 December 1952.

When Bosse prepared to move to Norway, she faced a decision about publication and safekeeping of the debated letters. Since she did not feel strong enough to work on a new book, by January 1954 she was ready to sell. When he learned that Bosse had used the sum received in 1949 to purchase an annuity for her daughter, head librarian Nils Afzelius was sympathetic about her financial needs. Officially the library continued to maintain that those letters were not Bosse's property because they had never been mailed.[27] This proved true only of the letter from 1 January 1904, which Strindberg marked "unsent." Bosse and the library were at an impasse. In March 1954 she promised amicably to take the letters to Norway with the understanding that they should be returned to the Royal Library after her death. Soon she changed her mind and gave up the prospect of either selling the letters or keeping them for herself. On 22 May Dr. Fredbärj, representing Bosse, brought the "rediscovered letters" to the Royal Library.[28]

Since Strindberg never used them for a book called *Inferno II,* the unpublished letters were of potential interest to scholars and the public. Harriet Bosse chose to publish the "rediscovered" letters as a separate book. Although they would some day be included in the Strindberg Society's comprehensive edition, it was decided to issue this group of letters as a separate volume in 1955. In consultation with Bosse and Eklund, Åke Runnquist of Bonniers edited the letters and wrote an introduction to *De återfunna breven till Harriet Bosse.* She became upset when people suggested she did not have the right to publish them and when they doubted that the letters had been out of her hands for decades. For a while she considered withdrawing from the project, but she justified her decision to proceed by recalling that Strindberg often said, "Every word I write is literature and shall be published."[29]

All letters were written in 1901 except for the one from New Year's Day 1904. The contents confirm that Bosse inspired several characters in Strindberg's plays and that he wooed her by promising to pull strings so that she could star in productions. They also provide evidence of his vacillating moods of resentment, despair, and generosity, and of his struggle to see suffering as a spiritual test during the separation from 22 August to 6 October 1901. For scholars seeking the biographical circumstances under which Strindberg wrote works like *Queen Christina* and the poem "Chrysaëtos," this tiny volume was a welcome new source. Since the *Occult Diary* was not available, the letters served a more important function in 1955 than they do now. They present a vivid image of Strindberg's creative process and love for his third wife, ranging from rather adolescent adoration and delight through jealousy and disillusionment. Gunnar Brandell wrote in *Svenska Dagbladet* that the book did not present new aspects of Strindberg, but he called it "one of the most beautiful among this year's volumes" and "probably the richest in content."[30]

Bosse's own letters, which she demanded that Strindberg return after the divorce, would have complemented his, both in this volume and in the earlier one. There were about two hundred letters that people urged her to publish. She considered doing so but felt the letters were "childish" and without literary merit. Since they were not found among her papers after her death, it is believed that she burned them, against the advice of Torsten Eklund.[31]

When the "Inferno II" letters were published in 1955, Bosse experienced great distress and confusion. She insisted she had never received Strindberg's letters; yet there were nine letters extant that she had written in reply.[32] They had been copied by Professor Carlheim-Gyllensköld. Her letters from August and September 1901 helped Eklund to verify the dates of those from Strindberg. Despite her bewilderment, Bosse gave Eklund permission to publish the nine letters in the Strindberg Society's journal, *Meddelanden från Strindbergssällskapet,* in 1956. Also published with them was a beautiful letter written by Strindberg to his unborn child and sent to Bosse on 4 September 1901. Later she almost regretted having allowed her letters to be published.[33] They offer insight into Bosse's affection and regard for Strindberg, as well as her determination to preserve her self-respect and fond memories of the harmony they had briefly enjoyed. Whether to put career goals first or to consider the relationship with Strindberg her mission in life occupied Bosse's mind, along with apprehension about motherhood and conflicting advice from friends and family.

Bosse commented to Torsten Eklund that she had no reason to say anything negative about Strindberg, "since he never deliberately did me any harm."[34] She recalled his saying, "Child, if it should happen that my besmirched name can be of any use to you, use it."[35] She realized she would never be able to convince the public to accept her version of what had happened:

Strindberg writes that I "said this and that"—no, I am not so indiscreet and vulgar that I would touch upon such a sensitive question. But I *cannot* help it if Strindberg imagined a great deal. Poor fru von Essen when he wrote *A Madman's Defense*. I have not read it but I have heard people talk about it.

I think these letters I am publishing now are interesting and illuminating . . . many of the letters are beautiful.[36]

Despite the controversy and misinterpretation of her motives, Bosse was content with her two volumes of Strindberg letters, as she wrote to Jenny Bergqvist-Hansson: "In the book you arranged for, I have said that Strindberg was not mentally ill, that he was kind, and now in the latest letters that he was nice and thoughtful toward a young girl, as I was then." She felt that she had accomplished her "mission."[37]

ARVID PAULSON'S TRANSLATION

Another publication project occurred to Harriet Bosse as a means of sharing her version of the Strindberg story with a wider audience and providing some financial security for her daughter. She contacted a Swedish-American actor, Arvid Paulson, who had sent her a copy of his translation of *The Great Highway (Stora landsvägen)*. Bosse proposed publishing a selection of letters in English, sharing the royalties equally with Paulson. Beginning 29 March 1955, they began a correspondence which continued until August 1961.

Bosse had unrealistic expectations about the receptivity of American publishers to the proposed translation and what it might earn. Explaining that few Americans knew of Strindberg and that sales would be modest,

Paulson crushed her hopes of a steady income from royalties. He tried to persuade her that the payment she received was quite generous, considering that Strindberg had never won the Nobel Prize. She wanted to maintain control over the correspondence, but she followed Paulson's advice, reluctantly granting radio and television rights while declining to allow translation into other languages. Tempers sometimes flared, for both were sensitive and high-strung. Bosse usually accepted Paulson's views and smoothed over the points of conflict. He was shocked to learn she had sold the letters to the city of Stockholm; she reassured him that she still had publication rights. The book was delayed so long that Bosse began to doubt she would ever see it, but she hoped that it would at least bring her daughter some pleasure — and royalties.

Bosse worked diligently on the American edition, maintaining her preference for keeping the letters in chronological order. She sent a few photographs of herself and a list of sixteen letters from the "rediscovered" group, leaving the final selection to Paulson. Bosse checked on a number of factual details and tried to help him with words that were puzzling to decipher. He also consulted Torsten Eklund and Walter Berendsohn while preparing the volume. At her insistence, Paulson sent sample translations, which Bosse found "faithful and beautiful," "fine, correct and fluent," and which Anne Marie also approved.[38]

Paulson provided an introduction on Strindberg and a two-page note on Bosse. He explained that the volume includes almost all of the letters published by Natur och kultur in 1932, along with most of the "rediscovered" letters issued in 1955. For making the letters and commentary available to readers unable to enjoy them in Swedish, the volume deserves recognition. However, it is not a reliable source for scholars since Paulson omitted sentences, paragraphs, and entire letters without so indicating. He used ellipses freely, not necessarily when material is missing but as part of his liberal changes of the original punctuation. Paulson omitted passages referring to domestic matters, family visits, and references to literature, such as Strindberg's comparison of their love to that of Ferdinand and Miranda in *The Tempest*. Occasionally what was omitted expresses Strindberg's tormented emotions. Paulson tended to elaborate the style, adding length but diluting the vigor of the original, as when he translates "jag är Du" into "then sense it as if I were actually you."[39]

Anyone wanting the complete story of Strindberg's correspondence with Bosse must see the appropriate volume edited by Torsten Eklund. The letters, with detailed footnotes, appear in the collected *Brev*, volumes 13, 14,

and 15. In 1963 Eklund issued a collection of the correspondence interwoven with passages from the *Occult Diary;* an English translation by Mary
Sandbach appeared in 1965.[40] Since Eklund devoted years to Strindberg
scholarship and had access to the diary, he was much more precise than
Paulson about dating letters and identifying people and other references.
Bosse knew about the diary, but she probably never saw it. Her understanding of Strindberg's state of mind might have changed markedly if she had
read about some of his bitter attitudes and bizarre fantasies.

First published in hard cover by Thomas Nelson and Sons, the Paulson
edition was issued in paperback by Grosset and Dunlap in 1959. Harriet
Bosse was not pleased with the cover design, done in shades of blue and
lavender. It shows a handsome and brooding man bearing a remote resemblance to Strindberg, posed with his hands resting on several letters
handwritten in English. Behind him is the head of a pretty young woman
with blond hair. Bosse reluctantly accepted the design as an example of
"American taste," which probably also accounts for the subtitle *Love Letters
from a Tormented Genius.* When the book appeared, Bosse received only two
complimentary copies from the publisher. In June and August 1959 she
wrote to congratulate Paulson for the excellent review he had sent.

Arvid Paulson presented his correspondence with Bosse to the Drottningholm Theatre Museum in 1975. The letters have some interest beyond
the information they provide about the translation. The two shared comments on Eugene O'Neill, whose plays Bosse admired, and Sean O'Casey,
to whose work Paulson introduced her. She remarked on her dislike of the
music of Brahms and gave her opinion that Ingrid Bergman was highly
overrated. "Garbo, on the other hand, was a genius — she was wonderful."[41]
Themes that recur often in Bosse's letters are her loneliness, ill health, and
longing to escape the cold winters. Paulson assumed that she would be
acquainted with actress Tore Segelcke and producer Tancred Ibsen but she
confessed that she had no social life. She referred with pride to the career of
her grandson Arne Wyller, an astronomer. The final letter, on 23 August
1961, tells about a stay in the hospital, when doctors could not determine
why she was ill.

The letters also reveal how interested Bosse was in any news related to
Strindberg. In 1957 she was glad to hear about the ninety successful
performances of *Miss Julie* in Rome. She commented sometimes on translations of the plays, mentioning specifically that she did not like Elizabeth
Sprigge's use of "Thou" as Indra's Daughter addresses the god. She was
upset to learn of a scholar who had written a dissertation on Strindberg that

included quotations from the correspondence without Bosse's permission. She called Paulson's attention to a psychiatric study of Strindberg written by a doctor in Gothenburg *(Strindberg i skärselden* by Sven Hedenberg). It is clear that Bosse earnestly hoped American readers would appreciate the letters and that she had played her final role as guardian of the Strindberg legend conscientiously.[42] She had given away her last souvenir of their life together, the pen made from the eagle feather, but she still had her memories. Writing to Paulson about *A Dream Play,* she declared that it was "especially close to my heart because it was written during my time at Karlavägen." She praised the play as "the most beautiful S—g has done—it has humor, vigorous wit, and warmth—it is mild, something which was generally not abundant with S—g—it is simply the best thing Strindberg wrote—human, warm."[43]

TRIBUTES

Harriet Bosse died at Our Lady's (Vår Frues) Hospital in Oslo on 2 November 1961, at the age of eighty-three. Following her wishes, the family held a private funeral service on Tuesday, 7 November, with burial in the family plot at Our Savior's (Vår Frelsers) Cemetery.

Newspapers throughout Scandinavia carried lengthy stories about Bosse. It was assumed that the younger generation of theatregoers knew her only by name, but there were many loyal admirers who remembered her "Oriental beauty," distinctive voice, and remarkable diction. Many roles were mentioned, in plays by many authors, evidence of her impressive versatility. Looking back to the start of her career, it was evident that her beauty represented the turn-of-the-century ideal, a romantic image removed from the mundane. Critics sometimes commented about her captivating beauty that it was easy to understand the irrational and passionate behavior of her admirers in the plays. Determined to develop a personal style free from traditional mannerisms, she had asserted her originality with intelligence and good taste. Oscar Wieselgren recalled the powerful expressiveness of her eyes, "which with trembling intensity mirrored the inner movement of the soul." He often saw her at the Royal Library, where she came to do research on roles and to discuss the psychology of characters. Sometimes she worried about being inhibited and overly analytical, but restraint and simplification were characteristic of her art.[44] Concepts of realism change, and what looked revolutionary and simple to audiences at the beginning of the century seemed stylized and "technical" to the next generation. Still all the tributes to Bosse in 1961 granted her a prominent place in the history of Swedish theatre. Her individuality and achievements were in the spotlight again in 1978, when a Swedish broadcast observed the hundredth anniversary of her birth. Hans Christer Sjöberg featured interviews with people who had worked with her, and he kept the marriage with Strindberg in proportion as one important aspect of a long life.

THE IMAGE

The spotlight has dimmed on Bosse as an independent artist, but her relationship with Strindberg and its significance for his creative work has been studied over and over by biographers and critics. It even inspired a postage stamp that won an international competition in 1985: Bosse in elaborate period hat and costume in the lower right corner, and behind her a letter and envelope in Strindberg's handwriting.[45] Certain episodes, certain passages from their correspondence are treated in countless books, newspapers and journal articles, and program notes for productions. Bosse does not appeal only to the scholarly mind. A number of creative writers have used the material made familiar by literary historians to present a character named Harriet Bosse.

In 1970 Colin Wilson published a play entitled *Strindberg,* based on biographical and autobiographical material including the *Occult Diary.*[46] The play opens in Strindberg's bedroom in the Blue Tower, where he is being tormented by nocturnal fantasies of Harriet. She and other female characters are not individualized, but they represent the women in his life, sometimes speaking as they might in reality, sometimes becoming the temptresses and tormentors he imagined. Chronology and facts are used in a confusing fashion, with Harriet appearing in a scene in Paris in 1894 and her fiancé being referred to as Gunnar Castrén. The last female character to speak is Harriet, who asks, "Is it too late?"—to learn, to change one's life. "Oh, yes," Strindberg answers.

The Swedish novelist Ole Söderström was inspired to write two novels on Bosse and Strindberg: *The Red House (Röda huset)*, published in 1976, and *Victoria,* published two years later.[47] *The Red House,* set in the well-known apartment building that used to stand on Karlavägen, uses primarily the *Occult Diary* and the correspondence with Bosse's commentary. Söderström narrates the story from the playwright's point of view. The fictional Harriet Bosse is awestruck by the famous author's reputation. Sweet, naive, and anxious to please, she "acts" in her scenes with him and evaluates them afterward. The novel progresses from courtship through marriage, with the husband jealous and suspicious, the young wife fun-loving and sociable. Söderström emphasizes her dedication to the art of acting.

Bosse's ambition to achieve success as an actress and acclaim from the public receives more attention in *Victoria,* subtitled *Novel of an Actress' Marriage.* Söderström takes as his starting point four familiar photographs of Bosse, in which her moods range from disdain to listlessness to determination. The story of the relationship with Strindberg is told this time from her point of view. Bosse is often tender and sympathetic toward her husband, but also calculating, strong-willed, and restless. The book ends after Harriet has stood outside looking up at Strindberg's apartment, where he is entertaining Fanny Falkner. As she rides away, Harriet enjoys seeing that people recognize her. If anyone were to ask who she is, she would answer, "a brilliant artist" who has "played a decisive role in Strindberg's life."[48]

Harriet Bosse also appears as a character in the play *Lunatic and Lover* by Michael Meyer, translator of Strindberg plays and author of a Strindberg biography. The script was commissioned by the British Broadcasting Corporation for a radio broadcast in 1977; stage versions were presented in 1978 and 1981. The three wives confront Strindberg at the start of the play. Frida accuses him of exaggerating and Siri accuses him of lying, but Harriet, milder and more sympathetic, says, "You don't distinguish between reality and fantasy." Harriet summarizes the torment of their relationship: "We loved each other, and hated each other."[49] She is the last character to speak to him, offering consolation: "Remember what you wrote? It is the chosen ones who suffer."[50] As have so many authors, Meyer leaves Strindberg in the spotlight and Bosse a secondary figure in the shadows.

Nanny Westerlund made her debut as an actress at the Swedish Theatre in Helsinki in 1910. More than seventy years later, for the same theatre, she wrote and directed a play entitled *August Strindberg and Harriet Bosse,* which had its premiere on 15 January 1982, with Veronika Mattsson as Harriet. Later the play was presented in Stockholm at the Strindberg Museum. The script begins with Harriet's first visit to Strindberg's apartment in 1900 and ends with him alone in 1908. Creating credible dialogue from the standard biographical material, Westerlund presents a brilliant, erratic playwright and a vigorous, rational actress. Harriet accuses Strindberg of taking refuge from people and his own feelings in an ivory tower, declaring: "I don't need an ivory tower. The theatre needs no ivory tower. The theatre deals with people, who talk directly to people. Now I have chosen my way, and it leads to the people."[51]

In 1985 Swedish television presented a film of the life of Strindberg in six parts, codirected by Johan Bergenstråhle and Kjell Grede from a script by Per Olov Enquist.[52] Strindberg was played by Thommy Berggren and Harriet Bosse by the Norwegian actress Anne Krigsvoll. Harriet is introduced as she speaks one of Puck's monologues, dressed in a fanciful flowery costume quite different from the original modest sailor dress. Enquist imagines an episode of confrontation and mutual sympathy with Siri during Harriet's guest appearance in Helsinki. The character of Harriet has brief moments as an independent personality and stage artist, but for most of the film, she is seen through Strindberg's imagination, becoming part of the confused hallucinations of his deathbed before the final vision of his mild and forgiving mother.

Although Ole Söderström concluded his novel *Victoria* with the image of a proud and independent Harriet, he is typical of dramatists, novelists, and scholars who wrote about the actress. His purpose was "to see *him* [Strindberg] still more clearly. I don't mean that Bosse is not interesting enough in herself, no human being is uninteresting. But she is truly interesting in a deeper sense . . . as Strindberg's wife; as the costar in *his* drama she remains unique. . . ."[53]

Bosse's role in Strindberg's life was important. As others have done, he often thought of her as a fictional character, as the fluid image shaped by his psychological need and artistic imagination. Having traced the life of the "real" Harriet Bosse through years of hard work, artistic achievement, and bitter disappointments, we are ready to draw together the threads that interweave her life with Strindberg's.

CHAPTER ELEVEN

Inspiration and Interpreter

Having presented an account of Harriet Bosse's work in the theatre, it is appropriate now to emphasize that aspect of her career that earned her acclaim as an interpreter of Strindberg. The role she played as his muse and as an image in Strindberg's poetry, essays, and fiction and his role as her mentor provided the foundation for her interpretations. We must view them as independent artists and as a man and woman caught up in a complex relationship.

This chapter provides a description of that relationship, from both a personal and professional perspective. A chronological history of Bosse's stage interpretations of Strindberg is organized into two sections—the minor roles and the major roles. The chapter—and the book—concludes with thoughts about Bosse's achievements and the transitory nature of her art.

STRINDBERG AND WOMEN

"Man loves and woman hates; man gives and woman takes; man sacrifices and woman devours." When consumed by resentment and loneliness, August Strindberg saw all men as the victims and slaves of women. While men longed for a peaceful domestic life, women seemed to be born "for the theatre, the restaurant, and the street."[1] At times bitterness and anger provoked him to create images of women as shallow and cruel, as sphinx or witch. However, there were other periods when Strindberg believed he could find happiness with a woman who conformed to his ideal of purity and perfection.[2] Harriet Bosse was asked by French director Gregory Chmara why Strindberg hated women. She answered: "He hated only deceitful, depraved women. For him, a woman should be above all a mother, and a friend to her husband."[3]

Scholars have traced Strindberg's yearning for an idealized woman to his childhood and to his memories of his mother, Ulrika Eleonora. She was a beautiful, pious woman, who died when Strindberg was thirteen. He was never able to achieve a harmonious relationship with his stepmother, Emilia Charlotta. Martin Lamm has written, "Throughout his life he felt a sense of loss and longed for an ideal maternal figure, an ideal maternal embrace, in which his stormy emotions could be cradled to rest."[4] In October 1901, when Strindberg felt that Harriet might never return to him, he wrote: "You were my child, my daughter. Now, mother, now I am your child."[5]

Harriet Bosse resembled other women in Strindberg's life. Her appearance was reminiscent of that of his mother, Frida Uhl, his sister Anna, and a Madame Lecain he had known in Paris. Like his first two wives, she was an ambitious career woman. The incarnation of youth, Harriet seemed to offer him a healthy alternative to a life of contemplation and loneliness. Perhaps their relationship was doomed because of a problem psychiatrist Donald L. Burnham has called the "need-fear dilemma." Strindberg seemed to feel safer when he kept people at a distance, even though he could occasionally be gracious to friends and family. The blissful moments he shared with Harriet were followed by disillusionment, for no real person could correspond for long to the ideal he imagined.[6]

MUSE AND IMAGE

Harriet Bosse was the inspiration for many of Strindberg's works. Sometimes he presented her in a favorable light; at other times he vented his anger or resentment by presenting an exaggerated, almost grotesquely negative image.

This book focuses on Bosse as actress and Strindberg as playwright, but we should remember that Strindberg was a prolific writer in other genres. Two of Strindberg's major works of poetry are associated with Bosse, "The Golden Eagle" ("Chrysaëtos" or "Guldörnen") and "The Dutchman" ("Holländaren"). In the works of fiction, echoes of Bosse's qualities and actions may be found in *Fairy Tales (Sagor)*, *The Roofing Feast (Taklagsöl)*, *Alone (Ensam)*, *Black Banners (Svarta fanor)*, *The Scapegoat (Syndabocken)*, and *Fair Haven and Foul Strand (Fagervik och Skamsund)*.[7]

Harriet Bosse's image blends with that of other women in his life, but often in the literary works—in all genres—her personality is distinct and episodes she shared with Strindberg are recognizable. Their separation in the early fall of 1901 stimulated his creativity, for example when writing the historical drama *Engelbrekt*. The images inspired by Bosse may be classified into two major groups: beautiful/idealized and distorted/negative. Sometimes more than one image appears in the same work, as in "The Dutch-man," where the woman is represented as a golden eagle and as a figure with all the harmonious beauty of nature and the spheres, as an enslaver whom he calls Omphale, and as a seductive temptress or Eve figure. Stereotyped as a bad wife, the image of Bosse appears in *The Black Glove (Svarta handsken), Alone,* and *The Roofing Feast.* Of the beautiful images associated with Bosse, the best-known examples from dramatic works are the virgin princess in *Swan White* and the angelic mediator in *A Dream Play.*

Many examples of Strindberg's use of his experiences with Harriet are found in his essays in the volumes of *The Blue Book (Blåboken).* Martin Lamm has noted that Strindberg shared many thoughts inspired by his third marriage, writing of its beauty and sacredness as well as of the impossibility of cohabitation. Describing a walk with his wife and child along the shore of an island, he wrote: "I had the impression it was heaven. Then, the dinner bell rang, and we were once again on earth, and directly after that, in hell."[8]

In *The Blue Book* Strindberg refers to the legend of "Undine" by the German poet Friedrich Heinrich Karl de la Motte Fouqué (1777–1843). He retold the story selectively to convey his disillusionment with women in general and with Bosse in particular. The sensitive, playful Undine is not unlike the nymphs and fairy tale princesses Bosse portrayed. Like Indra's Daughter, Undine has a powerful father, with a kingdom in the sea, who wants her to participate in human suffering by acquiring a soul. She does so by marrying the knight Huldbrand. Strindberg asks, "Who has not at some time encountered a little Undine?" The playwright compares himself to Pygmalion, breathing life into the beautiful, passive body. But, draining strength from the man, the woman develops the power to transform herself into a siren, an elf, or a witch. When the joy of being in love is replaced by the realities of marriage, the man realizes his bride has understood nothing he said but has simply been reflected in her lover's eyes. Like Undine, her counterpart drifts away. Olof Lagercrantz points out that the Undine image is a recurrent theme in Strindberg's thoughts. The work of a man of genius is not understood by his lover or spouse. Work triumphs, the woman is sacrificed, and her beauty remains a consoling memory.[9]

Other sections of *The Blue Book* develop the theme of domestic conflict, women's frivolity and inconstancy, and man's suffering and disillusion-ment.[10] When Strindberg describes telepathic contact with an actress performing at a theatre in Helsinki, window shopping with a young daughter while avoiding his estranged wife, or finding toys and withered bouquets in an attic, the memory of Harriet Bosse is vibrantly present.

Calling attention to Strindberg's use of autobiographical material under-lines Bosse's importance to him as an artist, but aesthetic considerations and a universal frame of reference are more important to literary critics today.

STRINDBERG AND THE ACTRESS

When Strindberg fell in love with Harriet Bosse, he found himself, iron-ically, in a situation with echoes from the past. He had encouraged Siri von Essen in her early efforts to become an actress and later to return to the stage, but his literary career, his wanderlust, and their family life took precedence over her theatrical career. In contrast to Siri, Harriet was well on her way to a successful career before she and Strindberg met. Once again he would have to tolerate the demands of a rehearsal schedule, the focusing of energy on performances, and the intrigues and social milieu of the theatre world. During their courtship and marriage, Strindberg tried to captivate and hold Harriet by doing what he could—through his writing and influence—to further her career. His efforts were in three areas: writing vehicles in which she might star, intervening on her behalf in casting decisions, and advising her about acting.

From the start of their acquaintance, Strindberg's courting of Harriet was interwoven with persuasion that she play The Lady in *To Damascus I* and Eleonora in *Easter*. He urged her to be patient during the frustration of playing bit parts, assuring her that he was "thinking and thinking" about how he could rescue her from that "purgatory."[11] He tried to obtain her agreement to play Kersti in *The Crown Bride* and the title role in *Swan White,* since he wanted to propose her for those roles to the management of the Royal Theatres (Dramaten and the Opera) and the Swedish Theatre. Strindberg could not understand her hesitation. Obviously not convinced that she should be identified primarily with Strindberg roles, Bosse was flattered by attention from other playwrights who were supposedly writing plays for her. During a crisis in April 1901 Strindberg went for a walk on Narvavägen and looked up at her bedroom window, overcome by tears. It tormented him that she could prefer any other playwright and fail to appreciate that his plays were innovative and modern. "You who are young should grow in the new century and turn your back on what has gone before. But you don't; instead you love the old, which was young twenty years ago!"[12]

Strindberg believed that Harriet Bosse could be as innovative in acting as he was in drama. In the 1880s, when he saw Sarah Bernhardt in Paris, he was appalled by her artificiality and mannerisms. Bosse shared with Strindberg a preference for motivated, believable acting. When *To Damascus* closed in December 1900, he sent her roses and wrote the oft-quoted challenge: "Become now for us the actress of the new century! You have allowed us to hear new tones, wherever you may have taken them from!"[13] Although he had failed in his own attempt to have a career on stage, Strindberg had interesting opinions about the art of acting. Some of them are known through the memos he sent to members of the Intimate Theatre.[14] He encouraged clear diction, spontaneity, and multidimensioned characterizations, as illustrated by his advice to Anna Flygare, when she was to play Alice in *The Dance of Death:* "Do not be too unsympathetic, so that you are lost to the audience! Keep all the sides of the role distinct; divide it up, so that it becomes a whole gallery of figures (incarnations) as people are in general. . . ."[15]

One of the earliest acting lessons to Bosse was given in his letter of 16 February 1901, when he ridiculed her "theory" that she could not play something outside her own experience: "You can't really mean that, can you? You have not experienced Puck's roguish tricks, or the dubious victories of *The First Violin,* have you? And yet you have acted them most successfully. Nor have you lived through The Lady's horrible Inferno journey with The Stranger (who now progresses with firm steps toward the cloister)."[16] If she was to prove worthy of the acclaim she had received, he urged her to reconsider and to discard her theory.

Bosse was greatly influenced by Strindberg; yet she was determined to maintain her individuality as an artist. She occasionally used the name Harriet Bosse Strindberg, but most of the time her independence was symbolized by use of her maiden name. At social gatherings Strindberg referred to her as "Fröken [Miss] Bosse."[17] Through the years of their relationship Strindberg molded her intellectual development. He also counseled her on how to interpret roles, but she recalled this being done only through letters, never in conversation.[18] Harriet was anxious about her throat, for she had been known to lose her voice during a performance. Knowing how worried she was, Strindberg wrote in August 1906: "Your throat? You speak too much, that is the whole thing; I remember when it began in *Venetian Comedy,* with straining and a new placement for your voice. You should get into one register and stay there."[19] Often Strindberg would offer Bosse guidance on how to negotiate with managers. For example, he encouraged her to try the engagement in Vienna with Richard Vallentin, and he pushed her toward working for Albert Ranft at the Swedish Theatre.[20]

Strindberg never went to Bosse's opening nights, even in his own plays. He would pace from room to room in their apartment during the performance, eager to hear about it when she arrived home. They read the reviews together, and he shared her disappointment or joy.[21] On rare occasions Strindberg attended the theatre with his wife, as when they saw Gerhart Hauptmann's *Beaver Coat (Bäfverpelsen)*.[22] Strindberg tried to show an interest in her work in plays by other dramatists, especially Mæterlinck. In June 1904 he read *Sakuntala,* in which she would appear the following spring, and was struck by the fact that the number of the book in the publisher's series, 2751, was similar to 5172, the number on his engagement ring. After spending a day reading the play, he commented, "It was a remarkable story which resembles ours."[23]

Some of Strindberg's ideas for Bosse's career never materialized. In 1905 he was enthusiastic about writing monodramas for her to perform "in a great new style to be played with screens." He planned to rewrite *A Dream Play* as a monodrama called *Indra's Daughter,* and to adapt dramas by other playwrights, such as *Macbeth* or Schiller's *Maria Stuart.* The performance of a play by one artist was in vogue at this time, partly because of August Lindberg's successful solo interpretation of *The Tempest.* Strindberg suggested to Bosse that she might appear at the auditorium of the Academy of Science (Vetenskapsakademien), as the Danish actress Charlotte Wiehe had done in 1904.[24] Realizing that the form of monodrama is extremely limiting, Strindberg proposed organizing a theatre ensemble with three people, and going on tour with Bosse to play "with screens and a curved backdrop."[25]

Harriet Bosse was the inspiration for several Strindberg plays that did not become part of her repertory. When he finished the history play *Engelbrekt* in the fall of 1901, he wrote to tell her, "It deals with us—with our parting—but grandly and lovingly—not a word of hatred, not a smile, no banality . . . Heavy as sorrow, the sorrow of the dead one still living."[26] "The Dutchman" is a fragment of a dramatic poem, a tribute to Harriet's beauty, with a tantalizing heroine named Lilith. Their marriage is mirrored in the sequence of infatuation, marriage, a mutual sense of imprisonment, and the woman's departure. *The Black Glove,* completed in 1909, traces its origin to an episode when Bosse lost a ring and suspected that a maid had stolen it. The wife in the play is beautiful but petty and irritable; an angel teaches her a lesson so that she will be ready to celebrate Christmas in the proper mood.

The most important role inspired, but never performed, by Bosse was Swan White. The play is a charming love story, written in 1901, at a time when Strindberg could easily visualize Bosse as a fairy-tale princess, the epitome of love and purity. Strindberg was eager to see Harriet in the lead, perhaps as her first major role after the birth of their daughter, but she never played it. Bosse interceded on behalf of the playwright, to persuade Jean Sibelius to compose music to accompany the play.[27] When the world premiere took place in Helsinki in 1908, Strindberg wrote to Bosse of "your Swan White, which I received from you, and you from me, and which you did not get to play."[28] The manuscript remained in Bosse's possession for many years, as a reminder of the happy months when she and Strindberg were in love.

BOSSE IN STRINDBERG PLAYS: MINOR ROLES

Harriet Bosse played eight Strindberg roles that may be considered minor, either because the character appears briefly or has a secondary function in the play, or because her interpretation did not receive a great deal of attention. The roles are discussed in chronological order, dating from the first known performance by Harriet Bosse.

Thérèse—7 September 1898

The first minor role belongs to Bosse's apprenticeship in Norway. She entered carrying a rat trap, according to the script, dressed in a robe, with her hair down. The character was Thérèse, youngest daughter in the naturalistic one-act play *Facing Death* (*Inför döden* in Swedish; *Ved dødens port* in Norwegian). The play was on a bill at the Central Theatre on 7 September 1898, with Hans Aanrud's *Stork* (*Storken*). Since Alma Fahlström had met the playwright in Paris, she probably felt a sense of mission in producing the first play by Strindberg to be presented on a Norwegian stage. With this early experiment in naturalism, Alma in part laid the foundation for her later achievement in directing Gorky's *Lower Depths*.

Written in 1892, *Facing Death* is one of a group of experimental plays that Stindberg labeled "out of cynical life."[29] There are familiar elements of family conflict. A long-suffering and bitter husband recalls the deceptions and injustices perpetrated by his deceased wife. Now he is ready to give up the struggle of running a boardinghouse in Switzerland, where he lives with three selfish and cruel daughters. Bosse played the youngest daughter, who is her father's favorite even though she lies, flirts shamelessly with a young lieutenant, and threatens her father with starvation. Not a typical sweet ingenue, Thérèse allowed Bosse to soften, show affection, and beg her father for forgiveness—before leaving him alone to die in the fire he sets so that his daughters may inherit his insurance money. Although Strindberg may have been inspired by *King Lear* when he wrote the play, the resulting small "tragedy in nine scenes" evokes distaste rather than pathos.[30]

Seen in relation to Bosse's other Strindberg roles, Thérèse is atypical in its harshness and pettiness. Always appreciative of Bosse's talent, Sigurd Bødtker wrote of the premiere, "As the youngest daughter Thérèse, Miss Harriet Bosse shows an ability for vigorously aggressive characterization, which one is inclined to believe is foreign to her: in the farewell scene with her father, where suddenly a bright daughterly instinct emerges from the darkness in her soul, Miss Bosse manages to give Thérèse's words a ring of touching helplessness."[31]

Emerentia Polhem—*21 August 1902*

Charles XII (Karl XII) is an unusual history play set in the years 1715–18, showing the warrior king toward the end of his life—weary, dejected, and bitter. Surrounded by advisors who do nothing to solve his political and economic problems, he is haunted by those who have suffered because of his actions. In act 4 the king, who has never married, encounters three challenging women. The most petty and foolish is Emerentia Polhem, a woman engaged to—but not at all fond of—the philosopher Swedenborg. Having vowed to bring the king to her feet, Emerentia presents herself to Charles against her fiancé's wishes. She attempts to charm him with a bouquet of flowers and a flattering speech. Although he finds her childish impudence diverting for a moment, the king is irritated when she throws herself at his feet. Later he carries through on his threat to tell Swedenborg that she is not worthy of him.

Strindberg wrote *Charles XII* in June 1901, during the weeks when Harriet was in Denmark without him. Later in the summer he confessed that he wondered whether she might have played with his feelings like Emerentia Polhem, and sworn to "see me at your feet."[32] Emerentia appears briefly, yet Strindberg wanted his wife in the role. Convinced that she would contribute to the success of the production, he asked the director, Emil Grandinson, to cast her as Emerentia. She was willing, but Dramaten postponed the premiere from 30 November 1901 until 13 February 1902, less than six weeks before the birth of Anne Marie. Having waited as long as she could, Bosse requested sick leave as of 3 February.[33] At the premiere Emerentia was played by Constance Sjöberg, and later by Margot Rolén, who would one day marry the provincial impressario Allan Ryding. Emil Grandinson won praise for his direction, and August Palme for an interpretation of the title role that endowed the unhappy, isolated ruler with tragic greatness.[34]

Harriet Bosse finally appeared in *Charles XII* at the start of the next season, giving three performances in August 1902. There was limited enthusiasm for the play and the production, so the assurance and vitality Bosse brought to the performance was welcome. In her hands the cameo role was artistic and believable. Bosse's Emerentia was not just a foolish child. She became "the intoxicating and dangerous woman the author visualized," combining exquisite beauty with treachery, her "laughter . . . as poisonous as it is bewitching."[35]

Biskra — 22 October 1902

Written in 1889 for his experimental theatre, *Simoon* was written to star Siri von Essen. Instead the intense one-act play was performed in Stockholm in 1890, but it proved difficult to produce successfully. Poet Gustaf Fröding praised its lyricism and dramatic form: "Revenge has perhaps never been depicted with such concentration and power as in this wild, fantastic work."[36] The play takes place in an Algerian sepulchre, into which the howling desert wind has blown sand. Biskra is determined to win revenge for the death of Ali. She assures her fiancé Youssef that her hate is "boundless as the desert, scorching as the sun, and stronger than my love."[37] Calling herself "despised, ugly, but strong," Biskra is confident that her skill in ventriloquism and hypnotism, combined with heat from the blazing sun, will achieve her purpose. The Zouave lieutenant Guimard enters, staggering and confused from the effect of the storm. Giving him sand instead of water to quench his thirst, Biskra drives Guimard to madness and death. She sings a haunting incantation (presumably to a melody composed by Strindberg), accompanying herself on the guitar. Youssef joins in the song from offstage. Her most effective strategy is to conjure images of the lieutenant's home and family, suggesting his wife's infidelity and his son's death. She even creates the illusion of Guimard's own corpse. The play ends in a mood of barbaric victory, as Youssef acclaims Biskra to be stronger than the violent storm — "stronger than Simoon." Strindberg considered the play a brilliant imitation of the work of Edgar Allan Poe.

As the companion piece to Thore Blanche's *Monument (Monumentet),* *Simoon* was performed at Dramaten for three evenings in October 1902. The combined bill was pronounced a waste of time for the audience and a failure for the theatre. Criticism of *Simoon* concentrated on the play more than the performance. Critics described it variously: "an unreadable horror- and robber-story," "a meaningless jest," "a scene of devastating and consuming fire," "bizarre form."[38] Those who did not totally dismiss the work found its effect powerful and nearly unbearable. In fact the audience could scarcely applaud when the curtain fell. "You sat and literally felt the hot sand of the desert storm in your mouth."[39]

The play required only fifteen minutes of playing time. *Stockholmsbladet's* critic found it too unpleasant and improbable to be worthy of Bosse's efforts. Nevertheless, the actress gave an intense performance that some found superb. According to the script, Biskra enters in a burnoose and kneels on a prayer mat to chant. Bosse wore a brown turban, red and white jacket, white vest, wide white pants, brown stockings, and sandals.[40] The costume suggested an Arabian style, but with a simplicity and a lack of adornment appropriate to Biskra's lower-class status. The critic for *Dagens Nyheter,* describing the character as "the fury of hate in the figure of a little Arabian girl," said Bosse's performance was so strong "one almost had to shield oneself against it." If the stage directions were followed literally, the actress drew on her musical talent to sing and play a guitar and flute. Another critic thought Bosse had captured Biskra's fanaticism, but that she did not create the proper fear in the audience, "and that was just as well, since otherwise there would have been panic." Even so, one reviewer wrote that the play was almost painfully frightening; afterward one had to "shake off the impression like the memory of a horrible dream."[41]

Harriet Bosse may have come "as close as possible to the author's intentions" in her "almost sublime" depiction of hate. Critics remarked that Bosse played with her usual intelligence, thoughtfulness, and poetic temperament. Sven Söderman considered *Simoon* "proof of this highly talented and technically perfect young actress' ability to create individual life and evoke fascinating moods." The atrocity in the action, which could have been repugnant, in Bosse's interpretation achieved "a conciliatory justification through her fanatic dedication and fatalistic faith." Vocal control was her primary means of dampening the horror. "She understood through delicate changes in her voice how to soften Strindberg's harsh speeches and round off many of their sharp edges."[42] In this instance Bosse's art seems to have surpassed her husband's.

Bertha—1919

Comrades (Kamraterna), a domestic comedy, was written when Strindberg felt the need for revenge against the outspoken champions of feminism whom he considered his enemies. His first version of the script, called *Marauders (Marodörer)*, was written in 1886; when published in 1888, the play was retitled *Comrades.* The leading characters are Axel and his wife Bertha, both painters. They have agreed to a nontraditional marriage in which each is a free individual. The husband secretly submits one of his works under his wife's name to a Paris salon competition. His generous gesture backfires when the painting wins. Bertha plans to celebrate what she thinks is her triumph and to gloat over her husband's defeat, only to discover it was her painting that the salon rejected. In the end Axel drives his wife out of the house and reclaims his male prerogatives. Strindberg preferred that Bosse not appear in his plays from the 1880s, but people considered Bertha's role quite suited for her talents.

Adolf Paul, a Finnish-Swedish writer, appears in fictional form as Ilmarinen in Strindberg's autobiographical novel *The Cloister.* In 1930 Paul wrote a book about Strindberg, presenting his own version of the events fictionalized in *The Cloister.*[43] Although Strindberg undoubtedly distorted episodes for the novel, he and others in the Berlin artists' colony in the early 1890s found Paul unpleasant and self-effacing.[44] Despite the negative aspects of their relationship, Paul remained interested enough in Strindberg's dramas to ask Harriet Bosse to appear in them in Berlin.

Paul visited Bosse, probably early in 1919, in her home on Narvavägen. She adamantly refused to appear on the Berlin stage, saying that no matter how well she might learn German, she would feel confined and her acting would suffer. Paul pointed out that Danish actress Betty Hennings and Finnish actress Ida Aalberg had both performed successfully in German, but Bosse is supposed to have declared, "I shall never play in a foreign language."[45]

If Paul's account is accurate, Bosse expressed interest in acting in a German film. Having recently made her screen debut in *The Ingmarssons*, she may have been contemplating the advantages of film as a medium for reaching foreign audiences. She proposed that Paul adapt one of Strindberg's plays for the screen. He suggested *Miss Julie*, but Bosse vetoed that idea—because she had promised Strindberg never to play Julie and because Asta Nielsen had already done the role on film. Bosse told Paul that the Strindberg heirs had decided not to release movie rights for any of the major plays. Only *Comrades* was available. Paul promised to undertake the project on behalf of a production company in Berlin for which he was artistic director. Once negotiations were completed, he set to work adapting the script to the visual medium of the silent film. Recalling that Strindberg had told of a first act that had been cut and woven into the action of the second act, Paul tried to recreate events that are only narrated in the play. If Paul had had access to the first version, *Marauders,* he would have discovered that it set a bright comic tone, satirizing the reversal of sex roles and fashions.[46]

Treated graciously while in Berlin, Harriet Bosse may have been unaware of impending financial catastrophe. The first two films produced by the small firm had used up most of their capital. It was impossible to meet commitments to the cast for salaries or to pay for settings and costumes ordered for *Comrades.* Luckily a businessman who owned a large cinema agreed to finance the production, but further problems with financing and legal rights proved as dramatic as anything the public saw on the screen. Despite complications after the film was edited, Paul sold it to investors for distribution in Sweden and Germany, identified as a production of Centaur Films.[47]

The director was Dr. Johannes Guter, whose movie career continued intermittently until 1944. One of his silent films was *Grand Hotel,* produced in 1927. In 1919 he was directing three other productions besides *Comrades.*[48] A critic observed that Guter used too many close-ups, thus restricting the Strindberg film. Hannes Bloch, the cinematographer, achieved sharp and clear images, but there were limited technical effects. Considering Harriet Bosse's description of working conditions, it is amazing that anyone could concentrate: "We are working in a big facility, where four other films are also housed. So you can understand that there is an infernal uproar here — next to us they are dancing and playing music, alternating with howls and pistol shots; God knows it isn't easy to collect one's thoughts during all this racket." Bosse found that the producers totally misunderstood Strindberg's conception of an intimate Bohemian party in the artists' studio. Instead they arranged a "grand gala — hundreds of people, large orchestra." The filming moved rapidly, for Bosse needed to be in Berlin only eighteen days.[49]

One of 480 films produced in Germany in 1919, *Kameraden* was released in October and first shown at the Tauentzienpalasttheater in Berlin.[50] It came at a time of "antiliterary" sentiment among filmgoers. *Comrades* was relatively popular, the Strindberg play produced most often in German theatres from 1905 to 1927.[51] The film was expected to appeal especially to viewers who had never experienced Strindberg on stage. Paul was credited with writing a film "which perhaps no longer has much in common with Strindberg's *Comrades,* but will succeed as a film." He used the text sparingly and toned down the unflattering presentation of women, so that only Bertha was seen in a negative light. One critic wrote, "The action is exciting, it flows well, and the ending is satisfying."[52]

Bosse's costar was Alfred Abel. He began his acting career in 1913, played in more than fifty major films, and directed four films before his death in 1937.[53] Abel was acknowledged to be an excellent partner for Bosse, and his acting was called "unsurpassable." He was praised for certain moments when an expressive smile or tired gesture suggested "the spirit of Strindberg."[54]

The character of Bertha as it appears in the play is an aggressive, selfish wife who fails to appreciate her husband's self-sacrifices. Bosse undoubtedly drew upon her familiarity with the stage version. However, while the play endows Bertha with a cruel and shallow personality, an extant still from the film gives a different impression: Harriet Bosse is dressed in a modest evening dress with a black cape and a feathered headpiece. She looks delicate and sad and is deferring to Alfred Abel, as though pleading for his good will, while he gazes straight ahead, looking sardonic and unsympathetic.

Bosse's remarkable acting seems to have been the most successful aspect of the film.[55] The critic for *Der Kinematograph* thought Bosse maintained the comical tone compatible with Strindberg's conception, but another critic thought she was too pathetic and guilty. Bosse had at her disposal the means of a mature actress. She used her skill to create an ordinary, middle-class woman who longs to be out in the world and to win recognition in artistic circles. Bosse made the character realistic, rather than theatrical. One critic assumed she was drawing on her own experience: "Twenty years ago this woman lived next to Strindberg, and today she bases her acting on her own life and experience."[56] Bosse was still learning silent film technique; one reviewer found she moved her lips too much. Still she was praised for her breeding, temperament, youthfulness, and "elegant and agile figure." She played naturally, sometimes expressing feeling through just the widening of her eyes.[57]

The film received a lukewarm reception in Sweden, where it was considered an interesting experiment. Having to read rather than hear the Strindberg dialogue was disappointing. "As a film the play is acceptable, but as a Strindberg film . . . it is too small a cage for such a large lion."[58] The Swedish critics found Harriet Bosse well suited for the role of Bertha, "with the right sort of softness and falsity." The critic for *Svenska Dagbladet* described Bosse as "the typical little Strindberg female parasite — sly, willful, seductive." While critics disagreed as to whether Bosse's performance was superficial or carefully thought through, she was praised for the wide range of her facial expressiveness and pantomime. Alfred Abel was well received by the Swedish critics, who suggested that he and Bosse could have been outstanding if they had worked with a more capable director.[59]

While making *Kameraden,* Harriet Bosse committed herself to five more years of movie making in Berlin.[60] Considering Adolf Paul's account of the legal and financial complications involved in marketing the film, one assumes that the company went out of business. If only Bosse's contract had been with a well-managed firm, her career might have developed in a new direction with international recognition.

Judith — September 1921

Strindberg's *Dance of Death (Dödsdansen)* is a play whose interest centers mainly on part 1 and the spiteful married couple, Edgar and Alice. Part 2 brings their dueling to an end when Edgar dies. It also introduces a younger generation, their daughter Judith and her cousin Allan. On first acquaintance Judith may seem to be a pleasant and saucy ingenue; during the play she leaves childhood behind and becomes a woman. Her life is complicated by the sparring and vengefulness of her parents, and we sense that in the future she might become just as heartless and manipulative as her mother. Strindberg thought Judith was a wonderful character, and he hoped that Bosse would play her. In the fall of 1921 while on tour with Allan Ryding, she finally did appear as Judith, a role which was by then out of her age range. It gave her the opportunity to play with intensity and a wide spectrum of emotions.[61]

The Lady — 15 October 1926

During their courtship Strindberg was eager for Bosse's reaction to the draft of *To Damascus III.* He wrote on 1 March 1901: "Come and tell me your impression of *Damascus III* before it is erased by something else. I regard your opinion so highly, since you played the role of The Lady, you understand."[62]

Twenty-five years later Bosse finally appeared in a production of *To Damascus III,* advertised with the title *The Cloister.* As one of Per Lindberg's productions at the Concert House Theatre, this was a major event but an experiment that was not completely successful. Making drastic cuts in the script, Lindberg did not achieve the grandeur and sweeping movement of his *Antony and Cleopatra* a month earlier, but he and designer Jon-And found a way to establish the abstract and ghostly atmosphere of the script with a rugged cubistic setting. On the large open concert stage the exterior scenes were played among platforms and three-dimensional triangular shapes suggesting mountains, lit in green and other hues typical of the palette of expressionistic theatre.[63] Some locations were indicated with projections, but interior settings were quite realistic and naive. Trying to match the visual expressionism with stylized acting was not effective. Speech patterns sounded unnatural and strained to some ears. The actors at times contended with the distracting and powerful effect of Ture Rangström's organ music in the background; still the tones of the organ added an inspiring and spiritual dimension to the production.[64]

The first two parts of *To Damascus* might be combined in one evening, but part III needs to be presented independently. It provides a kind of synthesis of the conflicts developed in the first two parts. Although the trilogy uses many episodes from Strindberg's brief marriage to Frida Uhl, experiences with all three wives are dramatized. Details of the relationship with Harriet Bosse may be discovered in part III, such as the husband's jealousy at hearing the tones of other men in her voice when the wife plays and sings banal melodies at the grand piano. Like Strindberg, The Stranger preferred that his wife play classics.[65] The autobiographical elements struck some Swedish critics as a shameful example of exhibitionism. The plays also represent an interesting experiment in style. Influenced by medieval drama, Strindberg in effect wrote "a monologue, divided for many voices, as when a musical motif is arranged for orchestra." The structure of the play also resembles the "bizarre logic" of a dream, in which The Stranger, a dramatic image of Strindberg, takes a pilgrimage where he encounters ghosts from his past as he wanders toward the refuge of the cloister.[66]

The production opened on 15 October 1926, with Olof Sandborg and Ingolf Schanche in the two major men's roles. Sandborg did not bring The Stranger to life convincingly. His performance was "natural and truthful," but rather weak and colorless.[67] Sandborg realized he had not been successful. He begged Lindberg not to judge him by this performance, since the role is difficult "and does not really lie within my range—unfortunately."[68] The dominating aspect of the production was Norwegian actor Ingolf Schanche's appearance as The Tempter, dressed with "satanic elegance" in top hat, tails, and gloves. With his flexible movements and expressive face,

Schanche established the "irony and bravura" in the role, broke up the rather monotonous tone of the performance, and brought clarity to the action.[69]

Probably no one in the audience saw Bosse simply as an actress creating a new role. They knew she had played The Lady in part 1 at Strindberg's request; they knew that she had lived through some of the marital discord in the play. Bosse faced a dilemma: Should she play the role in a way that was credible to her or as the author had imagined it?[70] Anders Österling wrote: "It is not easy to express a critical opinion about Harriet Bosse's interpretation of The Lady; the actress has a privileged relationship to the drama and maintains it honorably. All her inflections did not sound genuine; but the truth is that Strindberg also put into *To Damascus* a great deal that is false."[71]

Harriet Bosse seemed deeply moved during the performance, which affected the audience through its charm and the warmth of her vocal tones.[72] She was praised by Erik Wettergren for the naturalness and sincerity of the confrontations between The Lady and The Stranger: "In these scenes the busy lighting effects and staging faded away and what remained was an inspired confession from one who had been involved, but who now had achieved a distance that allowed her to speak quietly of what had happened."[73] Sven Stål asserted that to regard Bosse's participation as a kind of penance was inappropriate. The focus should be on her performance, where at least in her first scene she established "a tone which she had not used since the very start of her stage career. She spoke simply, unaffectedly, and the way in which she harmonized with the scenery was incomparably beautiful."[74]

Margit — October 1928

Sir Bengt's Wife from 1882 is a play about marriage, set in the early Reformation. The female lead of Margit was conceived as a vehicle for Siri von Essen, who played the role successfully. Despite the historical setting, this play is a response to *A Doll House,* concerned with the problems of marriage in the 1880s. Margit is a refined and high-strung young woman, who for a while is blissfully ignorant of her husband's problems. She and Sir Bengt come close to parting, but they decide they can continue their marriage on a more mature and honest basis.

In the fall of 1928 Harriet Bosse starred with Carl Johan Fahlcrantz in *Sir Bengt's Wife* on a Ryding tour which began in Gävle. The role of Margit had probably never been played this way before, according to Vagn Børge. In the first act Bosse was mature and technically proficient, but unconvincing as a novice in a convent. She was somewhat more believable as the happy bride in act 2, and she continued to build the character in the remaining acts. Combining coquetry and "tender maternal feelings," she built to the confrontation with her husband and "finally the victory over herself." Børge evaluated her performance as "interesting but not really harmonious." Per Lindberg as director and Jon-And as designer seemed to deserve more praise than did the cast.[75]

Gerda — *30 August 1933*

Storm Weather was the first "chamber play" intended for performance at the Intimate Theatre. Strindberg wrote the play in January and February 1907, when he realized that Harriet had grown away from him and that soon she and his daughter might be sharing their lives with another man. Gunnar Ollén calls this "his last 'warning drama'"—an effort to warn Harriet against remarriage.[76] The play takes place at an apartment house in a fashionable neighborhood, where a distinguished retired civil servant talks with his maid, his brother, and a confectioner. The Gentleman has settled quietly into a shadowy, emotionally detached existence—keeping life at a distance. On the second floor live a singer, his wife, and his daughter. For a week he has been running a rather questionable social club with drinking and gambling. Like a gathering storm, the complications of life threaten to shatter the play's quiet. The singer runs away with the baker's teenaged daughter, taking the child with them. Left behind is his young wife Gerda, who is the former wife of the aging gentleman. On her first entrance Gerda is disheveled and upset. She deserves some sympathy, for her husband has struck her, but she speaks coarsely about her former husband's reputation and their child's welfare. The Gentleman catches sight of Gerda during a sudden flash of lightning, but does not realize she is his new neighbor until she comes to ask him hesitantly for help. Gerda obviously is patterned on Harriet—being young, playing the piano, having worked at a theatre, having planted doubt about the paternity of her child, being jealous of The Gentleman's maid. In a highly dramatic scene, she begs him for help. The little girl is rescued and the teenager returns home safely, but The Gentleman has had ample opportunity to recall the suffering of his marriage and divorce. The play ends with a restoration of tranquillity, painful memories receding as the darkness of early autumn descends.

Contrary to Strindberg's wishes, Harriet saw the play at the Intimate

Theatre in the spring of 1908, and was distressed by the unflattering implications about Gunnar Wingård in the portrait of the singer. Strindberg protested in a letter on 8 April that he had advised her to stay away from *Storm Weather,* which he had written as therapy to rid his heart of Harriet and Anne Marie. Twenty-five years later Harriet seized an opportunity to show that the play should not be taken literally, but seen as a grotesque distortion written out of jealousy.

For its premiere at Dramaten on 30 August 1933, Alf Sjöberg directed *Storm Weather* in a style that appeared to have been influenced by Max Reinhardt's "ghost sonata" approach to Strindberg's chamber plays.[77] The set, designed by Sjöberg, was in an eerie shade of blue, creating a gloomy and supernatural atmosphere but failing to establish a distinct style. On the whole critical response was negative. Anders Österling called it "insensitive and unimaginative," and said not even Bosse's acting could save the production, which ran for six evenings in Stockholm before going on tour.[78] Carl Browallius was morose and stodgy as The Gentleman, playing a supporting role since the focus of attention was on Harriet Bosse. The production was likely to confirm the public's misconception of Strindberg's drama as dark and disharmonious.[79]

It had been Sjöberg's idea to ask Bosse if she would play a woman at the opposite range of the spectrum from the idealized goddess of *A Dream Play.* After he offered her the role, Bosse stared at him in astonishment and asked, "But don't you know that Strindberg was writing about me?" After considering the invitation, she agreed to be in *Storm Weather,* inquiring if it would be acted realistically. Sjöberg replied, "No, there are other ways." Bosse set one condition: that she be allowed through her interpretation to present a self-defense. She wanted to show that she understood how Strindberg, obsessed by a desire for revenge, had written the play as an indictment, presenting not a realistic portrait of her, "but his vision, his image." Sjöberg realized that the production would be several steps removed from reality: "an image of an image which is an image." At first it was difficult at rehearsals for Bosse to speak the dialogue. The only way she could handle the irrational material was by developing a very obvious stylization. Sjöberg knew this would probably kill the "human tone" in the play, and indeed the effect was unpleasant.[80]

Photographs show that Bosse made herself look like a caricature of a fallen woman, with garish makeup and a sleazy costume of verdigris green and poppy red. In fact she allowed herself to look less attractive here than in any other role she played. Reviews described her as "poisonous," "a demon," "sensual and horrid."[81] As though pursued by the Furies, she played with too much pathos and hysteria. Obviously critics hesitated to fault her interpretation, which drew upon "inner authority" and "so many costly experiences." It was diplomatically suggested that as part of the realistic group of characters, "a rather more bourgeois profile would also have been appropriate for Gerda."[82]

BOSSE IN STRINDBERG'S PLAYS: MAJOR ROLES

The Lady—19 November 1900

The world premiere of *To Damascus I* on 19 November 1900 is of interest to theatre historians more because of its scenic and lighting effects than because of Harriet Bosse's performance. Strindberg had many suggestions for director Emil Grandinson on how to achieve and sustain the mood of this "dream play" through music, limited intermissions, and smooth scene changes. The sets were placed on an inner stage behind a false proscenium. On photographs Bosse's petite figure in the prim costumes is seen against painted backdrops—the town square by the church, the waves of the sea, imposing mountains. There is also a famous role portrait from the hotel room scene that is a work of art in itself. She is dressed in a simple, dark velvet dress; her hair is parted in the center and softly frames her face. She looks down at a flower, her luminous beauty more striking in close-up than when she is surrounded by the large painted sets from the Grabow atelier.[83] We see that Harriet Bosse endowed The Lady (Damen) with sweetness and quiet charisma.

All episodes of *To Damascus* are concentrated on the central character, The Stranger, and seen through his eyes. Retracing his life in a process of humiliation, he goes through mystical stages of self-examination reminiscent of a medieval morality play. His encounter with The Lady at the beginning of the play is both playful and serious, "one of the most sublimely poetic scenes in dramatic literature."[84] She is willing to accompany him on the pilgrimage, becoming his wife and suffering through episodes based on the marriage with Frida Uhl. The Lady is not an individualized character, for she represents mythical figures such as Eve and a madonna who leads The Stranger to reconciliation—to the door of the church. It was easy to be engulfed by the serious mood of the play, but Strindberg assured Bosse that a smile and "a little of Puck" would be appropriate for her character.

It is doubtful that Bosse used any of Puck's playfulness as The Lady. Critics commented that she was calm, subdued, and intelligent. Bosse was developing her own individual style, but her calm movements and quiet speech were coached by Grandinson. He helped her emphasize the neutrality of the character revealed in the line "I am nothing." This speech was chosen by the director as the key to The Lady; he instructed Bosse to speak it "with a strange, deliberate, half smile."[85] Bosse's method of acting made August Palme's portrayal of The Stranger seem warmer and more human, but also somewhat melodramatic. Not everyone was ready for the new style: Miss Bosse "should have been less reserved in order to succeed fully. The theatre has a couple of other artists who would have been suited for this character, but Strindberg himself had wanted the young, talented actress." The fact that she was young and inexperienced was mentioned in several reviews. This was a difficult play, so intense and serious that the audience hesitated to applaud. After the final curtain they called for the playwright, but he was not there to accept their acclaim.[86]

Strindberg was grateful for the efforts of everyone involved in the world premiere. He cherished memories of the production, sometimes referring to himself as The Stranger and Harriet as The Lady.[87] Bosse realized that she had not been ready for the role, stating years later "that The Lady in *To Damascus* exceeded my capacity and that I had only been partly successful in my interpretation of this role."[88] Nevertheless, Strindberg was delighted with his protégée. A few days after the opening he wrote to August Palme to ask for photos, "especially of Miss Bosse something good, preferably in the black-white suit."[89]

When Bosse played The Lady in Helsinki in 1904, she had become more assured and the play more respected. One of the most detailed reviews was written by Gunnar Castrén, who appreciated both the mysticism and the reality of the seventeen symmetrically arranged tableaux. Although The Stranger, played by Konrad Tallroth, should have been the central figure, most of the attention focused on Bosse. With delicacy and subtlety, Castrén wrote, she established "a pure, clear beauty—a figure controlled by a strange quiet rhythm which slipped in among the agony and agitation."[90] Another Helsinki critic described the stylization, her intelligence, her graceful movement, "the large, deep eyes which spoke their clear language; the pale face, surrounded by dark hair"—every detail contributing to a beautiful image of the mysterious character. Yet another critic called Bosse "a vision, elevated and mild as the holy Madonna."[91]

Eleonora—4 April 1901

Even before *To Damascus I* opened, Strindberg was eager to persuade the management of Dramaten and Bosse herself that she was the perfect choice to play the sensitive daughter in *Easter,* which he wrote in the autumn of 1900. Admitting his "weakness for Miss Bosse," Strindberg praised her unique qualities of "poetic charm and 'seriousness'" and childlike appearance, which would perfectly suit "a girl with braids down her back." He requested Nils Personne's permission to let Bosse read the play, remarking that a role can never be given out too soon if an actor is to allow a character to grow and mature slowly.[92]

While writing this drama of a family haunted by their father's disgrace and fearful of creditors, Strindberg was inspired by his unfortunate sister Elisabeth, who was confined to a mental hospital in Uppsala. After she died in 1904, Strindberg remarked that he had felt as though she were his twin. Eleonora has also been confined to a hospital, but she unexpectedly returns home for the Easter weekend to bring healing peace and love to her family.

The complex and sensitive character at first intimidated Bosse. To encourage her, Strindberg suggested a long list of books she should read by Balzac, Swedenborg, Mæterlinck, and others. He offered advice about Eleonora's scenes with the schoolboy Benjamin, to whom she should be kind and gentle, prattling like a girl playing "little mama." He advised her to convey the serene essence of Eleonora's nature, creating an impression of brightness, gentleness, and faith in a forgiving God. Making the same allusion he had with The Lady, Strindberg encouraged Bosse to use some of the playful, humorous quality he had admired when he saw her as Puck. He warned her not to give a traditional rendering of someone mentally ill, but of this he was sure there was no danger, "since you seem to be born with all the thoughts of the new century."[93] Although Bosse pleaded to have the role given to an actress with more experience and technical skill, Strindberg charmed her into continuing the role—and becoming his fiancée.

Emil Grandinson directed the production, faithfully following the script without cuts or changes. The first reading rehearsal was held 4 February 1901, and rehearsals on stage began 11 March. When a reporter asked about the new play, Bosse said: "I have never before read anything so beautiful."[94] In all there were nineteen rehearsals, more than usual at that time.[95] *Easter* had its premiere at a matinee on Maundy Thursday, 4 April 1901. Actually the production was not completely successful, although Bosse was praised for her beautiful performance.

In critical commentary we discover two dichotomies: one between sides of Eleonora's character and the other between styles of acting. Eleonora is viewed by most critics as an original and exquisite character and by some as the only justification for performing the play. An actress must present the naive, innocent, optimistic childlike nature of the personality and also show the visionary, hypersensitive, Christ-like identification with the suffering of her family and all of creation. Though burdened with sorrow, Eleonora possesses a glowing faith that promises comfort and atonement. The tension in styles was between what the critics called "natural" and what they considered "stylized." Bosse's determination to play in a restrained, subtle style was disconcerting to some members of the audience. The critic for *Social-Demokraten* found the production underrehearsed and the play itself puzzling. For him the "artificiality" of Bosse's interpretation simply added to the confusion. Actually her approach was compatible with Grandinson's, as Ingrid Hollinger has explained: "One can assume that he and Harriet Bosse found it easy to work together—they were both striving in the same direction, away from grand acting for effect and toward consistency, clarity, simplicity."[96]

Opinion was divided about the effectiveness of Bosse's voice. Tor Hedberg thought it sounded strained, tiresome, and false, but other reviewers described her spontaneous and sincere line-reading and sweet voice.[97] There was more agreement on her physical expressiveness. Blocked by Grandinson to move restlessly, she presented imaginative and exquisite details of pantomime. On the line that begins, "Poor daffodil," for example, she walked behind Benjamin, caressed the flower pot, and pressed it to her breast.[98] Bosse's performance moved the audience to tears and evoked a warm tribute at the final curtain. The delicacy and mysticism of her portrayal are captured in a role portrait showing her in a simple striped blouse, hair framing her face, eyes lowered, and hands held as though in prayer.

Harriet Bosse kept Eleonora in her repertory until 1930, playing the role many times in many places. In Finland in 1906 she presented successfully the two sides of the character: the shy, frightened girl who has matured too soon because of the suffering she has witnessed, and the abnormally sensitive, clairvoyant mystic. Her voice, they said, was like the delicate and trembling tone of a violin. Others' performances in the production seemed pale in comparison with Bosse's radiant portrayal.[99] Clearly, in these early years Harriet Bosse as Eleonora was what Sven Stål has called "a miracle of inner and outer beauty."[100]

Continuing to play Eleonora when in her forties and fifties, Bosse was an impressive artist more than the embodiment of a saintly child. *Easter* had been the most popular play in the repertory of Strindberg and Falck's Intimate Theatre. Anna Flygare was so natural and inspired in the role that people recalled her beautiful performance, especially her wonderfully expressive eyes, to Bosse's disadvantage during the revival of *Easter* at the new Intimate Theatre in 1921. Bosse was too calculated, the shift from the childlike to the visionary too obvious, the naïveté too artificial. It was conceded that her playing was brilliant, though lacking spontaneity and charm.[101] During her visit to Gothenburg in 1921 H. Wigert-Lundström wrote: "Through the years she seems to have become even simpler and more heartfelt. Her voice still has its quiet music and can both rejoice and lament as before, with just a minute shift of pitch and volume."[102] Critics in Copenhagen in April 1925 saw too much technique and refinement in her performance, yet they credited Bosse with bringing out the fine qualities of the script and creating a reverent mood.[103] Obviously it can be misleading to summarize reviews, for there is rarely concensus when individuals respond to a performance. While her technical mastery may have grown more pronounced, Bosse always presented a beautiful interpretation of Eleonora.

Eleonora was perhaps Strindberg's most sympathetic portrait of a woman, and Harriet Bosse will always be remembered as the first actress to bring her to life. Following a rehearsal of *Easter* at the Intimate Theatre seven years after the world premiere, Strindberg noted in his diary, "Flygare played Harriet's role."[104]

Kersti—24 April 1906

Strindberg wrote the role of Kersti in the fall of 1900 for his daughter Greta, who eventually played it successfully. After he became aware of Bosse's talent, he wanted her to play the tormented girl in the 1901–2 season. During their courtship he waited for Bosse to agree to accept the role. He had sent her the manuscript hoping she would like it, reassuring her that Kersti is not "incurably wicked." The playwright told Bosse that he was trying to emulate Mæterlinck and enter into his "wonderful realm of beauty, omitting analyses, questions and viewpoints, seeking only beauty in depiction and mood."[105]

Strindberg submitted the play to Chamberlain Axel Burén at the Opera, who decided the script was more appropriate for the dramatic stage. Strindberg also talked to Nils Personne of Dramaten about a production. Before he began campaigning on Bosse's behalf, he asked her to sing a simple song, so that he would know she could do the folk melodies in the play. Her ability to sing was not, however, as important as the "primitive essence of tragedy" that he felt only she could bring to the role.[106] In a letter on Easter Monday, 8 April, Strindberg expressed his humiliation and jealousy of other playwrights because she was keeping him waiting for an answer about Kersti. Harriet Bosse did not have an opportunity to play in *The Crown Bride* until her guest appearance in Finland in April 1906. She repeated the role in 1907, 1917, and 1918.

The Crown Bride is a romantic play, inspired by folk music and a vogue for the culture of the Dalarna area. In its setting, the murder of an infant, and the imprisonment of the child's mother, the play bears a relationship to the film *The Ingmarssons*. Although Strindberg's first impulse was to write a bright play like his *Midsummer (Midsommar)*, *The Crown Bride* evolved into a haunting treatment of guilt. Kersti and Mats have a child, which she kills so that she can marry wearing the silver crown symbolizing virginity. Confessing her crime at the wedding, she is sentenced to prison, and the young couple's families revive an old feud. Seeing Christ in a vision, Kersti finds forgiveness and peace of mind. After she drowns in an icy lake, the families are reconciled. Strindberg had grand ideas for the setting and special effects, but they were almost impossible for a theatre to achieve in the early part of this century. He also tried a unique approach to the dialogue, avoiding the authentic Dalarna dialect by using what he called an "Icelandic" style to give the effect of peasant speech.

The world premiere of *The Crown Bride* took place on 24 April 1906. Bosse deserves credit for the event, for she proposed the play to Conny Wetzer when negotiating about the repertory for her second visit to Helsinki. In early January she suggested opening with *Pelléas and Mélisande*, continuing with *A Midsummer Night's Dream*, and "then *The Crown Bride*, which I should be very much interested in doing; it is the most beautiful [play] written on the depiction of Swedish folk life. I am sending the book, in case it should also interest you to read both the other plays in the same volume. Staging *The Crown Bride* is certainly a little complicated, but not *expensive*."[107] Gunnar Wingård played the male lead, Mats, and Ida Brander did the challenging role of the midwife. Bosse's admirer Gunnar Castrén wrote eloquently of the play and the performance, which he deemed "a great success." Bosse's Kersti was as excellent as her Juliet and Eleonora, and yet a fresh and individual character. "Fru Bosse's greatest gift is perhaps her captivating, pure lyricism, and it flowed here as clearly as ever, but in new forms and new tones: it was stronger, with more of the feel of fresh air than in previous roles. . . ."[108] Other reviews praised the beauty and rich details of her work, the stages of suffering, and the final regaining of peace of mind and reconciliation with God.[109]

When the play was produced at the Swedish Theatre in Stockholm on 14 September 1907, Bosse, Wingård, Ida Brander, and Ernst Malmström all repeated their roles from the Helsinki premiere. Critical reaction was mixed about both the play and the performance. The six tableaux were divided by two intermissions. Although the program listed the performance time from 7:30 to about 10:30 P.M., the audience actually did not leave until almost midnight. Director Victor Castegren was criticized for using lighting that was too dim. There was little fault to find with Harriet Bosse. Bo Bergman described the memorable image of her face frozen in anxiety, with her eyes staring blindly. "The diction was, as usual, exemplary."[110] Carl Laurin remarked that she was not a convincing peasant, but "a suffering and tormented woman bearing the millstone of the pangs of conscience. . . ."[111]

The Crown Bride is a play with music. Strindberg used authentic folk melodies and contributed a composition of his own. While reviews do not comment on Bosse's singing voice, one assumes that she sang Kersti's songs. One of the most attractive scenes takes place at dusk. The mother has left Kersti alone, reminding her to say evening prayers. She plays on the *lur,* a birchbark horn used by country women to call the cows. Actually Bosse only held the instrument while someone played a French horn backstage.[112] Then an antiphonal effect begins, as Mats sings a lullaby about the child sleeping in the forest and she answers. Kersti's part in the key of E minor is a charming melody that would not have made undue demands on someone who had appeared in a number of recitals while earning her diploma in voice.

In October 1917 Bosse appeared as Kersti at the Lorensberg Theatre in Gothenburg. Director Gustaf Linden succeeded in capturing the authentic Dalarna milieu as well as Strindberg's mysticism in beautiful stage pictures. The production as a whole, as well as its star, was warmly praised. John Atterbom wrote a detailed description of specific moments:

her tormented pain when she holds the little dead child to her breast, or the endlessly suffering expression which came over her face when everything seemed to break within her, the rigid apathy which gripped her and made her insensitive to all the harsh words which were hurled at the unfortunate girl, finally the glow of understanding which brightened the pained expression and radiated her whole being when the help comes from above in the bright image of the white child.

Atterbom went on to describe other moving episodes, building to the high point of Bosse's performance when, "freed from her chains, she sinks to her knees with thanks to the Highest," the religious mood reinforced by swelling tones from an organ. At the close of the performance there were two minutes of silence before the applause began. Then Harriet Bosse was called out for ten curtain calls and inundated with flowers.[113]

When *The Crown Bride* was produced at Dramaten in 1918, the musical score combined folk melodies and selections from an opera written by Ture Rangström. Olof Molander did not like the weak, gentle character of Mats, but he was flattered that director Tor Hedberg wanted him in the role. Harriet Bosse was alarmed and wrote to Hedberg that she would almost rather not do the play at all. It was being scheduled too late, "since *The Crown Bride* is absolutely too serious for a spring play. . . . I think the whole thing is unfair—so much more since I have just found myself having to play opposite actors who will *not* be advantageous either for my part or the play."[114] She had to make the best of the situation. This turned out to be Molander's last role before he suffered facial paralysis and was forced to give up his acting career.[115] On the whole the critics reacted more favorably than they had in 1907. Mysterious and frightening effects were emphasized by unusual lighting in shades of green and red.[116] Bo Bergman called the play "a national poem by our most national genius."[117] Maria Schildknecht was praised for her striking and grotesque portrayal of the midwife. Harriet Bosse's performance was admirable and deeply moving, although it struck one critic as too "intellectual" in the early scenes.[118] Most reviews recalled Bosse as Kersti in 1907, finding that she now played with more depth.

In her role gallery Kersti must rank high among Harriet Bosse's achievements. Her musical voice, expressive pantomime, and emotional power brought to life the heroine of the play Strindberg called "the most Swedish" of all that he wrote.

Indra's Daughter—17 April 1907

Strindberg considered *A Dream Play* his greatest drama. The Oriental quality of Harriet Bosse's beauty inspired him to create the role of Indra's

Daughter, a goddess who is sent to earth by her father to hear and interpret the laments of mankind. She wanders through a world in which time is distorted and real objects are fantastically transformed from scene to scene to create the atmosphere of a dream. By assuming the identity of a human being named Agnes, she experiences the constraints and disillusionment of marriage. She encounters several characters—the Officer, the Lawyer (her husband), the Poet—who guide her through the maze of human suffering. At the end the Daughter presides over a ritual fire and leaves earth, promising to convey the prayers of mankind to her father.[119] Details from Bosse's life with Strindberg appear, primarily as the Officer waits outside the theatre for Victoria, the opera singer who never appears, while the Officer ages and his bouquet withers. The playwright had waited at the Dramaten stage door for Siri twenty years before he found himself meeting another actress wife at the same place. Strindberg used in the play a door with a puzzling aperture shaped like a four-leaf clover, which Bosse knew that he had seen at the theatre.

A Dream Play evolved as Strindberg longed for Harriet to return to him and await the birth of their child. He sent a letter on 12 September 1901: "I am writing *The Growing Castle*—grand, beautiful, like a dream . . . It is, of course, about you—Agnes—who shall liberate the Prisoner from the castle."[120] Bosse's return and their divorce intervened before *A Dream Play* was produced in 1907 at the Swedish Theatre in Stockholm. By then Strindberg had added a prologue set in heaven, believed to be part of the monologue "Indra's Daughter" planned for Bosse.[121] The play was an innovative masterpiece in symphonic form, making technical demands beyond the resources of the Swedish Theatre and the directorial imagination of Victor Castegren. Its visual richness and dreamlike atmosphere would be better realized by later directors, including Max Reinhardt, Olof Molander, and Ingmar Bergman. Castegren rejected Strindberg's suggestions to use projections and limelight spots and relied on limited lighting, painted backdrops by Carl Grabow, and a false proscenium of red poppies to suggest the dreamlike environment. He neglected to suggest that objects in one scene are transformed into elements of following scenes. The director admitted to Strindberg a few days after the premiere that the sets and lights were not successful.[122]

Because the production was ambitious and the script unique, critical comments tend to deal with the 1907 production in broad terms. There was nearly a consensus that the play did not belong on stage. The three major men's roles were played by Ivan Hedqvist (the Poet), Ivar Kåge (the Officer), and Tore Svennberg (the Lawyer). The cast seems to have been at a loss as to how to act in a "dream play." Some used stylized speech; others spoke naturally. Harriet Bosse's performance received brief critical mention; yet we can sense its spiritual qualities from extant role portraits and recordings she made later. She wore an unadorned, shapeless white gown. All attention must have been on her serene face, distinctive hair style, elaborate earrings, metal ornament decorating her forehead, as well as on the lyrical intonations of her compassionate and poetic speeches.[123] Tor Hedberg found Bosse's diction "empty and strained" at times, but in the grotto scene "it was elevated to great beauty." Bo Bergman wrote that Bosse was most in harmony with the spirit of the play: "Her pure diction shone as always, and her soft, slightly swaying walk had the right ethereal quality. . . ."[124]

There had been a gentle snowfall on the morning of 17 April. That evening, as usual on the occasion of a premiere, Strindberg waited at home for news. He placed a laurel wreath on the bust of Beethoven, in gratitude for the music accompanying the drama. At 11:00 P.M. a telephone call from the theatre announced that the performance had gone well.[125] After twelve performances Harriet Bosse never appeared in *A Dream Play* again, but it remained close to her heart.[126]

Henriette — 27 April 1916

Bosse's last appearance in a Strindberg play was as Henriette in *Crimes and Crimes* in the fall of 1936. With the costumes and setting updated to the 1930s and Bosse looking sultry and dangerous, the performance demonstrated once again the charisma of her personality and the highly polished craftsmanship she had mastered. Sten Selander praised her authenticity and naturalness: "No one masters the special Strindberg style so completely in every detail as she does. And what superb diction fru Bosse has. She succeeded fully in getting you to forget the sound of the writing desk which Strindberg's language . . . often has, and made the speeches sound almost natural."[127]

Crimes and Crimes, written in 1899, exemplifies Strindberg's fascination with the power of the mind to affect human destiny through wishes and thoughts. The central character in this four-act "comedy" is Maurice, a writer who is having a play produced successfully in Paris. During the course of the action he neglects his devoted mistress and child and whiles away some time with Henriette, an alluring and demonic woman. The death of the child, which for a while is suspected to be a murder, brings Maurice a sense of guilt and causes Henriette to reflect upon the harm others may have suffered because of her malice and amorality. In a humiliating scene she is accused by a policeman of being a prostitute. Henriette and Maurice consider marrying, but realizing that would be torment, they part. Henriette leaves to come to terms with her conscience, and Maurice starts a new life of worldly success and spiritual rebirth.

Harriet Bosse had been impressed by Augusta Lindberg's interpretation of Henriette in the world premiere in 1900. She did not want to do the role—"for personal reasons"—when she received the assignment at Dramaten in 1916.[128] The production, which opened 27 April, was directed by Gustaf Linden, and Ivan Hedqvist played Maurice. Whenever Bosse played Henriette, critics were divided on one main issue: whether she was successful in conveying both the seductive abandon of the first part of the play and the introspective penitence of the latter part. In 1916 her work in the restaurant scene of act 2 was described as "the high point of her psychologically thorough but intuitively spontaneous acting. The scene with the champagne . . . has a distinctive realism in a kind of half visionary chiaroscuro, which truly sends shivers down the spectator's spine."[129] Critics did not agree on what they wanted of Henriette. Bosse was too sweet and childlike for Henriette, according to Bo Bergman. She had "sensual allure and charming inflections," but she was too soft and helpless to be the least bit "demonic."[130] Another critic found her cheerful and uncorrupted but somewhat vulgar in the first part of the play, so that later she was unconvincing as a penitent.[131]

That spring Bosse played Henriette in Oslo, where Sigurd Bødtker pointed out how different her interpretation was from that of Johanne Dybwad, whose unhappy fate was foreshadowed from the first moment she appeared. Bosse was a much more lighthearted Parisian lady.

Her Henriette stayed within the frame of the Parisian milieu. She let herself be tempted by life. She followed Maurice's voice because it called to her—why should there be negative consequences—? For that reason Henriette's inner being was *surprised* when the misfortune occurred. Only afterward did she give in to it with despair and patience. Fru Dybwad's Henriette responded to the misfortune as if it were expected. She screamed in opposition which she knew was to no avail.[132]

From Bosse's tour with Ryding in 1921, an extant photograph shows her dressed in a contemporary décolleté evening dress, smoking a cigarette. She was totally believable in the early seductive scenes, with her "half-open mouth, the enticing, passionate eyes, the cat-like movements of her whole body." The final moments were effective also, as her "pale face shone with the beautiful melancholy of a resignation one cannot forget."[133]

Bosse played Henriette at Dramaten again in 1924 for the seventy-fifth anniversary of Strindberg's birth and next did the role at the Dagmar Theatre in Copenhagen in 1925, where one critic saw her as a seductive Bohemian type from a bygone era. *Berlingske Tidende* found her more successful in the first half of the play, with its erotic passion. *Politiken* praised her both as the siren of early scenes and later when "she was no longer the extroverted Delilah. Her deathly pale face stiffened, she cried without tears, transformed herself into the tragic muse."[134]

By the time Bosse played Henriette for Dramaten and the traveling Swedish National Theatre in 1936, she was almost sixty, yet, as Carl Björkman wrote, "Who calculated Harriet Bosse's age?" She played the restaurant scene with "artistic enthusiasm" and was "neither too old nor too young." Bosse looks dynamic on a photograph where she stands in a dark, sequined evening dress, her head and arms flung back in abandon. Uno Henning kneels before her, his arms around her waist and his head to her midriff. Gunn Wållgren has described her in that production: "She made an unforgettable impression when she entered; everyone was drawn to her as to a magnet."[135] On the key issue Olof Hillberg has written that she brought out "both the hardness of the type of woman who will crush everything in her path, and the mood of penitence which emerges from the transformation of her mind."[136] This complex image was the last a theatre audience saw of Harriet Bosse in a play by Strindberg. Alf Sjöberg directed the play in what was called "a lightly subdued Strindberg style." How appropriate in the role of Henriette to see Bosse, the artist who was "to the very highest degree identical with the Strindberg style."[137]

Christina — 23 March 1926

In September 1901 Strindberg wrote *Queen Christina*, one of his impressive and highly original groups of plays on figures from Swedish history. It served as an outlet for frustration about his failing marriage and as part of his strategy to win back Harriet Bosse. Letters during the separation in late summer reveal his enthusiasm about the new script and his eagerness to discuss it with Harriet. He sent her progress reports as each act was finished, and he wished especially that she would visit and talk about the ending of the play. Strindberg suggested books for her to read about the queen, who reigned from 1644 to 1654, and he asked her to study portraits—but only beautiful ones from Christina's younger years. Theatregoers remembered Lina Sandell the previous year as an aging, ugly Christina in *A Phantom* by Knut Michaelson.

Strindberg knew how to appeal to an actress: this would be the greatest and most profound woman's role ever written, one for which he was using "a completely new technique." Amy van Marken claims that the "new technique" is revealed in the 212 unusually detailed stage directions Strindberg provided for Christina, revealing the psychological state of the character by suggesting gestures, actions, facial expressions, line readings, and pauses for the actress.[138] He promised she would get to wear five beautiful costumes, including a masquerade dress as Pandora that they had considered using in *Swan White*. Nils Personne received the manuscript before the end of September. Strindberg hoped that Queen Christina would be the first part Bosse would play after the birth of their child, unless she preferred Swan White, but Dramaten never featured her in either play. In his exuberance Strindberg imagined that Bosse could create this great role in Germany and go on to play Christina in Denmark and Norway. He would immediately have the play translated into French so that she could also play the role in Paris.

Although Strindberg was inspired by his love for Harriet when writing this play, he also drew upon negative feelings, especially his sense that she was like an actress in real life, guilty of flirtation, intrigue, and deception.[139] Shortly before her marriage to Wingård, Strindberg reminded Bosse that he had always understood her personality and inclinations: "In *Christina* I have explained it."[140] The queen is really an "actress," playing roles for her courtiers, giving in to irrational impulses, but as her abdication draws near in the final scenes, she acquires dimensions of greatness. Christina is surrounded by men, advisors and admirers whom she treats variously, as she plays the roles of imperious ruler, irresponsible child, and yielding lover. She is most dignified and serious with Klas Tott, but in the end she will face the future alone.

Strindberg was right. Christina was a great role, and many Swedish actresses have brought her to life. The first was Manda Björling at the Intimate Theatre in 1908, in a production condemned by critics because they disliked the play. Influenced by authentic portraits, Björling used makeup to convey the ugliness of the real Christina. She was tall and majestic, and the playwright advised August Falck to have her play the role "like an Amazon" but to make the character pleasant. The dramatist had visualized a petite Christina—like Bosse in size. In 1911 Strindberg wrote to

Tor Hedberg that the role had been written for Bosse and that she was the only actress who could interpret the role.[141] Unfortunately, Bosse never during Strindberg's lifetime played the role about which he wrote: "What luck for the unfortunate queen that I still possessed the beautiful image of yourself in the portrait I have of you—and . . . in my heart—now that I have portrayed her. And that you, as an actress, are here with us! (The new century's!)"[142]

On 23 March 1926, Harriet Bosse demonstrated how brilliantly she could play Christina. She did the role at the Lorensberg Theatre in Gothenburg, and later on tour with Allan Ryding. The femininity, sense of isolation, playfulness, and tension of the complex personality were all conveyed. The production, directed by Rudolf Wendbladh, was successful, with the possible exception of the last act. Bosse evoked sympathy for Christina's "struggle between the woman and the queen, in which the woman triumphs, only to taste the bitterness of defeat." According to *Ny Tid,* Bosse was more convincing when harsh and "heartless" than in the weaker moments.[143] Several critics disliked the play, but they credited Bosse with virtuoso acting that was compatible with the author's intentions and made them acknowledge the play's effectiveness on stage. Birger Bæckström praised the humanity and seriousness of Bosse's portrayal, noting that she did not hide Christina's faults: "Everything that the role contains of unreliable and diabolical feminine traits, she presented with an almost dazzling boldness—and with superior technical mastery."[144]

Bosse finally got to play Christina in Stockholm in 1928, at the Concert House Theatre under the management of Ernst Eklund, with Rudolf Wendbladh once again as director. She was nervous before the premiere on 16 March, writing to her sister Dagmar, "Think of me then!"[145] As she had in Gothenburg, Bosse used a German accent, which was biographically justifiable but not universally accepted by the critics. Any difficulty the critics had were with the character more than its interpretation. Bosse was not historically correct in appearance, but she was true to the playwright's original depiction of Christina's personality. "She played resolutely a Christina which it amused her to play, and which would certainly have charmed Strindberg to see."[146]

THE TRANSITORY ART

Her having played the role of muse in Strindberg's life and fourteen of his characters on stage, screen, and radio is reason enough to remember Harriet

Bosse, but we must not limit our picture of her. She could never escape her identity as the third wife of Strindberg, yet she told a journalist in 1929 that she had no favorite playwright and no favorite role: "I can have a period when I am loyal to Ibsen, then I perhaps move over to Mæterlinck, only after a time to return to Strindberg. And the roles—well, among Strindberg's things, I think Christina has been most enjoyable to do. . . ." Bosse asserted that it is not helpful for an actor to be close to an author during the rehearsal period, for there is danger of becoming a "gramophone record" or a parrot. Bosse considered Strindberg's works the most difficult to play: "And it is possible that is because I had him too close to me during the time I learned them." The playwright should not see the actor's work until opening night. An actor works with an image and creates something that Bosse believed is more richly faceted and deeper than the author's conception.[147]

Determination to be an independent artist, the pressure of financial need, and the giant shadow cast by a brilliant playwright are intrinsic elements of Harriet Bosse's life story. She lived in a society and worked in a field dominated by men. Although not politically active as a champion of women's rights, she demonstrated talent, intelligence, and courage during five decades of work. Once the embodiment of a romantic ideal, Harriet Bosse enjoyed the praise of critics and the warm response of audiences at happy times during her career. Then there was a beautiful voice and a vibrant presence; now we encounter her only through photographs and words.

Appendixes
Abbreviations
Notes
Bibliography
Index

First Performances of Roles Played by Harriet Bosse

This list is arranged alphabetically by the first name of the character. There are cross references between some familiar English names and the Scandinavian equivalent. The title of the play, author, theatre, city where the theatre is located, and date of the first known performance are provided. Consistent with how the production was advertised, the title is given in Norwegian or Swedish, followed by an English translation and the original title in a non-Scandinavian language, when known. The name of the theatre is translated in the first reference. The city where each theatre is located is listed in each reference, except for the Royal Dramatic Theatre in Stockholm, which is given as "Dramaten."

Acacia in *Mors rival (Mother's Rival; La Malquerida)* by Jacinto Benavente, Dramaten, 27 March 1924.

Ada Törne in *Två mödrar (Two Mothers)* by Nanna Wallensteen, Dramaten, 30 March 1900.

Agda Gauvin in *Johan Ulfstjerna* by Tor Hedberg, Svenska teatern (The Swedish Theatre), Stockholm, 12 March 1907.

Aline Solness in *Byggmästare Solness (The Master Builder)* by Henrik Ibsen, Dramaten, 13 February 1937.

Ann Whitfield in *Mannen och hans öfverman (Man and Superman)* by George Bernard Shaw, Svenska teatern, Stockholm, 27 September 1907.

Anna Möller in *Första fiolen (First Violin)* by Gustav Wied and Jens Petersen, Dramaten, 19 April 1900.

Anna Worthley in *Mrs. Dot (Worthley's Entire)* by W. Somerset Maugham, Svenska teatern, Stockholm, 25 February 1909.

Annette in *Den gamla paviljongen (The Old Pavilion)* by Gustav Wied, Dramaten, 9 May 1905.

Belle Schlessinger in *Guldbröllop (Dear Octopus)* by Dodie Smith, Dramaten, 1 September 1939.

Benjamine Lapistone in *Chokoladprinsessan (The Chocolate Princess)* by Paul Gavault, Svenska teatern, Stockholm, 7 May 1910.

Berenike in *Titus* by Arvid Järnefelt, Dramaten, 29 August 1911.

Bertha Alberg in *Kameraden [Kamraterna] (Comrades)* by August Strindberg, Centaur film, Berlin, 1919.

Bessy in *Miss Hobbs* by Jerome K. Jerome, Dramaten, 4 September 1902.

Biskra in *Samum (Simoon)* by August Strindberg, Dramaten, 22 October 1902.
Brita in *Ingmarssönerna (The Ingmarssons)* by Selma Lagerlöf, Svenska Bio (film), 1918.
Brown, Mrs., in *Claudia* by Rose Franken, Dramaten, 6 February 1942.
Capulet, Lady, in *Romeo och Julia (Romeo and Juliet)* by William Shakespeare, Dramaten, 4 April 1936.
Chitra in *Chitra* by Rabindranath Tagore, Intima teatern (The Intimate Theatre), Stockholm, 15 April 1921.
Christina (Kristina) in *Drottning Kristina (Queen Christina)* by August Strindberg, Lorensbergsteatern (The Lorensberg Theatre), Gothenburg, 23 March 1926.
Clarissa Caerleon in *Valet (The Choice)* by Alfred Sutro, Dramaten, 17 February 1922.
Clärchen (Klärchen) in *Egmont* by Johann Wolfgang von Goethe, Kungl. Teatern (The Royal Opera), Stockholm, 2 April 1903.
Claudine van Zuylen in *Trohetseden (The Oath of Allegiance)* by Oskar Blumenthal, Svenska teatern, Stockholm, 13 September 1909.
Cleopatra (Kleopatra) in *Antonius och Kleopatra (Antony and Cleopatra)* by William Shakespeare, Konserthusteatern (The Concert House Theatre), Stockholm, 14 September 1926.
Cleopatra (Kleopatra) in *Cæsar och Kleopatra (Caesar and Cleopatra)* by George Bernard Shaw, Lorensbergsteatern, Gothenburg, 21 February 1927.
Daisy in *Öster om Suez (East of Suez)* by W. Somerset Maugham, Komediteatern (The Comedy Theatre), Stockholm, 20 August 1923.
Damen (The Lady) in *Till Damaskus I (To Damascus I)* by August Strindberg, Dramaten, 19 November 1900.
Damen (The Lady) in *Till Damaskus III* by August Strindberg, Konserthusteatern, Stockholm, 15 October 1926.
Ebba Örnflyckt in *Min niece (My Niece)* by Gustaf von Horn, Svenska teatern, Stockholm, 28 December 1910.
Edit Morland in *Mikael* by Tor Hedberg, Svenska teatern, Stockholm, 28 October 1908.
Edna Marasso in *Lögnens ansikten (The Faces of the Lie)* by Stellan Rye, Svenska teatern, Stockholm, 10 April 1911.
Elektra in *Elektra* by Hugo von Hofmannsthal, Dramaten, 19 November 1912.
Eleonora in *Påsk (Easter)* by August Strindberg, Dramaten, 4 April 1901.
Elga in *Elga* by Gerhart Hauptmann, Svenska teatern, Stockholm, 3 April 1908.
Elisabeth in *Gösta Berlings saga (Gösta Berling's Saga)* by Selma Lagerlöf, Svenska teatern, Stockholm, 4 March 1911.
Elise Thiers (Madame Thiers) in *Nederlaget (The Defeat)* by Nordahl Grieg, Dramaten, 15 April 1939.
Eliza Doolittle. *See* Liza.
Elsa in *Pension Bellevue* by Ernst Didring, Dramaten, 9 March 1922.
Elsa Båge in *Den stora skuggan (The Big Shadow)* by Carlo Keil-Möller, Dramaten, 9 April 1943.
Else in *Konstnärslif (Artist's Life)* by Adolf Wilbrandt, Dramaten, 16 December 1903.

Emerentia Polhem in *Karl XII (Charles XII)* by August Strindberg, Dramaten, 21 August 1902.

Erika Larsson in *Blommor i drifbänk (Hothouse Flowers)* by Frans Hedberg, Dramaten, 16 December 1915.

Erna Wahl in *Det vida landet (The Far Country; Das weite land)* by Arthur Schnitzler, Dramaten, 23 November 1915.

Esther in *Innanför murarna (Within the Walls)* by Henri Nathansen, Dramaten, 12 February 1913.

Eva Webster in *Den nya bibliotekarien (The New Librarian)* by Gustav von Moser, Dramaten, 19 December 1899.

Fiametta in *Den stora mängden (The Masses)* by Rudolph Lothar and Leopold Lipschutz, Svenska teatern, Stockholm, 8 September 1908.

Flickan (The Girl) in *Himlens hemlighet (The Secret of Heaven)* by Pär Lagerkvist, Intima teatern, Stockholm, 15 April 1921.

Francine Margerie in *Den heliga lunden (The Sacred Grove;* American adaptation: *Decorating Clementine; Le bois sacré)* by G.A. de Caillavet and Robert de Flers, Svenska teatern, Stockholm, 13 September 1910.

Françoise in *Skyltdockan (The Mannequin; La figurante)* by François de Curel, Dramaten, 14 May 1904.

Franskan in *Bombi Bitt och jag (Bombi Bitt and I)*, Triangelfilm, November 1936.

Gerda in *Oväder (Storm Weather)* by August Strindberg, Dramaten, 30 August 1933.

Germaine in *Cornevilles klokker (The Bells of Corneville; Les cloches de Corneville)* by Robert Planquette, Centralteatret (The Central Theatre), Kristiania, 12 November 1897.

Germaine in *Familjeband (Family Ties; La conscience de l'enfant)* by Gaston Devore, Dramaten, 7 January 1901.

Germaine de la Cognac in *Äruns fält (What Price Glory?)* by Maxwell Anderson and Laurence Stallings, Dramaten, 5 October 1929.

Giselle Vaudreuil in *Kvinnans vapen (Woman's Weapon; L'Eventail)* by G. A. de Caillavet and Robert de Flers, Svenska teatern, Stockholm, 8 May 1908.

Grace de Plessans in *Bröllopsmarschen (The Wedding March; La Marche nuptiale)* by Henri Bataille, Dramaten, 12 February 1918.

Greta in *Stigare-Mats (Mats the Climber)* by Ernst Didring, Dramaten, 6 October 1899.

Grusinskaja in *Grand Hotel* by Vicki Baum, Vasateatern (The Vasa Theatre), Stockholm, 18 March 1933.

Gulnare in *Aladdin* by Adam Oehlenschläger, Dramaten, 6 March 1914.

Halla in *Berg-Eyvind och hans hustru (Berg-Eyvind and His Wife)* by Johann Sigurjonsson, Dramaten, 19 November 1913.

Hedvig in *Vildanden (The Wild Duck)* by Henrik Ibsen, Dramaten, 20 March 1903.

Hélène de Trévillac in *Äfventyret (The Adventure; La belle Aventure)* by G. A. de Caillavet, Robert de Flers, [and Étienne Rey], Dramaten, 25 February 1915.

Henriette in *Brott och brott (Crimes and Crimes)* by August Strindberg, Dramaten, 27 April 1916.

Hero in *Mycket väsen för ingenting (Much Ado About Nothing)* by William Shakespeare, Dramaten, 1 November 1902.

Hilda in *Byggmästare Solness (The Master Builder)* by Henrik Ibsen, Intima teatern, Stockholm, 1 February 1919.

Hrafnhildur in *Hadda Padda* by Gudmundur Kamban, Dramaten, 13 April 1915.

Hustrun (The Wife) in *Ledaren (The Leader)* by Rudolf Värnlund, Dramaten, 15 May 1935.

Ilka Etvös in *Krig i Fred (War in Peace; Krieg im Frieden)* by Gustav von Moser and Franz von Schönthan, Dramaten, 1 January 1903.

Ilona in *Anatol* by Arthur Schnitzler, Dramaten, 21 March 1912.

Indras dotter (Indra's Daughter) in *Ett drömspel (A Dream Play)* by August Strindberg, Svenska teatern, Stockholm, 17 April 1907.

Isotta in *En Veneziansk komedi (A Venetian Comedy)* by Per Hallström, Dramaten, 1 March 1904.

Jacqueline Gautier in *En hustru för mycket (One Wife Too Many; La passerelle)* by Francis de Croisset [Franz Wiener], Cirkus (Circus), Gothenburg, 24 September 1915.

Jeanne in *Arftagaren (The Heir)* by Pierre Soulaine, Dramaten, 15 February 1904.

Jeanne Raymond in *Sällskap där man har tråkigt (The Boring Society; Le Monde où l'on s'ennuie)* by Eduoard Pailleron, Dramaten, 12 September 1911.

Joan of Arc (Johanna) in *Sankta Johanna (Saint Joan)* by George Bernard Shaw, Lorensbergsteatern, Gothenburg, 9 February 1926.

Johanne in *Lögnens ansikten (The Faces of the Lie)* by Stellan Rye, Svenska teatern, Stockholm, 10 April 1911.

Jolanta in *Kung Renés dotter (King René's Daughter)* by Henrik Hertz, Dramaten, 13 December 1901.

Minor role in *Jomfru Askepot (Cinderella)* by Bonnami, Centralteatret, Kristiania, 3 January 1898.

Judith in *Dödsdansen (The Dance of Death)* by August Strindberg, Ryding tour, September 1921.

Julia in *Balkongen (The Balcony)* by Gunnar Heiberg, Intima teatern, Stockholm, 1 April 1919.

Julie (also Julia; Juliet) in *Romeo og Julie (Romeo and Juliet)*, Tivoli, Kristiania, 16 August 1896.

Kate Hardcastle in *Värdshuset Råbocken (She Stoops to Conquer)* by Oliver Goldsmith, Dramaten, 8 December 1923.

Kersti in *Kronbruden (The Crown Bride)* by August Strindberg, Svenska teatern (The Swedish Theatre), Helsinki, 24 April 1906.

Kitty Tattenberg in *Sodoms undergång (The Fall of Sodom; Sodoms Ende)* by Hermann Sudermann, Svenska teatern, Stockholm, 8 February 1907.

Kleo in *Lysistrate (Lysistrata)* by Aristophanes, Dramaten, 16 November 1934.

Kleopatra. *See* Cleopatra.

Klärchen. *See* Clärchen.

Kristina. *See* Christina.

Lady, The. *See* Damen.

Lazarillo in *Don Cesar de Bazano (Don Cesar de Bazan)* by Philippe François Demanoir and Adolphe Philippe Dennery, Dramaten, 21 January 1901.

Lena in *Faddergaven (The Christening Gift)* by Peter Egge, Centralteatret, Kristiania, 24 November 1897.

Lenander, fru (Mrs. Lenander) in *Appassionata*, Film A.B. Lux, 2 February 1944.

Leonore in *Pernilles korte Fröykenstand (Pernille's Brief Time as a Lady)* by Ludvig Holberg, Centralteatret, Kristiania, 16 September 1897.

Liza Doolittle in *Pygmalion* by George Bernard Shaw, Dramaten, 7 April 1914.

Louise Strandberg in *Den bergtagna (The Enchanted)* by Ernst Ahlgren and Axel Lundegård, Svenska teatern, Stockholm, 15 March 1910.

Loyse in *Gringoire* by Théodore Faullain de Banville, Dramaten, 22 August 1899.

Löwenfeldt, Friherrinnan (Baroness Löwenfeldt) in *Anna Lans,* Film A.B. Lux, 20 August 1943.

Lucienne in *Vännen Lorel (Friend Lorel)* by Vély and Géradet, Lorensbergsteatern, Gothenburg, on tour, 3 April 1925.

Magda in *Kärlekens krokvägar (The Pathways of Love)* by Tor Hedberg, Svenska teatern, Stockholm, 1 March 1910.

Malin in *Evas systrar (Eve's Sisters)* by Edvard Bäckström, Dramaten, 6 December 1899.

Margit in *Herr Bengts hustru (Sir Bengt's Wife)* by August Strindberg, Ryding tour, October 1928.

Marguerite Gautier in *Kameliadamen (The Lady of the Camellias; La Dame aux camélias)* by Alexandre Dumas *fils*, Ryding tour, October, 1920 (also 1919?).

Maria in *Tjänaren i huset (The Servant in the House)* by Charles Rann Kennedy, Svenska teatern, Stockholm, 15 April 1909.

Maria Hamilton in *Nils Ehrensköld* by Gustaf von Horn, Svenska teatern, Stockholm, 30 March 1910.

Maria Stuart (Mary Stuart) in *Maria Stuart i Skotland (Mary Stuart in Scotland)* by Bjørnstjerne Bjørnson, Dramaten, 25 October 1911.

Marianne von Hohenberg in *Melinit* by Max Ritter, Dramaten, 28 January 1904.

Marie in *Konserten (The Concert; Das Konzert)* by Hermann Bahr, Svenska teatern, Stockholm, 10 November 1910.

Marie-Louise in *Mammon* by Henrik Christiernsson, Dramaten, 6 February 1901.

Marie-Louise Voyasin in *Tjufven (The Thief; Le Voleur)* by Henri Bernstein, Svenska teatern, Stockholm, 14 February 1908.

Marie Walewska in *Marie Walewska* by Johan Bojer, Dramaten, 23 October 1913.

Märta Dohna in *Gösta Berlings saga (Gösta Berling's Saga)* by Selma Lagerlöf, Dramaten, 25 February 1936.

Marthe Bourdier in *Kungen (The King; Le Roi)* by G. A. de Caillavet, Robert de Flers, and Paul Arène, Svenska teatern, Stockholm, 6 October 1909.

Mélisande in *Pelléas och Mélisande (Pelléas and Mélisande)* by Maurice Mæterlinck, Stora teatern (The Large Theatre), Gothenburg, 24 October 1905.

Mikaela Bonalt in *En hederlig man (An Honorable Man)* by Sigfrid Siwertz, Dramaten, 22 October 1934.

Monique Felt in *Eldprofvet (Trial by Fire; La Flambée)* by Henry Kistemaeker, Dramaten, 7 September 1912.

Morehead, Mrs., in *Kvinnorna (The Women)* by Clare Booth Luce, Dramaten, 1 September 1938.

Naemi in *Jefta* by Ernst Didring, Dramaten, 14 March 1913.

Nennele in *Som blad för stormen (As Leaves Before the Storm; Como le foglie)* by Guiseppe Giacosa, Dramaten, 22 April 1903.

Nerissa in *Köpmannen i Venedig (The Merchant of Venice)* by William Shakespeare, Dramaten, 13 December 1904.

Nju in *Nju* by Ossip Dymov, Intima teatern, Stockholm, 21 January 1921.

Nora in *Ett dockhem (A Doll House)* by Henrik Ibsen, premiere in Norrköping, 6 September 1924.

Olga Ramsing in *Örnarna (The Eagles)* by Ernst Didring, Svenska teatern, Stockholm, 16 April 1910.

Olivia in *Familien Jensen (The Jensen Family)* by Edgar Høyer, Centralteatret, Kristiania, 8 February 1898.

Page in *Cyrano de Bergerac* by Edmond Rostand, Dramaten, 9 March 1901.

Parisina in *Parisina Malatesta* by Hjalmar Bergman, Dramaten, 28 April 1915.

Phaethusa in *Skomakar Aiolos (Aiolos the Shoemaker)* by Arnold Kübler, Dramaten, 22 March 1923.

Polja in *Småborgare (The Bourgeoisie)* by Maxim Gorky, Svenska teatern, Stockholm, 15 November 1906.

Prinsessen (Prinsessan; The Princess) in *Der var engang— (Once Upon A Time—)* by Holger Drachmann, Centralteatret, Kristiania, 17 August 1897.

Puck in *En midsommarnattsdröm (A Midsummer Night's Dream)* by William Shakespeare, Dramaten, 6 February 1900.

Rautendelein. *See* Skovstjernelil.

Robina Pennicuick in *Dufslaget (The Dovecote,* or *Robina in Search of a Husband)* by Jerome K. Jerome, Dramaten, 3 September 1903.

Rosalind in *Som Ni behagar (As You Like It)* by William Shakespeare, Dramaten, 21 April 1922.

Sakuntala in *Sakuntala* by Vasantasena, adapted by Max Müller, Dramaten, 28 March 1905.

Salome in *Johannes* by Hermann Sudermann, Svenska teatern, Stockholm, 26 November 1907.

Sara in *Glada fruar (Merry Wives)* by Jonas Lie, Svenska teatern, Helsinki, 23 March 1906.

Silvia in *Giorgione* by Tor Hedberg, Dramaten, 21 November 1903.

Skovstjernelil (Rautendelein) in *Klokken som sank (The Sunken Bell; Die versunkene Glocke)* by Gerhart Hauptmann, Centralteatret, Kristiania, 17 August 1898.

Sophie in *Spelet om kärleken och döden (The Play of Love and Death)* by Romain Rolland, Riksteatern tour, 1937–38.

Steinunn in *Önskningen (The Wish)* by Johann Sigurjonsson, Dramaten, 1 February 1917.

Suzanne Leblanc in *Aigretten (The Plume; L'Aigrette)* by Dario Niccodemi, Intima teatern, Stockholm, 10 February 1920.

Suzy Courtois in *Topaze* by Marcel Pagnol, Dramaten, 18 January 1930.

Thea Elvsted in *Hedda Gabler* by Henrik Ibsen, Dramaten, 11 April 1918.

Thérèse in *Ved dødens port (Facing Death; Inför döden)* by August Strindberg, Centralteatret, Kristiania, 7 September 1898.

Thérèse in *Michel Perrin, eller Polisspion utan att veta det (Michel Perrin, or the Unwitting Police Spy)* by Joseph-Anne-Honoré Mélesville Duveyrier, Dramaten, 20 December 1900.

Tiden (Time) in *En vintersaga (A Winter's Tale)* by William Shakespeare, Sveriges Radio (Swedish Radio), 18 January 1938.

Tilda in *Hårt mot hårt (Holding Firm)* by Edvard Brandes, Dramaten, 18 November 1904.

Tilda in *Heder för två (Honor for Two)* by Anna Wahlenberg, Dramaten, 16 March 1905.

Tove in *Gurre* by Holger Drachmann, Svenska teatern, Stockholm, 22 October 1906.

Trévillac, fru de (Madame de Trévillac) in *Äfventyret (The Adventure; La belle Aventure)* by G. A. de Caillavet, Robert de Flers, [and Étienne Rey], Dramaten, 31 August 1940.

Tro (Faith) in *Det gamla spelet om Envar (Everyman)* by Hugo von Hofmannsthal, Dramaten, 27 January 1916.

Valborg in *Axel og Valborg (Axel and Valborg)* by Adam Oehlenschläger, Central-teatret, Kristiania, 17 October 1897.

Valentine in *Charlataner (Charlatans; Cahotins)* by Edouard Pailleron, Central-teatret, Kristiania, 27 September 1898.

Valentine Bourjon in *Herrens vingård (The Lord's Vineyards; Les vignes du Seigneur)* by Robert de Flers and Francis de Croisset, Nils Ekstam tour, June 1939.

Varvara Aleksejevna in *Labyrinten (The Labyrinth)* by S. L. Poljakov, Dramaten, 5 January 1923.

Victoria in *Änkleken (Home and Beauty* or *Too Many Husbands)* by W. Somerset Maugham, Intima teatern, Stockholm, 16 March 1920.

Viola in *Trettondagsafton eller Hvad Ni vill (Twelfth Night)* by William Shakespeare, Dramaten, 1 March 1912.

Vita Binder in *Hjälpen (The Rescue)* by P. A. Rosenberg, Dramaten, 6 December 1904.

"Strindberg as I Knew Him" by Harriet Bosse

How often have I not received inquiries from private individuals and people in medicine, as to whether I did not see Strindberg act in a way which indicated insanity. I have always answered that during all the years we had contact, I never once heard or saw anything in him that could indicate madness. Some have gotten hold of the fact that Strindberg mentioned that "the Powers" ordered something or other. Well, then what? If he during a certain period of his life listened to and believed in "powers," does he have to be labeled "mad" for that? How many religions are there not where they believe in what seem to us ridiculous things? There are Moslems, Jews, Catholics, Protestants, Pentacostalists, Baptists, Buddhists, some who believe in a stone and some who believe in a piece of wood, etc., and these are not generally considered "insane." During the years I knew and was married to Strindberg I saw only a completely natural, kind, honorable, faithful man—a "gentleman." Whether Strindberg was "crazy" before my time, I can naturally not comment on. It is possible that while in Berlin and Paris he drank and raised cain, but he was not the only one. There was a whole coterie of artists who did not live such a terribly proper life, but none of these has later been considered "mad." The first to characterize Strindberg as "insane" were some German psychiatrists. But they like to think that great men are mad.

I have felt the need—while I live—to *expressly* say to those who still consider Strindberg abnormal: "It is a pity for him, and unfair that these unwarranted allusions to his emotional illness shall be associated with his memory."

This statement is my translation of a typed statement in the collection of Anne Marie Wyller Hagelin.

ABBREVIATIONS

Of the Names of Libraries, Archives, and Private Collections

DTM	Drottningholms Teatermuseum, Stockholm
Film	Svenska Filminstitutet, Stockholm
Film/DDR	Staatliches Filmarchiv der Deutschen Demokratischen Republik, Berlin
GTM	Göteborg Teatermuseum, Gothenburg
Hagelin	Anne Marie Wyller Hagelin collection, Sigtuna
KB	Kungliga Biblioteket, Stockholm
KDT	Kungliga Dramatiska teatern (Dramaten), Stockholm
Sibelius	Sibeliusmuseum (Musikvetenskapeliga institutionen vid Åbo Akademi), Turku
SLF	Svenska litteratursällskapet i Finland, Helsinki
SMA	Svenska Musikaliska Akademien, Stockholm
Stad	Stockholms Stadsarkivet
Sv Mus	Svensk Musik Arkiv
Sv teatern	Svenska teatern, Helsinki
UB (Goteborg)	Göteborg Universitetsbiblioteket, Gothenburg
UB (Lund)	Lund Universitetsbiblioteket
UB (Oslo)	Universitetsbiblioteket i Oslo
UB (Uppsala)	Uppsala Universitetsbiblioteket
Wingård	Randi Wingård collection, Oslo

NOTES

1. Debut of a Princess

1. Sigurd Bødtker, *Kristiania-premierer gjennem 30 aar: Sigurd Bødtkers teaterartikler*, ed. Einar Skavlan and Anton Rønneberg (Kristiania/Oslo: Aschehoug, 1924), 2: 218.

2. Birth certificate, Jakobs Menighed i Kristiania, 11 Oct. 1892, Wingård.

3. Erich Kramer, *Die "Bosse": Beitrag zur Geschichte eines Mansfelder Rittergeschlechts und seines Sippenkreises* (Glücksburg: C.U. Starke, 1952), 78. Although Kramer gives Hattorf as the birthplace, Harriet Bosse said her father was born in Celle. Supplementing Kramer's genealogical study, information about the family comes primarily from interviews with Anne Marie Wyller Hagelin, Randi Wingård, and Dagny Bull Heyerdahl.

4. Harriet Bosse, "Både—och: Några skisser," 5. These memoirs exist only as manuscripts in the possession of the family (Hagelin and Wingård). Although they are incomplete and unpolished, they provide insight and interesting details, and they have furnished material used throughout this book.

5. Miss Bugge's School for Girls and the New Middle School for Young Girls in Kristiania; kindergarten and the Normal School for Girls on Riddargatan in Stockholm.

6. Bosse, "Semesterbrevet," *Svenska Dagbladet*, 11 July 1943; Bosse, "Både—och," 5.

7. Lists of students, 1894–97, *Kongl. Musikkonservatorium: Hösttermin 1894* (Stockholm, 1894), etc., and other documents, SvMus.

8. Olallo Morales and Tobias Norlind, *Kungl. Musikaliska Akademien: 1771–1921* (Stockholm: Lagerströms, 1921), 227.

9. "Ellen Bergman," *Svensk musiktidning*, 15 Dec. 1899, 149–50.

10. Tammelin taught declamation at the conservatory from 1879 to 1906 (Morales and Norlind, 229); "Musikföredrag af Konservatoriets Elever: 1896," "Kongl. Musik-Konservatorium Offentlig Uppvisning" (program), December 1896, and various programs in scrapbook, SMA.

11. Alma Fahlstrøm, *17 Portrettmedaljonger: Fra det gamle Christiania Theater* (Oslo: Aschehoug, 1944), 95–100; Obituary, unidentified newspaper, Fahlstrøm scrapbook, UB (Oslo); Morales and Norlind, 142, 227, 230. Dagmar's first husband was Count Adolf von Sterky. Her second marriage was to architect Carl Möller.

12. Anne Marie Wyller Hagelin, letter to the author, 15 Mar. 1981.

13. Gunnar Brandell, *Strindberg—ett författarliv* (Stockholm: Alba, 1983), vol. 3, *Paris, till och från 1894–1898*, 87–91; Alma Fahlstrøm, *To norske skuespilleres liv og de Fahlstrømske teatres historie: 1878–1917* (Oslo: Gyldendal, 1927), 95–96.

14. Inez (1865–1947) became a widow after eleven months of marriage to Knut Ahlqvist. She was a modest and generous woman who supported herself and her son Alf by managing two glove shops in Stockholm.

248

15. Heinrich (1871–1911) worked as a journalist in Kristiania. He immigrated to Brooklyn and worked for the *Nordisk Tidende* newspaper, for which he wrote reviews of concerts and theatrical performances.

16. Letter to Inez Ahlqvist, 18 Aug. 1896, Hagelin, quoted in part in Olof Molander, *Harriet Bosse: En skiss* (Stockholm: Norstedts, 1920), 6–7; Telegram in Bosse scrapbook, KDT; *Dagens Nyheter*, 31 May 1914.

17. Letter to Inez Ahlqvist and handwritten diary, Wingård. Pages in the diary are unnumbered.

18. Clippings of reviews identified in Harriet Bosse's handwriting, from *Buskeruds Tidende, Fredrikstads Avis, Drammens Blad, Morgenbladet, Landsbladet, Dagbladet, Vårt land*, etc. in Bosse scrapbook, KDT.

19. Renovations were designed by Henrik Bull. The Fahlstrøms operated the Central Theatre for two seasons.

20. Rudolf Rasmussen, *Salong og foyer* (Oslo: Gyldendal, 1943), 17; *Aftenposten*, 18 Aug. 1897.

21. Molander, *En skiss*, 8–10; Bosse scrapbook, KDT; Joachim Lampe, *Revyen*, 18 June 1898; Bødtker, 2:215. In 1903, when the Fahlstrøms revived the production for the opening of the Fahlstrøm Theatre, Dagny Backer was cast as the Princess. She was the daughter of Johanne Marie Bosse (1856–1936) and August Berntsen. Dagny's performance could not compete with the memory of her Aunt Harriet's "charm and rich personality" (*Morgenbladet*, 22 Aug. 1903).

22. Molander, *En skiss*, 9.

23. Bosse, "Både—och," 7.

24. Rasmussen, *Salong*, 14, 16. See also Sophus Dahl, *Teaterminner: Fra Nasjonalturnéens dager* (Oslo: Dreyers, 1959), 85–87.

25. [Lampe], *Revyen*, 18 June 1898.

26. Gerda Ring, interview, 14 July 1983; Thit Jensen, "I et norsk kunstnerpars hjem," *Dannebrog*, 24 Nov. 1907, Fahlstrøm scrapbook, UB (Oslo); Rasmussen, *Salong*, 12.

27. On Holberg premiere 16 September 1897, clippings from *Verdens Gang, Morgenbladet, Eidsvold, Social-demokraten*, Bosse scrapbook, KDT.

28. F. [Nissen], *Social-demokraten*, 25 Nov. 1897.

29. [Lampe], *Revyen*, 11 June 1898; script of *Axel og Valborg*, Centralteatret collection, UB (Oslo); Fahlstrøm, *To norske*, 149.

30. Hagelin.

31. The portrait, in an ornate gilded frame, was given to the Nordiska Museet by Alma Fahlstrøm in 1945.

32. Fahlstrøm, *To norske*, 147–48, 158.

33. Album, Hagelin.

34. Bødtker, 2:218.

2. Debut in Sweden

1. Personal anecdotes are from the section entitled "Parisresan," in Bosse, "Både—och," 9–14.

2. Molander, *En skiss*, 16.

3. Jules Martin, *Nos artistes: Annuaire des théâtres et concerts 1901–1902* (Paris: Ollendorff, 1901), 153; André Antoine, *Le théâtre* (Paris: Éditions de France, 1932), 1:373; Stephen Murray Archer, "Visiting French Repertory Companies in New York: 1900 to March, 1964," (Ph.D. diss., University of Illinois, 1964), 70–71.

4. Bosse, "Både—och," 10.

5. Bosse, "Både—och," 12.

6. Paul Sérusier, letter to Bosse, 8 Jan. 1899, Hagelin.

7. O.R., *Svenska Dagbladet,* 15 Feb. 1901.

8. Bosse, draft of letter to André Antoine, Hagelin.

9. O.R., *Svenska Dagbladet,* 17 Aug. 1904.

10. Pierre Aimé Touchard, *Grandes heures de théâtre à Paris* (Paris: Perrin, 1965), 253, 341.

11. Touchard, *Grandes heures,* 423–25. Information on the repertory in Paris in 1899 is derived primarily from Antoine, *Le théâtre,* 1:360–84; *Le Temps* Jan.–May 1899; and Charles Beaumont Wicks, *The Parisian Stage: Part V (1876–1900)* (University: University of Alabama, 1979).

12. Marvin Carlson, *The French Stage in the Nineteenth Century* (Metuchen, N.J.: Scarecrow, 1977), 215.

13. A. Joannidès, *La Comédie-Française de 1680 à 1900: Dictionnaire général des pièces et des auteurs* (Paris: Plon-Nourrit, 1901; Geneva: Slatkin, 1970); Christian Genty, *Historie du théâtre national de l'Odéon (Journal de Bord) 1782–1982* (Paris: Fischbacher, 1981), 87.

14. Bosse, "Både—och," 13.

15. O.R., *Svenska Dagbladet,* 17 Aug. 1904; Philippe Van Tieghem, *Les Grands Acteurs contemporains (1900–1960)* (Paris: Presses Universitaires de France, 1960), 21.

16. Molander, *En skiss,* 12; O.R., *Svenska Dagbladet,* 15 Feb. 1901. The offer from Bjørnson may have come in 1901.

17. Rudolf Rasmussen, letter to Bosse, 17 Mar. 1899, Hagelin.

18. Strindberg, *Strindbergs brev till Harriet Bosse* (Stockholm: Natur & kultur, 1932), 17; Bosse, "Både—och," 15.

19. Bosse, "Både—och," 15–16; Strindberg, *Strindbergs brev till Harriet Bosse,* 17.

20. Bosse, letter to Sven Brun, 22 Sept. 1899, UB (Oslo).

21. O.R., *Svenska Dagbladet,* 15 Feb. 1901.

22. Roll-Bok, 1863–84, KDT.

23. The historical summary is based on: Claes Rosenqvist, *Hem till historien: August Strindberg, sekelskiftet och "Gustaf Adolf,"* Umeå Studies in the Humanities 66 (Umeå [Stockholm]: Almqvist & Wiksell International, 1984), 56–70; Claes Hoogland and Gösta Kjellin, eds., *Bilder ur svensk teaterhistoria* (Stockholm: Sveriges Radio, 1970); Gösta M. Bergman and Niklas Brunius, eds., *Dramaten 175 år: Studier i svensk scenkonst* (Stockholm: Norstedts, 1963); P.G. Engel and Leif Janzon, *Sju decennier: Svensk teater under 1900-talet* (Stockholm: Forum, 1974); Frederick J. Marker and Lise-Lone Marker, *The Scandinavian Theatre: A Short History* (Oxford: Basil Blackwell, 1975); Tom J.A. Olsson, "Facts about the Royal Dramatic Theatre" (Stockholm, n.d.); Gunnar Richardson, *Oscarisk teaterpolitik: De kungliga teatrarnas omvandling från hovinstitution till statliga aktiebolag,* Studia historica Gothoburgen-

sia, 5 (Göteborg: Akademiförlaget, 1966); Birgitta Steene, "Royal Dramatic Theatre," in *Theatre Companies of the World*, ed. Colby H. Kullman and William C. Young (Bridgeport, Conn.: Greenwood, 1986), 491–94; Erik Wettergren and Ivar Lignell, eds., *Teater i Sverige sista 50 åren* (Stockholm: Svensk litteratur, 1940); Stig Torsslow, *Dramatenaktörernas republik: Dramatiska teatern under associationstiden 1888–1907*, Dramatens skriftserie, 2 (Stockholm: Kungl. Dramatiska teatern, 1975); Eric Wennerholm, *Anders de Wahl: Människan bakom maskerna* (Stockholm: Bonniers, 1974).

24. On Josephson see Walter Johnson, *Strindberg and the Historical Drama* (Seattle: University of Washington Press, 1963) and T. Blanc, *Christiania Theaters historie, 1827–1877* (Christiania: Cappelens, 1899).

25. Ingrid Hollinger, "Regi och spelstil på Dramatiska teatern 1900–1910 speglade genom några uppsättningar av Emil Grandinson och Gustaf Linden" (Thesis, University of Stockholm, 1973), 58–59; Inga Tidblad, *Om Ni behagar* (Stockholm: Hökerbergs, 1963), 183; Cläes Lundin, "Nils Personne," *Teatern*, nr. 10 (Nov.–Dec. 1901): 2–4; Tor Hedberg, *Ett decennium: Uppsatser och kritiker i litteratur, konst, teater M.M.* (Stockholm: Bonniers, 1912), 3:96–97.

26. Gustaf Fredrikson, *Teaterminnen* (Stockholm: Bonniers, 1918), 211; K.A. Winter-Hjelm, *Af Kristiania teaterliv i den seneste tid* (Kristiania: Cappelen, 1875), 127–30; Evert Sprinchorn, "Ibsen and the Actors," in *Ibsen and the Theatre: The Dramatist in Production*, ed. Errol Durbach (New York: Macmillan, 1980), 120.

27. On directing see Hollinger, "Regi och spelstil"; Marker and Marker; and Carla Waal, "William Bloch's *The Wild Duck*," *Educational Theatre Journal* 30 (1978):495–512.

28. T. Hedberg, "Teatersäsongen," *Ord och bild* 11 (1902): 110–11.

29. Ingrid Ödeen, "Elise Hwasser: Spelstil och utveckling" (Report, Theatre History Seminar, University of Stockholm), /4, DTM; Emil Grandinson, *Teatern vid Trädgårdsgatan: 1842–1902* (Stockholm, 1902), 17.

30. Georg Nordensven, *I rampljus: Svenska teaterstudier* (Stockholm: Bonniers, 1900), 191–97; Georg Nordensvan, "Lina Sandell," *Teatern*, Nr.1 (May 1899): 4–6; Karl Hedberg, *Ord och bild* 9 (1900): 288–89; Johannes Svanberg, *Kungl. teatrarne under ett halft sekel 1860–1910* (Stockholm: Nordisk Familjeboks Förlag, 1917–), 200–201.

31. Nordensvan, *I rampljus,* 173–79; Ingrid Qvarnström, *Svensk teater i Finland* (Stockholm: Wahlström & Widstrand, 1946), 1:153–54; Georg Nordensvan, *Svensk teater och svenska skådespelare från Gustav II till våra dagar, 1842–1918* (Stockholm: Bonniers, 1917–18), 2:421; Svanberg, 138–42.

32. O.R., *Svenska Dagbladet*, 15 Feb. 1901.

33. Dora Söderberg, interview, 23 Mar. 1981.

34. Helge Cohn, interview, 4 Feb. 1981; Herbert Grevenius, interview, 24 Mar. 1981; Mimi Pollak, telephone interview, 13 Apr. 1981.

35. Herbert Grevenius, "Sekelvändan 1900," in *Bilder ur svensk teater historia*, ed. Claes Hoogland and Gösta Kjellin (Stockholm: Sveriges Radio, 1970), 228.

36. Hollinger, "Regi och spelstil," 37–38.

37. Strindberg, *Strindbergs brev till Harriet Bosse*, 18–19.

38. Torsslow, 131.

39. Torsslow, 131.
40. Hollinger, "Regi och spelstil," 17.

3. The Ingenue and the Playwright

1. For chronology see Walter Johnson, *August Strindberg* (Boston: Twayne, 1976), 13–18.
2. Ulf Boëthius, *Strindberg och kvinnofrågan: Till och med Giftas I* (Stockholm: Prisma, 1969), 149.
3. A judicial separation was granted on 24 March 1891. The divorce became final 4 April 1893 (Register över skilsmässor 1800–1916, Stad).
4. Frida [Uhl] Strindberg, *Strindberg och hans andra hustru*, 2 vols. (Stockholm: Bonniers, 1933–34); *Lieb, leid und zeit: Eine unvergessliche Ehe: Mit zahlreichen unveröffentlichten Briefen von August Strindberg* (Hamburg, Leipzig: H. Govert, 1936); *Marriage with Genius*, ed. Frederich Whyte, with the assistance of Ethel Talbot Scheffauer (London: Jonathan Cape, 1937).
5. Olof Lagercrantz, *August Strindberg*, trans. Anselm Hollo (New York: Farrar Straus Giroux, 1984), 235.
6. Bosse, "Både—och," 17.
7. Photograph in *Teatern*, nr. 6 (Mar. 1901): 7.
8. The adaptation, first produced at Dramaten in 1853, was based on a German version for the stage, and used in part an earlier adaptation by C. A. Hagberg (Emil Michal, "Tal- och sångpjäser, uppförda å Stockholms samtliga teatrar och öfriga lokaler spelåren 1863–1913," entry 736, KDT.
9. Prompt script, *En midsommarnattsdröm*, KDT.
10. Bosse, "Både—och," 1.
11. Anna Maria Strindberg von Philp and Nora Strindberg Hartzell, *Strindbergs systrar berättar om barndomshemmet och om bror August* (Stockholm: Norstedts, 1926), 70–71. Bosse may have previously been introduced to Strindberg at a party she attended with the Möllers. See Valdemar Lindholm, "Hur Strindberg fann Harriet Bosse," *Nya Thalia* 5 (1931), clipping, GTM.
12. Von Philp and Hartzell, 71; Strindberg, *Strindbergs brev till Harriet Bosse*, 19.
13. nn, clipping, 8 Feb. 1903, DTM; Algot Ruhe, "Från Stockholms teatrar," *Ord och bild* 12 (1903): 364. The production was revived in 1903, with insufficient rehearsals, as a vehicle for Ferdinand Thegerström, who played Egeus.
14. Strindberg, *De återfunna breven till Harriet Bosse* (Stockholm: Bonniers, 1955), 111.
15. Strindberg, *Strindbergs brev till Harriet Bosse*, 17–18.
16. Strindberg, *Strindbergs brev till Harriet Bosse*, 19–21. The pen is now at the Strindberg Museum in the Blue Tower in Stockholm. Bosse may have been mistaken in her recollection of the date when she gave Strindberg the feather.
17. Bosse, letter to Nils Personne, KB.
18. See Lagercrantz, 296–313.
19. A detailed account of the production and those of other Strindberg plays in which Bosse starred is found in the final chapter.

20. Strindberg, *Strindbergs brev till Harriet Bosse,* 22.

21. Bosse, "Både—och," 2.

22. Roll-Bok II B, KDT.

23. Strindberg, *De återfunna breven,* 37; René [Anna Branting], "Harriet Bosse," *Idun,* 17 Mar. 1904, 132.

24. Details of daily life were recorded by Strindberg in *Ockulta dagboken* (Stockholm: Gidlunds, 1977).

25. This drawing may be seen at KB.

26. *Letters of Strindberg to Harriet Bosse: Love Letters from a Tormented Genius,* ed. and trans. Arvid Paulson (New York: Grosset & Dunlap, 1959), 56–57.

27. Strindberg, *Letters,* 95.

28. Strindberg, *Letters,* 70.

29. Arvid Selling, *Teaterfolk* (Stockholm: Hiertas, 1912), 45.

30. Strindberg, *Letters,* 80.

31. Letter to Bonde, 10 Nov. 1902, KDT.

32. Torsslow, 88–89; *Nya Dagligt Allehanda,* 11 Dec. 1902; *Expressen,* 11 Dec. 1902.

33. Torsslow, 99–101.

34. Torsslow, 207.

35. Torsslow, 208.

36. Strindberg, *Letters,* 24.

37. Review of *Första fiolen,* 20 Apr. 1900, clipping, DTM.

38. Fix., "Teaterkåseri," 5 Sept. 1902, clipping, DTM.

39. nn, 23 Apr. 1903, clipping, DTM.

40. Per Hallström, letter to Personne, 15 Feb. 1903, KB. His second choice for the role was Hilda Borgström.

41. Bosse, letter to Conny Wetzer, 26 July 1904, SvTeatern.

42. Torsslow, 133.

43. Matteo Bandello, *The Novels of Matteo Bandello Bishop of Agen,* trans. John Payne (London: Villon Society, 1890), 1:186–219.

44. E.A., *Dagens Nyheter,* 2 Mar. 1904.

45. Bosse, "Både—och," 18.

46. E.A., *Dagens Nyheter,* 2 Mar. 1904.

47. Helge Wahlgren, "Harriet Bosse: En studie," *Scenisk konst,* nr. 10 (1911): 90; Strindberg, *Ockulta dagboken,* 77.

48. Agne Beijer, "Svensk teater efter sekelskiftet från Stockholms horisont," in *Teater i Sverige sista 50 åren,* ed. Erik Wettergren and Ivar Lignell (Stockholm: Svensk litteratur, 1940), 545.

49. René, *Idun,* 17 Mar. 1904, 131–32.

50. *Teatern,* nr. 11 (Sept. 1904): 6.

51. *Svenska Dagbladet,* 18 Feb. 1903.

52. Hans-Eric Holger, "Din ödmjuke förrädare," *Vecko Journalen,* 26 Nov.–3 Dec. 1955, 22–23, 44, 45, clipping, GTM.

53. O.R., *Svenska Dagbladet,* 15 Feb. 1901.

54. O.R., *Svenska Dagbladet,* 17 Aug. 1904.

4. *Reaching Out*

1. O.R., *Svenska Dagbladet,* 17 Aug. 1904.

2. Ester-Margaret von Frenckell, *ABC för teaterpubliken* (Helsingfors: Söder-ström, 1972), 159.

3. Qvarnström, 1:171, 202–06; 2:190.

4. Qvarnström, 2:31.

5. Karin Smirnoff, *Strindbergs första hustru* (Stockholm: Bonniers, 1925), 344–50, 367, 372–73; Frenckell, 98, 121; Harry Jacobsen, *Strindberg og hans første hustru* (København: Gyldendal, 1946), 23.

6. Frenckell, 82, 115, 142, 199; "En svensk-finsk skådespelerskas jubileum," *Scenen,* 1 Oct. 1927, 591–92.

7. Bosse, letter to Conny Wetzer, 26 July 1904, SvTeatern.

8. Baal, *Hufvudstadsbladet,* 13 Oct. 1904.

9. Habitué, *Helsingfors-Posten,* 10 Sept. 1904.

10. Hj. L., *Hufvudstadsbladet,* 17 Sept. 1904.

11. Frenckell, 161.

12. Habitué, *Helsingfors-Posten,* 29 Sept. 1904.

13. Qvarnström, 2:18–21.

14. Bosse, letter to Anne Marie Strindberg, 8 Oct. 1904, Hagelin.

15. Bosse wore her costumes from Dramaten. Bosse, letter to Conny Wetzer, 26 Jan. 1906, SvTeatern.

16. Bosse, letter to Nina Lindfors, 12-1-1904 (probably 12 Jan. 1905), SvTeatern.

17. Habitué, *Helsingfors-Posten,* 20 Oct. 1904.

18. *Helsingfors-Posten,* 21 Oct. 1904.

19. See Gunnar Castrén, *Den nya tiden (1870–1914),* vol. 7 of *Illustrerad svensk litteraturhistoria,* ed. Henrik Schück and Karl Warburg, 3d ed. (Stockholm: H. Geber, 1926–52); Gunnar Castrén, *Humanister och humaniora: Tryckt och talat från sex decennier,* Skrifter utgivna av Svenska litteratursällskapet i Finland, 368 (Helsingfors: Svenska litteratursällskapets i Finland Förlag, 1958).

20. Strindberg, *August Strindbergs brev,* ed. Torsten Eklund, Strindbergssällskapets skrifter (Stockholm: Bonniers, 1976), 15:327.

21. Nineteen letters from Bosse to Castrén are in Helsinki in the archives of the Svenska litteratursällskapet i Finland.

22. Gunnar Castrén, "Fru Bosses gästspel, II," *Euterpe,* nr. 33 (1904): 397.

23. Bosse, letter to Gunnar Castrén, 3 Apr. 1905, SLF.

24. O.R., *Svenska Dagbladet,* 17 Aug. 1904.

25. Bosse, letter to Gunnar Castrén, 3 Apr. 1905, SLF.

26. Her salary was six thousand crowns. She had permission in advance to be away from 1 Sept. through 14 Oct. without pay for a visit to Finland. Contract signed by Gustaf Fredrikson, 11 Mar. 1904, Dramatiska Teatern, Wingård.

27. Torsslow, 208–09.

28. Bosse, letter to Gunnar Castrén, 3 Apr. 1905, SLF.

29. Bosse, letter to Gunnar Castrén, 28 Feb. 1906, SLF. Eysoldt (1870–1955) made her debut in 1890. Among her roles were Lulu, Salome, Nora, Elektra, Puck,

Cleopatra, and Miss Julie. Most of her work was at the Deutsches and Lessing Theatres in Berlin.

30. *Nordisk Familjebok: Konversationslexikon och realencyklopedi,* rev. ed. (Stockholm: Nordisk Familjeboks Förlag, 1915), 3:1259.

31. Bosse, letter to Gunnar Castrén, 27 July 1905, SLF.

32. Bosse, letter to Gunnar Castrén, 27 July 1905, SLF.

33. Frenckell, 149.

34. Caption on photograph exhibited at GTM, 1981.

35. Guillaume, *Göteborgs-Posten,* 16 Sept. 1905.

36. A. Jonason, "Fru Harriet Bosse som Mélisande," *Scenisk konst,* nr. 1 (1906): 3; T.S.K., *Göteborgs-Tidningen,* Parvus [Gustaf Blom], *Ny Tid,* and E.A. [Edvard Alkman], *Göteborgs–Posten,* 25 Oct. 1905.

37. Bosse, letter to Strindberg, 15 Sept. 1905, KB.

38. Bosse, letter to Conny Wetzer, 2 Jan. 1906, SvTeatern.

39. O.R., *Svenska Dagbladet,* 17 Aug. 1904.

40. Strindberg, *Brev,* 14:347.

41. Bosse, "Både—och," 19–21; Bosse, letter to Gunnar Castrén, 20 Jan. 1907, SLF; Molander, *En skiss,* 42; Gottfried Reinhardt, *The Genius: A Memoir of Max Reinhardt* (New York: Alfred A. Knopf, 1979), 273.

42. Bosse, letter to Conny Wetzer, 3 Mar. 1905, SvTeatern.

43. Bosse, letters to Conny Wetzer, 1 Apr., 9 and 30 Nov. 1905, SvTeatern.

44. Bosse, letter to Conny Wetzer, 2 Jan. 1906, SvTeatern.

45. Bosse, letter to Conny Wetzer, 9 Mar. 1906, SvTeatern.

46. Bosse, letter to Gunnar Castrén, 5 May 1906, SLF.

47. Hj. L., *Hufvudstadsbladet,* [18 Mar. 1906].

48. See Carla Waal, *Johanne Dybwad: Norwegian Actress* (Oslo: Universitetsforlaget, 1967).

49. Thf., *Nya Pressen,* [21 Mar. 1906].

50. Bosse, letter to Gustaf Fredrikson, 15 Jan. 1906, KDT.

51. Thf., *Nya Pressen,* 24 Mar. 1906.

52. *Hufvudstadsbladet,* 30 Apr. 1906. Bosse's visits to Helsinki received little attention in the Finnish-language press. In 1906 *Helsingin Sanomat* noted her performances briefly and reported that Bosse gave "a very vivid reading" in Norwegian of a story by Bjørnstjerne Bjørnson for a charity performance (Clas Zilliacus, letter to the author, 11 June 1981).

53. *Hufvudstadsbladet,* 20 Oct. 1904; Frenckell, 150.

54. Qvarnström, 1:211.

55. Obituaries disagree as to whether Wingård was born in Stockholm or Sundsvall. Stockholm is correct.

56. Bo Wingård, letter to the author, 30 Oct. 1983.

57. *Dagens Nyheter,* 8 Oct. 1912.

58. Kaarlo Bergbom, "Hedvig Charlotte Winter-Hjelm," in *Af Kristiania teaterliv i den seneste tid,* by K. [Kristian] A. Winter-Hjelm (Kristiania: Cappelen, 1875), 132–37; *Svenska män och kvinnor,* 8:403.

59. *Life in the Country* is based on a novel by H. L. Ch. Fritz Reuter, translated into Swedish by Frans Hedberg from a Danish adaptation by P. Fristorp. On

Wingård see Rudolf Björkman, "In Memoriam," *Scenisk konst,* nr. 15–16 (1912): 157; "Våra favoriter," *Dagens Nyheter,* 8 Dec. 1910; *Dagens Nyheter,* 8 Oct. 1912.

60. Review in *Finsk Tidskrift,* quoted in Ernst Ahlbom, *Minnen och anteckningar från en trettiofemårig teaterbana* (Helsingfors: Söderström, 1919), 1:169.

61. Ahlbom, *Minnen,* 1:169; Qvarnström, 1:206.

62. On roles see Marianne Lüchou, *Svenska teatern i Helsingfors: Repertoar, styrelser och teaterchefer, Konstnärlig personal 1860–1975* (Helsingfors: Stiftelsen för Svenska teatern, 1977).

63. Frenckell, 101, 150, 155, 167, 194; Lüchou, 106; Qvarnström, 1:218.

64. Bosse, letter to Gunnar Castrén, 5 May 1906, SLF.

65. Bosse, "Semesterbrevet," *Svenska Dagbladet,* 11 July 1943, clipping, Hagelin.

5. Stardom

1. Anne Marie Wyller Hagelin, interview, 4 June 1983.

2. Walborg Hedberg and Louise Arosenius, *Svenska kvinnor från skilda verksamhetsområden: Biografisk uppslagsbok* (Stockholm: Bonniers, 1914).

3. A.N. Kiær, "Indtægtsforhold i Sverige og Norge for personer av forskjellig kjön, alder og ægteskapelig stilling," reprint from *Statsvetenskapelig tidskrift* (1914): 228.

4. Kerstin Moberg, *Från tjänstehjon til hembiträde: En kvinnlig låglönegrupp i den fackliga kampen 1903–1946* (Uppsala: Almqvist & Wiksell International, 1978), 33–35.

5. Claes Rosenqvist, "Ministerlöner och svältlöner: Anteckningar om skådespelarkårens ekonomiska förhållanden vid 1900-talets början," in *Sättstycken och stickrepliker: Drama- och teaterstudier tillägnade Sverker Ek på 50-årsdagen 19 januari 1980,* ed. Dag Nordmark (Umeå: Institutionen för litteraturvetenskap, 1980), 216–17, 219–20; Bengt Idestam-Almqvist [Robin Hood], *När filmen kom till Sverige: Charles Magnusson och Svenska Bio* (Stockholm: Norstedts, 1959), 287; Gustaf Uddgren, quoted in Michael Meyer, *Strindberg: A Biography* (New York: Random House, 1985), 490.

6. *Aftonbladet,* 14 Oct. 1910; Rosenqvist, "Ministerlöner," 214–15, 218, 220.

7. Olga Raphael, *Skiftande spel: Minnen* (Stockholm: Norstedts, 1960), 142.

8. Michael Hays, *The Public and Performance: Essays in the History of French and German Theatre 1871–1900,* Theatre and Dramatic Studies 6 (Ann Arbor: UMI Research Press, 1981), 44.

9. Hays, 100.

10. Agne Beijer, "Svensk teater," 536–38.

11. Ranft's theatres in Stockholm were the Swedish Theatre, the Vasa Theatre, the Oscar Theatre, the South Theatre (Södra Teatern), the Djurgård Theatre, the Östermalm Theatre, and the Opera (Operan). Engel and Janzon, 20–21; Nordensvan, *Svensk teater,* 2:450–64; Svanberg, 39–41; Albert Ranft, *Albert Ranfts memoarer: Första delen* (Stockholm: Norstedts, 1928).

12. Engel and Janzon, 20–21; Beijer, "Svensk teater," 549; Kaifas [Erik Ljungberger], "Till ett 25-års jubileum," *Scenen,* 1 Dec. 1931, 647.

13. Nordensvan, *Svensk teater,* 2:393–447; Marker and Marker, 197.

14. Engel and Janzon, 21.

15. *Dagens Nyheter,* 26 Aug. 1904.

16. Engel and Janzon, 21.

17. Bosse, letter to Gunnar Castrén, 15 Sept. 1906, SLF.

18. Bosse, letters to Gunnar Castrén, 11 Nov. 1906 and 20 Jan. 1907, SLF.

19. Sven Söderman, *Melpomene och Thalia: Från Stockholms teatrar, studier och kritiker* (Stockholm: Åhlén & Åkerlund, 1919), 158.

20. Bosse, "Både—och," 21–22.

21. [Vilain Quatorze], "Drachmann i Stockholm," [*Hufvudstadsbladet,* clippings, 23 Oct. 1906], DTM; Carl Laurin, *Ros och ris från Stockholms teatrar* (Stockholm: Norstedts, 1921), 1:141.

22. Bosse, letter to Gunnar Castrén, 11 Nov. 1906, SLF.

23. Tor Hedberg, 3:282.

24. Laurin, *Ros och ris,* 1:145.

25. Bosse, "Både—och," 32.

26. Gustaf Collijn, "Tonfall," *Thalia,* 1 Dec. 1911, 7.

27. Bosse, "Både—och," 21, 32. The score includes seven interludes, two "melodramas" to accompany dialogue, and a song for Mélisande to sing. Critics did not comment on Bosse's singing. Harold L. Johnson, *Sibelius* (London: Faber and Faber, 1959), 106–7.

28. *Thalia,* 19 Nov. 1910, 6.

29. Regan [Elin Brandell], "Våra favoriter," *Dagens Nyheter,* 8 Dec. 1910.

30. In Helsinki, during the first two weeks of June 1909, Bosse appeared in *The Servant in the House (I en tjänares skepnad)* and *Mrs. Dot.*

31. Regan, *Dagens Nyheter,* 8 Dec. 1910; *Dagens Nyheter,* 8 Oct. 1912; Jes, *Scenisk konst,* nr. 5 (1908):3.

32. Selling, 41.

33. Bosse, letter to Gunnar Castrén, 1 Jan. 1907, SLF.

34. Bosse, letter to Strindberg, 13 June 1907, KB.

35. Bosse, letter to Gunnar Castrén, 13 Mar. 1908, SLF.

36. Strindberg, letter to Bosse, 8 Apr. 1908, KB.

37. Bosse, letter to Strindberg, 4 May 1908, KB.

38. Bosse, letter to Strindberg, 13 May 1908, KB.

39. "En celeber teaterförlofning i går," *Dagens Nyheter,* 5 Apr. 1908; Randi Wingård, interview, 12 July 1983; church records, Hedvig Eleonora.

40. Gunilla Lidbeck, "En dotters försvarstal," *Månads Journalen,* 6 June 1982, 85.

41. Födelsebok for Oscarförsamling; Inflyttningsbok, Oscarförsamling. Bosse took only a brief maternity leave, for *Mrs. Dot* opened six and a half weeks after Bo's birth.

42. Selling, 38–40.

43. *Gwen.,* "Moderna damdräkter," *Scenisk konst,* nr. 12 (1908):2–7.

44. Bosse had already decided to leave the Swedish Theatre, but she told Bojer she would have produced the play herself for a tour. Bosse, letter to Johan Bojer, 9 Apr. 1910, UB (Oslo).

45. Brita Hebbe, *Wendela: En modern 1800–talskvinna* (Stockholm: Natur & kultur, 1974), 284.

46. Raphael, 70.

47. Brita Hebbe, 283–98; *Svenskt biografiskt lexikon* (Stockholm: Bonniers [Norstedts], 1918–   ), 18:373–75.

48. Laurin, *Ros och ris,* 1:194.

49. Hermann Sudermann, *John the Baptist: A Play,* trans. Beatrice Marshall (London: John Lane, 1909), 185.

50. Bosse, letter to Gunnar Castrén, 2 Dec. 1907, SLF.

51. Bosse, letter to Gunnar Castrén, 9 July 1907, SLF.

52. Nordensvan, *Svensk teater,* 2:462; Laurin, *Ros och ris,* 1:188; Sven Söderman, quoted in Erik Ljungberger, *Harriet Bosse* (Stockholm: Hasse W. Tullbergs, 1917), 9.

53. Bosse, letter to Gunnar Castrén, 2 Dec. 1907, SLF.

54. A.B—s. [August Brunius], *Svenska Dagbladet,* 26 Feb. 1909.

55. Oscar Wieselgren, "Dramatiska teatern 25 år," in *Kungliga dramatiska teatern 25 år* (Stockholm: Norstedts, 1933), 3.

56. Fallström, *Stockholms-Tidningen* [?], 7 Oct. 1909.

57. Bosse, letter to Gunnar Castrén, 2 Dec. 1907, SLF.

58. Bosse, "Både—och," 55.

59. Strindberg, *Open Letters to the Intimate Theater,* trans. Walter Johnson (Seattle: University of Washington Press, [1966]).

60. August Falck, *Fem år med Strindberg* (Stockholm: Wahlström & Widstrand, 1935), 74, 76.

61. John Landquist, introduction, *Fanny Falkner och August Strindberg,* by Stella Falkner-Söderberg (Stockholm: Rabén & Sjögren, 1970), 6–13.

62. Strindberg, letter to John Dondorff, 22 Nov. 1911, KB.

63. Stockholms rådhusrätts 6:e avdelnings protokoll för Brottmål 1911 5:e delen, nr. 393, quoted in Anna-Lena Järvstrand, letter to the author, 10 June 1984; Register över skilsmässor 1800–1916, Stad.

64. Randi Wingård, interview, 12 July 1983.

65. Various Dramaten programs, DTM.

66. Regan, "Våra teaterfavoriter," *Dagens Nyheter,* 15 Dec. 1910.

67. *Scenisk konst,* nr. 10 (1911): 88; Kaifas, Dec. 1910, clipping, DTM.

68. Regan, *Dagens Nyheter,* 15 Dec. 1910. Bosse was reported to have demanded an annual salary of 15,000 crowns (*Aftonbladet,* 14 Oct. 1910).

69. Engel and Janzon, 33.

70. Bosse, "Semesterbrevet," *Svenska Dagbladet,* 11 July 1943, clipping, Hagelin.

6. *Reign at the Royal Theatre*

1. The ten theatres were the People's House (Folkets Hus), the Intimate Theatre, the Oscar Theatre, the Vasa Theatre, the Swedish Theatre, Dramaten, the Folk Theatre, the Marionette Theatre, the Opera, and the South Theatre.

2. Sverker Ek et al., eds., *Teater i Stockholm 1910–1970,* Umeå Studies in the Humanities, 45 (Stockholm: Almqvist & Wiksell International, 1982), I (nr. 1): 14, 18, 24; Engel and Janzon, 28–29, 32–33.

3. Grevenius, "Sekelvändan 1900," 242–43.

4. *Ridå,* 28 Jan. 1914, 14.

5. Molander, *En skiss,* 142.

6. Bosse, "Både—och," 23.

7. Selling, 42–43.

8. Bosse, letters to Strindberg, 12 Nov. and 13 Dec. 1911, KB.

9. Bosse, letter to Strindberg, 4 Mar. 1912, KB. After the death of Gunnar Wingård, his brother Nils Åke, with wife and son, came to visit a few times. Bo had no other contact with Wingård relatives.

10. Vagn Børge, *Kvinden i Strindbergs liv og digtning* (København: Levin & Munksgaard; Lund: Gleerups, 1936), 399.

11. *Dagens Nyheter,* 8 Oct. 1912.

12. A.B—s. [August Brunius], *Svenska Dagbladet,* 8 Oct. 1912, clipping, KB; *Dagens Nyheter,* 8 Oct. 1912; Dödslistor 1912, 174, Stad.

13. Anne Marie Wyller Hagelin, interview, 10 Feb. 1981.

14. Pauline Brunius, *Osminkat* (Stockholm: Bonniers, 1931), 198.

15. A.B—s. [August Brunius], *Svenska Dagbladet* and B.B—n. [Bo Bergman], *Dagens Nyheter,* 8 Oct. 1912.

16. "In Memoriam," *Scenisk konst,* nr. 15–16 (1912): 157.

17. *Dagens Nyheter,* 11 Oct. 1912.

18. *Dagens Nyheter,* 8 Nov. 1912.

19. Ljungberger, 10.

20. Bosse, "Semesterbrevet," *Svenska Dagbladet,* 11 July 1943, clipping, Hagelin.

21. *Scenisk konst,* nr. 4 (1912): 38.

22. *Göteborgs Morgonposten,* 28 Sept. 1914.

23. Kjell R.G. Strömberg, "Richard III och fru Bosses gästspel," *Forum,* 23 Feb. 1918, clipping, Collijn collection, KB.

24. In 1912, 1916, and 1923.

25. Bosse, "Både—och," 23.

26. Quoted in Molander, *En skiss,* 55.

27. 8 [Nils Vogt], *Morgenbladet,* 1 June 1916.

28. Einar Skavlan, *Dagbladet,* 1 June 1916.

29. 8, *Morgenbladet;* Bødtker, 2:218; Nils Kjær, *Aftenposten,* 1 June 1916.

30. Btt., clipping, 20 Nov. 1912, DTM; Helge Krog, *Tidens Tegn* and A—t, *Morgenbladet,* 14 May 1923.

31. Bosse, "Både—och," 54.

32. Btt.; Fernanda Nissen, *Social-Demokraten,* 3 June 1916; Bødtker, 2:218.

33. Molander, *En skiss,* 70–71; Kjær, *Aftenposten,* 1 June 1916.

34. Ljungberger, 10.

35. S.T. [Stig Torsslow], *Svenska män och kvinnor,* 1:420.

36. Bosse, "Både—och," 25.

37. Playbills, 1913–14, KDT.

38. Hugo Vallentin, letter to Tor Hedberg, 16 June 1914, KDT. Shaw also sent word that the theatre must not use the ending added in Germany because it distorts Eliza's character (Hugo Vallentin, letter to Tor Hedberg, 4 June 1914, KDT).

39. A.B., *Svenska Dagbladet,* 8 Apr. 1914, clipping, DTM.

40. *Stockholms-Tidningen*, 8 Apr. 1914, clipping, DTM.
41. Söderman, 224.
42. A.L., *Svenska män och kvinnor*, 6:438–39.
43. Bosse, "Både—och," 31. Further details on her work with Ryding are found on pages 29–31 of the memoirs.
44. Nitouche, "I Erika Larssons klädloge," *Göteborgs-Posten*, 4 Oct. 1917.
45. In August 1914, prior to joining Ryding, Bosse appeared in *Pygmalion* with the Dramaten ensemble in Malmö (Bosse, letter to Tor Hedberg, 6 June 1914, KDT).
46. Nitouche, *Göteborgs-Posten*, 4 Oct. 1917.
47. *Politiken*, 1 Dec. 1914; Haagen, *Nationaltidende* and M. Carreau, *Berlingske Tidende*, 2 Dec. 1914.
48. J.C., *Berlingske Tidende*, S.L., *Politiken*, and H.F., *Nationaltidende*, 3 Dec. 1914.
49. Gunnar Heiberg, quoted in Knut Nygaard, *Gunnar Heiberg: Teatermannen*, Bergens Teatermuseums Skrifter 2 (Bergen: Universitetsforlaget, 1975), 209.
50. Bosse, "Både—och," 24.
51. Bødtker, 2:215–18.
52. Bosse, "Både—och," 24.
53. *Dagbladet*, 25 May 1916.
54. Bosse, "Både—och," 24.
55. Clipping, 10 Jan. 1916, Strindberg Museum, Stockholm.
56. Clipping, 8 Dec. 1916, DTM.
57. Bosse, letter to Tor Hedberg, 26 July 1916, KDT.
58. Bosse, "Både—och," 28.
59. Bosse's salary in 1915–16 was thirteen thousand crowns (contract, Wingård).
60. *Dagens Nyheter*, 25 Oct. 1916; Bosse, letter to Tor Hedberg, 13 Oct. 1916, KDT.
61. Clipping, 22 Oct. 1916, DTM.
62. Bosse had previously proposed to alternate in the title role of *Madame Sans Gêne;* this did not take place (Bosse, letter to Tor Hedberg, 18 Nov. 1914, KDT).
63. p., *Stockholms Dagblad*, 23 Oct. 1916.
64. Freddie Rock [Rokem], *Tradition och förnyelse: Svensk dramatik och teater från 1914 till 1922* (Stockholm: Akademilitteratur, 1977), 52–60.
65. Nordensvan, *Svensk teater*, 2:481–83.
66. *La Marche nuptiale*, L'Illustration théâtrale nr. 19 (18 Nov. 1905) (Paris: L'Illustration, 1905), Lilly.
67. Laurin, *Ros och ris*, 2:308–9.
68. *Nordisk Familjebok*, 3:1259.
69. *Svenska män och kvinnor*, 1:420.
70. H—d B—d, *Vecko-Journalen*, 20 Feb. 1918[?], clipping, GTM.

7. The Turning Point

1. Elisabeth Liljedahl, quoted in Ek et al., *Stockholm* 1 (nr. 1):25.
2. Carl David Marcus, quoted in Rock, 22.

3. On the film-theatre debate see Elisabeth Liljedahl, *Stumfilmen i Sverige—kritik och debatt: Hur samtiden värderade den nya konstarten,* Skrifter från Dokumentationsavdelningen, nr. 18 (Stockholm: Proprius & Svenska Filminstitutet, 1975), 153–68.

4. Svenska Biografteatern (Svenska Bio), the producers, released the film to English-language audiences with the title *Dawn of Love.* Parts 1 and 2 were combined as a one-hundred-minute film shown in February 1977 at the Museum of Modern Art in New York City under the title *The Ingmarssons* (publicity release from The Museum of Modern Art Department of Film, Film).

5. *Svenska Dagbladet,* 2 Jan. 1919. This clipping and other items on *Ingmars-sönerna* are in the collection of the Swedish Film Institute in Stockholm (Film).

6. Sun Gynt, *Filmen,* nr. 3 (1919): 4.

7. Bengt Forslund, *Victor Sjöström: Hans liv och verk* (Stockholm: Bonniers, 1980), 323.

8. For more on the film see Bengt Idestam-Almqvist [Robin Hood], *Den svenska filmens drama: Sjöström-Stiller* (Stockholm: Åhlén & Söner, 1939), 151–58.

9. Bengt Forslund, "Victor Sjöström: Bergman's Mentor, Chaplin's Favorite," *Scandinavian Review* 70, nr. 1 (1982): 64–75.

10. Selma Lagerlöf, *Jerusalem: A Novel,* trans. Velma Swanston Howard (Garden City, N.Y.: Doubleday, Page, 1916), 8, 42, 44.

11. One of Bosse's costumes was the same as she had worn at Dramaten in *The Crown Bride* (Idestam-Almqvist, *Sjöström-Stiller,* 157).

12. Contemporary newspapers give her age as eighty-four. Idestam-Almqvist says she was seventy-five and living in a retirement home (*Sjöström-Stiller,* 156).

13. "Med fru Bosse och Victor Sjöström i Ingmarssönernas land," *Filmen,* nr. 1 (1918):24.

14. if, "Harriet Bosse om sin första filmning," [*Dagens Nyheter*], 22 Aug. 1918.

15. *Maudlin,* "Fru Bosse om filmkonsten," brochure for *Ingmarssönerna,* 5, Film.

16. Idestam-Almqvist, *Sjöström-Stiller,* 157.

17. "Kritikens blick," clipping, Film.

18. *Svenska Dagbladet* and *Aftonbladet,* 2 Jan. 1919.

19. *Maudlin,* "Fru Bosse," 4-5.

20. rf, "Fru Bosse och filmen," *Dagens Nyheter,* 2 Dec. 1918.

21. Sun Gynt, *Filmen,* nr. 3 (1919):3–4.

22. On vignettes see H. M. Geduld and R. Gottesman, *An Illustrated Glossary of Film Terms* (New York: Holt, Rinehart & Winston, 1973), 178.

23. rf, *Dagens Nyheter,* 2 Dec. 1918.

24. Bosse, "Både—och," 45.

25. Wennerholm, 86.

26. Oscar Wieselgren, Förord to *Intiman: Historien om en teater,* by Gustaf Collijn (Stockholm: Wahlström & Widstrand, 1943), 9–10.

27. Engel and Janzon, 32.

28. "Teaterpublik i Stockholm och Göteborg," clipping, [15 Mar. 1918], DTM.

29. Ruben G:son Berg, quoted in Collijn, 212–13.

30. Agne Beijer, "Svensk teater," 561–62.

31. Bo Bergman, quoted in Collijn, 250.

32. Bosse, letter to Gustaf Collijn, 21 Dec. 1918, KB. She had hoped to appear also in a comedy or farce. See Bosse, letter to Gustaf Collijn, 1 May 1918, KB.

33. Collijn, 213.

34. *Stockholms-Tidningen,* [2 Feb. 1919].

35. Collijn, 211–17; clippings, Collijn collection, KB.

36. Margit Siwertz, *Lars Hanson* (Stockholm: Norstedts, 1947), 142–43; Collijn, *Intiman,* 217–19; clippings, Collijn collection, KB.

37. Söderman, 146.

38. Bosse, letter to Gunnar Heiberg, 3 May 1919, UB (Oslo).

39. Bosse, letter to Gustaf Collijn, 28 Dec. 1919, KB.

40. Collijn, 223–25.

41. Bosse, letter to Vetterlund, 18 Mar. 1920, KB.

42. Edvin Adolphson, *Edvin Adolphson berättar: Om sitt liv med fru Thalia fru Filmia och andra fruar* (Stockholm: Bonniers, 1972), 76–77, 82.

43. Collijn, 233–35; Adolphson, 82–85.

44. Inga Tidblad, *En bukett* (Stockholm: Hökerbergs, 1967), 180–81.

45. Adolphson, 80.

46. Rabindranath Tagore, *Collected Poems and Plays* (New York: Macmillan, 1937), 149–73.

47. Collijn, 246–47; "En recett," *Svenska Dagbladet,* 21 Apr. 1921.

48. Pär Lagerkvist, letters to Gustaf Collijn and Arvid Fougstedt, quoted in Rock, 84.

49. *Svenska Dagbladet,* 21 Apr. 1921.

50. Bosse, "Både—och," 35; Lagerkvist, *Modern Theatre* (Lincoln: University of Nebraska Press, 1966), 73–91; Carl G. Laurin, *Minnen* (Stockholm: Norstedts, 1932), 3:186; Ejnar Smith, Rbs. [Olof Rabenius], J.D—n [Johan Danielson], R.G.B. [Ruben G:son Berg] et al., reviews, 16 Apr. 1921, Collijn collection, KB.

51. Bosse, letter to Gustaf Collijn, 1 Nov. 1943, KB.

52. *Hvar 8. Dag,* 16 Mar. 1919, 370.

53. Ek et al., *Stockholm,* 1:30.

54. Adolphson, 76–78.

55. Olof Hillberg, *Teater i Sverige utanför huvudstaden* (Stockholm: Svensk litteratur, 1948), 426.

56. Ann Mari Engel, *Teater i Folkets Park 1905–1980. Arbetarrörelsen, folkparkerna och den folkliga teatern, En kulturpolitisk studie,* Theatron-serien (Stockholm: Akademilitteratur, 1982), 2:33–51.

57. Bosse, letter to Gustaf Collijn, 13 Sept. 1920, KB.

58. Bosse, "Både—och," 31.

59. Allan Ryding, letter to the editor, [*Svenska Dagbladet*], 1 Dec. 1920.

60. Bosse, letter to Ellen Collijn, 9 July 1923, UB (Uppsala).

61. *New York Times,* 5 and 6 May 1924. This was not the first time the arrival of a Strindberg widow had been heralded. Frida Uhl Strindberg came to New York in January 1916, with the intention of producing and directing a series of Strindberg plays. She would begin with *Easter,* "exactly as it was staged in Stockholm, where more than 200 performances were given at the Strindberg Theatre under the poet's

own direction" (*New York Times,* 19 Jan. 1916). Frida, referred to as "Mme. August Strindberg," also made the news when she heckled a suffragette speaker at Carnegie Hall (*New York Times,* 15 Jan. 1915).

62. Bosse, "Både—och," 38–39.

63. Bosse does not name the managers with whom she talked. Bernhardt's first New York managers were Sam and Lee Shubert and William F. Connor; later she dealt with Martin Beck (Archer, 17; Bosse, postcard to Ellen Collijn, 17 May 1924, UB [Uppsala]).

64. In the late 1930s Ewald Bosse was director of his own Institute for the Study of Organizations and Labor. He wrote a number of books on labor and economics, including *Arbeidslæren: Det økonomiske arbeide* (Oslo: Nye Nordiske forlag, 1927), *Retten til arbeide* (Oslo: Fabritius, 1933), and *Fattigdommen som samfundsfenomen* (Oslo: Fabritius, 1939).

65. Anne Marie Wyller Hagelin, letter to author, 19 June 1983; Bosse, postcards to Ellen Collijn, 28 May, 8 and 13 June 1920, UB (Uppsala).

66. Bosse, letter to Ellen Collijn, 11 June 1922, UB (Uppsala).

67. Bosse, letter to Ellen Collijn, 9 July 1923, UB (Uppsala).

68. Bosse, letter to Ellen Collijn, 9 July 1923, UB (Uppsala).

69. Engel and Janzon, 16–17, 53–54. Dramaten's management was displeased that Bosse agreed to perform for Eklund for a month at the start of a season in which she was under contract to them. Her subsequent contracts with Dramaten contained a clause stipulating that she would not appear on any other stage in Stockholm (see correspondence and contracts from files of Lidforss and Levy, KB).

70. Bosse was paid two thousand crowns per month, with a bonus for each performance and a guarantee of fifty performances.

71. Bosse, letter to Telemak Fredbärj, 3 Feb. 1958, Wållgren.

72. *Dagens Nyheter,* 10 Mar. 1922.

73. J. D—n, *Social-Demokraten,* 5 Jan. 1923.

74. Rbs., *Nya Dagligt Allehanda,* 17 Feb. 1922.

75. Sminx, "Masker: En rimpokal," *Svenska Dagbladet,* 8 Mar. 1922.

76. Hollinger, "Regi och spelstil," 46–47.

77. Gösta M. Bergman, *Den moderna teaterns genombrott: 1890–1925* (Stockholm: Bonniers, 1966), 529–34.

78. Molander, *En skiss,* 45–46.

79. An anecdote relates that Bosse exclaimed at a performance of Picard's play in honor of Albert Ranft's sixty-fifth birthday, "Thalia is dying," to which Gösta Ekman is supposed to have responded, "But Ranft lives." This performance took place on 23 November 1923, after her short essay was published in *Scenen.* The anecdote is told in Per Lindberg, *Gösta Ekman: Skådespelaren och människan* (Stockholm: Natur & kultur, 1942), and retold in Bengt Forslund, *Från Gösta Ekman till Gösta Ekman: En bok om Hasse, far och son* (Stockholm: Askild & Kärnekull, 1982), 51.

80. Bosse, "Thalia dör," *Scenen,* 15 Oct. 1923, 227.

81. Sven Stål, *Rep i hängd mans hus: Teaterkritiska artiklar* (Stockholm: Svenska Andelsförlaget, 1925), 39–44.

8. Independence

1. Adolphson, 84.
2. Adolphson, 136–37.
3. *Samling av uppgifter till äktenskapsregistret 1927*, nr. 255:22, Stad.
4. Adolphson, 33, 148.
5. Staffan Tjerneld, *Stockholmsliv: Hur vi bott, arbetat och roat oss under 100 år: Birgerjarlsgatan och Östermalm* (Stockholm: Norstedts, 1951), 58–59.
6. Bosse, letter to Dagmar Möller, 16 Mar. 1928, Wingård.
7. Babette [Ellen Liliedahl], "Om tonfilm, talfilm och teater" (interview), *Scenen*, 1 Sept. 1929, 458–60.
8. Borghild Freudin, "Diktaren och skådespelerskan," *Nya Dagligt Allehanda*, 6 Oct. 1929.
9. Forslund, *Gösta Ekman*, 67, 70; Adolphson, 153, 163.
10. Anna-Lena Järvstrand, letter to the author, 16 May 1984. Bosse moved to an apartment at Uplandsgt. 7 in 1933.
11. Olof Lagercrantz, *Eftertankar om Strindberg* (Stockholm: Författarlaget, 1980), 74; Randi Wingård, interviews, 27 Mar. and 3 June 1981.
12. Nils Beyer, *Skådespelare* (Stockholm: Kooperative Förbundets Bokförlag, 1945), 23.
13. Viveca Lindfors, *Vevika . . . Viveca: An Actress . . . A Woman* (New York: Everest House, 1981), 78–79.
14. Einar Sundström, Arne Lindenbaum, and Åke Vretblad, eds., *Svenska konstnärer inom teaterns, musikens och filmens värld* (Stockholm: Mimer, 1943), 212.
15. For an analysis of Adolphson's acting, see Beyer, *Skådespelare*, 11–37. Adolphson's third wife was Mildred Folkestad Mehle, and his fourth wife was Ulla Balle-Jensen. He died in 1979.
16. Bosse, letters to Dagmar Möller, 14 Jan. and 2 Feb. 1928, Wingård.
17. Bosse, letter to Dagmar Möller, 11 Apr. 1928, Wingård.
18. Bosse, letter to Dagmar Möller, 14 Jan. 1928, Wingård.
19. Bosse, letter to Ellen Collijn, 12 Aug. 1927, UB (Uppsala).
20. Lagercrantz, *Agnes von Krusenstjerna* (Stockholm: Bonniers, 1980), 8, 219, 247; Bosse, "Både—och," 27–28; Olof Lagercrantz, interview, 19 Feb. 1981.
21. "En debut som direktris," *Svenska Dagbladet*, [?] Aug. 1924, clipping, DTM.
22. Bosse, letter to Ellen Collijn, 29 July 1924, UB (Uppsala).
23. Englund, "Några extra rader . . . ," typescript, Sveriges Radio.
24. "På turné 1924 med Harriet Bosse," *Södermanlands Nyheter* (Nyköping), 9 Mar. 1978.
25. Ragnar Falck, ed., *Teaterhistorier* (Stockholm: Wahlström & Widstrand, 1947), 94.
26. Lindberg manuscript collection at DTM and UB (Lund); *En bok om Per Lindberg* (Stockholm: Wahlström & Widstrand, 1944); Ulla Britta Lagerroth, *Regi i möte med drama och samhälle: Per Lindberg tolkar Pär Lagerkvist* (Stockholm: Rabén & Sjögren, 1978); Marker and Marker, 209–17; Rock, 15–49.
27. Herbert Grevenius, "Den göteborgska talscenen," in *Teater i Sverige sista 50 åren*, ed. Erik Wettergren and Ivar Lignell (Stockholm: Svensk litteratur, 1940), 620–22.

28. Bergman, *Genombrott,* 536.

29. Bosse, "Både—och," 23.

30. E.B. [Erik Brogren], *Göteborgs Morgenpost,* 10 Feb. 1926. Reviews of Bosse's performances in Gothenburg are found in the clipping collection of the Gothenburg Theatre Museum (GTM).

31. B. B—m. [Birger Bæckström], *Göteborgs Handels- och Sjöfartstidning,* 10 Feb. 1926.

32. E.W., *Ny Tid,* 10 Feb. 1926.

33. E.A. [Edvard Alkman], *Göteborgs-Posten, B. B—m, Göteborgs Handels- och Sjöfartstidning,* and K [Carl Kullenbergh], *Göteborgs Aftonblad,* 10 Feb. 1926. After Bosse left, Elsa Widborg stepped into the title role.

34. Bosse, letter to Ellen Collijn, 16 Feb. 1926, UB (Uppsala).

35. Bosse, letter to Ellen Collijn, 16 Feb. 1926, UB (Uppsala).

36. B. B—m., *Göteborgs Handels- och Sjöfartstidning,* 22 Feb. 1927; "Är gästspel en oart eller en nödvändighet?," [Mar. 1927], clipping, GTM.

37. Bosse, letter to Ellen Collijn, 25 Feb. 1927, UB (Uppsala).

38. Elis Andersson, *Tjugofem säsonger: Pjäser och föreställningar på Lorensberg-steatern och Göteborgs Stadsteater 1926–1951* (Göteborg: Erik Hoglunds, 1957), 27–28.

39. E.B., *Göteborgs Morgonposten,* 22 Feb. 1927.

40. Herbert Grevenius, "Den stora folkteatern," in *En bok om Lindberg* (Stockholm: Wahlström & Widstrand, 1944), 110–12.

41. Bosse, letter to Per Lindberg, 13 Feb. 1926, UB (Lund). At this time Bosse was hearing members of the Lorensberg Theatre ensemble talk about leaving Gothenburg to work with Lindberg in the coming season (letter to Ellen Collijn, 16 Feb. 1926, UB [Uppsala]).

42. Bosse, letter to Per Lindberg, 21 Feb. 1926, UB (Lund).

43. Axel L. Romdahl, "Lorensbergsteatern 1919–1923," in *En bok om Lindberg* (Stockholm: Wahlström & Widstrand, 1944), 46–47.

44. Mimi Pollak, *Teaterlek: Memoarer* (Stockholm: Askild & Kärnekull, 1977), 91.

45. [Isaac Grünewald], manuscript, "Utdrag ur Isaacs tal vid Pelles bår," UB (Lund).

46. Sven Stål, *Krut: Teaterkritik* (Stockholm: Svenska Andelsförlaget, 1927), 19.

47. Pollak, 91.

48. Bosse, "Både—och," 37.

49. Pollak, 92.

50. Sven Stål, *Teater–nihilism?: Teaterkritiska artiklar* (Stockholm: Svenska Andelsförlaget, 1926), 203; Siwertz, *Scenen,* 1 Oct. 1926, 570; Erik Wettergren, *Scenerier: Resor/konst/teater* (Stockholm: Norstedts, 1927), 257–58.

51. Bosse, letter to Per Lindberg, 3 Mar. 1927, UB (Lund); Bosse, letter to Dagmar Möller, 11 Apr. 1928, Wingård; Bosse, "Både—och," 36.

52. Freudin, *Nya Dagligt Allehanda,* 6 Oct. 1929.

53. Grevenius, "Stora folkteatern," 114–17; Engel and Janzon, 54–55.

54. Bosse, "Semesterbrevet," *Svenska Dagbladet,* 11 July 1943, clipping, Hagelin.

55. Bosse, letter to Ellen Collijn, 12 Aug. 1927, UB (Uppsala).

56. "Är gästspel en oart," clipping, GTM.

57. E.H. [Ernst Emil Hallin], *Göteborgs-Posten*, 19 Jan. 1928.

58. Laurin, *Ros och ris*, 4:98; Göran Lindblad, *Våra Nöien*, [? Jan. 1925], clipping, KB; A. B—s., *Svenska Dagbladet*, 11 Jan. 1925.

59. Plus, *Nya Dagligt Allehanda*, [? Jan. 1925], clipping, DTM; *Scenen*, 1 Feb. 1925, 49; Stål, *Teater-nihilism?*, 138; "Varför fru Bosse så plötsligt har lämnat Dramaten," 26 Jan. 1925, clipping, DTM. See also correspondence and drafts of letters from Dramatens styrelse, Tor Hedberg, Gustaf Linden, Carl Möller, and Harriet Bosse in Lidforss and Levy collection, KB.

60. Bosse, letters to Ellen Collijn, 29 July 1924 and 12 Aug. 1927, UB (Uppsala).

61. Bosse, letter to Dagmar Möller, 14 Jan. 1928, Wingård. Bosse occasionally presented a "one-woman show," such as the varied program at the Royal Academy of Music in 1925. It included "A Half Sheet of Paper," a story by Strindberg that she read on numerous occasions (program, Kungl. Musikaliska Akademien, 3 Mar. 1925, SMA).

62. Jean, *Politiken*, 13 Nov. 1925.

63. *Nationaltidende*, 22 Apr. 1925.

64. *Berlingske Tidende*, 12 Nov. 1925.

65. Bosse, postcard to Ellen Collijn, 17 Nov. 1925, UB (Uppsala).

66. *Scenen*, 15 Mar. 1924, 92. Tore Svennberg played Henri in the original production.

67. Bosse, letter to Dagmar Möller, 8 Mar. 1928, Wingård. Anders de Wahl played Henri from 7 Feb. to 9 Apr. 1928.

68. Bosse, letter to Telemak Fredbärj, 3 Feb. 1958, Wållgren.

69. Agne Beijer, *Teaterrecensioner 1925–1949: Jämte en översikt av teater och drama i Sverige under seklets förra hälft*, Skrifter utgivna av Föreningen Drottningholmsteaterns vänner, 10 (Stockholm, 1954), 44–45; August Brunius, *Scenen*, 15 Mar. 1924, 82–84.

70. Bosse, letters to Dagmar Möller, 11 Apr. and 30 May 1928, Wingård; Alma Braathen, "Harriet Bosse om Strindbergsbreven," *Hvar 8. Dag*, 24 Apr. 1932, clipping, GTM.

71. Freudin, *Nya Dagligt Allehanda*, 6 Oct. 1929.

72. Freudin, *Nya Dagligt Allehanda*, 6 Oct. 1929.

73. Artur Möller, *Scenen*, 15 Oct. 1929; Carl G. Laurin, "Från Stockholms teatrar," *Ord och bild* 39 (1930): 113.

74. g, [1930], clipping, DTM.

75. Gösta Richter, letter to Bosse, 16 Nov. 1930, Wingård; Bosse, letter to Erik Wettergren, 3 Dec. 1930, KDT; Bosse, "Både—och," 42–44.

76. Laurin, *Ros och ris*, 5:395.

77. *Vagabonde, Scenen*, 1–12 Apr. 1933, 16–17.

78. *Nationaltidende*, 22 Apr. 1925.

79. *Berlingske Tidende*, 13 Nov. 1925.

80. Adolphson, 164–66.

81. Martin Lamm, *Strindbergs dramer* (Stockholm: Bonniers, 1924–26). Lamm also wrote *August Strindberg*, 2 vols. (Stockholm: Bonniers, 1940–42); for American edition see *August Strindberg*, trans. and ed. Harry G. Carlson (New York: Benjamin Blom, 1971).

82. Margareta Brundin, "Hur förvarade Strindberg sina manuskript?," in *Kungl. bibliotekets årsberättelse 1981* (Stockholm, 1982), 66.
83. Bosse, letter to Martin Lamm, 30 May 1922, KB.
84. Bosse, letter to Dagmar Möller, 14 Jan. 1928, Wingård.
85. Strindberg, letter to Bosse, 10 Apr. 1908, quoted in Margareta Brundin, "Kungliga Bibliotekets Strindbergssamlingar," in *Strindbergiana: Första samlingen,* ed. Anita Persson and Karl-Åke Kärnell (Stockholm: Strindbergssällskapet, 1985), 64–65.
86. Torsten Eklund, letter to KB handskriftsavdelningen, 21 Nov. 1977, KB; Brundin, "Strindbergssamlingar," 64; confirmed by Brundin in telephone interview with Eklund, 11 Feb. 1981.
87. Randi Wingård, interview, 12 July 1983. These are probably the letters to which Bosse referred in an interview with *Nordstjernan,* 19 Jan. 1950, when she said that there were "three which, out of consideration to others, I shall never make public" (Bosse, letter to Jenny Bergqvist-Hansson, 7 Oct. 1955, Eklund collection, KB).
88. Bosse, letter to Arvid Paulson, 19 June 1956, DTM.
89. Braathen, *Hvar 8. Dag,* 24 Apr. 1932.
90. "Förord," in *Strindbergs brev till Harriet Bosse,* 11–13.
91. Bosse, letter to Martin Lamm, 15 Apr. 1932, KB.
92. John Landquist, review, *Aftonbladet,* 17 Apr. 1932.
93. For other reviews see T. F—t. [Torsten Fogelqvist], *Dagens Nyheter* and Anders Österling, *Svenska Dagbladet,* 17 Apr. 1932. The last verse of Karl-Gerhard's "Ännu en vår" from *Karl-Gerhards kupletter* (Stockholm: Affärstryck, 1932) contains the lines:

Strindbergs brev som han till Bosse skrev
har gjort att på vår boklådsdisk med Giftas viftas
   A-u-gust en renässans fått just. . . .

Strindberg's letters, which he wrote to Bosse,
have caused at our bookstores, with *Married* carried,
   A-u-gust to enjoy a renaissance. . . .

94. Bosse, letter to Arvid Paulson, 16 Nov. 1956, DTM.
95. Freudin, *Nya Dagligt Allehanda,* 6 Oct. 1929.
96. Dorothy Dix played Laura. In 1927 *The Father* was presented with George Bernard Shaw's *Overruled* as a curtain raiser. In 1929 J. M. Barrie's *Barbara's Wedding* was the curtain raiser. By playing two totally different characters, Loraine achieved a tour de force.
97. *Times* (London), 4 Aug. 1927; P.M. —W., *Daily Chronicle,* 15 Aug. 1929; *Sunday Graphic,* 18 Aug. 1929.
98. Miriam Lewes played Alice, and Edmund Gwenn was Curt (*Times,* 17 Jan. 1928); Quex., *Evening News,* 17 Jan. 1928.
99. Herrström tried to persuade Bosse to convert to Christian Science. Although she made an effort, Bosse could not accept its principles (Hagelin, interview, 4 June 1983; Bosse, letter to Ellen Collijn, 12 Aug. 1927, UB [Uppsala]).
100. According to Hagelin, the Swedish Ambassador arranged for Bosse and Loraine to meet (Letter to the author, 19 June 1983).

101. Bosse, "Både — och," 40–41.
102. Lagerroth, 269–71; Grevenius, "Stora folkteatern," 135–36.
103. Bosse, letter to Cyril Holm, and Holm, letter to Johan Hansson, 10 Sept. 1932; receipt signed by Bosse and Hansson, 30 Nov. 1932, UB (Lund).
104. Grevenius, "Stora folkteatern," 142–44.
105. Bosse, letter to Dram. Teaterns Chef och Styrelse, 11 May 1932, KDT.

9. Bitter Homecoming

1. Bosse, letter to Oscar Wieselgren, 4 Feb. 1949, KB.
2. Bosse, letter to Oscar Wieselgren, 4 Feb. 1949, KB.
3. Pauline Brunius, 143, 167; Georg Rydeberg, Ridån går alltid ner: Memoarer (Stockholm: B. Wahlströms, 1979), 93.
4. Beijer, Teaterrecensioner, 45; Sundström, Lindenbaum, and Vretblad, 259–60.
5. Lindfors, 66.
6. Herbert Grevenius, Dagen efter: Premiärer och mellanspel, 1944–50 (Stockholm: C.E. Fritze, 1951), 290–91; Rydeberg, 88.
7. Bosse, letters to Pauline Brunius, 8 Feb. 1941 and 5 May 1943, KDT.
8. For overview of the prewar period see Engel and Janzon, 63–83; Marker and Marker, 232–36; Nils Beyer, "Stjärnspel och regiteater," in De 50 åren: Sverige 1900–1950, ed. Jan Cornell, Bengt Olof Vos, and Märtha Ångström-Wilson (Stockholm: Åhlén & Åkerlund, 1950), 135–64.
9. Oscar Wieselgren, "Dramatiska teatern," 3–6.
10. Beyer, "Stärnspel," 164.
11. Artur Möller, Göteborgs-Posten, 18 Apr. 1939; B. B — n, Dagens Nyheter and PGP [P.G. Pettersson], Aftonbladet, 16 Apr. 1939.
12. B. B — n, Dagens Nyheter, S. S — r [Sten Selander], Svenska Dagbladet, and S. [Sanfrid] Neander-Nilsson, Nya Dagligt Allehanda, 14 Feb. 1937; Beijer, Teaterrecensioner, 241.
13. Signe Hasso, telephone interview, 17 May 1981.
14. Sven Erik Skawonius, interview, 20 Jan. 1981.
15. Gunn Wållgren, interview, 24 May 1981; Bosse, letter to Telemak Fredbärj, 3 Feb. 1958, Wållgren.
16. For a thorough account of Carlheim-Gyllensköld's work with the Strindberg papers, see Brundin, "Hur förvarade Strindberg," 61–97.
17. Five volumes were planned; two were actually published by Bonniers in 1918–19 (Brundin, "Hur förvarade Strindberg," 64–65).
18. Bosse, letter to Arvid Paulson, 20 Nov. 1959, DTM.
19. Margareta Brundin, letter to author, 22 Mar. 1985.
20. Quelqu'une [Märta Lindquist], "Återfunna Strindbergsbrev," Svenska Dagbladet, 7 Apr. 1935.
21. KB handskriftsavdelningens depositionsjournal, nr. 37, 2 Feb. 1925 and 10 Aug. 1928.
22. Oscar Wieselgren, letter to Bosse, 10 Feb. 1938, KB. It is possible that Wieselgren had put all the letters together; see Nils Afzelius, letter to Torsten Eklund, 7 Jan. 1954, KB.

23. Harald Dahlin, letter to Isak Collijn, 5 Feb. 1938; Bosse, drafts of letter to Isak Collijn, 5 Feb. 1938; Isak Collijn, letter to Wenner-Grenska Stiftelsen, 7 and 9 Feb. 1938; Oscar Wieselgren, letter to Wenner-Grenska Stiftelsen, 9 Feb. 1938, all at KB.

24. Bosse, letter to Torsten Nothin, 21 Oct. 1938, Lund (UB).

25. Bosse, letter to Karl-Gerhard, 18 Mar. 1937, Hagelin. It is possible that this letter was never sent.

26. Selm., *Göteborgs Handels- och Sjöfartstidning,* 26 Jan. 1937.

27. Later the film was reedited for children, but that version was not successful (Staffan Grönberg, ed., *Svensk filmografi* [Stockholm: Svenska Filminstitutet, 1979], 3:302–4).

28. Contract with Triangelfilm, Wingård.

29. *Kristianstads Läns Tidning,* 22 July 1936.

30. Axon, *Nya Dagligt Allehanda,* 1 Dec. 1936.

31. Notes from screening at the Swedish Film Institute, 27 June 1983.

32. Axon, *Nya Dagligt Allehanda,* 1 Dec. 1936.

33. *Dramaten spelar,* nr. 2 (Dec. 1936): 15.

34. Rydeberg, 94–95.

35. Jobs-Berglund, interview, 13 May 1981.

36. Ann Mari Engel, 2:65.

37. Clipping collection, Folkparkernas Centralorganisation.

38. Helene Høverstad, letter to author, 4 May 1981; Bosse, letter to Per Lindberg, 19 July 1933, UB (Lund).

39. Catalog, Sveriges Radio arkiv, lists Bosse on ten programs, 1934–42. In 1983 a musical setting by Miklós Maros of "Stora grusharpan" was broadcast in Sweden, introduced by Bosse's reading from 1937. For an analysis of Bosse's reading of Shakespeare, see Jacqueline Martin, *Eloquence Is Action: A Study of Form and Text's Influence on the Vocal Delivery Style of Shakespeare in Sweden, 1934–1985* (Stockholm: Institutionen för teater- och filmvetenskap, University of Stockholm, 1987), 59, 86.

40. Gunnar Ollén, *Strindbergs dramatik,* 4th ed. (Stockholm: Sveriges Radio, 1982), 282.

41. Olle Hilding, interview, 10 Apr. 1981.

42. Gerda Ring, interview, 14 July 1983.

43. Jørgen Wyller, interview, 14 July 1983; Anne Marie Wyller Hagelin, interview, 10 Feb. 1981.

44. Anders Wyller, *Kjempende humanisme: Taler og artikler* (Oslo: Aschehoug, 1947).

45. Bosse, letter to Ellen Hagen, 19 Dec. 1940, KB.

46. Tom J.A. Olsson, interview, 20 Jan. 1981.

47. Bosse, letter to Telemak Fredbärj, 3 Feb. 1958, Wållgren.

48. Bosse, letter to Oscar Wieselgren, 4 Feb. 1949, KB.

49. Raphael, 212.

50. Bosse, letter to Oscar Wieselgren, 4 Feb. 1949, KB.

51. Bosse, letter to H. Lettström, 5 Jan. 1940 and H. Lettström, letter to Bosse, 9 Jan. 1940, Pauline Brunius file, KDT.

52. Bosse, letter to Arvid Paulson, 20 May 1956, DTM.

53. Carlo Keil-Möller, "Den stora skuggan," typescript, KDT, 103.
54. Olof Bergström, telephone interview, 2 June 1983; Bosse, "Både—och," 62–63; Bosse, letter to Pauline Brunius, 5 May 1943, KDT.
55. Gvs., *Stockholms-Tidningen*, 7 June 1943, clipping, DTM.
56. *Lill.*, "Kvartetten som lämnar Dramaten," *Svenska Dagbladet*, 13 June 1943.
57. Manuscript, Stockholms Stadsfullmäktige Presidiet, Bosse collection, DTM. After Bosse's death Bo Wingård donated her Litteris et Artibus and S:t Eriks medal to Drottningholms Teatermuseum.
58. Bosse, letter to Fredrik Ström, 2 June 1944, UB (Göteborg).

10. After the Final Curtain

1. Jon Olsson, *Svensk spelfilm under andra världskriget* (Lund: Liber Läromedel, 1979), 8; Bertil Wredlund and Rolf Lindfors, eds., *Långfilm i Sverige, 1940–1949* (Stockholm: Proprius, 1981), 7.
2. Grönberg, 4:285–87, 344–47.
3. Viveca Lindfors, telephone interview, 12 Dec. 1982.
4. Comments based on videotape at Institutionen för Teater- och filmvetenskap, University of Stockholm.
5. Georg Funkquist, telephone interview, 13 Apr. 1981.
6. At this time Bosse was living at Norr Mälarstrand 76. Greta Gerell, interview, "Harriet Bosse 100 år," Sveriges Radio, 19 Feb. 1978; Dramaten styrelse, letter to Bosse, 7 Dec. 1950, KDT.
7. "Harriet Bosse ger porträtt och far till Kanarieöarna," *Göteborgs Handels- och Sjöfartstidning*, 13 Dec. 1950, clipping, GTM; Jørgen Wyller, interview, 14 July 1983.
8. Bosse, letter to Fredrik Ström, 14 May 1945, UB (Göteborg).
9. Anne Marie Wyller Hagelin, letter to author, 2 Feb. 1984.
10. Henrik Haugstøl, *Aftenposten*, 14 May 1955.
11. Bosse, letter to Arvid Paulson, 23 Sept. 1956, DTM.
12. Bosse, letter to Telemak Fredbärj, 3 Feb. 1958, Wållgren.
13. Mentz Schulerud, interview, 2 June 1981; Bo Wingård, interview, 5 Aug. 1983.
14. Jørgen and Wenche Wyller, interview, 14 July 1983.
15. *Arbeiderbladet*, 26 Sept. 1958.
16. Jørgen and Wenche Wyller, interview, 14 July 1983.
17. "Både—och," 53, 58–59.
18. Bosse, letters to Fredrik Ström, 7 Feb. and 25 May 1943, UB (Göteborg).
19. Bosse, letter to Fredrik Ström, 14 May 1945, KB.
20. Zeth Höglund, letter to Uno Willers, 10 Nov. 1952, KB.
21. Margareta Brundin, letter to author, 22 Mar. 1985.
22. Ruben Eriksson, 29 Mar. 1950, KB dagbok.
23. Margareta Brundin, letter to author, 22 Mar. 1985; Harry Järv, interview, 15 Apr. 1981.
24. Oscar Wieselgren, letter to Bosse and list, 14 Jan. 1943, KB; Bosse, letter to Oscar Wieselgren, 17 Jan. 1943, KB.
25. Ruben Eriksson, 8 Feb. 1950, KB handskriftsavdelningens dagbok.

26. Nils Afzelius, 22 Oct. 1952, KB dagbok; Zeth Höglund, letter, 10 Nov. 1952. The letters had probably been misplaced after use by Eklund in writing *Tjänstekvinnans son* and "rediscovered" once more, according to Nils Afzelius, 26 Nov. 1952, KB dagbok. On 22 Mar. 1953 *Dagens Nyheter* noted that this group of letters was not included in the KB collection.

27. Nils Afzelius, 22–23 Jan., 8 and 15 Feb. 1954, KB dagbok; Nils Afzelius, letter to Eklund, 27 Jan. 1954, KB.

28. Nils Afzelius, 12 Mar. and 22 May 1954, KB dagbok.

29. Bosse, letters to Jenny Bergqvist-Hansson, 12 Oct. and 4 Nov. 1955, KB; Bosse, letters to Torsten Eklund, 11 Mar., 13 Oct., and 16 Nov. 1955, KB.

30. Gunnar Brandell, "De fyrtio dagarna," *Svenska Dagbladet,* [25?] Nov. 1955.

31. Margareta Brundin, telephone interview with Torsten Eklund, 19 Mar. 1981; Brundin, "Strindbergssamlingar," 64; Torsten Eklund, letters to Anne Marie Wyller, 3 and 28 Jan. 1963; Anne Marie Wyller, letter to Torsten Eklund, 6 Jan. 1963; Bosse, letters to Torsten Eklund, 6 Dec. 1955 and 19 Oct. 1956, all letters at KB.

32. Åke Runnquist, letter to Torsten Eklund, 5 Oct. 1955, KB.

33. Torsten Eklund, "Strindbergs tredje äktenskap i ny belysning," *Meddelanden från Strindbergssällskapet* 19 (1956): 4–8.

34. Bosse, letter to Torsten Eklund, 4 July 1948, KB.

35. Bosse, letter to Jenny Bergqvist-Hansson, 29 Sept. 1955, KB.

36. Bosse, letter to Jenny Bergqvist-Hansson, 25 Oct. 1955, KB.

37. Bosse, letter to Jenny Bergqvist-Hansson, 27 Nov. 1955, KB.

38. Bosse, letters to Arvid Paulson, 16 Nov. and 11 Dec. 1956, 9 July 1958, DTM.

39. Strindberg, *Letters,* 146.

40. Strindberg, *Brev; From an Occult Diary: Marriage with Harriet Bosse,* ed. Torsten Eklund, trans. Mary Sandbach (New York: Hill and Wang, 1965).

41. Bosse, letter to Arvid Paulson, 15 Mar. 1957, DTM

42. On 4 June 1960, Bosse wrote to John Landquist about some errors in an article he had written. She was anxious to correct the impression that it was her idea to give the eagle feather to Strindberg. "I was too shy for that. Strindberg asked for it" (letter, KB).

43. Bosse, letters to Arvid Paulson, 13 Oct. 1958 and 5 Apr. 1960, DTM.

44. Oscar Wieselgren, *Svenska Dagbladet,* 6 Nov. 1961 and "Harriet Bosse: Några minnesord," *Meddelanden från Strindbergssällskapet,* nr. 29 (1961): 2–3.

45. *Politiken,* 24 Nov. 1985.

46. Colin Wilson, *Strindberg* (London: Calder & Boyars, 1970).

47. Ole Söderström, *Röda huset* and *Victoria: Roman om en skådespelerskas äktenskap* (Stockholm: Norstedts, 1976, 1978).

48. Söderström, *Victoria,* 235.

49. Michael Meyer, *Lunatic and Lover: A Play about Strindberg* (London: Methuen, 1981), 31.

50. Meyer, 32.

51. Nanny Westerlund, "August Strindberg and Harriet Bosse: Skådespel i 2 akter," typescript (Helsingfors: Svenska teatern, 15 Jan. 1982), SvTeatern.

52. Typescript, Produktion: Svenska Teaterklubben Kammerteatern, TV 1. The script was adapted into novel form and published as *Strindberg: Ett liv* (Stockholm: Norstedts/TV 1 Fiction, 1984) by Per Olov Enquist.

53. Matts Rying, "Strindberg och Harriet Bosse," *Horisont* 26, nr. 5 (1979): 15–16.

II. Inspiration and Interpreter

1. August Strindberg, "The Crooked Rib" and "White Slavery," in *Zones of the Spirit: A Book of Thoughts,* trans. Claud Field (New York: G.P. Putnam's Sons, 1913), 174–75.

2. For more on Strindberg and women see Boëthius; Børge, *Kvinden.*

3. Gregory Chmara, letter to Anthony Swerling, quoted in Swerling, *In Quest of Strindberg* (Covent Garden: Trinity Lane, 1971), 57.

4. Lamm, *Strindberg,* 5.

5. Strindberg, *De återfunna breven,* 114.

6. Donald L. Burnham, "Strindbergs kontaktdilemma studerat i hans förhållande till Harriet Bosse," *Meddelanden från Strindbergssällskapet,* nr. 50 (1972): 8–26. On the marriage see also Brita M. E. Mortensen and Brian W. Downs, *Strindberg: An Introduction to His Life and Work* (Cambridge: Cambridge University Press, 1965), 68–73, and Elizabeth Sprigge, *The Strange Life of August Strindberg* (New York: Russell & Russell, 1972), 188–215.

7. On the nondramatic works see Eric O. Johannesson, *The Novels of August Strindberg* (Berkeley: University of California Press, 1968).

8. August Strindberg, *Samlade skrifter,* ed. John Landquist, 55 vols. (Stockholm: Bonniers, 1912–20), 46:175, quoted in Lamm, *Strindberg,* 516. See also Strindberg, *Zones,* 180.

9. Lagercrantz, *Eftertankar,* 103–7; August Strindberg, "Undine," *En blå bok,* 2, in *Samlade skrifter* 47:641–44.

10. In Strindberg, Zones, variations on the theme may be found in the sections "White Slavery," "The Crooked Rib," "The Jewel Casket or His Better Half," "The Mummy-Coffin," and "The Sculptor."

11. Strindberg, *De återfunna breven,* 25.

12. Strindberg, *De återfunna breven,* 31–32.

13. Strindberg, *Brev,* 13:347.

14. See Evert Sprinchorn, *Strindberg as Dramatist* (New Haven: Yale University Press, 1982), 30–33, and Strindberg, *Open Letters.*

15. Margit Siwertz, "Strindberg och skådespelarna," *Svenska Dagbladet,* 31 Dec. 1948.

16. Strindberg, *Letters,* 22.

17. René, *Idun,* 17 Mar. 1904, 131.

18. Hans-Eric Holger, "Din ödmjuke förrädare," *Vecko-Journalen,* 26 Nov.–3 Dec. 1955, 44.

19. Strindberg, *Brev,* 15:298.

20. Strindberg, *Brev,* 15:214, 244.

21. Molander, *En skiss,* 34.

22. Strindberg, *Ockulta dagboken,* 163.

23. Strindberg, *Brev,* 15:32.

24. Strindberg, *Brev,* 15:166–67, 174.

25. Strindberg, *Brev*, 15:169.

26. Strindberg, *Letters*, 58.

27. Bosse, letter to Jean Sibelius, 31 Apr. 1906, Sibelius family; Erik Tawastjerna, *Jean Sibelius*, trans. Erkki Salmenhaara (Helsinki: Otava, 1972), 3:114–15.

28. Ollén, 401.

29. See preface and translation in August Strindberg, *Plays from the Cynical Life*, trans. and ed. Walter Johnson (Seattle: University of Washington Press, 1983).

30. Ollén, 210–11.

31. Sigurd Bødtker, *Verdens Gang*, 9 Sept. 1898, quoted in Fahlstrøm, *To norske*, 150.

32. Strindberg, *De återfunna breven*, 52.

33. Bosse, letter to Nils Personne, 4 Feb. 1902, KB.

34. Yngve Hedvall, *Strindberg på Stockholmsscenen, 1870–1922: En teaterhistorisk översikt* (Stockholm: Lundström, [1923]), 136–37.

35. *Vårt Land*; —d—n; D. S—l, *Svenska Dagbladet*, all 22 Aug. 1902, clippings, DTM.

36. Hedvall, *Stockholmsscenen*, 80.

37. Strindberg, *Cynical Life*, 140.

38. Hedvall, *Stockholmsscenen*, 81.

39. *Dagens Nyheter*, [23 Oct. 1902].

40. "Gamla listor," 22 Oct. 1902, KDT.

41. D. B—n [*Aftonbladet?*] and unidentified clipping [23 Oct. 1902], DTM.

42. Söderman, *Stockholms Dagblad*, clipping, DTM; Algot Ruhe, "Från Stockholms teatrar," *Ord och bild* 11 (1902): 608.

43. Adolf Paul, *Min Strindbergsbok: Strindbergsminnen och brev* (Stockholm: Norstedts, 1930).

44. August Strindberg, *The Cloister*, trans. Mary Sandbach (New York: Hill and Wang, 1966), 158, n.4.

45. Paul, 183.

46. On *Comrades* see Lamm, *Strindberg*, 199–201 and Ollén, 78–88.

47. Paul, 184–89.

48. Johan Casper Glenzdorf, *Internationales film-Lexikon: Biographisches Handbuch für das gesamte Filmwesen* (Badmünder [Deister]: Prominent-Filmverlag, 1960), 565; Gerhard Lamprecht, *Deutsche Stummfilme, 1919* (Berlin: Deutschen Kinemathek, 1968), 177, 304, 312.

49. Bosse, letter to Ellen Collijn, 25 Aug. 1919, UB (Uppsala).

50. Lamprecht, 356.

51. Ollén, 88.

52. *Der Kinematograph*, nr. 668, 22 Oct. 1919, typescript, Film/DDR.

53. Director Lichtenstein, Staatliches Filmarchiv der Deutschen Demokratischen Republik, Berlin, letter to author, 10 May 1982.

54. *Der Kinematograph*, nr. 668, 22 Oct. 1919; *Der Film*, nr. 43, 26 Oct. 1919, typescripts, Film/DDR.

55. Excerpt from *Illustrierte Film Woche*, nr. 44, 1919, typescript, Film/DDR.

56. *Der Film*, nr. 43, 26 Oct. 1919, typescript, Film/DDR.

57. *Berliner Tageblatt*, clipping, Hagelin. Also in the cast were Lotte Stein as Abel, Hans Wolden as Willmer, and Willi Schröder as Dr. Östermark.

58. [Julius Regis], "Strindberg om igen," *Film-journalen*, nr. 19 (1920), clipping, Film; Ollén, 88.

59. Clippings, Film.

60. Bosse, letter to Ellen Collijn, 25 Aug. 1919, UB (Uppsala).

61. Ollén, 374; Strindberg, *Brev*, 14:22, 27.

62. Strindberg, *De återfunna breven*, 28.

63. Grevenius, "Stora folkteatern," 113–14. *To Damascus III* had been produced at the Lorensberg Theatre in Gothenburg in 1922 with Elsa Widborg as The Lady.

64. Anders Österling, *Tio års teater: 1925–1935* (Stockholm: Bonniers, 1936), 40–41; Daniel Fallström, *Stockholms-Tidningen*, 16 Oct. 1926, DTM.

65. Børge, *Kvinden*, 253.

66. Österling, 39–40.

67. Österling, 41; Fallström, *Stockholms-Tidningen*, 16 Oct. 1926.

68. Olof Sandborg, letter to Per Lindberg, 20 Nov. 1928, UB (Lund).

69. Österling, 41; Carl J. Laurin, *Ros och ris*, 4:241; Gunnar Klintberg, *Scenen*, 1 Nov. 1926, 645–46. Also in the cast were Nils Arehn as the Confessor, Märta Ekström as Sylvia, and Doris Nelson as the first wife.

70. Laurin, *Ros och ris*, 4:241.

71. Österling, 41.

72. B. B—n. [Bo Bergman], *Dagens Nyheter*, 17 Oct. 1926; Fallström, *Stockholms-Tidningen*, 16 Oct. 1926; Klintberg, *Scenen*, 1 Nov. 1926, 645.

73. Wettergren, 263.

74. Stål, "Formalism eller titskåp?," *Krut*, 29.

75. "Harriet Bosse i en ny Strindbergsroll," *Scenen*, 1 Nov. 1928, 596.

76. Ollén, 499.

77. Ollén, 504.

78. *Svenska Dagbladets årbok* (Uppsala: Almqvist & Wiksell, 1933), 11:178.

79. Herbert Grevenius, *I afton klockan 8: Premiärer och mellanspel* (Stockholm: C.E. Fritze, 1940), 61–62.

80. Hans Christer Sjöberg, broadcast, Sveriges Radio, 19 Feb. 1978.

81. *Stockholms-Tidningen*, 31 Aug. 1933; Grevenius, *I afton*, 60.

82. C. B—n [Carl Björkman?], 31 Aug. 1933, clipping, DTM. When visiting the Gothenburg City Theatre in 1950, Bosse observed a rehearsal of *Storm Weather*, but she refused to comment on the play (*Göteborgs Handels- och Sjöfartstidning*, 13 Dec. 1950).

83. For photographs and an account of the production, see Ingrid Hollinger, "Urpremiären på Till Damaskus," in *Dramaten 175 år: Studier i svensk scenkonst*, ed. Gösta M. Bergman and Niklas Brunius (Stockholm: Norstedts, 1963), 296–325.

84. Sprinchorn, *Dramatist*, 100.

85. Hollinger, "Regi och spelstil," 98, 133–34.

86. Don Diego [Fredrik Nycander], *Dagen*, 20 Nov. 1900.

87. Strindberg noted in his diary in 1903 how pleasant it was when Bosse played for him the Beethoven sonata that had been the overture to the production (*Ockulta dagboken*, 170).

88. Strindberg, *Letters,* 23.
89. Strindberg, *Brev,* 13:341.
90. Castrén, "Fru Bosses gästspel," 397.
91. A. S — m, *Hufvudstadsbladet* and Habitué, *Helsingfors-Posten,* 29 Sept. 1904.
92. Strindberg, *Brev,* 13:335, 338.
93. Strindberg, *Letters,* 19–20, 23–24.
94. O.R., "Plats, plats för de unga . . . ," *Svenska Dagbladet,* 15 Feb. 1901.
95. Hollinger, "Regi och spelstil," 147.
96. Hollinger, "Regi och spelstil," 162.
97. *Svenska Dagbladet,* 6 Apr. 1901.
98. Hollinger, "Regi och spelstil," 159.
99. Thf., *Nya Pressen* and Hj. L., *Hufvudstadsbladet,* 11 Apr. 1906.
100. Sven Stål, "Från andra radens fond," *Scen och salong* 65, nr. 11–12 (1980): 31.
101. Daniel Fallström, *Stockholms-Tidningen;* B. B — n, *Dagens Nyheter;* J. D — n, *Social-Demokraten;* K.B., *Dagens Tidning,* all 9 Feb. 1921.
102. rt., *Göteborgs Morgonposten,* 14 Sept. 1921.
103. Børge, *Kvinden,* 298; V. C — n, *Politiken;* J.C., *Berlingske Tidende,* all 24 Apr. 1925.
104. August Strindberg, *Ur ockulta dagboken: Äktenskapet med Harriet Bosse,* ed. Torsten Eklund (Stockholm: Bonniers, 1963), 126.
105. Strindberg, *Letters,* 20.
106. Strindberg, *Letters,* 20–21
107. The other plays were *A Dream Play* and *Swan White* (letter to Conny Wetzer, SvTeatern).
108. Gunnar Castrén, *Svenska Dagbladet,* byline 25 Apr. 1906.
109. Hj. L., *Hufvudstadsbladet* and Thf , *Nya Pressen,* 25 Apr. 1906.
110. Bo Bergman, *Dagens Nyheter,* 15 Sept. 1907.
111. Laurin, *Ros och ris,* 1:182.
112. Penman, *Göteborgs Aftonblad,* 10 Nov. 1917.
113. John Atterbom, *Göteborgs Handels- och Sjöfartstidning* and H — d, *Göteborgs Aftonblad,* 24 Oct. 1917.
114. Bosse, letter to Tor Hedberg, 23 Feb. 1918, KDT.
115. Molander, *Detta är jag . . .* (Stockholm: Bonniers, 1961), 125–26.
116. *Kronbruden,* prompt script, KDT.
117. Hedvall, *Stockholmsscenen,* 143.
118. Gunnar Bjurman, 27 Apr. 1918, clipping, DTM.
119. For an interpretation of the mythical dimensions of the script, see Harry G. Carlson, *Strindberg and the Poetry of Myth* (Berkeley: University of California Press, 1982), 137–90.
120. Strindberg, *Letters,* 61. Note that Paulson gives the date as 4 Sept., but Eklund identifies it as 12 Sept. (Strindberg, *Brev,* 14:131).
121. Olof Molander suspected that the prologue was added for Bosse's benefit to augment her role so that she would dominate the performance; she did not recall the circumstances (Bosse, letter to Torsten Eklund, 16 June 1957 and Olof Molander, letter to Torsten Eklund, 18 Feb. 1965, KB).

122. Richard Bark, *Strindbergs drömspelsteknik—i drama och teater* (Lund: Studentlitteratur, 1981), 83–84.

123. In 1981 a recording of Bosse reading the prologue was an important element in the experimental production of *A Dream Play* presented by Teater 9 in Stockholm.

124. Tor Hedberg, 3:304; Bark, 86.

125. Strindberg, *Zones,* 7–8.

126. Bosse, letter to Arvid Paulson, 19 Feb. 1960, DTM.

127. *Svenska Dagbladet,* [4?] Dec. 1936, clipping, DTM.

128. [*Stockholms Dagblad?*], 21 Oct. 1916, clipping, DTM.

129. G.B., [28] Apr. 1916, clipping, DTM.

130. *Dagens Nyheter,* 28 Apr. 1916, clipping, DTM.

131. K.B., [28] Apr. 1916, clipping, DTM.

132. Bødtker, 2:217.

133. *Östergötlands Dagblad,* quoted in Ollén, 278.

134. J.C., *Berlingske Tidende* and V. C—n, *Politiken,* 14 Nov. 1925.

135. Gunn Wållgren, interview, 24 May 1981.

136. Hillberg, 306.

137. "Två höstsuccéêr," *Dramaten spelar,* 2 (1936):15.

138. Amy van Marken, "Strindbergs *Kristina:* En ny teknik," *Annali-Studi Nordici* (Istituto Universitario Orientale di Napoli) 22 (1979):165–76.

139. On the historic Christina as actress, see Monica Setterwall, "Queen Christina and Role Playing in Maxim Form," *Scandinavian Studies* 57 (1985): 162–73.

140. Ollén, 427.

141. Børge, *Kvinden,* 354; Ollén, 427.

142. Strindberg, *Letters,* 66, 69. See various letters from Sept. 1901.

143. E.W., *Ny Tid,* 24 Mar. 1926.

144. *Göteborgs Handels- och Sjöfartstidning,* 24 Mar. 1926, clipping, GTM.

145. Letter to Dagmar Möller, 16 Mar. 1928, Wingård.

146. Artur Möller, *Scenen,* 1 Apr. 1928, 217.

147. *Nya Dagligt Allehanda,* 6 Oct. 1929.

BIBLIOGRAPHY

The bibliography has been alphabetized according to the Swedish system.

BOOKS AND ARTICLES

Scandinavian Theatre, Film, and Society

Adolphson, Edvin. *Edvin Adolphson berättar: Om sitt liv med fru Thalia fru Filmia och andra fruar.* Stockholm: Bonniers, 1972.

Ahlbom, Ernst. *En skådespelares minnen.* Helsingfors: Söderström, 1931.

———. *Minnen och anteckningar från en trettiofemårig teaterbana.* Vol. 1. Helsingfors: Söderström, 1919.

Ahlenius, Holger. *Fem år med Thalia: Från Stockholms teatrar 1948–1953.* Stockholm: Bonniers, 1954.

Andersson, Elis. *Tjugofem säsonger: Pjäser och föreställningar på Lorensbergsteatern och Göteborgs Stadsteater 1926–1951.* Göteborg: Erik Hoglunds, 1957.

Beijer, Agne. "Svensk teater efter sekelskiftet från Stockholms horisont." In *Teater i Sverige sista 50 åren,* edited by Erik Wettergren and Ivar Lignell, 535–619. Stockholm: Svensk litteratur, 1940.

———. *Teaterrecensioner 1925–1949: Jämte en översikt av teater och drama i Sverige under seklets förra hälft.* Skrifter utgivna av Föreningen Drottningholmsteaterns vänner, 10. Stockholm, 1954.

Bergbom, Kaarlo. "Hedvig Charlotte Winter-Hjelm." In *Af Kristiania teaterliv i den seneste tid,* by K. [Kristian] A. Winter-Hjelm, 132–37. Kristiania: Cappelen, 1875.

Bergman, Gösta M. *Den moderna teaterns genombrott: 1890–1925.* Stockholm: Bonniers, 1966.

———, ed. *Svensk teater: Strukturförändringar och organisation 1900–1970.* Stockholm: Almqvist & Wiksell, 1970.

Bergman, Gösta M., and Niklas Brunius, eds. *Dramaten 175 år: Studier i svensk scenkonst.* Stockholm: Norstedts, 1963.

Beyer, Nils. *Skådespelare.* Stockholm: Kooperativa Förbundets Bokförlag, 1945.

———. "Stjärnspel och regiteater." In *De 50 åren: Sverige 1900–1950,* edited by Jan Cornell, Bengt Olof Vos, and Märtha Ängström-Wilson, 135–64. Stockholm: Åhlén & Åkerlund, 1950.

———. *Teaterkvällar: 1940–1953.* Stockholm: LTs, 1953.

Blanc, T. *Christiania Theaters Historie: 1827–1877.* Christiania: Cappelens, 1899.

Brunius, August. *Ansikten och masker: Modern litteratur, konst och teater.* Stockholm: Norstedts, 1917.

Brunius, Pauline. *Osminkat.* Stockholm: Bonniers, 1931.

Bødtker, Sigurd. *Kristiania-premierer gjennem 30 aar: Sigurd Bødtkers teaterartikler.* Edited by Einar Skavlan and Anton Rønneberg. 3 vols. Kristiania/Oslo: Aschehoug, 1923–29.

Castrén, Gunnar. *Den nya tiden (1870–1914).* Vol. 7 of *Illustrerad svensk litteraturhistoria.* Edited by Henrik Schück and Karl Warburg. Stockholm: H. Geber, 1926–52.

————. *Humanister och humaniora: Tryckt och talat från sex decennier.* Skrifter utgivna av Svenska litteratursällskapet i Finland, 368. Helsingfors: Svenska litteratursällskapets i Finland Förlag, 1958.

Cohn, Helge. *Nu, nyligen och länge sen.* . . . Stockholm: Norstedts, 1977.

Collijn, Gustaf. *Intiman: Historien om en teater.* Stockholm: Wahlström & Widstrand, 1943.

Cornell, Jan, Bengt Olof Vos, and Märtha Ängström-Wilson, eds. *De 50 åren: Sverige 1900–1950.* Stockholm: Åhlén & Åkerlund, 1950.

Dahl, Sophus. *Teaterminner: Fra Nasjonalturnéens dager.* Oslo: Dreyers, 1959.

Dahlgren, F.A. *Förteckning öfver svenska skådespel uppförda på Stockholms theatrar 1737–1863 och Kongl. theatrarnes personal 1773–1863.* Stockholm: Norstedts, 1866.

Ek, Sverker, et al., eds. *Teater i Göteborg 1910–1975.* Umeå Studies in the Humanities, 20. 3 vols. Stockholm: Almqvist & Wiksell International, 1978.

————. *Teater i Stockholm 1910–1970.* Umeå Studies in the Humanities, 45. 4 vols. Stockholm: Almqvist & Wiksell International, 1982.

En bok om Per Lindberg. Stockholm: Wahlström & Widstrand, 1944.

Engel, Ann Mari. *Teater i Folkets Park 1905–1980: Arbetarrörelsen, folkparkerna och den folkliga teatern. En kulturpolitisk studie.* Theatronserien. 2 vols. Stockholm: Akademilitteratur, 1982.

Engel, P. G., and Leif Janzon. *Sju decennier: Svensk teater under 1900-talet.* Stockholm: Forum, 1974.

Erbe, Berit. *Bjørn Bjørnsons vei mod realismens teater.* Bergen: Universitetsforlaget, 1976.

Evensmo, Sigurd. *Det store tivoli: Film og kino i Norge gjennom 70 år.* Oslo: Gyldendal, 1967.

Fahlstrøm, Alma. *17 Portrettmedaljonger: Fra det gamle Christiania Theater.* Oslo: Aschehoug, 1944.

————. *To norske skuespilleres liv og de Fahlstrømske teatres historie: 1878–1917.* Oslo: Gyldendal, 1927.

Falck, Ragnar, ed. *Teaterhistorier.* Stockholm: Wahlström & Widstrand, 1947.

Forslund, Bengt. *Från Gösta Ekman till Gösta Ekman: En bok om Hasse, far och son.* Stockholm: Åskild & Kärnekull, 1982.

————. "Victor Sjöström: Bergman's Mentor, Chaplin's Favorite." *Scandinavian Review* 70 (1982): 64–75.

————. *Victor Sjöström: Hans liv och verk.* Stockholm: Bonniers, 1980.

Fredrikson, Gustaf. *Teaterminnen.* Stockholm: Bonniers, 1918.

Frenckell, Ester-Margaret von. *ABC för teaterpubliken.* Helsingfors: Söderström, 1972.

Fromell, Axel. *Stora Teatern i Göteborg, 1893–1929: Några blad ur dess historia.* Göteborg: Axel Fromell, 1929.

Gjesdahl, Paul. *Centralteatrets historie,* med tillegg og registre ved Øyvind Anker. Oslo: Gyldendal, 1964.

Grandinson, Emil. *Teatern vid Trädgårdsgatan: 1842–1902.* Stockholm: n.p., 1902.

Grevenius, Herbert. *Dagen efter: Premiärer och mellanspel. 1944–1950.* Stockholm: C. E. Fritze, 1951.

————. "Den göteborgska talscenen." In *Teater i Sverige sista 50 åren,* edited by Erik Wettergren and Ivar Lignell, 620–29. Stockholm: Svensk litteratur, 1940.

————. "Den stora folkteatern." In *En bok om Per Lindberg,* 105–56. Stockholm: Wahlström & Widstrand, 1944.

————. *I afton klockan 8: Premiärer och mellanspel.* Stockholm: C.E. Fritze, 1940.

————. "Sekelvändan 1900." In *Bilder ur svensk teaterhistoria,* edited by Claes Hoogland and Gösta Kjellin, 227–50. Stockholm: Sveriges Radio, 1970.

Grönberg, Staffan, ed. *Svensk filmografi.* Vols. 3–4. Stockholm: Svenska Filminstitutet, 1979, 1980.

Hebbe, Brita. *Wendela: En modern 1800–talskvinna.* Stockholm: Natur & kultur, 1974.

Hedberg, Frans. *Vid skrifbordet och bakom ridån: Minnen från flydda teatertider.* Stockholm: Bonniers, 1908.

Hedberg, Tor. *Teater.* Vol. 3 of *Ett decennium: Uppsatser och kritiker i litteratur, konst, teater M.M.* Stockholm: Bonniers, 1912.

Hedberg, Walborg, and Louise Arosenius. *Svenska kvinnor från skilda verksamhetsområden: Biografisk uppslagsbok.* Stockholm: Bonniers, 1914.

Hedvall, Yngve. *Ivan Hedqvist som skådespelare och människa.* Publikens gunstlingar, 4. Stockholm: Lars Hökerbergs, 1918.

Hillberg, Olof. *Teater i Sverige utanför huvudstaden.* Stockholm: Svensk litteratur, 1948.

Hjorth-Jensen, Egil. *Norsk skuespillerforbund gjennom 50 år: 1898–1948.* Oslo: Gyldendal, 1948.

Hollinger, Ingrid. "Urpremiären på Till Damaskus." In *Dramaten 175 år: Studier i svensk scenkonst,* edited by Gösta M. Bergman and Niklas Brunius, 296–325. Stockholm: Norstedts, 1963.

Homén, Olaf. *Från Helsingfors teatrar: Essayer och kritiker.* 3 vols. Helsingfors: Söderström, 1915–19.

Hoogland, Claes, and Gösta Kjellin, eds. *Bilder ur svensk teaterhistoria.* Stockholm: Sveriges Radio, 1970.

Idestam-Almqvist, Bengt [Robin Hood]. *Den svenska filmens drama: Sjöström-Stiller.* Stockholm: Åhlén & Söner, 1939.

————. *När filmen kom till Sverige: Charles Magnusson och Svenska Bio.* Stockholm: Norstedts, 1959.

Jensson, Liv. *Biografisk skuespillerleksikon.* Oslo: Universitetsforlaget, 1981.

Jeppsson, Ann-Lis. *Tankar til salu: Genombrottsidéerna och de kommersiella lånbiblioteken.* Skrifter utgivna av Litteraturvetenskapliga institutionen vid Uppsala universitet, 13. Uppsala, 1981.

Johnson, Harold L. *Sibelius.* London: Faber and Faber, 1959.

Just, Carl. *Schrøder og Christiania Theater: Et bidrag til norsk teaterhistorie.* Oslo: Cammermeyers, 1948.

Karl-Gerhards kupletter. Stockholm: Affärstryck, 1932.

Kiær, A.N. "Indtægtsforhold i Sverige og Norge for personer av forskjellig kjön, alder og ægteskapelig stilling." Reprint from *Statsvetenskapelig tidskrift* (1914): 224–41.

Kungliga dramatiska teatern 25 år. Stockholm: Norstedts, 1933.

Lagercrantz, Olof. *Agnes von Krusenstjerna.* Stockholm: Bonniers, 1980.

Lagerkvist, Pär. *Modern Theatre*. Lincoln: University of Nebraska Press, 1966.

Lagerroth, Ulla Britta. *Regi i möte med drama och samhälle: Per Lindberg tolkar Pär Lagerkvist*. Stockholm: Rabén & Sjögren, 1978.

Lange, Sven. *Meninger om Teater*. Edited by Oskar Thyregod. København: Gyldendalske Boghandel, 1929.

Laurin, Carl G. *Minnen*. 4 vols. Stockholm: Norstedts, 1932.

———. *Ros och ris från Stockholms teatrar*. 6 vols. Stockholm: Norstedts, 1918–39.

Lewenhaupt, Inga. *Signe Hebbe (1837–1925): Skådespelerska, operasångerska, pedagog*. Stockholm: Institutionen för teater- och filmvetenskap, University of Stockholm, 1988.

Liljedahl, Elisabeth. *Stumfilmen i Sverige—kritik och debatt: Hur samtiden värderade den nya konstarten*. Skrifter från Dokumentationsavdelningen, nr. 18. Stockholm: Proprius & Svenska Filminstitutet, 1975.

Lindberg, Per. *August Lindberg: Skådespelaren och människan. Interiörer från 80- och 90-talens teaterliv*. Stockholm: Natur & kultur, 1943.

———. *Gösta Ekman: Skådespelaren och människan*. Stockholm: Natur & kultur, 1942.

Lindfors, Viveca. *Viveka . . . Viveca: An Actress . . . A Woman*. New York: Everest House, 1981.

Ljungberger, Erik. *Harriet Bosse*. Sceniska konstnärer. Stockholm: Hasse W. Tullbergs, 1917.

Lüchou, Marianne. *Svenska teatern i Helsingfors: Repertoar, styrelser och teaterchefer. Konstnärlig personal 1860–1975*. Helsingfors: Stiftelsen för Svenska teatern, 1977.

Marker, Frederick J., and Lise-Lone Marker. *The Scandinavian Theatre: A Short History*. Oxford: Basil Blackwell, 1975.

Martin, Jacqueline. *Eloquence Is Action: A Study of Form and Text's Influence on the Vocal Delivery Style of Shakespeare in Sweden, 1934–1985*. Stockholm: Institutionen för teater- och filmvetenskap, University of Stockholm, 1987.

Maudlin. "Fru Bosse om filmkonsten." Brochure for *Ingmarssönerna*, 4–5. Film.

Moberg, Kerstin. *Från tjänstehjon til hembiträde: En kvinnlig låglönegrupp i den fackliga kampen 1903–1946*. Uppsala: Almqvist & Wiksell International, 1978.

Molander, Olof. *Detta är jag . . . .* Stockholm: Bonniers, 1961.

———. *Harriet Bosse: Eine Studie von Olof Molander*. Translated by Heinrich Goebel. Leipzig: H. Haessel, 1922.

———. *Harriet Bosse: En skiss*. Stockholm: Norstedts, 1920.

Morales, Olallo, and Tobias Norlind. *Kungl. Musikaliska Akademien: 1771–1921*. Stockholm: Lagerströms, 1921.

Nordensvan, Georg. *I rampljus: Svenska teaterstudier*. Stockholm: Bonniers, 1900.

———. *Svensk teater och svenska skådespelare från Gustav III till våra dagar, 1842–1918*. Vol. 2. Stockholm: Bonniers, 1917–18.

Nordisk familjebok: Konversationslexikon och realencyklopedi. Rev. ed. 38 vols. Stockholm: Nordisk Familjeboks Förlag, 1915.

Nordmark, Dag, ed. *Sättstycken och stickrepliker: Drama- och teaterstudier tillägnade Sverker Ek på 50-årsdagen 19 januari 1980*. Umeå: [Institutionen för litteraturvetenskap], University of Umeå, 1980.

Noreng, Harald. *Bjørnsons skuespill på svensk scene.* Oslo: Gyldendal, 1967.

Nygaard, Knut. *Gunnar Heiberg: Teatermannen.* Bergens Teatermuseums Skrifter, nr. 2. Bergen: Universitetsforlaget, 1975.

Olsson, Jon. *Svensk spelfilm under andra världskriget.* Lund: Liber Läromedel, 1979.

Olsson, Tom J.A. "Facts about the Royal Dramatic Theatre." Stockholm, n.d.

———. *O'Neill och Dramaten: En studie kring arbetet med och mottagandet av fjorton olika O'Neill-uppsättningar på Dramatiska teatern åren 1923–1962.* Stockholm: Akademilitteratur, 1977.

Pollak, Mimi. *Teaterlek: Memoarer.* Stockholm: Askild & Kärnekull, 1977.

Qvarnström, Ingrid. *Svensk teater i Finland.* 2 vols. Stockholm: Wahlström & Widstrand, 1946.

Ranft, Albert. *Albert Ranfts memoarer: Första delen.* Stockholm: Norstedts, 1928.

Raphael, Olga. *Skiftande spel: Minnen.* Stockholm: Norstedts, 1960.

Rasmussen, Rudolf. *Rulle: De andre.* Oslo: Johan Grundt Tanum, 1936.

———. *Salong og foyer.* Oslo: Gyldendal, 1943.

Richardson, Gunnar. *Oscarisk teaterpolitik: De kungliga teatrarnas omvandling från hovinstitution till stagliga aktiebolag.* Studia historica Gothoburgensia, 5. Göteborg: Akademiförlaget, 1966.

Rock [Rokem], Freddie. *Tradition och förnyelse: Svensk dramatik och teater från 1914 till 1922.* Stockholm: Akademilitteratur, 1977.

Romdahl, Axel L. "Lorensbergsteatern 1919–1923." In *En bok om Per Lindberg,* 37–82. Stockholm: Wahlström & Widstrand, 1944.

Rosenqvist, Claes. "Ministerlöner och svältlöner: Anteckningar om skådespelarkårens ekonomiska förhållanden vid 1900-talets början." In *Sättstycken och stickrepliker: Drama- och teaterstudier tillägnade Sverker Ek på 50-årsdagen 19 januari 1980,* edited by Dag Nordmark, 213–29. Umeå: [Institutionen för litteraturvetenskap], University of Umeå, 1980.

———, ed. *Den svenska nationalscenen: Traditioner och reformer på Dramaten under 200 år.* Stockholm: Wiken, 1988.

Rydeberg, Georg. *Ridån går alltid ner: Memoarer.* Stockholm: B. Wahlströms, 1979.

Rønneberg, Anton. *Nationaltheatret gjennom femti år.* Oslo: Gyldendal, 1949.

Schildknecht-Wahlgren, Maria. *Minnesbilder.* Göteborg: Bergendahls, 1959.

Schiller, Harald. *Thalia i Malmö och andra essayer.* Malmö: Sydsvenska Dagbladets Aktiebolag, 1948.

Selling, Arvid. *Teaterfolk.* Stockholm: Hiertas, 1912.

Siwertz, Margit. *Lars Hanson.* Stockholm: Norstedts, 1947.

Siwertz, Sigfrid. *Nils Personne.* Stockholm: Norstedts, 1967.

Sjöberg, Alf. *Teater som besvärjelse: Artiklar från fem decennier.* Edited by Sverker R. Ek et al. Stockholm: Norstedts, 1982.

Sprinchorn, Evert. "Ibsen and the Actors." In *Ibsen and the Theatre: The Dramatist in Production,* edited by Errol Durbach, 118–30. New York: Macmillan, 1980.

Steene, Birgitta. "Royal Dramatic Theatre." In *Theatre Companies of the World,* edited by Colby H. Kullman and William C. Young, 491–94. Bridgeport, Conn.: Greenwood, 1986.

Stål, Sven. *Krut: Teaterkritik.* Stockholm: Svenska Andelsförlaget, 1927.

———. *Rep i hängd mans hus: Teaterkritiska artiklar.* Stockholm: Svenska Andelsförlaget, 1925.

———. *Teater-nihilism?: Teaterkritiska artiklar.* Stockholm: Svenska Andelsförlaget, 1926.

Sundström, Einar, Arne Lindenbaum, and Åke Vretblad, eds. *Svenska konstnärer inom teaterns, musikens och filmens värld.* Stockholm: Mimer, 1943.

Svanberg, Johannes. *Kungl. teatrarne under ett halft sekel 1860–1910.* Stockholm: Nordisk Familjeboks Förlag, 1917– .

Svenska Dagbladets årbok. Vols. 1–14. Uppsala: Almqvist & Wiksell, 1924–37.

Svenska män och kvinnor. 8 vols. Stockholm: Bonniers, 1942–55.

Svenskt biografiskt lexikon. Stockholm: Bonniers [Norstedts], 1918– .

Söderman, Sven. *Melpomene och Thalia: Från Stockholms teatrar, studier och kritiker.* Stockholm: Åhlén & Åkerlund, 1919.

Söderström, Ole. *Farväl Sverige.* Stockholm: Norstedts, 1980.

Tawastjerna, Erik. *Jean Sibelius.* Translated by Erkki Salmenhaara. Vol. 3. Helsinki: Otava, 1972.

Tidblad, Inga. *En bukett.* Stockholm: Hökerbergs, 1967.

———. *Om Ni behagar.* Stockholm: Hökerbergs, 1963.

Tjerneld, Staffan. *Stockholmsliv: Hur vi bott, arbetat och roat oss under 100 år: Birgerjarlsgatan och Östermalm.* Stockholm: Norstedts, 1951.

Torsslow, Stig. *Dramatenaktörernas republik: Dramatiska teatern under associationstiden 1888–1907.* Dramatens skriftserie, 2. Stockholm: Kungl. Dramatiska teatern, 1975.

Waal, Carla. *Johanne Dybwad: Norwegian Actress.* Oslo: Universitetsforlaget, 1967.

———. "William Bloch's *The Wild Duck.*" *Educational Theatre Journal* 30 (1978): 495–512.

Wahlström, Lydia. *Den svenska kvinnorörelsen: Historisk översikt.* Stockholm: Norstedts, 1933.

Wallin, Gunnar. *Teaterhumor: Thalias tjänare berättar roliga upplevelser från scen och salong.* Malmö: Bernces, 1961.

Wennerholm, Eric. *Anders de Wahl: Människan bakom maskerna.* Stockholm: Bonniers, 1974.

Werner, Gösta. *Den svenska filmens historia: En översikt.* 2d rev. ed. Stockholm: Norstedts, 1978.

Wettergren, Erik. *Scenerier: Resor/konst/teater.* Stockholm: Norstedts, 1927.

Wettergren, Erik, and Ivar Lignell, eds. *Teater i Sverige sista 50 åren.* Stockholm: Svensk litteratur, 1940.

Wiers-Jenssen, H. [Hans] *Nationalteatret gjennem 25 aar: 1899–1924.* Kristiania: Gyldendalske Bokhandel, 1924.

Wiers-Jenssen, H. [Hans], and Joh. Nordahl-Olsen. *Den nationale Scene: De første 25 aar.* Bergen: John Griegs, 1926.

Wieselgren, Greta. *Den höga tröskeln: Kampen för kvinnas rätt till ämbete.* Kvinnohistoriskt Arkiv, 7. Lund: Gleerups, 1969.

Wieselgren, Oscar. "Dramatiska teatern 25 år." In *Kungliga dramatiska teater 25 år,* 3–6. Stockholm: Norstedts, 1933.

————. Förord to *Intiman: Historien om en teater,* by Gustaf Collijn. Stockholm: Wahlström & Widstrand, 1943.

————. "Harriet Bosse: Några minnesord." *Meddelanden från Strindbergssällskapet,* nr. 29 (1961): 1–3.

Winquist, Sven G., and Torsten Jungstedt. *Svenskt filmskådespelarlexikon.* Stockholm: Forum, 1973.

Winter-Hjelm, K. [Kristian] A. *Af Kristiania teaterliv i den seneste tid.* Kristiania: Cappelen, 1875.

Wredlund, Bertil, and Rolf Lindfors, eds. *Långfilm i Sverige, 1940–1949.* Stockholm: Proprius, 1981.

Wyller, Anders. *Kjempende humanisme: Taler og artikler.* Oslo: Aschehoug, 1947.

Aabel, Hauk. *Moro var det lell: Mine første tyve år på scenen.* Oslo: Gyldendal, 1935.

Österling, Anders. *Tio års teater: 1925–1935.* Stockholm: Bonniers, 1936.

Non-Scandinavian Works Consulted

Antoine, André. *Le théâtre.* 2 vols. Paris: Éditions de France, 1932.

Archer, Stephen Murray. "Visiting French Repertory Companies in New York: 1900 to March, 1964." Ph.D. diss., University of Illinois, 1964.

Bandello, Matteo. *The Novels of Matteo Bandello Bishop of Agen.* Translated by John Payne. London: Villon Society, 1890.

Carlson, Marvin. *The French Stage in the Nineteenth Century.* Metuchen, N.J.: Scarecrow, 1977.

Geduld, H.M., and R. Gottesman. *An Illustrated Glossary of Film Terms.* New York: Holt, Rinehart & Winston, 1973.

Genty, Christian. *Histoire du théâtre national de l'Odéon (Journal de Bord) 1782–1982.* Paris: Fischbacher, 1981.

Glenzdorf, Johan Casper. *Internationales film-Lexikon: Biographisches Handbuch für das gesamte Filmwesen.* Badmünder [Deister]: Prominent-Filmverlag, 1960.

Hays, Michael. *The Public and Performance: Essays in the History of French and German Theatre 1871–1900.* Theatre and Dramatic Studies 6. Ann Arbor: UMI Research Press, 1981.

Joannidès, A. *La Comédie-Française de 1680 à 1900: Dictionnaire général des pièces et des auteurs.* Paris: Plon-Nourrit, 1901; Geneva: Slatkin, 1970.

Kramer, Erich. *Die "Bosse": Beitrag zur Geschichte eines Mansfelder Rittergeschlechtz und seines Sippenkreises.* Glücksburg: C.U. Starke, 1952.

Lamprecht, Gerhard. *Deutsche Stummfilme, 1919.* Berlin: Deutschen Kinemathek, 1968.

Martin, Jules. *Nos artistes: Annuaire des théâtres et concerts, 1901–1902.* Paris: Ollendorff, 1901.

Reinhardt, Gottfried. *The Genius: A Memoir of Max Reinhardt.* New York: Alfred A. Knopf, 1979.

Sudermann, Hermann. *John the Baptist: A Play.* Translated by Beatrice Marshall. London: John Lane, 1909.

Tagore, Rabindranath. *Collected Poems and Plays.* New York: Macmillan, 1937.

Taranow, Gerda. *Sarah Bernhardt: The Art Within the Legend.* Princeton, N.J.:
   Princeton University Press, 1972.
Touchard, Pierre Aimé. *Grandes heures de théâtre à Paris.* Paris: Perrin, 1965.
Van Tiegham, Philippe. *Les Grands Acteurs contemporains (1900–1960).* Paris: Presses
   Universitaires de France, 1960.
Wicks, Charles Beaumont. *The Parisian Stage: Part V (1876–1900).* University:
   University of Alabama, 1979.

Strindberg: Works

SWEDISH EDITIONS
August Strindbergs brev. Edited by Torsten Eklund. Strindbergssällskapets skrifter.
   Vols. 13–15. Stockholm: Bonniers, 1972–76. Strindberg's correspondence.
De återfunna breven till Harriet Bosse. Stockholm: Bonniers, 1955.
Ockulta dagboken. Stockholm: Gidlunds, 1977. Strindberg's diary.
Samlade skrifter. Edited by John Landquist. 55 vols. Stockholm: Bonniers, 1912–20.
   Collected works.
Strindbergs brev till Harriet Bosse. Stockholm: Natur & kultur, 1932.
Ur ockulta dagboken: Äktenskapet med Harriet Bosse. Edited by Torsten Eklund.
   Stockholm: Bonniers, 1963.

OTHER EDITIONS
Bekenntnisse an eine Schauspielerin. Edited and translated by Emil Schering. Mit
   verbindendem Text von Harriet Bosse. Berlin: Oswald Arnold, 1941.
The Cloister. Translated by Mary Sandbach. New York: Hill and Wang, 1966.
Days of Loneliness. Translated by Arvid Paulson. New York: Phaedra, 1971.
Five Plays. Translated by Harry G. Carlson. Berkeley: University of California Press,
   1983; New York: New American Library, 1984.
"The Flying Dutchman." Translated by Carl Lindin. *The Wild Duck* 5, nr. 6 (1916):
   n.p.
From an Occult Diary: Marriage with Harriet Bosse. Edited by Torsten Eklund.
   Translated by Mary Sandbach. New York: Hill and Wang, 1965.
Letters of Strindberg to Harriet Bosse: Love Letters from a Tormented Genius. Edited and
   translated by Arvid Paulson. New York: Grosset & Dunlap, 1959.
Lettres à Harriet Bosse. Edited by Torsten Eklund. Translated by Jacques Naville.
   Paris: Mercure de France, 1971.
Open Letters to the Intimate Theater. Translated by Walter Johnson. Seattle: Univer-
   sity of Washington Press, [1966].
Plays from the Cynical Life. Edited and translated by Walter Johnson. Seattle:
   University of Washington Press, 1983.
Selected Plays. Translated by Evert Spinchorn. Minneapolis: University of Minnesota
   Press, 1986.
Zones of the Spirit: A Book of Thoughts. Translated by Claud Field. New York: G.P.
   Putnam's Sons, 1913.

Strindberg: Biography and Criticism

Bark, Richard. *Strindbergs drömspelsteknik—i drama och teater.* Lund: Studentlitteratur, 1981.

Blackwell, Marilyn Johns, ed. *Structures of Influence: A Comparative Approach to August Strindberg.* Chapel Hill: University of North Carolina Press, 1981.

Boëthius, Ulf. *Strindberg och kvinnofrågan: Till och med Giftas I.* Stockholm: Prisma, 1969.

Brandell, Gunnar. *Paris—till och från 1894–1898.* Vol. 3 of *Strindberg—ett författarliv.* Stockholm: Alba, 1983.

————. *Strindbergs infernokris.* Stockholm: Bonniers, 1950.

Brundin, Margareta. "Hur förvarade Strindberg sina manuskript?" In *Kungl. bibliotekets årsberättelse 1981,* 61–97. Stockholm, 1982.

————. "Kungliga Bibliotekets Strindbergssamlingar." In *Strindbergiana: Första samlingen,* edited by Anita Persson and Karl-Åke Kärnell, 50–70. Stockholm: Strindbergssällskapet, 1985.

Burnham, Donald L. "Strindbergs kontaktdilemma studerat i hans förhållande till Harriet Bosse." *Meddelanden från Strindbergssällskapet* 50 (1972): 8–26.

Børge, Vagn. *Kvinden i Strindbergs liv og digtning.* København: Levin & Munksgaard; Lund: Gleerups, 1936.

————. *Strindbergs mystiske teater: Æstetisk-dramaturgiske analyser med særlig hensyn tagen til drömspelet.* København: Munksgaard, 1942.

Carlson, Harry G. *Strindberg and the Poetry of Myth.* Berkeley: University of California Press, 1982.

Collis, John Stewart. *Marriage and Genius: Strindberg and Tolstoy. Studies in Tragi-Comedy.* London: Cassell, 1963.

Eklund, Torsten. "Strindbergs tredje äktenskap i ny belysning." *Meddelanden från Strindbergssällskapet* 19 (1956): 4–8.

Falck, August. *Fem år med Strindberg.* Stockholm: Wahlström & Widstrand, 1935.

Falck, Johan. "Kring Strindbergs Oväder." Skrifter utgivna av Teaterhistoriska samfundet i Göteborg, 5. Göteborg, 1972.

Falkner, Fanny. *August Strindberg i Blå Tornet.* 2d ed. Stockholm: Norstedts, 1921.

Falkner-Söderberg, Stella. *Fanny Falkner och August Strindberg.* Stockholm: Rabén & Sjögren, 1970.

Hedenberg, Sven. *Strindberg i skärselden.* Göteborg: Akademiförlaget-Gumperts, 1961.

Hedvall, Yngve. *Strindberg på Stockholmsscenen, 1870–1922: En teaterhistorisk översikt.* Stockholm: Lundström, 1923.

Jacobsen, Harry. *Strindberg och hans første hustru.* København: Gyldendal, 1946.

Johannesson, Eric O. *The Novels of August Strindberg.* Berkeley: University of California Press, 1968.

Johnson, Walter. *August Strindberg.* Boston: Twayne, 1976.

————. *Strindberg and the Historical Drama.* Seattle: University of Washington Press, 1963.

Lagercrantz, Olof. *August Strindberg*. Stockholm: Wahlström & Widstrand, 1979; Translated by Anselm Hollo, New York: Farrar Straus Giroux, 1984.

———. *Eftertankar om Strindberg*. Stockholm: Författarlaget, 1980.

Lamm, Martin. *August Strindberg*. 2 vols. Stockholm: Bonniers, 1940–42; Edited and translated by Harry G. Carlson, New York: Benjamin Blom, 1971.

———. *Strindbergs dramer*. Stockholm: Bonniers, 1924–26.

Landquist, John. Introduction to *Fanny Falkner och August Strindberg,* by Stella Falkner-Söderberg. Stockholm: Rabén & Sjögren, 1970.

Meyer, Michael. *Strindberg: A Biography*. New York: Random House, 1985.

Mortensen, Brita M.E., and Brian W. Downs. *Strindberg: An Introduction to His Life and Work*. Cambridge: Cambridge University Press, 1965.

Ollén, Gunnar. *Strindbergs dramatik*. 4th ed. Stockholm: Sveriges Radio, 1982.

Paul, Adolf. *Min Strindbergsbok: Strindbergsminnen och brev*. Stockholm: Norstedts, 1930.

Philp, Anna Maria Strindberg von, and Nora Strindberg Hartzell. *Strindbergs systrar berättar om barndomshemmet och om bror August*. Stockholm: Norstedts, 1926.

Rosenqvist, Claes. *Hem till historien: August Strindberg, sekelskiftet och "Gustaf Adolf."* Umeå Studies in the Humanities 66. Umeå [Stockholm]: Almqvist & Wiksell International, 1984.

Rying, Mats. "Strindberg och Harriet Bosse." *Horisont* 26, nr. 5 (1979): 10–17, 21.

Setterwall, Monica. "Queen Christina and Role Playing in Maxim Form." *Scandinavian Studies* 57 (1985): 162–73.

Smirnoff, Karin. *Strindbergs första hustru*. Stockholm: Bonniers, 1925.

Sprigge, Elizabeth. *The Strange Life of August Strindberg*. New York: Russell & Russell, 1972.

Sprinchorn, Evert. *Strindberg as Dramatist*. New Haven, Conn.: Yale University Press, 1982.

Steene, Birgitta. *August Strindberg: An Introduction to His Major Works*. Stockholm: Almqvist & Wiksell International; Atlantic Highlands, N.J.: Humanities, 1982.

Stolpe, Sven. *Sven Stolpe berättar August Strindberg*. Svenska Folkets Litteraturhistoria. Stockholm: Askild & Kärnekull, 1978.

Strindberg, Frida [Uhl]. *Lieb, Leid und Zeit: Eine unvergessliche Ehe: Mit zahlreichen unveröffentlichten Briefen von August Strindberg*. Hamburg: H. Govert, 1936.

———. *Marriage with Genius*. Edited by Frederick Whyte, with the assistance of Ethel Talbot Scheffauer. London: Jonathan Cape, 1937.

———. *Strindberg och hans andra hustru*. 2 vols. Stockholm: Bonniers, 1933–34.

Swerling, Anthony. *In Quest of Strindberg*. Covent Garden: Trinity Lane, 1971.

Törnqvist, Egil. *Strindbergian Drama: Themes and Structure*. Stockholm: Almqvist & Wiksell International; Atlantic Highlands, N.J.: Humanities, 1982.

Uddgren, Gustaf. *Strindberg the Man*. Translated by Axel Johan Uppvall. New York: Haskell House, 1972.

Van Marken, Amy. "Strindberg's *Kristina*: En ny teknik." *Annali-Studi Nordici* (Istituto Universitario Orientale di Napoli) 22 (1979): 165–76.

Weaver, Donald K., ed. *Strindberg on Stage*. Stockholm: Svensk Teaterunion/Svenska ITI & Strindbergssällskapet, 1983.

Bosse and Strindberg in Drama and Fiction

Enquist, Per Olov. *Strindberg: Ett liv.* Stockholm: Norstedts/TV 1 Fiction, 1984.
Meyer, Michael. *Lunatic and Lover: A Play about Strindberg.* London: Methuen, 1981.
Söderström, Ole. *Röda huset.* Stockholm: Norstedts, 1976.
————. *Victoria: Roman om en skådespelerskas äktenskap.* Stockholm: Norstedts, 1978.
Westerlund, Nanny. "August Strindberg och Harriet Bosse: Skådespel i 2 akter." Typescript. Helsingfors: Svenskateatern, 15 Jan. 1982. SvTeatern.
Wilson, Colin. *Strindberg.* London: Calder & Boyars, 1970.

INTERVIEWS

Bergström, Olof. Telephone interview. 2 June 1983.
Bjälkeskog, Lars. Personal interview. 1 June 1983.
Cohn, Helge. Personal interview. 4 Feb. 1981.
Eklund, Torsten. Personal interview. 22 July 1968.
Funkquist, Georg. Telephone interview. 13 Apr. 1981.
Grevenius, Herbert. Personal interview. 24 Mar. 1981.
Hagelin, Anne Marie Wyller. Personal interviews. 10 Feb. 1981, 4 June 1983.
Hasso, Signe. Telephone interview. 1 May 1981.
Heyerdahl, Dagny Bull. Personal interview. 25 Mar. 1981.
Hilding, Olle. Personal interview. 10 Apr. 1981.
Jobs-Berglund, Lisskulla. Personal interview. 13 May 1981.
Järv, Harry. Personal interview. 15 Apr. 1981.
Lagercrantz, Olof. Personal interview. 19 Feb. 1981.
Lewenhaupt, Inga Grabe. Personal interview. 2 Mar. 1981.
Lindfors, Viveca. Telephone interview. 12 Dec. 1982.
Luterkort, Ingrid. Personal interview. 4 Apr. 1981.
Ollén, Gunnar. Personal interview. 9 Mar. 1981.
Olsson, Tom J.A. Personal interview. 20 Jan. 1981.
Persson, Anita. Personal interviews. 25 Jan. 1981, 30 June 1983.
Pollak, Mimi. Telephone interview. 13 Apr. 1981.
Rangström, Ture. Personal interview. 13 Feb. 1981.
Ring, Gerda. Personal interview. 14 July 1983.
Ringheim, Tage. Personal interview. 26 June 1983.
Rinman, Sven. Personal interview. 16 May 1983.
Schulerud, Mentz. Personal interview. 2 June 1981.
Skawonius, Sven Erik. Personal interview. 21 Jan. 1981.
Strandberg, Nikkan [Anna] Rosén. Personal interview. 10 May 1981.
Strindberg, Axel. Personal interview. 9 June 1983.
Stål, Sven. Personal interviews. 11 Mar. 1981, 24 June 1983.
Sundström, Frank. Personal interview. 20 Mar. 1981.

Söderberg, Dora. Personal interview. 23 Mar. 1981.
Söderström, Ole. Personal interview. 30 Jan. 1981.
Wennerholm, Eric. Telephone interview. 13 Feb. 1981.
Widgren, Olof. Personal interview. 29 June 1983.
Wingård, Bo. Personal interview. 6 Aug. 1983.
Wingård, Randi. Personal interviews. 27 Mar. 1981, 3 June 1981, 12 July 1983, 6 Aug. 1983.
Wyller, Jørgen, and Wenche Wyller. Personal interview. 14 July 1983.
Wållgren, Gunn. Personal interview. 24 May 1981.

NEWSPAPERS AND MAGAZINES

Because of the large number of newspapers, magazines, and clipping collections consulted, this list refers to the periodicals themselves rather than the many articles. The inclusive dates indicate that selected issues were consulted. Individual articles are identified in the notes.

Aftenposten (1896–1958)
Aftonbladet (1902–49)
Arbeiderbladet (1958)
Berliner Tageblatt (1919)
Berlingske Tidende (1914–25)
Borås Tidning (1961)
Bratsberg Amtstidende (1896)
Buskeruds Tidende (1896)
Dagbladet (1896–1923)
Dagen (1899–1910)
Dagens Nyheter (1900–1961)
Dagens Tidning (1921)
Dagsavisen (1897)
Daily Chronicle (1927–29)
Daily News (1928)
Daily Telegraph (1927–29)
Dannebrog (1907)
Dramaten spelar (1936)
Drammens Blad (1896)
Drammens Tidende (1896)
Eidsvold (1896–97)
Euterpe (1904)
Evening News (1928)
Evening Standard (1927)
Expressen (1902)
Der Film (1919)
Filmen (1918–19)
Film-journalen (1920)

Finsk Musikrevy (1905)
Folkets Dagblad (1921)
Forum (1918)
Fredrikstads Avis (1896)
Göteborgs Aftonblad (1914–39)
Göteborgs Dagblad (1919–21)
Göteborgs Handels- och Sjöfartstidning (1905–50)
Göteborgs Morgonposten (1905–27)
Göteborgs-Posten (1905–61)
Göteborgs-Tidningen (1905–26)
Hamar Stiftstidende (1896)
Helsingfors-Posten (1904)
Hufvudstadsbladet (1904–9)
Hvar 8. Dag (1919–32)
Idun (1900–1904)
Illustrierte Film Woche (1919)
Intelligenssedler (1896–97)
Der Kinematograph (1919)
Kristianstads Läns Tidning (1936)
Landsbladet (1896–97)
Morgenbladet (1896–1958)
Morgenposten (1897)
Morning Post (1928)
Månads Journalen (1982)
Nationaltidende (1914–25)
New York Times (1915–24)
Nordstjernan (1950)

Norsk Familie-Journal (1898)
Nyhetsbladet (1896)
Ny Tid (1905–57)
Nya Dagligt Allehanda (1899–1944)
Nya Pressen (1906–9)
Nya Thalia (1930–32)
Ord och bild (1900–39)
Politiken (1897–1985)
Revyen (1898)
Ridå (1905–15)
Scenen (1919–38)
Scenisk konst (1903–12)
Scen och salong (1980)
Social-Demokraten (Kristiania)
(1897–1916)
Social-Demokraten (Stockholm)
(1923–36)
Star (1927–29)
Stockholms Dagblad (1902–28)
Stockholms-Tidningen (1908–43)
Sunday Graphic (1927–29)

Svenska Dagbladet (1899–1961)
Svenska Teaterförbundets Medlemsblad
(1938–39)
Svensk musiktidning (1899)
Sydsvenska Dagbladet (1918–19)
Södermanlands Nyheter (1978)
Teatern (1899–1904)
Teatret (1917)
Le Temps (1899)
Thalia (1909–13)
Tidens Tegn (1923)
Times (London) (1927–28)
Trondhjems Adresseavis (1896)
Urd (1940)
Vecko-Journalen (1916–55)
Verdens Gang (1896–98)
Våra Nöien (1925)
Vårt land (1896–1902)
Weekly Dispatch (1928)
Örebladet (1897)

UNPUBLISHED SOURCES AND CLIPPING COLLECTIONS

The author has consulted unpublished letters, contracts, memoirs, scripts, musical scores, registers, theses, and other documents, as well as films, recordings, and pictorial materials, from the following libraries, archives, and collections:

Arkivet för ljud och bild, Stockholm
Drottningholms Teatermuseum, Stockholm
Folkparkernas Centralorganisation
Gustafson, Alrik, collection, University of Minnesota-Minneapolis
Göteborg Teatermuseum, Gothenburg
Göteborg Universitetsbiblioteket, Gothenburg
Hagelin, Anne Marie Wyller, collection, Sigtuna
Hedvig Eleonora församling, Stockholm
Institutionen för teater- och filmvetenskap, Stockholm
Kungliga Biblioteket, Stockholm
Kungliga Dramatiska Teatern (Dramaten), Stockholm

Lund Universitetsbiblioteket
Nordiska Museet, Stockholm
Norsk Rikskringkasting, Oslo
Oscarförsamling, Stockholm
Sibelius, Jean, family collection (Erkki Virkkunen), Helsinki
Sibeliusmuseum (Musikvetenskapeliga institutionen vid Åbo Akademi), Turku
Staatliches Filmarchiv der Deutschen Demokratischen Republik, Berlin
Stockholms Stadsarkivet
Strindbergsmuseet, Stockholm
Svenska Filminstitutet, Stockholm
Svenska litteratursällskapet i Finland, Helsinki
Svenska Musikaliska Akademien, Stockholm

Svenska Teatern, Helsinki
Svensk Musik Arkiv, Stockholm
Sveriges Radio, Stockholm
Universitetsbiblioteket i Oslo

Uppsala Universitetsbiblioteket
Waal, Carla, collection, Columbia
Wingård, Randi, collection, Oslo
Wållgren, Gunn, collection, Stockholm

INDEX

The index has been alphabetized according to the Swedish system.

Abel, Alfred, 215, 216
Adolphson, Gustav Edvin, 135–36, 147–49, 151, 152, 161, 164–65, 177, 180, 264n.15
Afzelius, Nils, 194, 271n.26
Ahlqvist, Inez Bosse, 5, 32, 60, 146, 248n.14
Anderson, Maxwell: *What Price Glory?* (*Ärans fält*), 162
Anna Lans, 186–87
Antoine, André, 13
Appassionata, 187
Arehn, Nils, 51, 60, 72, 274n.69

Bahr, Hermann: *The Concert* (*Konserten*), 59, 66
Bang, Herman, 20
Banville, Théodore Faullain de: *Gringoire,* 16–17, 27
Bataille, Henri: *The Wedding March* (*Bröllopsmarschen*), 73, 82, 138
Baum, Vicki: *Grand Hotel,* 163, 214
Beethoven, Ludvig von, 4, 66, 187, 230, 274n.87
Beijer, Agne, 38, 175
Benavente, Jacinto: *Mother's Rival (Mors rival),* 141, 142
Berendsohn, Walter, 197
Berg, Yngve, 136
Berggren, Thommy, 202
Bergman, Bo, 142, 227, 228, 230, 231
Bergman, Ellen, 3
Bergman, Gösta M., 171
Bergman, Hjalmar: *Swedenhielms,* 182
Bergman, Ingmar, 127, 229
Bergman, Ingrid, 149, 198
Bergqvist-Hansson, Jenny, 166, 192, 196
Bergström, Olof, 184
Bernhardt, Sarah, 14, 21, 22, 23, 76, 138, 139, 206–7, 263n.63
Bernstein, Henri, 15; *The Thief* (*Tjufven*), 60
Berntsen, Johanne Marie Bosse, 249n.21

Björling, Manda, 63, 65, 233
Bjørnson, Bjørn, 3, 8, 10, 15, 20
Bjørnson, Bjørnstjerne, 13, 19, 57, 173, 255n.52; *Maria Stuart in Scotland* (*Maria Stuart i Skotland*), 21, 36, 73, 82, 158
Bloch, Hannes, 214
Bloch, William, 20
Bojer, Johan: *The Eyes of Love* (*Kjærlighedens Øjne*), 62
Bolander, Hugo, 152, 163
Bombi Bitt and I (*Bombi Bitt och jag*), 178–79, 269n.27
Bonde, Carl Carlsson, 18, 19, 34, 35
Borgström, Hilda, 63, 67, 142, 161, 173–4, 175, 192, 253n.40
Bosse, Alma. *See* Fahlstrøm, Alma Bosse
Bosse, Anne Marie Lehman, 2, 32, 189
Bosse, Dagmar. *See* Möller, Dagmar Bosse
Bosse, Ewald, 3, 28, 140, 150, 165, 189, 263n.64
Bosse, Harriet: and Adolphson, 135–36, 147–49, 151, 152, 161, 164–65; and Anne Marie, 32, 33, 43–44, 47, 57, 62, 63, 71, 72, 140, 146–47, 165–66; "Både–och: Några skisser," 192, 248n.4; in Berlin, 48–49, 162–63, 254n.29; and Bo, 61–62, 66, 140–41, 147, 148, 150, 165, 257n.41; to Castrén, 45, 46–47, 57, 58, 60, 64, 65; at Concert House, 155–58; in Copenhagen, 78–79, 160; *De återfunna breven till Harriet Bosse,* 194–95; and Fahlstrøms, 4–11; in film, 126–32, 137, 178–79, 186–87, 226, 260n.4; in Gothenburg, 47–48, 78, 152–55, 265n.30; in Helsinki, 41–45, 47, 49–51, 255n.52; in Kristiania, 79–80; at New Intimate Theatre, 132–37; in Paris, 12–15; portraits of, 10, 188, 249n.31; on radio, 180–81, 182, 188, 190; and Strindberg, 1, 25–33, 38, 44–45, 48,

60, 61, 70–71, 138, 151, 163, 166,
177–78, 180, 188, 194, 195–96, 201;
and Strindberg papers, 163–64, 175–
78, 193, 196–99, 260n.87;
Strindbergs brev till Harriet Bosse, 163–
64, 165–68; at Swedish Theatre,
Stockholm, 52–68, 70; "Thalia is
Dying," 143–45, 263n.79; on tour, 5–
7, 8, 76–81, 132, 137–39, 150–52,
179–80, 218, 231–32, 260n.45; and
Wingård, 51–52, 59–62, 66, 72;
youth, 2–4. *See also* Dramaten, and
Bosse
Bosse, Heinrich, 5, 249n.15
Bosse, Inez. *See* Ahlqvist, Inez Bosse
Bosse, Johann Heinrich, 2, 4, 7, 189,
248n.3
Bosse, Johanne Marie. *See* Berntsen,
Johanne Marie Bosse
Brander, Ida, 42, 226, 227
Branting, Anna, 30, 38–39
Brogren, Erik, 155
Browallius, Carl, 220
Brunius, John, 158
Brunius, Pauline, 67, 72, 149, 158, 172–
73, 184
Bäckström, Oscar, 192
Bødtker, Sigurd, 8, 10, 79–80, 210, 231

Caillavet, G. A. de: *The Adventure (Åfven-
tyret),* 13, 77, 141, 174, 175, 182; *The
King (Kungen),* 13, 57, 62; *Woman's
Weapon (Kvinnans vapen),* 57, 62
Carlheim-Gyllensköld, Vilhelm, 175–76,
194, 195
Carlsten, Rune, 133, 134, 172, 173, 179,
186
Castegren, Victor, 47, 48, 52, 57, 58,
227, 229
Castrén, Gunnar, 45, 61, 200, 222, 226–
27; Bosse's letters to, 46–47, 57, 58,
60, 64, 65, 254n.21
Central Theatre, Kristiania, 7–10, 15,
249n.19
Charles XII (Karl XII) (August
Strindberg), 32, 34, 210–11
Christiania Theatre, Kristiania, 2, 3, 4, 8,
16
Christiansen, Halfdan, 182
Christiernsson, Henrik: *Mammon,* 29

Collijn, Ellen, 141, 150, 151, 154, 159–60
Collijn, Gustaf, 58–59, 69, 126, 132, 133,
134, 135, 137, 138
Collijn, Isak, 141, 177
Comédie-Française, Paris, 12, 14
Comedy Theatre, Stockholm, 141
Comrades (Kamraterna) (August
Strindberg), 213–16, 274n.57
Concert House, Stockholm, 155, 156,
157, 158, 159, 162, 216, 234
Coquelin, Constant, 14, 21, 76
Crimes and Crimes (Brott och brott) (Au-
gust Strindberg), 23, 79, 80, 160, 174,
179, 181, 230–32
Croisset, Francis de: *The Lord's Vineyards
(Herrens vingård),* 180; *One Wife Too
Many (En hustru för mycket),* 77
Crown Bride, The (Kronbruden) (August
Strindberg), 36, 50, 51, 59, 62, 64, 78,
82, 172, 177, 188, 193, 206, 225–28,
261n.11
Curel, François de: *The Mannequin
(Skyltdockan),* 44, 46; *The New Idol (La
Nouvelle Idole),* 13

Dagmar Theatre, Copenhagen, 78, 160,
232
Dance of Death, The (Dödsdansen) (August
Strindberg), 138, 161, 168–69, 207,
216
Després, Suzanne, 76
De Wahl, Anders, 23, 32, 57, 59, 63, 73,
132, 142, 150, 161, 162, 173, 174, 175,
181, 192, 266n.67
Didring, Ernst: *Midnight Sun (Midnattssol),* 52; *Pension Bellevue,* 142; *Two
Kings (Två konungar),* 61, 72
Drachmann, Holger: *Gurre,* 57–58, 66;
Once Upon a Time— (Der var engang—),
1, 7–8, 15, 82
Dramaten, Stockholm, 16–22, 23, 24, 35,
42, 50, 55, 57, 64, 65, 67, 76, 77,
127, 132, 142, 149, 161, 169, 172–75,
188, 258n.1; and Bosse (debut), 15–
24, 26–40, 46–47, 210–11, 212, 223–
24, (return), 66, 68–70, 72–76, 77,
81–83, 228, 231, (as guest), 141–43,
159–60, 162, 232, (final years), 161–
62, 164, 169–70, 172–75, 182–85,
219–20, 263nn. 69, 70; in Norway,

79–80; Strindberg and, 206, 223, 226, 229; and Swedish Theatre, 55, 57; on tour, 78, 260n.45

Dream Play, A (Ett drömspel) (August Strindberg), 46, 57, 64, 135, 161, 169, 172, 188, 199, 205, 208, 220, 228–30, 275nn. 107, 121, 276n.123

Dumas, Alexandre *fils: The Lady of the Camellias (Kameliadamen)*, 78, 138, 172

Duse, Eleonora, 21, 38, 59, 76, 139

Dybwad, Johanne, 3, 19, 38, 50, 76, 79, 80, 133, 231

Dymov, Ossip: *Nju,* 135

Dörum, Tyra, 192

Easter (Påsk) (August Strindberg), 29, 31, 34, 48, 50, 65, 66, 135, 136, 138, 151, 152, 160, 163, 169, 175, 188, 191, 206, 223–25, 227, 262n.61

Egge, Peder: *The Christening Gift (Faddergaven)*, 9

Eklund, Ernst, 141, 155, 156, 157, 158, 234, 263n.69

Eklund, Torsten, 193, 194, 195, 196, 197–98, 271n.26

Ekman, Gösta, 143, 149, 158, 163, 171, 263n.79

Ekstam, Nils, 180

Ekström, Märta, 142, 161, 170, 274n.69

Engberg, Arthur, 169, 172

Englund, Magda, 151

Enquist, Per Olov, 202

Erastoff, Edith, 132

Essen, Siri von, 25–26, 41–42, 70, 196, 201, 202, 206, 211, 218, 229

Eysoldt, Gertrude, 46, 254n.29

Facing Death (Inför döden) (August Strindberg), 8, 209–10

Fahlcrantz, Carl Johan, 218

Fahlstrøm, Alma Bosse, 2–3, 4–10, 22, 28, 41, 55, 140, 209, 249n.31

Fahlstrøm, Johan, 4–6, 7–8, 9–10, 28, 41, 140

Fahlstrøm Theatre, 249n.21

Falck, August, 65, 225, 233

Falkner, Fanny, 65, 66, 201

Fallstrøm, Daniel, 76, 133

Féraudy, Dominique-Marie-Maurice de, 12, 13

Flers, Robert de: *The Adventure (Åfventyret)*, 13, 77, 141, 174, 175, 182; *The King (Kungen)*, 13, 57, 62; *The Lord's Vineyards (Herrens vingård)*, 180; *Woman's Weapon (Kvinnans vapen)*, 57, 62

Flygare, Anna, 65, 207, 225

Folkets Parker (folk parks), 138, 180

Franken, Rose: *Claudia,* 174

Fredbärj, Dr. Telemak, 193–94

Fredrikson, Gustaf, 18, 19, 20, 23, 35, 42, 50

Free Theatre, Stockholm, 169, 170

Fröberg, Einar, 133, 136

Fröding, Gustaf, 211

Funkquist, Georg, 187

Garbo, Greta, 149, 198

Géradet: *Friend Lorel (Vännen Lorel)*, 152

Géraldy, Paul: *Love (Älska)*, 161

Gerell, Greta, 188, 190

Giacosa, Giuseppe: *As Leaves Before the Storm (Som blad för stormen)*, 36–37

Goethe, Johann Wolfgang von, 48; *Egmont,* 192; *Faust,* 19, 63

Gogol, Nikolai: *The Inspector (Revisorn)*, 52

Goldsmith, Oliver: *She Stoops to Conquer (Värdshuset Råbocken)*, 141, 142

Gorky, Maxim, 57, 58; *The Lower Depths,* 209

Gothenburg City Theatre, 152, 188, 274n.82

Grabow, Carl, 229

Grandinson, Emil, 27, 133, 210, 211, 221, 222, 223, 224

Grevenius, Herbert, 23, 184–85

Greig, Edvard: music of, 3, 4

Grieg, Nordahl, 182; *The Defeat (Nederlaget)*, 174

Grünewald, Isaac, 157

Gustav III, King, 17, 56

Guter, Dr. Johannes, 214

Hagelin, Anne Marie Strindberg Wyller, as a child, 31, 43–44, 47, 57, 60, 62, 72, 140, 220; and Strindberg, 32, 33, 48, 61, 70, 71, 190; as a woman, 146–47, 165–66, 182, 188, 189, 197, 210

Hallström, Per, 156; *A Venetian Comedy (En veneziansk komedi)*, 37–38, 42, 43, 46, 51, 207

Hammarén, Torsten, 152
Hanson, Lars, 54, 132, 133, 134, 142, 173, 174, 181
Hansson, Johan, 166, 169
Hansson, Valborg, 23, 29, 35, 71, 192
Hartman, Ellen, 21, 22
Hasso, Signe, 174, 175
Hautpmann, Gerhart: *The Beaver Coat (Bäfverpelsen)*, 208; *Elga*, 49, 62, 72; *The Sunken Bell (Klokken som sank)*, 9, 12; *The Weavers (Vävarna)*, 56
Hays, Michael, 55
Hebbe, Signe, 63, 77
Hebbel, Friedrich, 49, 82
Hedberg, Frans: *Hothouse Flowers (Blommor i drifbänk)*, 73, 78, 80
Hedberg, Stina, 73, 161
Hedberg, Tor, 20, 36, 39, 57, 58, 224, 230, 234; with Dramaten, 67, 69–70, 74, 80, 81, 82, 127, 132, 228; *Johan Ulfstjerna*, 67, 72, 79, 80
Hedqvist, Ivan, 48, 60, 75, 80, 142, 192, 229, 231
Heiberg, Gunnar, 20, 79, 80; *The Balcony (Balkongen)*, 133, 134, 152
Heidenstam, Verner von, 183–84
Henning, Uno, 232
Hennings, Betty, 19, 76, 213
Herrström, Sallie, 169, 267n.99
Hertz, Henrik: *King René's Daughter (Kung René's dotter)*, 34, 138
Hillberg, Emil, 192
Hirn, Julius, 43, 44, 51
Hofman, Holger, 78, 160
Hofmannsthal, Hugo von: *Elektra*, 49, 72, 73–75, 79, 80, 82, 83, 138; *Everyman (Det gamla spelet om Envar)*, 82, 174
Holberg, Ludvig, 133; *Pernille's Brief Time as a Lady (Pernille's korte fröykenstand)*, 8–9
Horn, Gustaf von: *My Niece (Min niece)*, 66
Hwasser, Elise, 21
Håkansson, Julia, 67, 142

Ibsen, Henrik, 19, 21, 57, 163, 235; *Brand*, 4; *A Doll House*, 9, 18, 20, 21, 151, 152, 159–60, 218; *An Enemy of the People*, 14; *Ghosts*, 21, 42, 51, 66, 141; *Hedda Gabler*, 56, 162; *John Gabriel Borkman*, 42, 66; *The Lady from the Sea*, 49; *Lady Inger of Östraat*, 18, 21; *Love's Comedy*, 21, 52; *The Master Builder*, 49, 133, 134, 137, 174, 175; *Peer Gynt*, 3, 161; *Rosmersholm*, 13; *The Vikings at Helgeland*, 18, 21; *The Wild Duck*, 9, 13, 18, 21, 35, 42, 43, 47
Intimate Theatre, 33, 65, 66, 207, 219–20, 225, 233, 258n.1
Intimate Theatre (New). *See* New Intimate Theatre

Jaenzon, Julius, 128
Janson, Amanda, 24, 35
Jerome, Jerome K.: *Miss Hobbs*, 34, 36
Jobs-Berglund, Lisskulla, 180
Jon-And, 217, 219
Josephson, Ludvig, 19, 20

Karl-Gerhard, 168, 177–78, 267n.93
Kavli, Karin, 174
Keil-Möller, Carlo, 175; *The Big Shadow (Den stora skuggan)*, 183–84
Kennedy, Charles Rann: *The Servant in the House (Tjänaren i huset)*, 59, 257n.30
Key, Ellen, 32
Kistemaeker, Henry: *Trial by Fire (Eldprofvet)*, 72, 73, 77, 192
Klintberg, Gunnar, 57, 67, 72, 163
Kolthoff, Signe, 73, 82, 142, 161
Krigsvoll, Anne, 202
Krusenstjerna, Agnes von, 150
Kübler, Arnold: *Aiolos the Shoemaker (Skomaker Aiolos)*, 141
Kåge, Ivar, 48, 60, 229

Lagercrantz, Olof, 26, 150, 205
Lagerkvist, Pär, 126, 133, 161, 171, 181; *The Secret of Heaven (Himlens hemlighet)*, 136
Lagerlöf, Selma: *Gösta Berling's Saga*, 174, 179; *The Ingmarssons (Ingmarssönerna)*, 127–32, 137, 213, 226, 261n.4; *Jerusalem*, 127, 128
Lagerwall, Sture, 178
Lamm, Martin, 151, 164, 165, 167, 177, 204, 205
Large Theatre, Gothenburg, 47, 56

Laurin, Carl, 58, 63, 83, 174, 227
Le Bargy, Simone, 15
Lenning, Hjalmar, 44, 50, 51
Lie, Jonas: *Merry Wives* (*Glada fruar*), 50, 51
Lindberg, August, 20, 51, 152, 208
Lindberg, Augusta, 23, 35, 66, 152, 192, 231
Lindberg, Per, 126, 152–53, 155–56, 157, 158, 161, 162, 169, 171, 180–81, 216, 217, 219
Linden, Gustaf (Muck), 75–76, 78, 150, 151, 152, 153, 159, 161, 162, 188, 227, 231
Lindfors, Viveca, 149, 173, 186, 187
Lindskog, Anna (Nickan), 73
Loraine, Robert, 168–69, 267nn. 96, 100
Lorensberg Theatre, Gothenburg, 78, 82, 147, 152–53, 154, 155, 156, 158, 227, 234, 265n.41
Luce, Clare Booth: *The Women* (*Kvinnorna*), 174
Lugné-Poe, Aurélien, 13, 14, 48, 58
Lundequist, Gerda, 63, 66, 159, 173

Mæterlinck, Maurice, 71, 193, 208, 223, 225, 235; *Pelléas and Mélisande* (*Pelléas och Mélisande*), 13, 36, 42, 43, 46, 48, 49, 50, 51, 58–59, 64, 135, 143, 226, 257n.27
Malmstrom, Ernst, 227
Masefield, John: *A Japanese Tragedy* (*En japansk tragedi*), 171
Mattson, Veronika, 201
Maugham, W. Somerset: *East of Suez* (*Öster om Suez*), 141; *Home and Beauty* (*Änkleken*), 134, 138–39; *Mrs. Dot*, 64, 257nn. 30, 41
Mendelssohn, Felix: music of, 27, 28, 82
Meyer, Michael: *Lunatic and Lover*, 201
Meyer-Foerster, Wilhelm: *Old Heidelberg* (*Gamla Heidelberg*), 32, 52, 57
Michaelson, Knut, 21, 67, 132, 133; *A Phantom* (*En skugga*), 21, 233
Moan, Henny, 191
Moissi, Alexander, 76, 141
Molander, Harald, 20, 41
Molander, Karin, 132
Molander, Olof, 8, 69, 73, 141, 161, 172, 173, 181, 187, 191, 228, 229,

275n.121; book about Bosse, 126, 142–43
Moser, Gustav von: *War in Peace* (*Krig i fred*), 43, 46, 48
Müller, Max, 46
Möller, Carl (Calle), 10, 30, 72, 183, 248n.11
Möller, Dagmar Bosse, 2, 3–4, 5, 7, 10, 16, 28, 31, 54, 72, 148, 150, 165, 189, 234, 248n.11

Nansen, Betty, 76, 160
National Theatre, Oslo, 10, 15, 79, 81, 138, 182
National Theatre, Sweden, 171, 179–80, 232
Nelson, Doris, 132, 157, 274n.69
New Intimate Theatre, 132, 133, 134, 137, 141, 147, 225
New Theatre, Stockholm, 18–19
Niccodemi, Dario: *The Plume* (*Aigretten*), 134
Nielsen, Asta, 213
Nissen, Dina, 10
Nissen, Fernanda, 9, 75

Oehlenschläger, Adam: *Aladdin*, 22, 75; *Axel and Valborg* (*Axel og Valborg*), 8, 9, 49
O'Neill, Eugene, 198; *Mourning Becomes Electra*, 149, 161, 169, 172; *Strange Interlude*, 161
Opera, Stockholm, 3, 18, 82, 206, 226, 256n.11, 258n.1
Oscar II, King, 2, 18
Oscar Theatre, Stockholm, 149, 158, 173, 256n.11, 258n.1
Oslo New Theatre, 160, 191

Pagnol, Marcel: *Topaze*, 162
Palme, August, 27, 28, 37, 192, 211, 222
Paul, Adolf, 23, 213–14, 216
Paulson, Arvid, 196–99
People's Theatre, Stockholm, 147
Personne, Nils, 16, 19–20, 23, 24, 29, 34, 35, 142, 192, 223, 226, 233
Petersen, Jens: *First Violin* (*Första fiolen*), 17, 28, 48, 49, 50, 73, 207
Petterson, Hjördis, 174
Philp, Anna von, 27, 33, 204

Picard, André: *A Gentleman in Tails* (*En herre i frack*), 143, 263n.79
Poe, Edgar Allan, 211
Poljakov, S. L.: *The Labyrinth* (*Labyrinten*), 141, 142
Pollak, Mimi, 157

Queen Christina (*Drottning Kristina*) (August Strindberg), 49, 65, 152, 153, 154, 156, 157, 159, 195, 232–34

Ranft, Albert, 52, 54, 55, 56, 57, 59, 62, 64, 153, 207, 256n.11, 263n.79; ensemble, 49, 67
Rangström, Ture: music of, 136, 217, 228
Raphael, Olga, 63, 73, 150, 182
Rasmussen, Rudolf, 15–16
Reinhardt, Max, 67, 69, 76, 137, 152, 220, 229
Rey, Étienne: *The Adventure* (*Äfventyret*), 13, 77, 141, 174, 175, 182
Richter, Gösta, 163
Ring, Gerda, 182
Rodin, Gösta, 178
Rolland, Romain: *The Play of Life and Death* (*Spelet om kärleken och döden*), 149, 179–80
Rostand, Edmond: *Cyrano de Bergerac*, 14, 20, 29, 30, 149, 168
Royal Dramatic Theatre, 16–19, 79–80. *See also* Dramaten.
Royal Opera. *See* Opera, Stockholm
Runnquist, Åke, 194–95
Rydeberg, Georg, 172, 180, 187
Ryding, Allan: tours, 77–78, 84, 138, 152, 211, 216, 218, 231–32, 234
Raa, Frithiof, 51

Sandborg, Olof, 155, 217
Sandell, Hugo, 52
Sandell, Lina, 21, 22, 67, 233
Sardou, Victorien: *Madame Sans-Gêne*, 21, 260n.62; *La Tosca*, 14
Saxe-Meiningen, Duke of: troupe, 21, 56
Schanche, Ingolf, 160, 217–18
Schering, Emil, 48
Schildknecht, Maria, 73, 163, 228
Schiller, Johann Christoph Friedrich von, 173; *Maria Stuart*, 51, 161, 208
Schnitzler, Arthur: *Anatol*, 82; *The Far

Country* (*Det vida landet*), 82
Schönthan, Franz von: *War in Peace* (*Krig i fred*), 43, 46, 48
Scribe, Eugene: *A Glass of Water*, 21
Selander, Hjalmar: traveling company, 51–52, 77, 141
Shakespeare, William, 19, 57; *Antony and Cleopatra*, 81, 155, 156, 157, 217; *As You Like It*, 79, 141, 142; *Hamlet*, 21, 157, 171; *King Lear*, 161; *Macbeth*, 51, 66, 162, 208; *Measure for Measure*, 14; *The Merchant of Venice*, 81, 142; *A Midsummer Night's Dream*, 17, 21, 26–28, 47, 49, 226; *Much Ado about Nothing*, 34; *Othello*, 51; *Romeo and Juliet*, 1, 4–7, 16, 35, 39, 42, 44, 47, 48, 50, 51, 174, 227; *The Taming of the Shrew*, 149; *The Tempest*, 197, 208; *Twelfth Night*, 20, 79, 80; *A Winter's Tale*, 181
Shaw, George Bernard, 57, 69, 76; *Caesar and Cleopatra*, 147, 153, 154–55; *Man and Superman*, 64, 168; *Pygmalion*, 75, 76, 77, 78–79, 82, 173, 259nn. 38, 45; *Saint Joan*, 153, 159
Sibelius, Jean: music of, 41, 48, 50, 59, 257n.27
Sigurjonsson, Johann: *Berg-Eyvind and His Wife* (*Berg-Eyvind och hans hustru*), 173
Simoon (*Samum*) (August Strindberg), 22, 34, 48, 49, 211–12
Sir Bengt's Wife (*Herr Bengts hustru*) (August Strindberg), 152, 218–19
Sjöberg, Alf, 173, 179, 220, 232
Sjöberg, Constance, 211
Sjöström, Victor, 83–84, 127–32, 137
Skandinavisches Theater, Berlin, 163
Skavlan, Einar, 75
Smaller Theatre, Stockholm, 19
Smith, Dodie: *Dear Octopus* (*Guldbröllop*), 174, 181
Stallings, Laurence: *What Price Glory?* (*Ärans fält*), 162
Stanislavsky, Constantin, 57, 172, 173
Stiller, Mauritz, 152
Stjernström, Edvard, 18, 19
Storm Weather (*Oväder*) (August Strindberg), 170, 179, 182, 219–21, 274n.82

Strindberg, Anna. *See* Philp, Anna von
Strindberg, Anne Marie. *See* Hagelin,
    Anne Marie Strindberg Wyller
Strindberg, August, 55, 57, 127; *Alone*
    (*Ensam*), 204, 205; and Anne Marie,
    31, 32, 33, 48, 61, 70, 190, 220; be-
    fore Bosse, 25–26; "The Big Gravel
    Screen" ("Stora grusharpan"), 181,
    269n.39; *The Black Glove* (*Svarta hand-
    sken*), 108, 204; *The Blue Book*
    (*Blåboken*), 204, 205, 272n.10; and
    Bosse, 1, 4, 22, 26–34, 36, 39, 45,
    60–61, 62, 204–8; "Chrysaëtos," 195,
    204; *The Cloister* (*Klostret*), 26, 213;
    death of, 66, 70, 71; and Dramaten,
    206, 223, 226, 229; "The Dutchman"
    ("Holländaren"), 193, 204, 205, 208;
    Engelbrekt, 204, 208; *The Father*
    (*Fadren*), 25, 168, 267n.96; *The Ghost
    Sonata* (*Spöksonaten*), 183; *The Great
    Highway* (*Den stora landsvägen*), 196;
    Gustav Vasa, 28, 56; "Inferno II," 176–
    77, 194, 195; and Intimate Theatre,
    33, 65, 66, 207, 219–20, 225; letters,
    143, 163–67, 177–78, 196; *Lucky Per's
    Journey* (*Lycko-Pers resa*), 32; *A Mad-
    man's Defense*, 196; *Master Olof*, 64;
    Midsummer (*Midsommar*), 226; *Miss
    Julie* (*Fröken Julie*), 13, 25, 198, 213;
    The New Kingdom (*Det nya riket*), 181;
    Occult Diary, 29, 195, 198, 200, 225;
    Open Letters to the Intimate Theatre,
    65; *The Red Room* (*Röda rummet*), 25;
    The Roofing Feast (*Taklagsöl*), 204, 205.
    See also Charles XII; *Comrades*; *Crimes
    and Crimes*; *Crown Bride, The*; *Dance of
    Death, The*; *Dream Play, A*; *Easter*; *Fac-
    ing Death*; *Queen Christina*; *Simoon*;
    Sir Bengt's Wife; *Storm Weather*; *Swan
    White*; *To Damascus*
Strindberg, Axel, 30, 32
Strindberg, Elisabeth, 29, 223
Strindberg, Emilia Charlotta, 204
Strindberg, Greta, 32, 41–42, 70, 225
Strindberg, Ulrika Eleonora, 204
Strindberg Society, 193, 194, 195
Ström, Carl, 180
Ström, Knut, 152, 153, 154
Stål, Sven, 144–45, 157, 218, 225
Sudermann, Hermann: *Johannes*, 22, 49,

62–64
Sundström, Frank, 178
Sutro, Alfred: *The Choice* (*Valet*), 142
Svennberg, Tore, 60, 64, 142, 153, 159,
    160, 161, 230, 266n.66
Swan White (*Svanevit*) (August
    Strindberg), 49, 65, 66, 160, 177, 183,
    193–94, 205, 206, 208–9, 233,
    275n.107
Swedish Theatre, Helsinki, 41–44, 47,
    49, 51, 52, 201
Swedish, Theatre, Stockholm, 19, 28, 49,
    53, 54–65, 66–67, 69, 70, 71, 72,
    133, 158, 161, 206, 207, 227, 229,
    256n.11, 257n.44, 258n.1
Söderman, Sven, 57, 64, 76, 134, 135, 212
Söderström, Ole: *The Red House* (*Röda
    huset*), 200–201; *Victoria*, 200, 201,
    202

Tagore, Rabindranath: *Chitra*, 22, 135,
    136
Tallroth, Konrad, 43, 222
Tammelin, Bertha, 3, 16, 248n.10
Tavaststjerna, Gabrielle, 50
Teje, Tora, 67, 73, 132, 142, 153, 161,
    162, 169, 170, 172, 175, 183, 184
Théâtre de l'Œuvre, Paris, 13, 14, 48
Theatre Guild, Stockholm, 169
Theslöf, Georg Henrik, 50
Thomas, Brandon: *Charley's Aunt* (*Char-
    leys tant*), 50, 52
Tidblad, Inga, 135, 149, 170, 180
To Damascus (*Till Damaskus*) (August
    Strindberg), 26, 218; *I*, 27, 29, 30,
    43–44, 45, 47, 49, 65, 206, 207, 221–
    23; *II*, 217; *III*, 156, 157, 216, 217,
    274n.63
Torsell, Astri, 32, 73

Uhl, Frida, 26, 30, 166, 201, 204, 217,
    221, 262n.61

Valberg, Birgitta, 174
Vallentin, Hugo, 76
Vallentin, Richard, 48–49, 207
Vasantasena: *Sakuntala*, 22, 46, 208
Vasa Theatre, Stockholm, 52, 59, 72, 147,
    163, 256n.11, 258n.1
Vély: *Friend Lorel* (*Vännen Lorel*), 152

Wendbladh, Rudolf, 154, 234
Wessel, Jessie, 73, 142
Westerlund, Nanny, 201
Wettergren, Erik, 157, 161, 170, 218
Wetzer, Conny (Konni), 41, 42, 43, 47, 49, 50, 52, 226
Wied, Gustav: *First Violin (Första fiolen)*, 17, 28, 48, 49, 50, 73, 207
Wiehe, Charlotte, 208
Wieselgren, Oscar, 176, 177, 194, 199
Wifstrand, Naima, 132
Wilde, Oscar: *Salome,* 49, 64, 161
Wilson, Colin: *Strindberg,* 200
Wingård, Anders Gunnar, 44, 45, 50–52, 59–60, 61, 64, 66, 67, 166, 220, 226, 227, 233; death of, 70, 71–72, 255n.55, 259n.9
Wingård, Bo Gunnarsson, 61–62, 66, 70, 140–41, 147, 148, 149, 150, 165, 190,

257n.41, 259n.9, 270n.57
Wingård, Carl-Gunnar, 141
Wingård, Nils Åke, 51, 259n.9
Wingård, Randi Iversen, 150, 190
Winterhjelm, Hedvig Charlotte, 51, 77
Wyller, Anders, 146–47, 165–66, 182
Wyller, Arne, 146, 165–66, 189, 198
Wyller, Janecke, 190, 191
Wyller, Jørgen, 146, 165–66, 182, 189, 190, 191
Wållgren, Gunn, 174, 175, 232

Zanderholm, Tyra, 141

Åhlander, Thekla, 142, 192
Aalberg, Ida, 76, 213
Aanrud, Hans: *The Stork (Storken)*, 209

Österling, Anders, 218, 220

Carla Waal is professor of theatre at the University of Missouri-Columbia, a position she has held since 1973. She has taught previously at Heidelberg College and the University of Georgia. Her graduate work was at the University of Virginia (M.A., 1957) and Indiana University (Ph.D., 1964).

Born in Milwaukee, Professor Waal is of Norwegian descent. She first visited Norway in 1959, as a student at the University of Oslo. Since then she has frequently returned to Scandinavia to do research in theatre history, contemporary theatre, and literature. She has published articles on the authors Henrik Ibsen, Knut Hamsun, and Bjørg Vik, and the director William Bloch. Her book *Johanne Dybwad: Norwegian Actress* was published in Oslo in 1967.

Carla Waal is an artist-scholar. She has played leading roles in such productions as *A Streetcar Named Desire, On Golden Pond,* and *Foxfire,* and she has directed many plays, including *Desire under the Elms, The Importance of Being Earnest,* and *The Lady from the Sea.* In 1989 Professor Waal did fieldwork in theatre anthropology at Den Nationale Scene in Bergen.